Early Modern Witches

The sixteen original pamphlets collected here describe fifteen English witchcraft cases in detail, vividly recreating events to give the reader the illusion of actually being present at witchcraft accusations, trials and hangings. Some of these original documents appear in print for the first time in three centuries, whilst others are newly edited to give a clearer picture of sources, generic developments in writing about witchcraft, the chronologies of cases, and the biographies of the people who are trying to tell us their stories. Presented in their original language, these legal cases provide a fascinating insight into this Elizabethan and Jacobean preoccupation and obsession.

As well as this engrossing recreation of dramatic events, *Early Modern Witches* draws on the latest research available, asking the reader to consider how much they are victims of literary manipulation by the pamphleteers, accusers, magistrates and witches themselves.

This book will be of use and fascinating to anyone interested in witchcraft, cultural history or literature. It combines original spelling editions of popular texts with scholarly annotation, and there are sections on further reading and sources for students as well as an introduction to each pamphlet.

Marion Gibson is Lecturer in English at the University of Exeter and her research interests are in witchcraft, the occult and biography. Her previous publications include *Reading Witchcraft* (Routledge, 1999).

Early Modern Witches

Witchcraft Cases in Contemporary Writing

Marion Gibson

London and New York

First published 2000
by Routledge
11 New Fetter Lane, London EC4P 4EE

Simultaneously published in the USA and Canada
by Routledge
29 West 35th Street, New York, NY 10001

Routledge is an imprint of the Taylor & Francis Group

Typeset in Garamond by
Florence Production Ltd, Stoodleigh, Devon
Printed and bound in Great Britain by
TJ International, Padstow, Cornwall

British Library Cataloguing in Publication Data
A catalogue record for this book is available from the British Library

Library of Congress Cataloging in Publication Data
Early modern witches : witchcraft cases in contemporary writing /
[compiled by] Marion Gibson.
p. cm.
Includes bibliographical references and index.
1. Witchcraft—England—History—16th century—Sources.
2. Witchcraft—England—History—17th century—Sources.
I. Gibson, Marion, 1970–

BF1581 .E37 2000
133.4′3′094209031–dc21
00–032828

ISBN 0–415–21579–x (hbk)
ISBN 0–415–21580–3 (pbk)

This book is dedicated to Barbara Rosen,
who modestly urged me not to do so.

It is also dedicated to the memory of Gareth Roberts.

Finally, it is for all those accused of witchcraft, especially those whose words and actions have contributed to the pamphlets contained in this book.

Margery Staunton
John Walsh
Mary Barber
Elizabeth Sawyer
Mother Nelson
Jennet Bierley
Alizon Device
Isabel Sidegraves
Henry Selles
Phillip Flower
Joan Upney
Cecily Glasenberye Arnold
John Bulcocke
Ales Nokes
Elizabeth Southerns Demdike
James Device
Margaret Grevell
Father Bill
Elizabeth Whale
Mother Margaret
Christopher Hargraves Jackes
Anne Baker
Alice Gray
Annis Herd
Grace Hay
Margaret Ewstace
Jennet Preston
Elizabeth Astley
Joan Waterhouse
Mother Dutten
Elizabeth Hargraves
Jennet Hargrieves
Agnes Waterhouse
Anne Crounckshey
Elizabeth Stile Rockingham
Jane Southworth
Ursley Kempe Gray
Ellen Greene
Joane Flower
Elizabeth Frauncis
John Ramsden
Lawrence Hay
Agnes Browne
Joan Robinson
Arthur Bill
Mother Sutton
Gamaliel Greete
Old Doewife
Joan Lucas
Jane Bulcocke
Ales Newman
Joan Pechey
Mother Devell
Elizabeth Device
Cysley Selles
Margaret Harkett
Mother Audrey
Christopher Howgate
Joan Cunny
Mother Rhodes
Margaret Pearson
Jane Boothman
Margaret Cunny
Mother Osborne
Joane Browne Vaughan
Elizabeth Ewstace
Katherine Mouldheeles Hewit
Alice Chaundeler
Mother Bill
Margery Sammon Barnes
Elizabeth Bennett
Alice Nutter
Katherine Gardener
Alice Stokes/Joan Harrison
Mother Atkins
Joan Prentis
Annis Glascocke
Elizabeth Mott
Hellen Jenkenson
Anne Redferne
Widow Loomeshaw
Joan Turner
Ellen Bierley
Margaret Flower
Widow Lord
Ales Hunt
Elizabeth Howgate
Father Roseman Osborne
Mother Barnes
Mary Sutton
Christian Stokes
Isabel Robey
Joan Willimot
Elleine Smithe
Ales Manfielde
Anne Whittle Chattox

Contents

Acknowledgements

Personal thanks to: Harry, Laura and Adam, Pippa, Carly and Micky, Kate and Rob, Katherine, Mark, Tom, George and Edward, Nathan, Becky, Paul, Mary, Angela, Robert, Stephanie, and Mum and Dad.

Academic thanks to: Gareth Roberts (who will be much missed), Diane Purkiss, Lyndal Roper, Jim Sharpe, Robert Mack, Barbara Rosen, Richard Strier, Jonathan Barry, J.S. Cockburn, J.M. Beattie, John Baker, Barbara Singleton, Winnifred Sullivan, Emma Wilby, Owen Davies, Nathan Johnstone, Harry Bennett, Robin Jacoby, Charles Taylor, Todd Gray, Anthony Musson, Alex Walsham and the students on the MA programme 'The History and Literature of Witchcraft' at the University of Exeter, especially Matthew, Jason, Nancy and Heidi who allowed me to try out my ideas on them.

Thanks to Exeter University Library, the Bodleian Library, the PRO, Trinity College, Cambridge, the Huntington Library, the British Library, the University Libraries of Edinburgh and East Anglia, Devon RO, Essex RO, Berkshire RO, Lambeth Palace Library, the Franke Institute, University of Chicago, and the College of Wooster Library, Ohio.

Editions used

The Examination and Confession of certaine Wytches (1566) Lambeth Palace, London.

The Examination of John Walsh (1566) British Library, London.

A Rehearsall both straung and true (1579) British Library.

A Detection of damnable driftes (1579) British Library.

Richard Galis, *A brief treatise* (1579) Bodleian Library, Oxford.

W.W., *A true and just Recorde* (1582) British Library and Trinity College, Cambridge.

The severall factes of Witch-crafte (1585) College of Wooster, Ohio.

The Apprehension and confession of three notorious Witches (1589) Lambeth Palace.

A Most Wicked worke of a wretched Witch (1592) Lambeth Palace.

A World of Wonders (1595) Trinity College, Cambridge.

The Most Cruell and Bloody Murther ('Johane Harrison') British Library.

The Witches of Northamptonshire (1612) Bodleian Library.

Thomas Potts, *The Wonderfull Discoverie* (1612) Bodleian Library, Oxford.

Witches Apprehended (1613) Huntington Library, California.

The Wonderful Discovery of the Witchcrafts of Margaret and Phillip Flower (1619) British Library.

Henry Goodcole, *The wonderfull discoverie of Elizabeth Sawyer* (1621) British Library.

Editorial practice

Abbreviated titles of reference works

Stationers' Register	Edward Arber, ed., *A Transcript of the Registers of the Company of Stationers in London. 1554–1640,* 5 vols, 1875–94 (Gloucester, Mass.: Peter Smith, 1967).
STC	A.W. Pollard, and G.R. Redgrave, with Katherine Pantzer, *A Short-title Catalogue of Books Printed in England, Scotland and Ireland 1475–1640* (*STC*), 2nd edn, 3 vols (London: Bibliographical Society, 1986–91).
OED	*Oxford English Dictionary*, ed. J.A. Simpson and E.S.C. Weiner, 2nd edn, 20 vols (Oxford: Clarendon Press, 1989).
Rosen	Barbara Rosen, *Witchcraft in England 1558–1618* (Amherst: University of Massachusetts Press, 1991).
Ewen	C. L'Estrange Ewen, *Witch Hunting and Witch Trials* (London: Kegan Paul, Trench, Trubner, 1929).
DNB	Leslie Stephen and Sidney Lee (eds) *The Dictionary of National Biography*, 22 vols (Oxford: Oxford University Press, 1921–2).

Spelling, early modern abbreviations and my substitutions

Punctuation, capitalisation and spelling are given in their original form. However, all contractions have been silently expanded (commaũds = commaunds, exãinate = examinate). The following changes have been made throughout where appropriate: + has been changed to &, f to s, i to j, u to v, vv to w, wc to which, wt to without, w to with, yt to that, y to ye etc.

Fonts

Italic in the original pamphlet is rendered as *italic*, blackletter as Roman, Roman as **bold**, except where the whole pamphlet is in Roman, as is sometimes the case after about 1590. Where this is so, continued use of bold would offend the reader's eye, so after an initial footnote of explanation, text is in non-bold font.

Legibility

Where the pamphlet is illegible or only semi-legible, every attempt has been made to reconstruct its spelling and punctuation from the clearest versions available. Complete certainty has, however, sometimes been impossible. The more difficult long sections of each pamphlet have been marked with square brackets [ ] so that readers are aware of their legibility problems and can decide to consult the original/s if necessary. In each case the clearest known copy has been used and extra details have been supplied from other versions.

Signatures

Page signatures are inserted in the texts with curly brackets { }.

Signatures in the earlier pamphlets are often expressed in Roman numerals, but, to avoid confusion between v = verso and v = 5, these have been changed to match the later pamphlets which use Arabic numerals. Where two signatures have the same letter, the second has been labelled 2 (e.g. A6v and 2A6v). Unnamed sections have been labelled a, b, etc.

Sources for students

Below is a short list of the most useful sources of general information about the pamphlets, and the background to their stories. A great deal of research still needs to be done on each witchcraft episode – readers will find my own sources below, in the footnotes and in the bibliography. This list is intended as a guide to where to begin further reading of your own.

General

Keith Thomas, *Religion and the Decline of Magic* (1971; London: Peregrine, 1978) and J.A. Sharpe, *Instruments of Darkness 1550–1750* (London: Hamish Hamilton, 1996) are the two best accounts of English witchcraft in the period of the pamphlets reproduced here. Marion Gibson, *Reading Witchcraft* (London and New York: Routledge, 1999) gives the most detailed interpretative reading of the pamphlets. Diane Purkiss, *The Witch in History* (London and New York: Routledge, 1996) gives incisive literary and psychoanalytic readings of a number of the pamphlets and their literary and cultural context – most notably *A true and just Recorde* (1582). Good accounts of the publishing world which produced the pamphlets are Sandra Clark, *The Elizabethan Pamphleteers: Popular Moralistic Pamphlets 1580–1640* (London: Athlone Press, 1983) and Tessa Watt, *Cheap Print and Popular Piety* (Cambridge: Cambridge University Press, 1991).

Bibliographical

Bibliographical information about the pamphlets themselves and their printers and publishers can be found in Edward Arber, ed., *A Transcript of the Registers of the Company of Stationers in London. 1554–1640*, 5 vols (1875–94; Gloucester, Mass.: Peter Smith, 1967), and A.W. Pollard and G.R. Redgrave with Katherine Pantzer, eds, *A Short-title Catalogue of Books Printed in England, Scotland and Ireland 1475–1640* (*STC*), 2nd edn, 3 vols (London:

Bibliographical Society, 1986–91), as well as R.B. McKerrow, ed., *A Dictionary of Printers and Booksellers in England, Scotland and Ireland, and Foreign Printers of English Books 1557–1640* (1910; London: Bibliographical Society, 1968), E. Gordon Duff, *A Century of the English Book Trade* (London: Bibliographical Society, 1905) and Henry R. Plomer, *A Dictionary of Booksellers and Printers Who Were at Work in England, Scotland and Ireland 1641–1667* (1907; London: Bibliographical Society, 1968).

Biographical

Biographical information on figures of national importance (judges, peers, some knights, some pamphleteers) is in Leslie Stephen and Sidney Lee, eds, *The Dictionary of National Biography*, 22 vols (Oxford: Oxford University Press, 1921–2), currently being revised to include more local and regional worthies. Some magistrates, clergymen and gentlemanly victims attended Cambridge or Eton and details of their later lives can be found in J. Venn and J.A. Venn, eds, *Alumni Cantabrigienses*, 4 vols (Cambridge: Cambridge University Press, 1927), C.H. Cooper and T. Cooper, eds, *Athenae Cantabrigiensis* (Cambridge, 1858) and/or Wasey Sterry, ed., *The Eton College Register 1441–1698* (Eton: Spottiswoode and Ballantyne, 1943). G.E. Cokayne, *The Complete Peerage*, ed. H.A. Doubleday and Lord Howard de Walden (London: St Catherine's Press, 1932) deals with the nobility, and the *Visitation* of each county (often published by scholarly societies such as the Camden or Chetham) gives genealogies of prominent families. The *Victoria County History* is the best place to look for local people not mentioned in any of these, followed by local histories and record offices. Where a person is mentioned in the text with minimal footnote information, the source will be their scattered and inspecific references in the *VCH*.

Legal

J.S. Cockburn, *A Calendar of Assize Records* (London: HMSO, 1975–85) reproduces indictments from the Home Counties in the reigns of Elizabeth I and James VI and I. His account, with its excellent introductory volume describing pre-trial and trial procedures, is indispensable in reading all the pamphlets which are based on legal records.

Introduction

A witchcraft renaissance

Interest in the subject of witchcraft has grown enormously in recent decades. Practising witches such as Starhawk describe it as 'reborn', 're-nascent' as a magical practice, whilst for others its renaissance lies in research and discussion of its history.[1] As it is remade and grows, it also changes. At present, witchcraft is less likely than at any time in its history to be seen as an exceptional matter, concerned with hysteria, cultic depravity, gynocide (the mass murder of women) or other extremes of human behaviour. Instead it is being reconstructed as part of a continuum of activities and beliefs worthy of exploration and investigation in both its historical and modern incarnations. 'Witchcraft studies' seems to have reached a moment of critical mass where it is noticed in and beyond the academic world as a coherent body of scholarship and as a subject in its own right. Public and academic curiosity have met in unexpected ways: enter 'witchcraft' as a search keyword on the world wide web, and both pagan networks and university resource centres will be listed. Several universities now run undergraduate modules and postgraduate programmes of study dealing partly or exclusively with the subject of witchcraft, and sustained interest from the academy, the media and the general public has fuelled a spate of theses, articles and books. Most bookshops now contain a section on occult and historiographic writings on the subject of witches – a section full of surprising contrasts, as Jim Sharpe notes in his 1996 history of English witchcraft, *Instruments of Darkness*.[2] Contemporary handbooks on Wicca, the Tarot, earth magic and palmistry sit cover to cover with severely rationalist texts, feminist readings of witchcraft plays and microhistories of significant cases several centuries old. Starhawk and Sharpe cohabit self-consciously on the shelf. This profusion and confusion of interest is reflected outside the bookshop, in a way which reinforces a growing perception

1 Starhawk (Miriam Simos), subtitled her *The Spiral Dance* (1979; New York: HarperCollins, 1999) with the words *A Rebirth of the Ancient Religion of the Great Goddess*.

2 J.A. Sharpe, *Instruments of Darkness: Witchcraft in England 1550–1750* (London: Hamish Hamilton, 1996), 294–7.

of the subject's allure and contemporaneity: the writer on witchcraft, whatever his or her views, is almost always sure of a response to the announcement that 'I'm interested in witchcraft'. This can range from the suspicious ('Do you believe in all that, then?'), to the delighted ('I've always found that fascinating myself!'). The knowledgability of those who respond in this way is usually surprising too – there seem to be few people who have not encountered a discussion or manifestation of witchcraft in some form, ancient or modern. An interest in sixteenth-century poetry, literary biography or British foreign policy in the 1920s seldom elicits the same flash of interest.

Why this edition?

In keeping with the wide-open nature of the field, this book does not set out to make judgements about witchcraft. What it does instead is to give the reader the opportunity to study, in their original language and in a format closely related to the original, some of the key writings on witchcraft from the early period of interest in the subject as a crime. The edition reproduces and annotates, in the light of the most recent scholarship, accounts by victims, legal officials and hack writers – and frequently the alleged words of witches are presented as part of the accounts. The notes in the edition help the reader to be constantly aware of whose words they are reading, how these are being represented, and how that affects the reader's perception of events. Thus it allows readers to form a precise judgement of what is written and of how that shapes what we believe about witchcraft. The reader can thus survey different sources of accounts of witchcraft, different stories told about it, and a wide range of ways of presenting those stories. The edition contains material never before published, and includes newly rediscovered works: so that it brings together complete texts of early pamphlet accounts of witchcraft and offers these, for the first time, to the reader's consideration as a genre in its own right. This genre contributes greatly (and sometimes too uncomplicatedly) to our understanding of what witchcraft was. The result is a vivid and highly complex picture of witchcraft and its prosecution in the late Tudor and early Stuart period.

Writing witchcraft: the reader, the text, the authors

As an undergraduate student, mesmerised by the vividness of the accounts, I felt that I heard the witches speak to their questioners, that I entered their homes and those of their alleged victims, and that I sorrowfully watched them hang. But although this impression was a source of inspiration, this edition, whilst it preserves for the reader a fresh and uninterrupted perspective on the texts, is also concerned to establish that what survives of the world of the past is a representation of it rather than a reflection. It is tempting to see the accounts collected here as windows on the world of witchcraft. But the pamphlets were written deliberately to create that impression. Produced for a variety of reasons (from the financial to the propagandist) and for a variety of readers, the texts display witchcraft as a coherent and explicable body of practices, and present its prosecution as a straightforward act. Modern readers will either accept this picture or wish to deconstruct it, and this edition tries to assist this process of exploration and rethinking by pointing out the influences of literary and cultural considerations on what we read, by emphasising authorial and other motivations, narrative contradictions and textual gaps, and by asking useful questions wherever these exist. These raise some basic issues about accounts of witchcraft which need to be considered in reading the texts which follow.

Each text is, to begin with, more than shaped by its author or authors. Its very content is determined by a complex series of exchanges between, for example, witness, magistrate, magistrate's clerk, and 'witch'. In an account based on pre-trial documents, an understanding of the process of bringing a suspected witch to trial is vital. The victim would come to the magistrate with a complaint against a suspect – essentially a narrative of hotly contested events, usually both perceived and put into words in circumstances of great stress and anxiety. The magistrate would question the victim, using questions likely to elicit a response which would be useful at the assizes (very properly, given his duty to commit suspected felons for trial). His clerk would write down, in a fairly formulaic way, the responses which those questions had both generated and shaped. This pre-trial document, an 'information' against the witch, would need to be coherent and specific, even if the victim had not been particularly clear in his or her narration. Finally, the accusations would be put to the suspected witch, whose responses would be recorded, in the same way, by the same clerk, as an 'examination'. On the basis of these accounts of events, the accused witch would be committed by the magistrate for trial at the next assizes – a period of waiting which he or she would pass in gaol. This series of exchanges and recordings – or re-tellings and re-interpretations – is the source of all those parts of the pamphlets which contain pre-trial documents, and it can be seen to constitute a kind of multiple authorship. What we are reading is a multi-layered series of documents prepared for a specific purpose by a process of dialogue and exchange which is far from straightforward.

When the suspected witch came to trial, the transmission of text from oral source to printed pamphlet might become even more complicated. The assizes had developed, of necessity, into a system designed to cover as many cases as possible in each geographical area within a three-day period. The enormous number of cases awaiting trial in each region had to be dealt with by judges who came 'down' to the country from London for two brief periods each year, at Lent and in summer – when legal work in London did not wholly occupy them. Two judges thus toured each circuit twice yearly, 'delivering' each county gaol by trying the cases of those imprisoned. It was customary for one judge to preside over civil, the other over Crown (criminal) cases. A system of grand

and petty juries operated: grand juries would inspect 'bills of indictment', or charges against the accused, and decide whether evidence and paperwork were in order. If they were, the jury would find that the bill before them was 'a true bill' and that the case should be passed to the petty jury. The petty jury would then hear the evidence, and make a judgement. There was no adversarial pitting of lawyers for the defence against the prosecution: there was no defence, and the truth of the matter was expected to emerge from the words of the accused, accuser and the witnesses alone. Pre-trial documents thus played a vital role in this frenzy of activity. They were used by clerks in court to draw up the indictments, and pre-trial documents would also be read out in court to help the jury make its decision. Juries would thus consider evidence given orally, in person, and evidence given on paper – and since they considered cases in batches rather than individually this profusion of material must have been confusing for both onlookers and participants. It was usual to deal with seven or eight prisoners, with entirely different cases, in quick succession and to give a judgement only when evidence against all of them had been presented. Then a new jury would be sworn in for the next batch of prisoners.[3] It is clear from some of the accounts given in pamphlets that pamphleteers were sometimes present in court, probably taking notes on the case for trial reports to appear in print. If they were not always clear about what was going on, or if they attempted to simplify their stories from the courtroom, it would hardly be surprising.

Reports from the assizes, which occur in several of the pamphlets collected here, often contain abbreviated versions of pre-trial documents and indictments, as well as eyewitness accounts of happenings in the courtroom. Some of the pamphleteers' laymen's accounts of legal procedures contribute layers of inexpert interpretation and confusion to several pamphlets. But in one case a court clerk himself is the author of the pamphlet. Thomas Potts's account of the Lancaster witch-trials of 1612 is distinguished by an expert knowledge of legal process. It is also, however, notable for its attempts to edit documents to provide an unnaturally clear and authoritative account, and to skew pre-trial documents into representing what went on in court (a task for which they are by nature unfitted). Potts also gives great prominence to 'evidence' of Catholic and other plots against the administration of justice in the north of England. His attempt to guide the reader through the case gives a wonderfully vivid picture of a witch-trial as a theatrical event, but is also deeply flawed as a recreation of assize realities, especially in less high-profile cases. The pamphlet intends to demonstrate the perfection of the system of justice, defending it against all comers – from papists to the aggrieved relatives of the condemned – and it is backed by powerful patrons in this task. This kind of polemical purpose, often anti-Catholic and often in evidence in the pamphlets, is a factor which brings further into

3 See J.S. Cockburn, *Introduction to Calendar of Assize Records. Home Circuit Indictments. Elizabeth I and James I* (London: HMSO, 1985) for a full account of assize procedures, and also note 4.

question any notion that we are looking through the texts into a real world beyond the text and unconstructed by language.

Even pamphlets whose structure appears simpler – third-person narrations of events, for example – might have equally complex multiple authorship. Here, the story to be told would emerge from oral and written conversation between the victim or victims, the writer or writers of the account, the publisher and the printer. As with modern documents such as statements to the police, or interviews with journalists, what the victim said (a story probably already shaped by consultation with friends, doctors, churchmen or even by the reading of demonologies) might be substantially changed in the narration set down by the writer. Tedious, but potentially illuminating, repetition might be omitted and contradictions harmonised. The publisher might colour the account with a polemical introduction, or ask further writers to contribute to the text. Finally, mistakes made by compositors, who turned manuscript into set type at the printers, might cloud or wrongly clarify the words at the moment when they entered print. As I have argued elsewhere, there might be up to eight levels of input in a given account, each with heavy interpretative gloss, and with mistakes and new readings: victim, questioner, clerk, witch, court clerk, shorthand writer, author or editor and printer.[4] This is before the pamphlet ever reaches a reader – who might have fancied that they would be the first to interpret this important historical source.

Printing, publishing and survival

The production of the pamphlets' content was thus a far from straightforward affair. The processes of printing in the early modern period have also left their mark heavily on their form. In editing them here, I have tried to reproduce as fully as possible their original style and form (although using modern fonts and layout for the sake of readability and easy annotation). For example, pamphlets were not usually given page numbers, and so they do not have page numbers here. Instead, their pages were organised into a coherent sequence after printing by the use of 'signatures'. These function as page numbers, but, because they come in groups, they can be confusing at first glance. In fact they worked very simply, as a guide to grouping sections of the text for binding. The first signature was usually 'A'. The first page was thus labelled 'A' and its back, or verso, side is known as 'Av'. The third page was 'A2' and its reverse 'A2v' – and so on through 'A3', 'A3v' and 'A4'. The signature would sometimes stop at 'A4v' and the next section of the pamphlet would be signature 'B', with pages labelled 'B', 'Bv' and so on. In other pamphlets the signature would run on until 'A8v' and then signature 'B' would begin. By reproducing signatures (in curly brackets in the text) this edition hopes to give a flavour of the original pamphlets. It is

4 Marion Gibson, *Reading Witchcraft: Stories of Early English Witches* (London and New York: Routledge, 1999), 46.

especially interesting to see how small some of their pages are, and how little text can be accommodated. Some pamphlets, on the other hand, waste space with large headings and blank pages: which would push up their price. These pamphlets seem likely to be aiming for a high-quality appearance. Many pamphlets, however, received little attention as they were being produced. Some were clearly dashed off far too quickly, and printed using inferior materials, with the result that their ink is smudged and has bled through the paper. Illegible passages in the main version used here have been marked with square brackets and the text supplied from another edition – where this is possible. All the material conditions of textual production, from confession to collation, are thus highlighted in this edition.

Despite the technical difficulties of printing, the system within which the pamphlets were published and distributed was quite simple in outline. Publishers and printers were responsible to the Company of Stationers in London for what they produced. Each work had to be licensed, upon payment of a fee, and its licensing to a particular publisher was recorded in the Stationers' Register for future reference. This gave publishers some control over any pirating of works licensed to them, but it gave the Company itself (and thus, indirectly, the government and the church) power over what was produced. Readers were employed to vet works, minimising the possibility that blasphemous, obscene or seditious material would reach the shops. However, not all works collected here have entries in the Register, reflecting gaps in its records as well as loopholes in the system. Once a work had been approved and printed, it would be sold in shops in London (often those owned by publishers and printers themselves) and distributed to the regions by chapmen carrying packs of pamphlets, ballads and broadsheets. Thus the story of witchcraft reached the public domain.

Most pamphlets were not expected to last in a readable form – topicality made them ephemeral, and they often had an afterlife as wrappers, wallpaper or absorbent wipes. It is not known in what quantities witchcraft pamphlets were originally produced, but the tiny number of survivals suggests either small print runs or a vast toll of destruction in the centuries since the last pamphlet collected here was published in 1621. It might be supposed that pamphlets reached a relatively small audience – literate Londoners for the most part – but it is probable that in fact they were available to more than those people who could read: reading aloud was common and pamphlets probably served as informative entertainment even to those who could not read them.[5] It is also clear from references in some of the pamphlets themselves, and in material surrounding possessions and witch-trials, that provincial people had read at least some of the pamphlets in this collection.[6] They were read from their first production by those who regarded them as 'histories', or signs of the times, rather than as factual accounts

5 The best account of publication, literacy and readership in the period is Tessa Watt, *Cheap Print and Popular Piety* (Cambridge: Cambridge University Press, 1991).

6 See for example, Richard Galis, *A brief treatise* (1579) and *The Wonderful Discovery of the*

of sensational events. The sceptical writer Reginald Scot read them to seek evidence of 'witchmongering', or the wanton persecution of witches. Early antiquarians such as John Aubrey and Francis Bacon were interested in changes in society and in the new sciences of the natural world. Like local historians, or chorographers, such as William Lambarde, these men would have been very likely to encounter and peruse pamphlets on contemporary events, and probably to preserve them.[7] The first interest in ephemera such as ballads and pamphlets as collectable was thus shown as early as the late sixteenth century. In the Restoration, Samuel Pepys, the civil servant and dabbler in scientific matters, collected ballads and short pamphlets, including a ballad on the case of the Flower family, accused of bewitching the children of the Earl of Rutland in 1618–19. His initial reason for collecting was an interest in music, but his acquisitive habit was also fed by historical and scientific impulses and his diary is full of references to his bookseller, new acquisitions, reading and singing.[8] The trade in pamphlets and ballads became brisker in the later eighteenth and nineteenth centuries. They were sold at auction by and to private collectors. Some appeared in print for the first time since the early modern period in works such as John Payne Collier's *Illustrations of Early English Popular Literature* (1863).[9] Some disappeared and have not yet resurfaced, a fact which was recorded regretfully by those who were not fortunate enough to become their owners.[10] It is always possible that some remain to be discovered in private collections. Pepys left his collection to his College library, and in a similar way witchcraft pamphlets have slowly drained from the private collections of antiquarians to the libraries of Oxford and Cambridge Universities and to the British Library. In many cases only one copy of each pamphlet survives. I have included in the introduction to each pamphlet a note on the text used, and its location.

Witchcrafts of Margaret and Phillip Flower (1619) for references to other pamphlets, and the case of Anne Gunter (described in J.A. Sharpe, *The Bewitching of Anne Gunter* [London: Profile, 1999], 7) for reference to a witchcraft pamphlet as a source for a 'victim' simulating possession.

7 See Stan A.E. Mendyk, *Speculum Britanniae: Regional Study, Antiquarianism and Science in Britain to 1700* (Toronto, Buffalo and London: University of Toronto Press, 1989) for an account of these men and their interests.

8 Samuel Pepys, *The Diary of Samuel Pepys*, ed. R. Latham and W. Matthews (London: Bell and Hyman, 1985).

9 John Payne Collier, *Illustrations of Early English Popular Literature*, 2 vols (1863; New York: Benjamin Blom, 1966).

10 See for example William Lowndes, *The Bibliographer's Manual of English Literature*. Rev. edn ed. Henry G. Bohn, 6 vols (London, 1890) for a snapshot of the trade in ephemera and the steady losses of surviving works.

Some signposts for the texts

The pamphlets' content, their production, their reception and survival thus can be seen to be determined by a large number of factors, rather than being stages in an organic process whereby events were transferred cleanly into text, conveyed directly to readers and so into 'history'. Trends in writing and publication, and public interest in the matter of witchcraft, clearly influenced the accounts in key ways and certain wider patterns can be noted, especially if the reader looks in chronological sequence at each work in this collection. For example, early Elizabethan accounts of witchcraft, from the 1560s to the 1590s, tend to consist of documents from the legal process against witches. After 1590 they are far more likely to be third-person narrations of events beyond the courtroom. Before 1590 accounts concentrate on the witch, but after 1590 they are more often concerned with the victim. Because of exceptions to this general chronological pattern, it is also possible to see that accounts by or concerning gentry and noble victims of witchcraft tend to stress the victims' blamelessness and the witches' innate criminality and corruption. Accounts based on legal documents far more frequently place an element of blame on the victim for initiating conflict with the witch, and give the witch a voice (even though much mediated) in examinations or other documents. Thus stories told of witches before 1590 and/or in accounts based on legal documents are more likely to focus on the traditional story of the witch being denied charity or abused in some way, and taking a legitimate revenge – whilst after 1590 and/or in narrative accounts of witchcraft, stories tend to be of motiveless witch-attack. Writers follow one another in this respect: there is evidence (particularly towards the end of the period covered here) that pamphleteers were familiar with the works of earlier writers in the genre, with writing in related crime genres, and sometimes with other works on witchcraft such as demonological treatises. All these sources of information shaped their writing and their view of what witchcraft was, and they also shaped the pamphleteers' view of the intended reader – matters which are touched on in the footnotes here. As the genre developed, pamphleteers evolved a widening range of ways of writing about witchcraft, and what they wrote became interdependent with considerations of form, function and fashion. Sources, authorship and readership therefore played a very important part in determining the content and shape of the story that we read now – and how we read it.

In this sense much of what we can learn from reading witchcraft pamphlets is about the pamphlets themselves. But in a wider context, we can also study how writers, markets and societies respond to events by putting them into text. One of the painful pleasures of reading these accounts is the sense of a mosaic being constructed before our eyes. Diverse impressions, intentions and chance happenings coalesce into a solid-seeming textual artefact which provides a coherent justification for the actions it describes and prescribes: actions ranging from godly exhortation to violent attack and execution. The ways in which this process is represented as truth-telling, and finally as history, are of concern to all. The transformation of the everyday into the extraordinary, and vice versa is an equally momentous issue, and here we have a privileged view of an element within the development of a very specific and enduring myth (or collection of myths) which intersects in increasingly complex ways with what we perceive to be the real. We can learn a good deal about witchcraft from the texts. But we can also see that the idea of witchcraft is a shape-shifting verbal-textual entity which reflects back on to us our own preconceptions and needs, as much as expressing its much-discussed self.

1

The Examination and Confession of certaine Wytches (1566)

The first witchcraft pamphlet to be published begins a long tradition of telling simple stories, complicated by the nature of their sources and by what storyteller and reader believe about what is told. The pamphlet tells of three accused Essex women, Agnes and Jone Waterhouse and Elizabeth Frauncis, and of their familiar Sathan, which turns from cat, to toad, to dog and commits various acts of *maleficium* (harmful witchcraft) in Hatfield Peverel. The women were tried at Chelmsford assizes on 26 July 1566, with one other, who is not mentioned in the pamphlet although she was tried by the same jury as Jone Waterhouse. Unusually, two witches pleaded guilty: Elizabeth Frauncis was imprisoned, Agnes Waterhouse hanged. Jone Waterhouse was found not guilty of disabling Agnes Browne by witchcraft on 17 July 1566 – a date which supports the pamphleteer's assertion that her actions brought about all three trials. Thus trial records corroborate most of the main assertions made by the pamphlet – which is itself made partly from pre-trial documents.

The pamphlet begins with poetic prefaces, at least one of which is by John Phillips, a writer of doggerel verse, and especially elegies – a *forte* which helps explain the gloomy tone of his work here. Phillips is sometimes credited with the authorship of the whole work, but, given its varied sources, this could be true only in a very loose sense. After his prefaces, the pamphlet's first main section is composed of apparently almost unaltered examination documents, with some third-person narration by a pamphleteer. It also gives, in a second section, an extraordinarily vivid account of court testimony supposedly given by a child victim, Agnes Browne. This twelve-year-old girl is 'haunted' by the familiar as an 'obsessing' (external, as opposed to internal 'possessing') spirit. It is hard to tell how far this account is based on a trial report, and how far it might be imaginatively enhanced. A third section describes the execution of the only witch to be sentenced to death. Thus we have three different types of source, all of which are related to the legal process. The accounts are likely to have originated with people close to the Essex court, rather than being conceived as a unified whole and created in London printshops. However, they have been polished and perhaps embellished in this setting – a process of creation which is characteristic of early witchcraft pamphlets.

This pamphlet, an octavo, was printed by William Powell for William Pickering, another printer who also published, and was entered in the Stationers' Register[1] in two parts, one with the pamphlet's current title, and one called 'the secounde examynation & confyson of Augnnes Waterhowse and Jone hyr Daughter'. The entries (13 August 1566) are separated by eleven other entries. This suggests that originally the pamphlet was conceived as two works, the second incorporating reiterated details of the examinations in Part One, and adding the trial report, which may therefore be from a different source. This separateness of the two parts can still be seen in that each ends with the publisher's and printer's details, as if the parts were designed for independent sale. The pamphlet's third section, describing the execution, doesn't have an entry in the Stationers' Register so may have been intended to be a short addition to Part Two. This pamphlet is the only one to be printed in such instalments. The text used here is in Lambeth Palace Library.

{A (title page)} The Examination and Confession of certaine Wytches at Chensforde in the Countie of Essex, before the Quenes majesties Judges,[2] the xxvi. daye of July. **ANNO.** 1566, at the Assise holden there as then, and one of them put to death for the same offence, as their examination declareth more at large.

{A2} *The Epistle to the Reader*

GOD whych of hys singuler goodnesse (as the sage philosopher Hermes hath plainly discribed) to each of his creatures hath added a reasonable soule, which is the chiefe and most excellent treasure that any man can be indued withall: Let us then consider gods inexplycable benefits alwaies of his owne free wyll (and not of our desertes) geven and bestowed upon us, and sith that the soule of man is of great estimation in his fatherly presence, let us endevour our selves to walke, that by continuall exercise of vertuous and holesome documents, I meane not onely by hearing of the sincere veritie: neither yet by much talkyng of the same to heare, and not to bear awaye is altogether frivolous: To babble and prate much of Christ and hys gospell (as though we would be counted ghostly gospellers) & to wante the chefest thing, I meane the frutes of well governed conversacion, and to be cleane voyde of integritie, and cleanesse of lyfe, in my judgement and as the sacred scripture verifieth, is nothynge but folly: (example) A tree that is altogether

1 See Edward Arber, ed., *A Transcript of the Registers of the Company of Stationers in London. 1554–1640*, 5 vols (1875–94; Gloucester, Mass.: Peter Smith, 1967).

2 John Southcote, a justice of the Queen's Bench since 1562 and from a local Essex family, and Gilbert Gerard, the Attorney General. Later knighted and appointed Master of the Rolls, Gerard was an eminent man, involved in many state trials (see *DNB* for both men). However, his presence here is a routine matter: he, like the other judges in the cases recorded in these pamphlets, had been appointed to 'do the rounds' on a particular circuit – here, the Home Circuit.

barren, and at {A2v} the required time destytute of fruyte having a trim shewe of leaves, deserveth to be hewed downe and made meete for the fier: so we wantinge fruites required, but having plenty of leaves be of lyke effect, and for all the outwarde shewe that we have, we shall in like case be cut downe & throwen into the fyer prepared for the devill and his aungelles, from which (gentell reader) God defende us all, and geve us suche grace that we maye henceforthe walke in our vocation, that god in al our workes may be unfeynedly glorified, and by thadmonition of this littel boke learne in such sorte to keepe our soules, by fixed and assured faith in Christ, from the stinking puddle of filthy pollution, then shal we escape that horrible place prepared for the ungodly and wycked livers, & as profitable servants be counted apt members to dwell wyth our Saviour Christ above the cloudes in his hevenly kingdome, to the which god for hys mercies sake bring us all. Amen.

{A3} The Preface.

MY tremblinge hande for feare doth quake,
my dolour doth excede:
My joyes decrese to tender teares
my sportes are turnd in dede.
The gredy gulfs of grysly griefe,
so gripe my restles harte:
yt my pore pen can scantly shewe,
the passions of my smarte.
Drawe nere you patrones with your babes,
come viewe this haples happe:
In flushing fluddes of fominge teares
your tender bewtyes lappe.
Ye matrones milde drawe nere in haste,
this yrksome acte beholde:
Then Nature shall her rufull playnts,
by you her Nimphes unfolde.
Eche wight in whom the skilfull skyll,
of natures arte is shown:
Surrender may themselves to me,
this cruell acte to mone.
The heapes of griefe so hugie are,
that sobbes must nedes abounde:
Yea shrilly shrickes to passe the skies,
your voyces shall redounde.
The dolour nowe so doubtfull is,
that skante my warbling penne:
Can forth expresse the sence thereof,
unto the sonnes of men.

Agayne the blubringe teares whych glide,
from my poore pincked eyes:
Besmerde my face that scarce I can,
my inwarde griefes supprise.[3]
One while I blushe for shame to showe,
these pageantes worthy blame:
Some other time my thoughtes me let,[4]
these bloddy factes to name.
{A3v} Thus as I stay in doubt alas,
my dompes are passinge great:
My clogged ioyntes benomd with feare,
have got Dame sorrowes seat
Her massy mace with direfull stroke,
hath stroke my members all:
But these Periphrases[5] I leave,
and will discourse my thrall.[6]
Which to conceave each reader wyll,
well way I do not doubt:
Of late in Chenceforde towne deare friendes,
before the noble route.
Of Judges just plast in that seate,
by our moste famous Queene:
Judgement to give as justice leades,
as daily well is seene.
The Sessions there by order kepte,
offenders to correct:
Thre feminine dames attached were,
whom Sathan had infect.
With Belials sprite whose sorcery did,
the simple so molest:
That when they woulde with present death.
they were full sore opprest.
Here after shall succede the actes,
that they them selves have wrought:
As they them selves confessed have,
to judgement being brought.
Which thing when thou hast viewed well,
good Reader do then praye:

3 A surprise attack, an overcoming. The poet presumably means that he cannot master and express his griefs.
4 Impede.
5 Circumlocutions, round-about ways of speaking.
6 Oppression, misery.

To God the Lorde that he from us,
woulde witches take away.
And thus I ende hoping thou wilte,
my travell well accept:
And judge the truth when thou hast hearde,
of this the full effect.
Finis Prolog.

{A4} An exhortacion to all faithfull men wyllinge them to set Gods feare before their eyes and Sathans practises utterly to despise annexed to the same, profitable for every Christian man to reade and to imbrace.

BEhold these acts & scan them well,
behold their pervers way:
these left ye lord these did his truth
which shold have ben their stay.
In them such power sathan had,
that Christ they did refuse:
his precious blud shed them to save
to much they did abuse.
Sin death and hell did spreade their flagge,
in them they bare the sway:
His worde was yrkesome to their hartes,
they walked farre astray.
What tender harte would god renounce,
who woulde his gospell leave:
What godly one woulde hate his lorde,
and unto Sathan cleave.
What wight woulde gods good benefites,
so lightly nowe esteme:
Which sent his Christ into the worlde,
from hell us to redeme.
Who by his might did vanquishe sinne,
and layed Sathan waste:
By whose dere death eternall lyfe,
his flocke shall surely taste.
His love to us his creatures did,
in ample wise excede:
{A4v} When by the paynes of paynefull death,
to save us he decrede.
What durat harte or selly brest,
coulde finde Christe to repaye:
With such contempte as did these ymphes,[7]

7 Imps.

which here beholde ye may.
What matrones harte woulde hyde the skyll,
of Nature that meke dame:
And toyle by such ungodly artes,
to extinquishe cleane the same.
I meane if God shoulde sende encrease,
and multiply her sede:
Woulde she frequent it to destroy,
by wicked meanes in dede.
I thinke no tender harte coulde finde,
an infantes bloude to spill:
Nor yet no spoused wife I thinke,
her husbande dere woulde kyll
Sith that by witchcraft witches use,
all evilles to sequest:
Let such as feare the livynge God,
their practises detest.
Sith whoredome in the same I saye,
her force doth plainly showe:
Let every wight the same abhorre,
and scape infernall wo.
Sith this arte doth such yll conteyne,
as swearinges manifolde:
Let faithfull hartes forsake the same,
and fixe on Christ their holde.
Sith by that practise vile dere frendes,
man slaughter put in ure:[8]
Let us contemne those godles actes,
and leade a life most pure.
Sith Christ the rocke of lastinge life,
must cleane renounsed be:
{A5} And Sathan as the governour,
must have the dignitie.
What cursed state shall they abyde,
Which Christ their guide refuse:
And study still the devilles minde,
by practise still to use.
Did Christ in vayne bestowe his bloude,
to save our soules from hell:
Did Christ in vaine prepare the heavens,
for his elect to dwell.
Not so I judge, why shoulde we then,

8 A legal term meaning 'use'.

his lawe and worde contemne:
The scripture doth rebellious folke,
everlastingly condemne.
I meane such as his worde detest,
his law condemneth playne:
To taste with him whom they do serve,
in hell eternall payne.
Such as do in sinne delighte,
frequenting mischiefe styll:
Be Sathans owne, for Jesus Christe,
for his deny them wyll.
Sith Christ in heaven will them forsake,
which him in earth denye:
Let us henceforthe learne so to walke,
his name to magnifye.
Let us that swearers be in dede,
our swearinge cleane refrayne:
So shall we scape the gredy gulphes,
of hell and burninge payne.
Let whoremongers which whoredome use,
cast cleane away the same:
And pardon crave, for Christ is prest,[9]
for to forgeve the blame.
Let such men as delight in sinne,
forsake their sinfull waies:
{A5v} And study nowe that all your actes,
may tende the Lorde to prayse.
Let filthy swynishe dronkardes nowe,
abhorred in Gods sight:
leave of their quaffing in excesse,
in modesty delight.
Then shall Gods armes be opened wide,
us wretches to embrace:
And with his sainctes in his kingedome,
he will us surely place.
To whych kingedome for Christes sake,
vouchsafe thy flocke to bringe:
That we as thy electes deare God,
to thee may prayses singe.
Finis. John Phillips.

9 Engaged.

{A6} The examination of them with their confession before Doctor Cole and master Foscue[10] at the same Sise verbatum[11] as nere as coulde be gathered, and firste of Elizabeth Frauncis who saide as here foloweth.

FYrst she learned this arte of witchcraft at the age of. xii. yeres of hyr grandmother whose nam[12] was mother Eve of Hatfyelde Peverell disseased.[13]

Item when shee taughte it her, she counseiled her to renounce GOD and his worde, and to geve of her bloudde to Sathan (as she termed it) whyche she delyuered her in the lykenesse of a whyte spotted Catte, and taughte her to feede the {A6v} sayde Catte with breade and mylke and she dyd so, also she taughte her to cal it by the name of Sathan and to kepe it in a basket. When this mother Eve had geven her the Cat Sathan, then this Elizabeth desired firste of the sayde Cat (callinge it Sathan) that she might be ryche and to have goodes, and he promised her she shoulde, askinge her what she would have, and she sayde shepe (for this Cat spake to her as she confessed in a straunge holowe voice, (but suche as she understode by use) & this Cat forthwith brought shepe into her pasture to the number of. xviii {A7} blacke and whyte, whych continued wyth her for a tyme, but in the ende dyd all weare awaye she knewe not howe.[14]

Item when she had gotten these shepe, she desired to have on[15] Andrew Byles to her husband, which was a man of some welth, and the cat dyd promyse she shold, but that he sayde she must fyrste consent that this Andrew shuld abuse her, and she so did.

10 Dr Thomas Cole, Archdeacon of Essex since 1559; Henry Fortescue of Faulkbourne, a justice of the peace from a neighbouring parish, and sheriff of the county in 1564 (see Alan Macfarlane, *Witchcraft in Tudor and Stuart England* [1970; Prospect Heights: Waveland, 1991], 73, 79 (although Macfarlane confuses assizes with pre-trial hearings); F.G. Emmison, ed., *Elizabethan Life: Wills of Essex Gentry and Merchants* (Chelmsford: Essex County Council, 1978), 84–5; J.S. Cockburn, *Calendar: Essex: Elizabeth* (London: HMSO, 1978) *nomina ministrorum* [lists of JPs] *passim*). The involvement of a religious figure is interesting: witchcraft was a matter still dealt with by ecclesiastical courts, despite its new status after 1563 as a secular offence, and Cole's presence in this secular arena might have helped determine the tone of the examination, with its focus on sin rather than crime.

11 The pamphleteer confuses magistrates and judges here. His first section is almost certainly based on written pre-trial documents taken before Fortescue and Cole, whilst the second section gives a rather more 'verbatum' account of the 'Sise' trial before the judges Gerard and Southcote. As the pamphlet indicates later, Gerard probably sat alone, as it was customary for the judges to divide. These particular felons had been referred to the assize court from quarter sessions (Macfarlane, 271, record 793) which may have added to the writer's confusion.

12 *Sic.*

13 Deceased. Hatfield Peverel is a village five miles north-east of Chelmsford.

14 This folktale-like story is interesting in the light of another such tale told by an examinate called Elizabeth Fraunces in *A Detection of damnable driftes* (1579), A5. Stories told by suspects and accusers may sometimes be based on readily available models as well as/rather than on experienced events.

15 *Sic.*

And after when this Andrew had thus abused her he would not mary her, wherfore she willed Sathan to waste his goodes, which he forthwith did, and yet not beyng contentid with this, she wild him to touch his body, whych he forthewith dyd whereof he died.
Item that every tyme that he did any thynge for her, she sayde that he required a drop of bloude, whiche she gave him by prycking herselfe, sometime in one place & then in an other, {A7v} and where she pricked herselfe there remayned a red spot, which was styl to be sene.
Item when this Andrew was dead, she douting her selfe with childe willed sathan to destroye it, and he bad her take a certayne herbe and drinke it whych she did, and destroyed the childe forthwyth.
Item when she desyred an other husbande, he promysed her an other, naminge this Frauncis whom shee nowe hath, but said he is not so rich as the other, willynge her to consent unto that Frauncis in fornycation which she did, and therof conceaved a daughter that was borne within a quarter of a yere after they were maried.
After they were maryed they lived not so quietly as she desyred, beinge stirred (as she said) to much unquietnes and moved to swearing and cursinge, wherfore she willed sathan her {A8} Cat to kyll the childe, beinge aboute the age of half a yere olde and he did so, and when she yet founde not the quietnes that she desyred, she wylled it to lay a lamenes in the leg of thys Frauncis her husbande, and it did in this maner. It came in a morninge to this Frauncis shoe, lying in it lyke a tode, and when he perceived it puttinge on his shoe, and had touched it with his fote, he being sodenly amased asked of her what it was, and she bad him kil it, and he was forthwith taken with a lamenes wherof he can not healed.[16]
After all this when she had kept this Cat, by the space of. xv. or xvi. yeare, and as some saye (though untruly) beinge wery of it, she came to one mother Waterhouse her neyghbour (a pore woman)[17] when she was going to the oven, and desired her to geve her a cake, & she wold geve her a thing that she should be the better {A8v} for so long as she lived, & this mother waterhouse gave her a cake, where upon she brought her this cat in her apron and taught her as she was instructed before by her grandmother Eve, tellig[18] her that she must cal him Sathan and geve him of her bloude and bread and milke as before, and at this examination woulde confesse no more.[19]
Mother waterhouse of Hatfylde peverell of the age of. lxiiii. yeares being examined the same day confessed as followeth, & the xxix. daye suffered.

16 *Sic.*

17 In *A Detection of damnable drifes* (1579) Elizabeth Fraunces says that Mother Waterhouse was her sister (A5).

18 *Sic.*

19 Elizabeth Frauncis pleaded guilty to bewitching a child, John Auger, and was imprisoned for a year (with four pillory appearances) as the penalty for a non-fatal first offence (Cockburn, *Calendar: Essex: Elizabeth,* record 273).

Fyrst she receyved this cat of this frances wife in ye order as is before sayde, who wild her to cal him sathan, and told her that yf she made muche of him he would do for her what she wolde have him to do.
Then when she had receyved him {B} she (to trye him what he coulde do) wyld hym to kyll a hog of her owne which he dyd, and she gave him for his labour a chicken, which he fyrste required of her & a drop of her blod. And thys she gave him at all times when he dyd any thynge for her, by pricking her hand or face & puttinge the bloud to hys mouth whyche he sucked, & forthwith wold lye downe in hys pot againe, wherin she kepte him, the spots of all the which priks are yet to be sene in her skin.
Also she saythe that another tyme being offended with one father Kersye she toke her catte Sathan in her lap and put hym in the wood before her dore, & willed him to kyll three of this father Kersyes hogges, whiche he dyd, and retourning agayne told her so, and she rewarded hym as before, wyth a chicken and a droppe of her bloud, which chicken he eate up cleane as he didde al the rest, and she {Bv} cold fynde neyther bones nor fethers.
Also she confessed that fallying out with one widdow Gooday she wylled Sathan to drowne her cow and he dyd so, and she rewarded hym as before.
Also she falling out wyth another of her neyboures, she killed her three geese in the same maner.
Item, shee confessed that because she could have no rest[20] (which she required) she caused sathan to destroye the brewing at that tyme.
Also beyng denyed butter of an other, she caused her to lose the curdes ii. or. iii. dayes after.
Item fallinge out with an other of her neybours and his wife, shee wylled sathan to kyll hym with a bluddye flixe,[21] whereof he dyed, and shee rewarded him as before.
Likewyse shee confessed, that because she lyved somwhat unquietly {B2} with her husbande she caused sathan to kyll hym, and he did so about. ix. yeres past, syth which tyme she hath lyved a widdow.
Also she said that when she wolde wyl him to do any thinge for her, she wolde say her Pater noster in laten.
Item this mother Waterhouse confessed that shee fyrst turned this Cat into a tode by this meanes, she kept the cat a great while in woll in a pot, and at length being moved by povertie to occupie the wol, she prai-{B2v}-ed in the name of the father, and of the sonne, and of the holy ghost that it wold turne into a tode, and forthwith it was turned into a tode, and so kept it in the pot without woll.
Also she said, that going to Brackstede[22] a lyttle before her apprehentyon, this Sathan wylled her to hye her home, for she shulde have great trouble,

20 Perhaps yest (yeast)? See *A Detection of damnable drifts* (1579), A4.
21 Flux – a bloody discharge or dysentery.
22 Great Braxted is a village three miles north-east of Hatfield Peverel.

and that shee shoulde be eyther hanged or burned shortly, more at this tyme she wolde not confesse.[23]
{B3} Jone Waterhouse, daughter to this mother Waterhouse, beinge of the age of. xviii. yeres, and examined, confesseth as foloweth.
FYrst, that her mother this laste wynter would have learned her this arte, but she lerned it not, neyther yet the name of the thinge. She saith she never saw it but once in her mothers hand, and that was in the likenes of a tode, and at that time comming in at a sodeyn when her mother called it oute to worke some thynge withall, she herde her to call it Sathan, for shee was not {B3v} at any tyme truely taught it, nor did never exercise it before this time as foloweth.[24]
Item she confessed that when her mother was gone to Breakstede, in her absence lacking breade, she went to a gyrle, a neighbours childe, and desired her to geve her a pece of bred and cheese, whiche when she denied and gave her not, or at the least not so muche as wolde satisfye her, shee goinge home dydde as she had seene her mother doe, callynge Sathan, whiche came to her (as she sayd) she thoughte out of her mothers shewe frome under the bedde, in the lykenes of a great dogge, demaundynge {B4} what she wolde have, wherewithall she beyng a fearde, sayd she wold have him to make such a gyrle a ferd naminge this gyrle, then asked hee her what she wolde geve hym, and she saide a red kocke, then sayde hee no, but thou shalt geve me thy body and sowle, whereby she beinge soore feared, and desyrous to be rydde of hym, sayd she wold: And herewith he went to this gyrle in the lykenes of an evyll favoured dogge with hornes on his head, and made her very muche afearde, and dothe yet haunt her, nowe can not these witches[25] (as they saye) cal hym in agayn, because they dyd not let hym out. And more (sayth shee) she never dydde, but this her doinge was the revealyng of all the rest.
FINIS.
{B4v} Imprynted at London by Willyam Powell for Wyllyam Pickeringe dwelling at Sainte Magnus corner and are there for to be soulde. Anno 1566. the. 13. August.[26]
{2A (second title page)} The second examination and Confession of mother Agnes Waterhouse & Jone her daughter, upon her arainement with the questions & answeres of Agnes Browne the childe, on whom the spirite haunteth

23 Agnes Waterhouse pleaded guilty to the murder by witchcraft of William Fynee (Cockburn, *Calendar: Essex: Elizabeth*, record 274).

24 After this full denial, confession of material more useful to a prosecution begins abruptly – because of pressure, or a change in questioning? Clearly something has happened behind the text and this is the ripple of that event – often all that we can detect.

25 Here the voice changes from Jone's examination narration to comment from the pamphleteer – note the echo about the 'haunted' child on the second title page. The narrative is being shaped more obviously here.

26 The pamphlet appears to be at an end here but another two sections are added, each beginning on a new A signature. These have been labelled by me as 2A and 3A. Perhaps the publisher acquired new material, or intended to spin out that which he had?

at this present, deliberately declared before Justice Southcote and master Gerard the quenes atturney, the. xxvii. day of July Anno. 1566. no lesse wonderfull then most true.

{2Av blank}

{2A2} The Confession of Agnes Waterhowse the. xxvii. daye of July in Anno. 1566. at Chelmsforde before Justice Southcote and M. Gerard the quenes Atturney.

FYrst being demaunded whether that shee were gyltye or not gilty upon her araynement of the murtheringe of a man, she confessed that she was gilty, and then uppon the evidence geven agaynst her daughter Jone Waterhouse, she sayde that she hadde a white Cat, and wylled her cat that he shuld destroy many of her neyghbours cattell, and also that {2A2v} he shoulde kyll a man, and so he dyd, and then after she must go. ii. or. iii. mile from her house, and then she toke thoughte howe to kepe her catte, then she and her catte concluded that he the sayde catte wolde become a tode, and then she shuld kepe him in a close house & geve hym mylke, and so he wolde continue tyll she came home againe,[27] and then being gone forth, her daughter having ben at a neyghbours house there by,[28] required of one Agnes Browne, of the age of xii. yeres or more, a peece of breade and cheese, and the sayde Agnes saide that shee {2A3} had none, and that she had not the key of the milkhouse dore, and then the said Jone went home and was angry with the said Agnes broun and she said that she remembred that her mother was wont to go up and downe in her house and to call Sathan Sathan & she sayde she wolde prove the like, & then she went up and downe the house and called Sathan, and then there came a black dogge to her and asked her what she woulde have, and then she saide she was afred and sayd I wold have thee to make one Agnes browne afrayde, and then he asked {2A3v} her what she wold give him and she saide she wolde geve hym a red kock, and he said he wolde have none of that, and shee asked him what he wolde have then, & he sayde he wold have her body and soule, and so upon requeste and feare together[29] she gave him her body and soule, and then sayde the quenes atturneye, **Ho*we* wylt thou do before god**.[30] O my lord, I trust god wyll have mercy upon mee, and then he saide, **thou saiste well**, and then he departed from her, and then she saide that she herde that he had made the sayde Agnes Browne a fearde.

27 A different telling of the earlier story – this seems like a paraphrase of Agnes Waterhouse's examination stories, perhaps by a court reporter or perhaps by the pamphleteers.

28 A paraphrase of Jone's stories follows here, presented as trial evidence and concluding with an intervention from the judge, Gerard. The detail of the milkhouse key was not mentioned by Jone before, but it is mentioned by Agnes Browne later. This suggests a mixture of sources here.

29 The pamphleteer seems to want to excuse Jone – perhaps a reflection of the jury's verdict. She was acquitted of bewitching Agnes Browne (Cockburn, *Calendar: Essex: Elizabeth*, record 263).

30 Original is in Roman font to set it apart from the surrounding blackletter.

{2A4} The said Agnes Brown was then demaunded and called for, and then she came in, and beinge asked what age she was of she sayde she thoughte she was, xii. yeres old,[31] and then the quenes atturney asked her what shee could say, and then she saide that at suche a day naming the daye certayne that shee {2A4v} was chirning of butter and there came to her a thynge lyke a blacke dogge with a face like an ape, a short taile a cheine and a sylver whystle (to her thinking) about his neck, and a peyre of hornes on his heade, & brought in his mouth the keye of the milkehouse doore, and then my lorde she saide, I was a fearde, for he skypped and leaped to and fro, and satte on the toppe of a nettle, and then I asked hym what he wolde have, and he saide he would have butter, and I said I had none for him and then he saide he wolde have some or he went, and then he {2A5} dyd run to put the keye into the locke of the mylkehouse dore, and I sayde he should have none, and he sayde he wolde have some, and then he opened the dore and went uppon the shelfe, and there upon a new chese laid downe the key, and being a whyle within he came out againe, and locked the dore and said that he had made flap[32] butter for mee, and so departed, and then she saide shee tolde her aunte of it, and then she sent for the priest, and when he came he had her to praye to god, and cal on the name of Jesus, and soo the nexte day my lord he came again[33] {2A5v} to me with the keye of oure milkehouse dore in his mouthe, and then I saide in the name of Jesus what haste thou there, and then he layed downe the key and sayde that I spake evyll woordes in speakynge of that name, and then hee departed, and so my aunte toke up the key for he had kept it from us. ii. dayes and a nyghte, & then we went into the milkhouse and there we did se[34] the print of butter upon the chese,[35] and then within a few daies after hee came againe with a beane pod in his mouth and then the queenes attourney asked what that was, and {2A6} so the other Justices declared,[36] and then shee sayde my lorde I saide in the name of Jesus what hast thou there and so then he laid it downe and saide I spake evil wordes and departed and came agayne by & by with a pece of breade in his mouth, and I asked hym what he wold have

31 This sounds like a trial transcript, unless one thinks this vivid recreation of childish speech is a little too perfect.

32 An unusual use of the word, according to the *OED* (*Oxford English Dictionary*, ed. J.A. Simpson and E.S.C. Weiner, second edn, 20 vols (Oxford: Clarendon Press, 1989). The closest uses recorded by the *OED* are 'faulty or improper'. Rosen suggests 'worthless, topsy turvy' (Barbara Rosen, *Witchcraft in England 1558–1618* (1969; Amherst: University of Massachusetts Press, 1991), 80, n. 10).

33 The account slips from third-person narration into a recreation of Agnes's words. The pamphleteer becomes as much dramatist as reporter, and the reader begins to experience the scene in a deceptively immediate way.

34 *Sic.*

35 As Rosen suggests, probably the print of the decorative butter moulder (80, n. 10).

36 Another detail suggesting that the author of this section actually attended Jone's trial, or, alternatively, that he may be a clever writer.

and he sayde butter it was that he wolde have, & so he departed, and my lord I dyd not se hym noo more tyll wenseday laste, whiche was the. xxiiii. day of July why said the quenes atturney was he with the[37] on wenseday last, ye she said, what did he then to thee sayde he, {2A6v} my lorde saide shee he came with a knyfe in his mouthe and asked me if I were not dead and I said no I thanked god, and then hee sayde if I wolde not dye that hee wold thrust his knife to my harte but he wold make me to dye, and then I sayde in the name of jesus lay down thy knyfe, and hee sayde he wolde not departe from his sweete dames knyfe as yet, & then I asked of hym who was his dame, and then he nodded & wagged his head to your house mother Waterhouse, then the queenes attourneye asked of the sayde Agnes Waterhouse[38] what {2A7} she saide to it, then she demanded what maner knife that it was, and Agnes Browne said it was a daggar knife, there thou liest saide Agnes Waterhouse, why quod the quenes atturney, mary my lord (quod she) she saith it is a daggar knif, and I have none suche in my house, but a greate knyfe, and therein she lieth, yea yea, my lorde, quoth Jone Waterhouse she lieth in that she saith that it hadde a face like an ape, for this that came to mee was like a dogge, well sayde the quenes attourney well, can you make it come before us nowe, if ye can we will dys-{2A7v}-patche you out of pryson by and by, no saith Agnes Waterhouse I can not, for in faith if I had let hym go as my daughter did I could make hym come by and by, but nowe I have no more power over him, then said the queenes atturneye, Agnes Waterhouse when dyd thye Cat suck of thy bloud never saide she, no saide hee, let me se, and then the jayler lifted up her kercher on her heade and there was diverse spottes in her face & one on her nose, then sayde the quenes atturney, in good faith Agnes when dydde he sucke of thy bloud laste, by my fayth {2A8} my lorde sayde she, not this fortnyght, and so the jurye went together for that matter.[39]

Imprynted at London by Willyam Powell for Wyllyam Pickeringe dwelling at Sainte Magnus corner and are there for to be soulde.

Anno 1566. the. 13. August.

37 *Sic.*

38 The account's dramatisation of what occurred in court may conflict with historic legal practice since because Agnes Waterhouse had pleaded guilty she would not have been tried, but set aside for judgement later. Therefore J.S. Cockburn argues that this 'protracted examination' of her seems unlikely to be a true report (J.S. Cockburn, *Calendar of Assize Records: Introduction* [London: HMSO, 1985], 98). However, if she was recalled to comment on evidence given at Jone's trial before a separate jury – for it was Jone and not her mother who was accused of attacking Agnes Browne – then the report may be a truthful account of exchanges with Gerard. The second part of the pamphlet is, after all, described as being based 'uppon the evidence geven agaynst her daughter Jone' (2A2).

39 Presumably to judge Jone. Agnes, because she had admitted her guilt, would not have received a jury trial. Again there is confusion over the transparency of the account.

{2A8v blank}
{3A} The ende and last confession of mother Waterhouse at her death, whiche was the xxix. daye of July. **Anno**. 1566.
FYrste (beinge redi prepared to receive her death) she confessed earnestly that shee had bene a wytche and used suche execrable sorserye the space of. xv. yeres, and had don many abhominable dede, the which she repented earnestely & unfaynedly, and desyred almyghty God forgevenes in that she had abused hys most holy name by {3Av} her devyllishe practyses, and trusted to be saved by his most unspekeable mercy. And being demaunded of the by standers, shee confessed that shee sent her sathan to one Wardol, a neibour of hers, beinge a tayler (with whom she was offended) to hurte and destroy him & his goodes. And this her Sathan went therabout for to have done her wyll, but in the ende he returned to her agayne, and was not able to do this myschiefe, she asked the cause, and he aunswered because the said Wardol was so strong in fayth that he hadde no power to hurt hym, yet she sent hym dyverse and sundry time (but all in vayne) to {3A2} have mischevid hym. And being demaunded whether she was accustomed to go to church to the common prayer or devine service, she saide yea & being required what she dyd there she saide she did as other women do, and prayed right hartely there, and when she was demanded what praier she saide, she aunswered the Lordes prayer, the Ave Maria, and the belefe, & then they demaunded whether in laten or in englyshe, and shee sayde in laten, and they demaunded why she saide it not in englyshe but in laten, seeing that it was set out by publike aucthoritie and according to goddes worde that all men shoulde pray in the englyshe & mother toung that they best understande, and shee sayde that sathan wolde at no tyme suffer her to say it in englyshe, but at all tymes in laten:[40] for these and many other offences whiche shee hathe commyted, done and confessed shee {3A2v} bewayled, repented, and asked mercy of God, and all the worlde forgyvenes, and thus she yelded up her sowle, trusting to be in joye with Christe her saviour, whiche dearely had bought her with his most precious bloudde. Amen.
Imprynted at London by Willyam Powell for Wyllyam Pickeringe dwelling at Sainte Magnus corner and are there for to be soulde.
Anno 1566. the. 23. August.[41]

40 Agnes apparently provides her Protestant questioners with the perfect justification for their views on the forbidden (Catholic) use of Latin. The pamphlet strikes the familiar anti-Catholic note.

41 Ten days after the first two sections. The first two sections have the same running title, 'The examination and Confession', but this last section's is 'The last ende of mother Waterhouse'.

2

The Examination of John Walsh (1566)

This very inky and sometimes barely legible octavo pamphlet, the sole surviving copy, is the only example of a church-court investigation of witchcraft finding its way into print. The original manuscript account, from which the pamphlet's main text was transcribed almost without change, is in a volume of similar cases in Devon Record Office (Chanter MS 855B, fos 310–12). It gives John Walsh's name as 'Welsh'. John Walsh is the only male 'witch' in this period to have an account devoted to his trial (although see the later 'life' of Dr Lambe, and Walsh's contemporary Francis Coxe for conjurors).[1] The anti-Catholic message of the pamphlet fits well with his masculine, semi-learned brand of magic, as it would not with more mainstream, predominantly female, witchcraft. Walsh learned his rituals from Sir Robert of Dreiton (Drayton), who, we are told, was a Catholic priest. Walsh's ritual – like Catholic ritual – is represented in this Protestant church-court document as evil and superstitious, connected with the devil and with beliefs about fairies which Walsh's questioners probably regarded as evidence of (papist) ignorance. The male 'witch' (more accurately, a conjuror, cunning man or village magician) is shown as half-educated, misled and yet powerful – a figure analogous to contemporary representations of Catholics, and quite unlike the traditional representation of the female witch.

The pamphlet has no entry in the Stationers' Register, but was printed and published by John Awdeley. Awdeley was also a writer, working throughout the 1560s and 70s, and is likely to be the author of the Preface to *The Examination of John Walsh.* His other works include the entertaining piece of character-writing, *The Fraternitye of Vacabondes* (1565), which catalogued the beggars and tricksters of Elizabethan London, and various anti-Catholic works such as the Protestant nationalist broadside *A Godly ditty or prayer to be song unto God for the preservation of his Church, our Queene and Realme against all Traytours, Rebels and papisticall enemies* (1569). Thus this pamphlet is in the

1 *A Briefe Description of the Notorious Life of John Lambe* ('Amsterdam', 1628), Francis Coxe, *A Short Treatise declaryinge the detestable wickednesse of magicall sciences* . . . (London, 1561).

mainstream of his publishing and writing interests. The text used here is in the British Library.

{A (title page)} The Examination of John Walsh, before Maister Thomas Williams, Commissary to the Reverend father in God William bishop of Excester,[2] upon certayne Interrogatories touchyng Wytchcrafte and Sorcerye, in the presence of divers gentlemen and others. The. xx. of August. 1566. Imprynted at London by John Awdely, dwelling in litle Britain street wythout Aldersgate 15[66] The. xxiii. of December.
{Av blank}
{A2} Here hast thou (gentle Reader) the examination of John Walsh of Netherbery in Dosetshiere,[3] touching Sorcerie and Witchcraft, which he learned (as hereafter is shewed) of a certayne Priest named syr Robert of Dreiton. Wherein thou mayest see the fruites of Papistes and papistrye, and their yll exercises of their ydle lyves, which hath bene no small hurt to all common weales. For hereby not onely the simple people have bene falsly seduced and superstitiously lead: but all estates have beene sore greeved and troubled by these their practises of Sorcery and Witchcraft.
It would be to tedious to shew but a few histories of their divelish practises, and to to horrible factes in murthers and other mischiefes: which not onely the fat belly fed Moonkes, flattering Friers, and idle lusty Priestes practised and used: but also the holy fathers themselves Popes, Cardinals, and Bishops were chiefly and wholye geven to the studye and exercise of these most wicked and divelish sciences, and by these meanes did worke to come to the Papall state, hie dignities, and great wealth. Which was (as the histories declare) wyth the murthering and poysoning prively one of anochrr.[4]
As first Pope Alexander the sixt,[5] having so-{A2v}-cietie with wicked Sprites and Divels, gave hymselfe body and soule unto them, upon condition he might attain to the Popes seate, and dignity: which they promised him and fulfilled, but he enjoyed it not long, contrarie to his expectation: For he being prively conveyed into a chamber in a certain place called Mount *Cavillus*, and ther questioning with his Demon how long hee shoulde raygne Pope, was aunswered that he should raigne. xi. and. viii. which this holy father understood to be so many yeares: but he was deceived. For after he

2 William Alley, bishop since 1560 – see George Oliver, *Lives of the Bishops of Exeter* (Exeter, 1861), 138–9.

3 *Sic.* Netherbury is a Dorset village some thirty-five miles east of Exeter. Perhaps Walsh was brought to Exeter because he was suspected within the diocese – his home village lies outside it.

4 *Sic.* Should presumably read 'another'.

5 Rodrigo Borgia, pope until 1503. Father of Lucrezia and Cesar, he had numerous enemies willing to defame him. It was also rumoured that he died of poison. Details of the popes are taken from *The Catholic Encyclopaedia*, 15 vols (New York: Robert Appleton, 1907–).

had raigned Pope xi. yeares and. viii. monethes, this Divel would no lenger be without hys praye, but strayght came to the Popes court deckt like a Courtier, and at the Popes chamber doore dyd knock very loudlye, saying that he must needes speake with his Fatherhood. The doore being opened, he came and spake with the Pope, al others being bid to avoyde. But they were so earnestlye talking together, that many did rightly conject that they were at contention. For the Pope stoutlye affirmed his time not to be expired. For (sayd he) I had promised me. xix. yeares (for. xi. and. viii. is. xix.) and of these. xix. yeares, I have raygned but. xi. yeares and. viii. monethes. But this courtierlike Devil replied and sayd, that he mistooke his wordes, for I sayd not (sayde he) xix. yeares, but I ment. xi. yeares and. viii. monethes, and therefore nowe thou must needes {A3} dye. Whereat the Pope being abashed, fell to entreating, but all was in vayne. For [as]soone as this Devil was gon, the soule of this Pope departed miserably from his body, wyth horrible cryes, fearefull groninges, and deadly bewaylinges. In this sort dyed this horrible Sorcerer (as sayeth *Hieronimus Marius* in his worke intituled *Eusebius Captivus*.)[6] In which worke the history of this wicked Pope Alexander is very lyvely set foorth, both as touching his wycked lyving and horrible factes. Whose terrible ende may be an example to all Sorcerers, Conjurers, and Witches.

Like unto hym was Pope Gregory the. vii. otherwyse called Hellybrand (Hildebrande I should say)[7] who was also a great Sorcerer and Nigromancer, as *Benno* the Cardinal doth declare in his worke of this Gregories life.[8] Saying that he also had a Familiar sprite, whereby he wrought manye mischiefes in the common weale of Rome, as well for the satisfieng of his fleshly and beastlye lust, as also for to encrease hys ryches and dignitie.

Platina[9] also writeth the lyke of Pope John. 8. Pope Silvester, Pope Bennet. 8.[10] with dyvers others, which were better practised in these divelish sciences then in godly divinitie.

Much like to these was Pope Paul the third,[11] who as *Sleidan*[12] declareth, exercised sorcerye and Witchcraft, and therby committed. ii. horrible {A3v}

6 Hieronymus Massarius, *Eusebius Captivus* (1553?), (Rosen, 66, n. 2).

7 The prefacer is not the first to spot this joke: Hildebrand, Pope Gregory VII, was known as Hell-brand to his (many) enemies. A reformer who excommunicated the German emperor, Henry IV, he was forced from office and replaced in the early 1080s.

8 Rosen suggests St Benno (66, n. 3), a contemporary of Gregory VII who opposed his policy towards Henry IV.

9 Bartolomeo Sacchi (Platina) was a Humanist opponent of various popes, although he eventually became papal librarian. His *Vitae Pontificum* or *Lives of the Popes* was published in 1479.

10 John VIII reigned from 872 to 882; Silvester may be Silverius (reigned 536–7); Benedict VIII reigned 1012–24.

11 Paul III, Alessandro Farnese, reigned 1534–49.

12 Johannes Sleidan (1506–56), Professor of Law at Strasbourg and author of *De Statu Religionis* (1555).

[murthers and poysoned his Mother and Nevew that he might enjoy hys inheritaunce the sooner. He poysoned also his own Sisters husband that he more freely might have her at hys wycked commaundement].

Pope Clement the. 8.[13] was also of this Fraternitie, as in the Comentaries upon the Articles of the Doctors of Paris is declared: where hys style is thus set foorth: that he was a Bastard, Empoysoner, Homicide, Bawd, Symoniacke, Sodomite, Perjurer, Whoremaster, Nigromancer, Church robber, and a practiser of all kinde of wyckednes.

These with a great many mor of that abhominable sea of Rome wer thus occupied, whose endes were most terrible, as their lives were most wicked. And these faculties their inferior sorte, as Moonkes, Friers, and Priestes also used, and would teach the same witchcraftes and Sorceries to such men and women as they had committed evyll wyth. As of late was confessed of a woman which used Witchcraft and Sorcerye, that she learned the same of a priest whose harlot she had bene many a yeare. I exhort all men therfore to flee from them and these dyvelish practises, as from Devils incarnate, least in following them with lyving here pleasantly a litle while, they be tormented with them in hell perpetually. Which God for hys Christs sake wythdraw and let[14] now and ever. Amen.

{A4} The examination of John Walsh of Dorsetshere touching Witchcraft and Sorcerie.

The Tewsday being the. xx. daye of August 1566. there was examined before maister Thomas Williams (Commissary to the reverend Father in God William Bishop of Excester) one John Walsh, upon certaine Interrogatories touchyng Wytchcraft, in the house of Mayster Thomas Sinkeler keeper of the Shiriffes warde, in the presence of John Butler, and Robert Buller, Gentlemen, William Blachford and John Bordfield.[15]

Hee being first demaunded of his habitacion, he said that he dwelt in a parish called Netherberry in Dorsetshere.

Secondly, beyng asked whether he were ever syr Robert Draitons man, he said that he was retaining unto him by the space of. vii. yeares.

{A4v} Thirdly, being demaunded whether he did practise any Phisicke or Surgery: he sayde that he doth practise both, for the Tisicke and the Agues, and that he hath practised thys Phisicke by the space of these. v. yeares, sithens his maister syr Robert of Dreiton died.[16]

13 Clement VIII did not become pope until 1592 – this could refer more plausibly to Clement VII, Giulio de Medici. Pope from 1523 to 1534, his parents were indeed unmarried. It was he who refused to grant Henry VIII his divorce from Catherine of Aragon and excommunicated him.

14 Prevent.

15 At this point the MS source for the pamphlet, an ecclesiastical record in Devon Record Office, gives the marginal information that Walsh was about 'L' (i.e. fifty) years of age (Chanter MS 855B, fo. 310).

16 Drayton is a village in Somerset, twelve miles north of Netherbury.

Fourthly, being demaunded of whom he learned his Phisicke and Surgery: he aunswered that he learned it of hys maister syr Robert of Dreiton.
Fiftly, being demaunded whether he doth it by Arte naturally, or els by anye other secrete or privy meanes: He aunswered that hee useth hys Phisicke or Surgerie by Arte, naturallye practised by him, as he sayth, & not by anye other yll or secrete meanes.[17] And yet he being demaunded whether he knew ye natural operation of ye herbs, as whether thei wer hot or cold and in what degre they wer hot or cold, he answered he could not tel.[18]
Sixtlye, he being demaunded whether he had a Familiar or not: he aunswered and denied utterlye that he had {A5} none about hym, neyther in anye other place of this worlde, eyther above the ground, or under the ground, either in any place secrete or open.
Seventhly, he being demaunded how he knoweth when anye man is bewytched: He sayth that he knew it partlye by the Feries, and saith that ther be. iii. kindes of Feries, white, greene, & black. Which when he is disposed to use, hee speaketh with them upon hyls, where as there is great heapes of earth, as namely in Dorsetshiere.[19] And betwene the houres of. xii. and one at noone, or at midnight he useth them. Whereof (he sayth) the blacke Feries be the woorst. Also he saith that he had a booke of hys said maister, which had great circles in it, wherein he would set two waxe candels a crosse of virgin waxe, to raise the Familiar spirite.[20] Of whom he woulde then aske for any thing stollen, who dyd it, and where the thing stollen was left, and thereby did know, and by the Feries he knoweth who be bewitched.
{A5v} Eightly, he being demaunded whether he had ever any Familiar or no: he sayth that he had one of his sayde mayster. Which Familiar (after his booke of Circles was taken from him by one Robert Baber of Crokehorne,[21] then beyng Constable, in the yeare. 1565) he coulde never do any thing touching his Familiar, nor the use thereof, but hys Familiar dyd then depart from him, and wyll never come to him agayne, as he sayth. And further he sayth upon his oth, that his Familiar would somtyme come unto hym lyke

17 This paragraph is very confused in the source MS – originally the question seems to have been recorded as whether 'he dothe yt by arte naturally or else by any familiar'. This final phrase was then crossed out, and other alterations made throughout the paragraph. Obviously this was felt by the recorder to be a key moment of clarification, and perhaps it indicates a concentration of questioning here. Mention of the familiar is deferred in the record until the next question – presumably not a true reflection of the actual moment when this idea was suggested.

18 Because Walsh is not educated in the prevailing medical orthodoxy of the humours, his source of skill is implicitly assumed to be the only conceivable alternative – magic.

19 Rosen plausibly suggests prehistoric burial mounds, sites of pagan spirituality, as the location for Walsh's fairies (68, n. 8).

20 Note the slippage (by the writer or Walsh?) into assumption of guilt – which the next question then probes.

21 Crewkerne, six miles north of Netherbury.

a gray blackish Culver,[22] and somtime lyke a brended Dog,[23] and somtimes lyke a man in all proportions, saving that he had cloven feete.

Ninthly, he being demaunded howe long he had the use of the Familiar: He sayd one yeare by his sayd maisters life, and. iiii. yeres after his death. And when he would call him for a horse stollen, or for any other matter wherein he would use him: hee sayth hee must geve hym {A6} some lyving thing, as a Chicken, a Cat, or a Dog. And further he sayth he must geve hym twoo lyving thynges once a yeare. And at the first time when he had the Spirite, hys sayd maister did cause him to deliver him one drop of his blud, whych bloud the Sprite did take away upon hys paw.

Tenthly, he sayth that when the Familiar should doo any thing at his commaundement in going anye arrant: he would not go, except fyrst two wax candels of Virgin waxe shoulde first have bene layd a crosse upon the Circle, wyth a little Frankensence,[24] and saynt Johns woorte, and once lighted, and so put out agayne: which Frankensence must be layd then at every end of the candel, as he saith a crosse, and also a litle Frankensence with saynt Johns woort burned upon the grounde, or ever the Familiar would go, and that would force hym to go the message, and returne agayne at the houre appoynted.

{A6v} Eleventhly, he being asked whether they yt do good to such as ar bewitched, cannot also do hurt if they list. Whereto he answered, he that doth hurt, can never heale againe any man, nor can at any time do good. Howbeit he saith that he wych hath but the gyft of healyng, may do hurt if he list, but his gift of healyng can never returne agayne to anye other persons use.

Twelftly, he being demaunded whether that any of the three kindes of Feiries when they did hurt, dyd it of theyr own malignity, or of the provocation of anye wicked man? He aunswered that they doe hurt of their owne malignitie, and not provoked by anye manne, and that thei have power upon no man, but upon suche as onelye doo want fayth, which is ye cause why they have power more of some persons then of anye others. Furthermore, he being demaunded to what end the Familiar dyd serve them? He aunswered that hee serveth {A7} for no purpose, but to search out things theft stollen, & for no other purpose at al. He being further demaunded to what end ye Spirits in the likenes of Todes and the pictures of man or woman made in wax or clay doo serve? He sayde, that[25] Pictures made in wax, wyll cause the partye (for whom it is made) to continue sycke twoo whole yeares: because it will be two whole yeares ere the wax wyll be consumed. And as for the

22 A pigeon or dove.

23 Brindled.

24 The MS records that the frankincense should be 'hallowyd' but this was then crossed out (fo. 311v).

25 MS reads 'theire temperature of pictures . . .' (fo. 311v).

Pictures of claye, their confection is after this maner. They use to take the earth of a new made grave, the ryb bone of a man or woman burned to ashes, if it be for a woman, they take the bone of a woman, if for a man, the bone of a man, and a blacke Spider,[26] with an inner pith of an elder, tempered all in water, in the which water the sayd Todes must fyrst be washed. And after al ceremonies ended, they put a pricke, that is, a pyn or a thorne in any member wher they wold have the party greved. And if the sayde {A7v} pricke be put to the hart, the party dieth within nine daies. Which Image they burne[27] in the moste moystest place they can finde. And as touching the using of the Todes, the which he sayth have several names: som they cal great Browning, or little Brownyng, or Bonne, great Tom Twite, or litle Tom Twite, with other like names: Which Todes being called the Witches strike with. ii. withie sperres on both sydes of ye head, and saith to the Spirit their Pater noster backward, beginning at the ende of the Pater noster, but they wyll never say their Creede. And when he is stricken, they commaunde the Tode to hurt such a man or woman as he would have hurted. Whereto if he swell, he will goo wher he is apointed, either to the deiry, brewhouse, or to the dry kill of malt, or to the Cattel in the field, to the stable, to the shepefold, or to any other like places, and so returne agayne to his place. The bodies of men or women bee hurt {A8} by the Images before named, & mens goods & Cattels[28] be hurt by the Todes, in commaunding and using them, as aforesaid, as he sayth. And if the Tode called forth, as aforesaid, do not swell, then will the Witch that useth them cal forth an other to do the act, which if hee do not, then will they spy an other tyme when they maye cause the partye to be found lacking fayth, or els to bee more voide of grace, where he or they may be hurt. Furthermore he saith, that who so doth once a day saye the Lordes prayer[29] and his Creede in perfite charitie, the Witch[30] shall have no power on hys body or goodes for that day.

Xiii. He beyng demaunded whether that those which doo heale men or women, being hurted by Witches, can find out those Images under ground, wher with they were tormented? He affyrmeth they can.

And. xiiii. he being demaunded whether he himselfe eyther hath or had at {A8v} any time any such Tode, or that ever he made anye suche Images to hurt man, woman or childe? He affirmeth by the othe which he hath taken that he never had suche Todes, or ever made suche Images.

26 MS reads 'athercobbe', a dialect term for a spider (fo. 312). The pamphleteer has altered this for his London audience.

27 Rosen suggests 'burie', 70, n. 15, which is confirmed by the MS (fo. 312).

28 Chattels (MS has 'cattales', fo. 312).

29 MS has 'pater noster' (fo. 312), and the substitution of the Protestant, vernacular 'Lordes prayer' in the printed version suggests the pamphleteer's propagandist editing skills at work.

30 MS has the 'devill', which was then crossed out (fo. 312).

And he being demaunded, whether that ever he dyd anye hurt to man, woman or childe, or to their goodes or Cattels? He sayth by the othe that he hath taken, that he never did any such hurt either in body or goodes.

3

A Rehearsall both straung and true (1579)

Published by Edward White the elder, who dealt largely in ballads and topical broadsides, and printed by John Kingston, this octavo pamphlet was registered by the Stationers' Company on 24 March 1579. The text used here is in the British Library.

The pamphlet is based – unusually – on a gaol examination of a witch, rather than a preliminary examination taken before the suspect was committed to gaol. This may be related to the fact that the Windsor witches were the subject of a letter from the Privy Council to local magistrates urging further investigation, on 16 January 1578/9, because of recent concern over attacks on the Queen by witchcraft. There are several discrepancies in the account of events given in the *Rehearsall* (1579), which in effect disguise Privy Council involvement.

For example, the Privy Council letter (to Sir Henry Nevell) is dated 16 January 1578/9, whilst Elizabeth Stile's gaol examination is dated 28 January. This gaol examination is described as being taken 'immediately after hir apprehension' (A4). But this seems unlikely: the Privy Council letter mentions that the Council have already considered elements of some witches' examinations before 16 January, and any witches dangerous enough to be reported to the Council would hardly have been left at large afterwards. Nevell had been aware of Stile's supposed activities with the same group of witches for years (see Richard Galis' *A brief treatise* (1579) for an account of their contacts), and even if the pamphlet is wrong in stating that the other witches were apprehended on Stile's evidence given in the 28 January examination (B2v – but the Council had considered the examinations of other 'wiches' by the 16th) it seems likely that Stile herself would have been in gaol before 28 January, as one of a known group of suspects. This is a complex knot of events, but they suggest that the document printed in *Rehearsall* (1579) is a gaol examination which may have been prompted by the Privy Council letter, and that political involvement was concealed – possibly by reordering events, but certainly by silence.[1]

1 See Rosen, 83, and *Acts of the Privy Council of England*, ed. J. R. Dasent. New Series, vol. 11 (1895; Mendeln/Liechtenstein: Kraus, 1974), 22.

The 'memorandum' at the end of the pamphlet contains two stories probably reported from the trial. Thus we have two different sources of information here, with the survival of another pamphlet about the case as a bonus.

{A (title page)} **A Rehearsall both straung** *and true, of hainous and horrible ac-*tes committed by Elizabeth Stile, *Alias Rockingham, Mother Dutten, Mo-*ther **Devell, Mother Margaret, Fower noto-***rious Witches, apprehended at winsore in the* Countie of Barks. and at Abbing-*ton*[2] *arraigned, condemned, and executed, on the 26. daye* **of Februarie laste** *Anno. 1579.*
Imprinted at London for Edward White at the little North-doore of Paules, at the signe of the Gun, and are there to be sold.
{Av blank}
{A2} **The Reader**
Among the punishementes whiche the Lorde GOD hath laied uppon us, for the manifest unpietie and carelesse contempt of his woorde, aboundyng in these desperate daies, the swarmes of Witches, and Inchaunters, are not the laste nor the leaste. For that old Serpent Sathan, suffred to be the scourge for our sinns, hath of late yeares greately multiplyed the broude of them, and muche encreased their malice. Whiche practize, he hath the more easely performed for that wholesome remedies, provided for the curing of such can-{A2v}-kers, are either never a whit, or not rightly applied: For albeeit the Justicer bee severe in executyng of the Lawes in that behalfe, yet suche is the foolishe pitie, or slackenes, or both of the multitude and under officers that thei most commonly are winked at, and so escape unpunished, to the dishonour of God, and imminente daunger on hir Majesties leige[3] people. Nay the fondnes and ignorance of many is such that they succour those Devilishe Impes, have recourse to them for the health of themselves or others and for thinges loste, callyng them by the honorable name of wise women. Wherin they know not what honour they doe to the devill. For it is Sathan, that doeth all that plageth with sicknes, that mayneth, {A3} Murdreth, and Robbeth, and at his lust restoreth. The Witche beareth the name, but the devill dispatcheth the deedes, without hym the Witche can contrive no mischief. He without the Witche can woorke treason to muche, to often, and to soone. If then by the lawe of the Lord of life, Witches, and Inchaunters, are accompted unworthy to live. If by the lawe of this Lande, they are to be done to death, as Traitors to their Prince, and felons in respect of her highnes subjectes, whosoever thou be, beware of ayding them, goe not with *Saule* the reprobate to aske counsaile

2 Abingdon, in Oxfordshire, would have hosted the assizes. It is thirty miles north-west of Windsor.

3 *Sic.*

4 King Saul, in 1 Samuel 28, went to 'inquire' of 'a woman that hath a familiar spirit' at Endor. Previously, he is said to have persecuted those with familiar spirits, and wizards, as readers here are exhorted to do – but he asked the woman to raise the spirit of Samuel, who then prophesied his downfall. Writers on witchcraft disputed endlessly the demonological

of them[4] neither for Christianitie sake, seeme to be more slack in a good purpose, then *Cicero* the Ethnique,[5] who plainely adviseth that Witches Poysoners .&c. are to be {A3v} rather shutte up in prison, and tied with fetters, then moved to amende with counsaile, and perswasions, only afterwardes suffered to escape whereby thei may renew their malicious, and treasonable driftes.

{A4} *1579. January the 28. daie.* **The true examination and** *Confession of Elizabeth Stile, alias* Rockyngham uttered at the Gaile *of Readyng,*[6] *in the Countie of Barke im-***mediately after hir apprehension** *in the presence of the per-*sons hereafter men**tioned.**

Eliazbeth Stile *ali.* Rockingham, late of Windesore widowe of the age of lxv. yeres or there aboute beeyng apprehended at Windsore aforesaid, and brought personally before the right worshipfull **Sir Henry Nevell**[7] knight beyng by him examined, and found by manifest and undeniable proffes[8] of her honest neighbors to be a leude, malitious, and hurtfull woman to the people and inhabitants thereaboutes, was thereupon committed to the common Gaile of Reading, there to remain untill the next great {A4v} Assises, there to bee holden that hir offence might be more straightly sifted, and she the offender to receive the guerdon due for hir demerites. Whither when she was come, and moved by the Gailer there named **Thomas Rowe** to turne hir self to God, from whome she had notoriously fallen, and mildely to beare the punishmente belongyng to hir deedes passed, and there withall urged in signe of hir repentaunce, to confesse hir former follies and facts, she seemed to have some remorse in conscience, and desired to have some talke with the saied **Thomas Rowe**. To whome with one **John Knight** the Counstable, **John Griffeth** an Inholder, and one **William Printall** being all fower presente she confessed as followeth.[9]

{A5} *And firste concernyng those persones that practice the damnable arte of Witchecraft, Sorcerie, or Inchauntement of her owne certaine knowledge, and voluntarie motion, she uttered to this effect ensuyng.*

In Primis that one father Rosimonde, dwellyng in Farneham Parishe,[10] beyng a widower, and also a daughter of his, are both Witches or Inchanters, which

implications of this story but here it is used with accessible simplicity, as a warning against the consultation of cunning people.

5 Heathen. This wonderfully dismissive labelling of Marcus Tullius Cicero, the prominent Roman Republican writer on law, oratory and ethics, suggests the pamphleteer's limitations.

6 The town of Reading is fifteen miles west of Windsor.

7 For Nevell see Richard Galis's much fuller account.

8 *Sic.*

9 This elaborate description of the circumstances in which this unusual document was produced suggests that the writer is justifying the motives of the examiners. The examination might have been made for any number of reasons, from the political to the merely curious, but it is given a most respectable veneer, and a religious context just like Henry Goodcole's 1621 gaol examination of Elizabeth Sawyer, in *The wonderfull discoverie of Elizabeth Sawyer, a Witch* (1621).

10 Farnham Royal, five miles north of Windsor.

Rosimond she saith hath and can transforme hymself by Divelishe meanes, into the shape and likenesse of any beaste whatsoever he will.

2 Item, that one Mother Dutten dwellyng {A5v} within one Hoskins in Cleworthe[11] Parishe, can tell every ones message, assone as she seeth them approche nere to the place of hir abroade,[12] and further, she keepeth a Spirite or Feende in the likenesse of a Toade, and fedeth the same Feende liyng in a border of greene Hearbes, within her Garden, with blood whiche she causeth to issue from her owne flancke.

3 Item, that one Mother Devell, dwellyng nigh the Ponde in Windesore aforesaied, beeyng a verie poore woman, hath a Spirite in the shape of a Blacke Catte, and calleth it Gille, whereby she is aided in her Witchcrafte, and she daiely feedeth it with Milke, mingled with her owne blood.

{A6} 4 Item, that one Mother Margaret dwellyng in the Almeshouse in Windesore, goeth with twoo Crouches, dooeth feede a Kitlyng or Feende by her named Ginnie, with croummes of bread and her owne blood.

5 Item, the saied Elizabeth Stile, **alias** Rockyngham, of her self confesseth that she the same Elizabeth, untill the tyme of her apprehension, kepte a Ratte, beeyng in very deede a wicked Spirite, namyng it Philip, and that she fedde the same Ratte with bloode, issuyng from her right handwrest,[13] the markes whereof evidently remaine, and also that she gave her right side to the Devill, and so did the residue of the Witches before named.

{A6v} *And thus far forthe touchyng the persones aforementioned in generall, now resteth her declaration of their detestable driftes, and devises in particuler.*

6 Furthermore, she confesseth that when she was apprehended, Mother Margaret came to her and gave her money, chargyng her in any wise not to detecte their secretes, whiche if she this prisoner did, the saied Mother Margarete threatened that she should be hardly entreated.[14]

7 And moreover, she saieth that Father Rosimond, with his daughter, mother Dutten, mother Devell, Mother Margaret, and her self the said Elizabeth Rockingham, did accustome to meete within the backeside of Maister Dodges in the Pittes there, and did in that place conclude upon hainous, and vilanous practises, suche as by them, or any of them before had bin devised, or determined.

8 Also she saieth, and confesseth that thei all purposed and agreed, by their Sorceries, and Inchauntementes, to dispatche privilie one Lanckforde a Fermour,[15] dwellyng in Windesore by the Thames side, and that they murde-{A7}-red hym accordinglie.

11 Clewer, an area bordering New Windsor.

12 Should presumably read 'abode'.

13 Wrist.

14 Treated harshly.

15 Farmer.

9 Thei also by their devillishe arte killed one Maister Gallis, who in times paste, had been Maior of Windesore.[16]
10 The like thei practized againste one of the saied Lanckfordes maides, whom by the mischevous meanes above expressed thei bereft of life.
11 Likewise A Butcher named Switcher, escaped not their treacherie, but was by their Witchcrafte brought to his grave.
12 Another Butcher named Mastlyn, was by them handeled in suche sorte, that he consumed awaie.
12 The maner of their Inchauntemente, whereby fower of the persones afore named were murdered was thus: Mother Dutten made fower pictures of Redde Wax, about a spanne long, and three or fower fingers broade for Lanckforde, for his Maide, for Maister Gallis, and for Switcher, and the saied Mother Dutten, by their counsaile and consente {A7v} did sticke an Hauthorne pricke, against the left sides of the breastes of the Images, directly there where thei thought the hartes of the persones to bee sette, whom the same pictures did represente, and thereupon within shorte space, the saied fower persones, beeyng sodainely taken, died.
14 As for Mastlyn the fifte man, she confesseth that he was bewitched, but howe or whether he dyed or no she uttreth not.
15 Further the same Elizabeth saieth, that her self did kill one Saddocke with a clappe on the shoulder, for not keepyng his promisse for an old Cloke, to make her a Saffegarde,[17] who presently wente home and died.
16 Further she saieth, that she and every of them, did over speake one Humfrey Hosie and his wife, and one Richard Milles, and one Jhon Mathynglise, that thei laye sicke in a straunge order a long tyme, but thei were recovered againe.
17 Further she saieth, that mother Devell did over speake one Wylliam Foster a Fi-{A8}-sher, and one Willies wife a Baker.
18 Further she saieth, that mother Dutten did give one Picture, but she knoweth not whether it was of a manne, or of a woman, and the man that had it of her, she thinketh to be deade, but she knoweth not his name.
19 Further she saieth, that one George Whittyng, servaunte to Matthewe Glover of Eaton,[18] had one Picture of her self for one Foster,[19] for that the saied George and Foster fell out at variaunce, and the Picture was made in mother Dottens house, and that mother Dutten, Mother Devell, and her self were at the makyng, and that Mother Devell did saie too her Bunne, or evil Spirite, Plague hym, and spare hym not, and she did thruste a Hauthorne pricke against the harte of hym, and so he laye at the poinct of death a long tyme, but Mother Dutten recovered hym againe.

16 See Richard Galis, *A brief treatise* (1579).
17 An overskirt.
18 Eton, a mile north of Windsor.
19 The fisher?

20 And in the ende, thei killed a Cowe of his by their Witchcrafte.
21 And further she saieth, that thei and every of them, if any had angred them, thei would go {A8v} to their Spirites and saie, suche a one hath angred me, goe dooe them this mischief, and for their hire, would give them a droppe of their owne blood, and presently the partie was plagued by some lamentable casualtie.
22 Elizabeth Stile also confesseth, that she her self hath gone to old Windsor, to the bedde makers there, to begge a messe of Milke, whiche she could not have, for that the maide was then Milkyng, but her Ratte had provided for her bothe Milke and Creame, againste her commyng home.[20]
23 Elizabeth Stile touched with more remorse saieth, that Mother Dutten, & Mother Devell, were her firste intisers to follie, and that she and every of them, did meete sometymes in maister Dodges Pittes, and somtyme aboute a leven of the Clocke in the night at the Pounde, and that Mother Dutten, and Mother Devell did perswade her, to dooe as thei had doen, in forsakyng God and his woorkes and givyng her self to the Devill.
24 Elizabeth Stile confesseth her self often tymes to have gon to Father Rosimund house {B} where she founde hym sittyng in a Wood, not farre from thence, under the bodie of a Tree, sometymes in the shape of an Ape, and otherwhiles like an Horse. She also confesseth her self to have tourned a childes hande in Windesor cleane backwardes, whiche was retourned to the right place by Mother Dutten.
25 Further she saieth, that she will stande unto her death, to all and every Article before rehearsed: and that father Rosimond can transforme hym selfe into the likenesse of an Ape, or a Horse,[21] and that he can helpe any manne so bewitched to his health againe, as well as to bewitche.
26 Further she saieth, that mother Seidre dwelling in the Almeshouse, was the maistres Witche of all the reste, and she is now deade.[22]

20 This, with its new style of starting each paragraph by naming the witch, is the first conventional story of the denial of charity in this pamphlet. The account does not begin conventionally, but opens with the description of magical practices and their victims. This unusual structure is probably connected to the circumstances of the questioning, in that the dialogue is obviously constructed to discover quickly the extent of the witchcraft being practised in Windsor, and to allow apprehension of any more dangerous witches (see B2v), instead of concentrating simply on the crimes of the witch who is already in prison. Note the change in the role of the familiar with the generic change in the type of story told by the witch: the spirit is no longer a magical tool for harming others here, but a nurturing friend to the poor and rejected witch. Perhaps two accounts are joined here, or perhaps the change in format and emphasis simply reflects a change in questioning?

21 This sounds like the response to a question from the examiners checking Stile's veracity: they are probably particularly incredulous of Rosimond's abilities.

22 This unusual statement, implying a hierarchy among a group of witches, suggests influences from the European centres of beliefs in 'covens', although it *may* be a native idea. The apparently foreign name of the mistress witch is probably misleading since Richard Galis's pamphlet alters her name to the more plausible 'Audrey' (B2, D3).

27 Further she saieth, that if she had bin so disposed, fower or five, or more of the best men in Windsor, should not have brought her to the Gaile, but that she came of her owne accorde, and by the waie as she came with Jhon Brome who brought her to the Gaile, her Bunne or Familier came to her in the likenesse of a black {Bv} Catte, and would have had her awaie, but she banished hym, hopyng for favour.

Memorandum, that besides the examination, and confession aforesaid, there was given in evidence, *viva voce*, at the Arraignement of the said Witches, one speciall matter by an Ostler of Windsore,[23] who affirmed upon his othe that the said Mother Stile using to come to his Maisters house, had often tymes reliefe given her by hym. And on a time not long sithens, she commyng to his Maisters house, when there was little left to be given her, for that she came somewhat late, yet he givyng her also somewhat at that tyme, she there-with not contented went her waies in some anger, and as it semed offended with the saied Ostler, for that she had no better Almes, and by the sequell, so it appered. For not long after, he had a greate ache in his limmes, that he was not able to take any reste, not to doe any labour, and havyng sought many meanes for remedie thereof, could finde none, at the laste he wente to a Wiseman, named Father Rosimonde, alias Osborne, who told hym that he was bewitched, and that there was many ill women in Windsore, and asked hym whom he did mistrust, and the saied Osteler aunswered one Mother Stile, one of the {B2} Witches aforesaied: well saied the Wiseman, if you can meete her, and all to scratche her, so that you drawe blood of her, you shall presently mende.[24] And the saied Osteler upon his othe declared, that he watchyng her on a tyme, did all too scratche her by the face, that he made the blood come after, & presently his paine went awaie, so that he hath bin no more greved sithens.

Moreover, on a tyme a mannes Soonne of Windsor, commyng to fetche water at a welle whiche was by the doore of the saied Mother Stile, and by chaunce hurlyng a stone uppon her house, she was there withall muche greeved and saied, she would bee even with hym, and tooke his Pitcher whiche he had brought from hym: the boye goyng home wardes, happened to meete his father, and tolde hym how that Mother Stile had taken awaye his Pitcher from hym, well saied his Father, you have doen her some unhappines, come on with me, and I will goe speake with her. And so the boye goyng with his Father towardes her house, did sodainly crie out: *O my hande my hande*, his father therewithall lookyng backe, and seeyng his Soonnes hande to tourne, and wende backwardes, laied holde thereupon, but he was not able to staye the tourning thereof, {B2v} besides a neighbour of his beeyng in his companie

23 Clearly a change of source, probably to a trial report taken down by someone at the assizes. Possibly this ostler is mentioned as 'Savoye Harvy' by Galis, D3v.

24 Note the slippage into dramatic recreation by the writer. He gives no precise dates, names or places, as a legalistic written source would, but is concerned with reporting a good story.

at that tyme, did also laye holde thereon, and notwithstandyng bothe their strengthes, the childes hande did tourne backwardes, and the palme thereof did stande, where the backe did, to the greevous torment of the saied childe, and vexation of his Father. The whiche hande was tourned againe to his right place, either by the saied father Rosimond, or the saied Mother Devell.[25] Also this is not to be forgotten, that the said Mother Stile, beeyng at the tyme of her apprehension, so well in healthe of bodie and limmes, that she was able, and did goe on foote, from Windsor unto Readyng unto the Gaile, whiche are twelve miles distaunt. Shortly after that she had made the aforesaied confession, the other Witches were apprehended, and were brought to the said Gaile, the said Mother Devell did so bewitche her and others (as she confessed unto the Jailer) with her Enchauntmentes, that the use of all her limmes and senses, were taken quite from her, and her Toes did rotte of her feete, and she was laied uppon a Barrowe, as a moste uglie creature to beholde,[26] and so brought before the Judges, at suche tyme as she was arraigned. Finis.

25 Presumably the incident referred to on B.

26 More evidence that the writer of this section was at the trial – he says he saw Elizabeth Stile. Possibly also a suggestion that he has talked to the gaoler, the source of part of this anecdote.

4

A Detection of damnable driftes (1579)

This octavo pamphlet is Edward White's second of 1579. It was entered in the Stationers' Register on 15 April, and printed by the same printer, John Kingston, as *A Rehearsall both straung and true*. Possibly it was prepared and prefaced by the same pamphleteer – his style, and especially the use of the word 'driftes' is reminiscent of the Windsor pamphlet.

It describes the trials of four witches from various Essex villages. The first, Elizabeth Fraunces, is almost certainly the same Elizabeth Frauncis/Fraunces as in the 1566 pamphlet. Elizabeth was hanged after this trial in 1579, for killing Alice Poole by witchcraft, a charge to which she pleaded not guilty. She was also tried in 1572 for what is rightly described in the court records as her second offence, but the indictment had to be redrafted, and when tried in 1573 for the same offence and found guilty she escaped death and was imprisoned and pilloried – the penalty for a first offence. The 1566, 1572 and 1573 Elizabeths are described as being the wife of Christopher Fraunces/Francys/Frances. In 1579 Elizabeth is described as a spinster, but must be the same woman since she mentions a 'Mother Waterhouse' as her sister. It is interesting that two pamphlets should relate so closely to the same witch over a period of a decade and a half: perhaps they have a source in common, although they were produced by different publishers.

The pamphlet is composed of an examination and informations, all of which informations seem to be paraphrased and reported from the trial or from gossip surrounding it. Trial records back up some of what is said about the witches and their alleged offences. Three of the women were hanged, whilst one (Margery Staunton) escaped trial because her indictment was found to be faulty. The pamphlet is, like the first Essex pamphlet, a fairly straighforward report of individual cases based on information from the pre-trial and judicial process. The text used here is in the British Library.

{A (title page)} **A Detection of damnable driftes, practi***zed by three*[1] *Witches arraigned at* Chelmisforde in Essex, at the laste Assises there holden, whiche were executed in Aprill. 1579.
Set forthe to discover the Ambushementes of Sathan, whereby he would surprise us lulled in securitie, and hardened with contempte of Gods vengeance threatened for our offences.
Imprinted at London for Edward White, at the little North-dore of Paules.
{Av blank}
{A2} **To the Reader.**
Accept this pamphlet (Christian Reader) view, and peruse it with discretion, and hedefulnesse. No trifles are therin conteined worthy to be contemned,[2] *nor pernicious fantazies deservyng to bee condemned. But contrariwise in this pretie plot may holsome hearbes of admonitions for the unwarie, and carelesse, and soote flowers to recreate the wearied senses, be gathered. For on thone*[3] *side the cleare sight maie espie the ambushmentes, whiche Sathan the secrete woorke-maister of* {A2v} *wicked driftes, hath placed in moste partes of this realme, either by craftie conveighaunces of the simple, or by apparaunt treacherie to undermine and spoile the states of suche as God permitteth him to have power over. And on the other side the eye that is wimpled, may hereby by advertised of the dark-enesse, wherewith his understandyng is overcast, and puttyng of the veile of vanities, maie reclaime his concept,*[4] *and esteeme of the impietie of the offendours and vilanie of their actes, accordyng to the woorde of God, and waightinesse of the case. And if in tyme past he hath escaped their Sorceries, let hym not the lesse* {A3} *feare the harmes that maie hereafter ensue. For the Devill by the sufferaunce of almightie God, is as well able to plague the persone, that moste presumeth of safetie, as any have bin who in this treatise are mentioned. Some with muche adoe can be awaked out of their drousie dreames, though thei bee tolde that their neighbours house is on fire. But when their owne walles are invaded with like flames, thei shall finde that it had bin better to have come an hower too soone, to quenche those forrein fires, then to have risen one minute too late to extinguishe the same, creepyng into their owne chambers. If therefore thou be assured that thy neighbour,* {A3v} *either in bodie, familie, or gooddes is impaired by damnable witchcrafte, or perceivest by information, or other wise ought of suche devises, intended to be practized, or likely presumption of suche Devilishe deedes contrived, for Charitie to thy Christian brother, and tender regard of thine own state, prevente or stop the mischief by all possible meanes. And for thyne owne parte with praier, and assured faithe in the merites of Christ Jesus shield thy self, so shal neither the Devill nor his Angelles have power, over thee, or thine. Farewell.*

1 Actually there are four, which may suggest hasty editing and addition of new material.
2 Despised – as opposed to condemned, disapproved of.
3 *Sic* – the one.
4 Conceit, idea – here right notion.

{A4} *The Confession of Elizabeth Fraunces, late of Hatfeelde in Essex.*[5]

Imprimis, the saied Elizabeth Fraunces confessed that about Lent last (as she now remembreth) she came to one Pooles wife her neighbour, and required some olde yest[6] of her, but beyng denied the same, she departed towardes one good wife Osbornes house a neighbour dwelling thereby of whome she had yest, and in her waie going towardes the saied goodwife Osbornes house, shee cursed Pooles wife, and badde a mischief to light uppon her, for that she would give her no yest, Whereuppon sodenly in the waie she hard a greate noise, and presently there appered unto her a Spirite of a white colour in seemyng like to a little rugged[7] Dogge, standyng {A4v} neere her uppon the grounde, who asked her whether she went? shee aunswered for suche thinges as she wanted, and she tolde him therewith that she could gette no yeest of Pooles wife and therefore willed the same Spirite to goe to her and plague her, whiche the Spirite promised to doe, but first he bad her give him somewhat, then she having in her hand a crust of white bread, did bite a peece thereof and threwe it uppon the grounde, whiche she thinketh he tooke up and so went his waie, but before he departed from her she willed hym too plague Pooles wife in the head, and since then she never sawe him, but she hath harde by her neighbours that the same Pooles wife was grevously pained in her head not longe after, and remayneth very sore payned still, for on saterdaie last past this Examinate talked with her.[8]

2 Item this Elizabeth Fraunces saieth further, that she knoweth one Elizabeth Lorde a widowe, dwellyng in the same parishe of Hatfielde and so hath doen of longe tyme, of whom she hard, that about seven or eight yeres paste she brought drinke in a crewse,[9] and gave it to one Jhon Fraunces servaunte to goodman {A5} Some of the same parishe, shortly after the taking of whiche drinke he sickened, and died.

3 Item she further confesseth that she likewise knoweth that the same Widowe Lorde, was saied to have bewitched one Jone Robertes, servaunte to old

5 See *The Examination and Confession of certaine Wytches* (1566) for Fraunces/Frauncis and Hatfield Peverel.

6 Yeast.

7 Shaggy.

8 Elizabeth Fraunces was passed from the magistrate who examined her to Chelmsford sessions (8 January 1578/9), and on to the higher assize court, and tried for bewitching Alice Poole so that she died on 1 November 1578 (J.S. Cockburn, *Calendar: Essex: Elizabeth*, record 1024, and Macfarlane, 273, record 812). Cockburn points out that if this is a report from the trial or after it, then the assertion that Elizabeth talked with her victim on the previous Saturday suggests alarming inaccuracy in either record or pamphlet (Cockburn, *Calendar of Assize Records: Introduction*, 98). But if this is a pre-trial document, the inaccuracy becomes less of a problem since the victim was probably still alive when it was taken (see Marion Gibson, *Reading Witchcraft* [London and New York: Routledge, 1999], 55–6 for further detail).

9 Cruse – a pot or bottle.

Higham, in a peece of an Apple cake whiche she gave her, upon the eatyng whereof she presently sickened, and not long after died.[10]

4 Item she also confesseth, that she knowes one Mother Osborne, a Widowe in the same toune to be a witche, and that she hath a marke in the ende of one of her fingers like a pitt, and an other marke uppon the outside of her right legge, whiche she thinketh to bee pluckt out by her Spirit: and that one Mother Waterhouse her owne sister (long since executed for Witchcrafte) had the self same markes, whiche she termeth (nippes) and she saieth that this Mother Osborne liyng lame, and complainyng of her sore legge, she the saied Elizabeth Fraunces came unto her, and required to see her leg, whiche beeyng shewed unto her, she the saied Elizabeth hadde to put it into the bedde again, saiyng: that she her self knewe that the same {A5v} came, by wante of well servyng of God. And thus muche for Elizabeth Fraunces.

The Evidence given against Elleine Smithe of Maldon.[11]

There was one Jhon Chaundeler dwellyng in Maldon, whose wife named Alice Chaundeler, was mother unto this Elleine Smithe, and for Witchcrafte was executed long before,[12] after whose execution he went unto his daughter in lawe[13] Ellein Smithe, and demaunded certaine money of her, whiche she had received of her mother his wife, by meanes of whiche money thei fell out, and in fallying out the saied Elline in greate rage saied unto hym, that it had been better for hym, he had never fallen out with her, and so it came to passe, for the same Jhon Chaundeler confessed before his death, that after that same hower that she had saied so unto hym, he never eate any meate that digested in hym, but ever it came up againe as soone as it was done, by whiche meanes he consumed, and wasted awaie to his death.

2 The sonne of the foresaid Ellen Smithe, {A6} of the age of thirteene yeres, or there aboutes, came to the house of one Jhon Estwood of Malden, for to begge an almose,[14] who chid the boye awaie from his doore, whereuppon he wente home and tolde his mother, and within a while after the said Estwood was taken with very greate paine in his bodie, and the same night followyng, as he satte by the fire with one of his neighbours, to their thinkyng thei did see a Ratte runne up the Chimney, and presently it did fall doune again in the likenesse of a Tode, and takyng it up with the tongges, thei thruste it into the fire, and so helde it in Forcesibly, it made the fire burne as blewe

10 Snow White – the second fairy-tale echo in a story told by Elizabeth Fraunces/Frauncis.

11 This suggests informations, but they appear to have been paraphrased (for example, the first 'informant' is unnamed, and the victim is dead) and are probably a trial report – see note 15. Maldon is a coastal town ten miles east of Chelmsford.

12 Cockburn, *Calendar: Essex: Elizabeth*, record 669. Alice was sent to the assizes of 24 March 1573/4 from Maldon sessions, accused of killing Mary Cowper, Robert Briscooe and Robert Brisco and his two children. She was, as the pamphlet suggests, found guilty. She also appeared before the borough court at Maldon (Macfarlane, 296, record 1141).

13 We would now say 'stepdaughter'.

14 Alms – an ecclesiastical term.

as Azure, and the fire was almoste out, and at the burnyng thereof the saied Ellen Smithe was in greate paine and out of quiete, whereuppon dissemblyngly she came to the house of the fore saied Jhon Estwood, and asked how all that were there did, and he saied well I thanke God, and she said, I thought you had not been well, and therefore I came to see how you did, and so went her waie.

3 Also it was avouched, and by this prisoner confessed,[15] that where as her daughter, and the daughter of one Widowe Webbe of Maldon aforesaied, did fall out and fight, the same El-{A6v}-lein Smithe offended thereat, meetyng good wife Webbes daughter the nexte daie, gave her a blowe on the face, whereupon so soone as the childe came home she sickened, and languishyng twoo daies, cried continually, awaie with the Witche, awaie with the Witch, and so died. And in the morning immediatly after the death of the same childe, the saied good wife Webbe espied (as she thought) a thyng like to a blacke Dogge goe out at her doore, and presently at the sight thereof, she fell distraught of her wittes.[16]

4 Besides the sonne of this Mother Smith, confessed that his mother did keepe three Spirites, whereof the one called by her greate Dicke, was enclosed in a wicker Bottle:[17] The seconde named Little Dicke, was putte into a Leather Bottle: And the third termed Willet, she kepte in a Wolle Packe. And thereuppon the house was commaunded to bee searched. The Bottles and packe were found, but the Spirites were vanished awaie.

The effecte of the Evidence againste Mother Staunton, late of Wimbishe[18] *in Essex, who was arraigned, but not executed, for that no manslaughter, or murder was objected against her.*[19]

{A7} Imprimis, this Mother Staunton, late of the parishe of Wimbishe in Essex, came to the house of one Thomas Prat of Broke Walden,[20] Jhon Farrour of Libleburie[21] beeyng presente, and one Thomas Swallowe, and the saied Mother Staunton, beyng demaunded by one of them how she did, she aunswered, that a knave had beaten her: saiyng she was a Witche, then saied

15 Confirmation that this is not a pre-trial document but connected to the trial itself – an important difference in timing, and perhaps even in what was confessed.

16 Ellein (Helen Smythe) was tried for killing Susan Webbe (aged four) and found guilty (Cockburn, *Calendar: Essex: Elizabeth*, record 1044).

17 Any type of container: here, a dwelling.

18 Wimbish is some twenty miles north-east of Chelmsford.

19 Actually Staunton's indictment was found insufficient by the grand jury and she could not be tried. Cockburn suggests that it may have been abandoned rather than redrafted (an option open to the court) because of judicial sympathy (*Calendar: Introduction*, 85). The accused was passed to the court from Braintree sessions (2 October 1578) and would have been tried for killing a gelding and a cow (Cockburn, *Calendar: Essex: Elizabeth*, record 1063, and Macfarlane, 273, record 810).

20 Part of Saffron Walden, two miles north-east of Wimbish.

21 Littlebury, three miles north-east of Wimbish.

he again,[22] in good faithe Mother Staunton, I thinke you bee no Witche, no Maister q[23] she, I am none in deede, although I can tell what belongeth to that practise, of whiche woordes, the goodman of the house tooke witnesse of the aforenamed parties, and delivered a bill subscribed with their handes thereof, to Maister George Nicolles.[24]

2 Item, the saied Mother Staunton came to his house an other tyme, and after certaine woordes of anger betweene hym and her, he raced her face with a Nedle, what quoth she, have you a Flea there: and the nexte night after, the saied Pratte was so greevously taken with tormente of his Limmes, that he never thought to have lived one hower longer, which also was subscribed and sent.

{A7v} 3 Item, she came the third tyme by his dore with Graines, and he demaundyng a fewe of her, she asked what he would doe with them, I will give them, saied he, to my Chickens, and snatchyng a handfull from her, did so. But after thei had tasted of them, three or fower dousen of them died, and onely one Chicken escaped of them all.

4 Item, she came on a tyme to the house of one Richard Saunder of Brokewalden, and beeyng denied Yeest, whiche she required of his wife, she went her waie murmuryng, as offended with her aunswere, and after her departure, her yonge child in the Cradle was taken vehemently sicke, in a merveilous strange maner, whereuppon the mother of the childe tooke it up in her armes to comforte it, whiche beyng doen, the Cradle rocked of it self, sixe or seven tymes, in presence of one of the Earle of Surreis[25] gentilmen, who seyng it stabbed his dagger three or fower tymes into the Cradle ere it staied: Merily jestyng and saiyng, that he would kill the Devill, if he would bee rocked there.

5 Item, the saied Mother Staunton, came on a tyme to the house of one Robart Petie of {A8} Brookewalden, and beyng denied by his wife diverse thynges, whiche she demaunded at once, and also charged with the stealyng of a Knife from thence, she wente her waie in greate anger, and presently after her departure, the little childe of the saied Petie fell so straungely sicke as for the space of a Weeke, as no bodie thought it would live.

6 Item, the saied Stauntons wife, came also to one Willyam Torners house of Brokewalden upon a Fridaie, as she had doen often in tymes paste, and

22 i.e. Thomas Swallowe replied.

23 Quoth.

24 A justice of the peace. Nicholls lived at Walden and probably also at Thaxted, a parish neighbouring Wimbish (see Emmison, *Elizabethan Life: Wills of Essex Gentry and Merchants*, *passim*).

25 This may date the story to before 1572, when Thomas Howard, Duke of Norfolk, was attainted and beheaded. His son, Philip Howard, was styled Earl of Surrey until then. By February 1579/80 he had become Earl of Arundel (G.E. Cokayne, *The Complete Peerage*, rev. edn ed. Vicary Gibbs and H. Arthur Doubleday, 13 vols (London: St Catherine's Press, 1910–59), vols XII, 514 and IX, 622–4).

beeyng denied of certaine thynges whiche she craved, as a peece of Leather &c. she asked the good wife how many children she had, who aunswered one, whiche childe beeyng then in perfite healthe, was presently taken with suche a sweate and coldnesse of bodie, and fell into suche shrickyng and staryng, wringyng and writhyng of the bodie to and fro, that all that sawe it, were doubtfull of the life of it.

7 Item, she came on a tyme to the house of Robart Cornell of Suersem,[26] and craved a Bottle of Milke of his wife, but beyng denied it, she departed for a little while, leavyng her owne Bottle behinde her, and tooke an other with her, that belonged to the afore saied Cor-{A8v}-nell, after three daies she came againe, and requested her owne Bottle, and restored the other, cravyng Milke as before, the wife of the house alwaies suspectyng her to bee a Witche denied her requeste, and barred the doores against her, whereupon she satte doune uppon her heeles before the dorre, and made a Circle uppon the grounde with a knife. After that she digged it full of holes with in the compasse, in the sight of the saied wife, her man, and her maide, who demaundyng why she she did so: She made aunswere, that she made a shityng house for her self after that sorte, and so departed, the nexte daie the wife commyng out at the same doore, was taken sicke, and began to swell from tyme to tyme, as if she had been with child, by whiche swellyng she came so greate in bodie, as she feared she should burste: and to this daie is not restored to healthe.

8 Item, she came often to the house of one Jhon Hopwood of Walden, and had continaally her requestes, at the laste beyng denied of a Leathern thong, she went her waie offended and the same night his Geldyng in the stable, beyng the daie before in very good case, died sodainly, and afterward beyng burdeined with all, she never denied it.

{B} Item, she commyng to the house of Jhon Cornell the yonger of Wimbishe, and beeyng denied her demaunde, she tooke offence, and immediatly after his cattell in steede of sweete Milke, yelded gore stinkyng blood, and one of his Kine fell into suche miserable plight, that for a certaine space, he could by no meanes recover her.

Item, she came on a tyme to the Vicars house at Wimbishe,[27] and beyng denied her errande by his wife (he beeyng as then from home) his little sonne in the Nurses lapp was taken with suche vehement sicknes, that the beholders supposed no lesse, but it would straight have died, the saied Mother Staunton sittyng by, and havyng touched the child before it grew sicke: but

26 Seward's End (Rosen, 97). An unlikely visual misreading, suggesting this information is reported from the trial as *heard*.

27 A strange glimpse of another literary world of which the pamphleteer seems quite unaware: the vicar was William Harrison, author of a number of topographical and historical writings including the *Description of England*. His wife was Marion Isebrande, whose family came from Picardy. Harrison had been Vicar of Wimbish since 1570–1 and resigned the vicarage in 1581 (see *DNB*).

within one hower after the Vicar came home the childe recovered perfectly, and plaied as before.

Item, also she came on a tyme to the house of one Robart Lathburie, of the same Toune, who dislikyng her dealyng, sent her home emptie, but presently after her departure, his Hogges fell sicke and died, to the number of twentie, and in the ende he burned one, whereby as he thinketh, he saved the reste: He also had a Cowe straungely caste into a narrowe {Bv} gripe, and beyng holpen out in the presence of maister Henry Mordaunt, notwithstandyng the diligent care that was takn of her, she was in fewe daies three tymes like to be loste in the mire. And thus muche for Mother Staunton.

The effecte of the Evidence geven in against Mother Nokes late of Lamberd[28] *Parishe in Essex.*

A Certaine Servant to Thomas Spycer of Lamberd Ende[29] in Essex yoman, sporting, and passing away the time in play with a great number of youth, chaunced to snatche a paire of Gloves out of the pockette of this Mother Nokes Daughter being a yong woman of the age of xxviii yeres, which he protesteth to have done in jest. Her Mother perceivyng it, demaunded the Gloves of him, but he geving no greate eare to her wordes departed towardes the feeldes to fetch home certeine Cattell. Immediately upon his departure quoth the same Mother Nokes to her Daughter, lette him alone, I will bounce him well enough, at what time he being soudainely taken, and reft of his limmes fell doune. There {B2} was a boye then in his companie by whome he sent the Gloves to Mother Nokes. Notwithstanding his Maister was faine to cause him to be set home in a Wheele Barrowe, and to bee laide into a bedde, where with his legges a crosse he lay beddred eight daies, and as yet hath not attayned to the right use of his lymmes.

Further it was avouched that mother Nokes had saied that her housbande laie with one Tailers wife of Lamberd Ende, and with reprochfull words reviled her saiyng at last: thou hast a Nurse childe but thou shalte not keepe it long, and presently thereupon the Childe died.

An other affirmed, that when he had repoved the said Tailers wife, and Mother Nokes as thei were at Churche, and willed them to agree better, the same Mother Nokes in a fume aunswereth that she cared for none of them all, as longe as Tom helde on her side, meanyng her Feende.

The same man having a servaunt of his at Plough, this Mother Nokes going by, asked the felowe a question but getting no aunswere {B2v} of him she went her way. Forthwith one of his horses fell doune. At his coming home to dynner, he tolde his Maister howe the same horse was swolne about the head. His Maister at first supposyng that it came by a strype,[30] was greately offended at the ploughman, but afterwardes understandyng of Mother Nokes

28 Lambourne, a village fifteen miles south-west of Chelmsford.

29 Lambourne End.

30 A blow of the whip.

goyng by, and the circumstance afore mentioned, went to the said Mother Nokes and chid and threatened to have her to her aunswere, howbeeit the Horse died.[31]

FINIS.

31 Alice Nokes was tried for killing Elizabeth Barfott and found guilty (Cockburn, *Calendar: Essex: Elizabeth*, record 1047).

5

Richard Galis, *A brief treatise* (1579)

Richard Galis was the son of a former mayor of Windsor of the same name. Galis senior allegedly fell victim to the witches described in *A Rehearsall both straung and true* (1579). His son wrote this pamphlet in response to the incomplete account of their crimes given in the *Rehearsall*, and his version was printed and published by John Allde in the same year. Allde produced topical ballads and ephemera, and his son Edward printed *The Apprehension and confession of three notorious Witches* (1589). There is only one surviving copy of the quarto of Galis's work, in the Bodleian Library, and its title page is missing – therefore the pamphlet is known by the title given to it in the Stationers' Register, where it was entered on 4 May: *A brief treatise conteyning the most strange and horrible crueltye of Elizabeth Stile alias Bockingham & hir confederates executed at Abington upon Richard Galis*.

Galis's work is highly unusual for its day: it is written by the supposed victim of witch-attack, it is highly literate and self-consciously artistic, and it reaches out to the reader with a personal appeal which is hard to resist. This type of writing, connected with increased interest in the victim rather than the witch, became more common in Jacobean pamphlets – but, even so, Galis's account is unique in its view of supposed events. His bizarre and violent response to visions and sicknesses which, he writes, were visited on him by the witches, leads the reader eventually to question his mental stability and trustworthiness as a reporter, so that the issues of fact and fiction surrounding this account of witches are far more complicated than before. It is not enough to determine context, text sources and authorship: clearly the pamphlet is a reasonably unified first-person narrative by a single author, incorporating edited text from the *Rehearsall* in its final section. It is the author's perspective on events which becomes the important – and elusive – matter of inquiry.

Richard Galis's account of witchcraft is the first of its kind to be written by a comparatively wealthy and reasonably learned victim. His version of events is the first expression of an attitude which will become common in later works. Firstly, he (articulately and at length) presents himself as reactive to events rather than initiating them. He thus presents the witches' attack on him as being motiveless. There is no story of his denying the witches charity, or otherwise justly angering them. This story of allegedly motiveless attack becomes increasingly common in narrations by, or written on behalf of, influential victims – pamphlets based on legal records, featuring victims of lower social status, continue to tell the traditional stories of the witch revenging an injury inflicted on them by the victim. On top of this alternative model of witchcraft, Galis also attempts to present himself as a godly hero, combatting the devil as part of a spiritual journey which becomes his autobiography. He does not see himself as being demonically possessed, but his story takes the same shape as that of a victim of possession would. His continual imprisonment by the authorities, and the apparent refusal of Windsor magistrates to take him seriously as an informant, further complicate the story since they suggest that Galis was regarded by his community as a nuisance rather than as a godly asset. Issues of local politics and religious conflict seem certain to be important in determining Galis's exclusion from power, but it is likely that he was also seen as a dangerously unpredictable person, and probably a melancholic. In view of his complete absence from the more 'official' story of the witches, in *A Rehearsall both straung and true*, it seems probable that his view of their activities was seen as invalid, and silenced. Combatting this rejection of his views is, he says, his motivation in writing the pamphlet. It is interesting that, in outline, his construction of himself as a blameless victim is one which does later accusers no harm at all. Neither was his accusation of these particular women implausible to his community, for they were (as we have seen) later accused by others, convicted and hanged. Other factors than the basic story of witchcraft seem to be key here: the credibility of the accuser, his religious stance and his place within the hierarchy of his community determine whether he is listened to, or not.

The pamphlet is little known, and there is no other modern edition of it. Its relation to the *Rehearsall* is particularly interesting: Galis has sources of information (but what are they?) which in his view correct and add to material in the earlier pamphlet, but his editing of it sometimes seems arbitrary and misleading. A comparison of the two pamphlets exemplifies the difficulties of reading the accounts in this edition – one feels that there are so many, equally rich and valid, tellings of each story of witchcraft that no definitive version can or should ever be constructed. In Galis's terms, therefore, there can never be a 'true edition' of a story of witchcraft.

{A2} *The Epistle* TO HIS SINGULER good Freend and looving Cuntreyman, *Maister Robert Handley Citizen and Grocer of* **London and Merchant Venterer into the Cuntries of Spaine**[1] **Richard Galis** wisheth long life and prosperitie to the pleasure of God and his soules helth.

1 Handley was presumably involved in the trade in luxury foodstuffs with Spain and her colonies, perhaps in oil and wine. As a member of the Grocers' Company he was a powerful merchant and would have had contacts throughout the trade: perhaps it was he who introduced Richard Galis to Stephen Heath, vintner (see D4v).

AFter I was given to understand of your safe return from Spanish soyle (moste deer and singuler good Freend) and of your happy arrival heer into this Cittie, I was often in hart more desirous, then in effects any wiaes[2] *able, with some small token of my good wil to gratulate your welcome home, and to thentent I might not be touched with that odible vice of Ingratitude (a vice of all men moste to be detested) I imagined many times with myself which way I might best frame myne habilitie, by using some parte of remuneration for your manifolde curtesies (aswel upon my self as for my sake upon my Freendes imployed) to avoid the same, emongst which my cogitations this handful of scribled and barren papers conteining the wunderfull and moste strange crueltie of Elizabeth Stile alias Rockingham and her associates lately at Abingdon rewarded with the guerdon due for their demerits,*[3] *came to my mind, which after I had finished albeit at the first deeming them unworthy of dedication to any: yet at the last incensed with the naturall* {A2v} *instinct of your gentle disposition I was imboldened (the rather for that you your self have tasted of their cup of displeasure) to commend the same beeing the first frutes of my labour to the gathering of your looving hands therby outwardly to shewe what the inwarde hart desireth if abilitie did not want, hoping that with the moste renowmed Persian King Artaxerxes you wil freendly vouchsafe thankfully to receive this handfull of colde water, the entire cognisaunce of my willing minde, offered unto you,*[4] *desiring you as leasure may serve you thorowly with your freends to peruse it, by revolving wherof if you finde any delight, gently to thinke of the writer who wisheth you encrease of health, welth and felicitie until the time that Atrapos shall cut of the thread of this your mortall life and that after you have passed the pace and run the race of this short voyage and journye and of this brittle frail and unconstant life yow may be placed, sociated, knit and comined in that glittering light and blesfull life of that celestiall Jerusalem amongst the company of heavenly Soules and holy mindes which do enjoy the life that only may be called life and only Emire*[5] *invincible.*

Your assured Freend in the Lorde Richard Galis.

{A3} *To the Reader.*

*AS thou hast all ready moste (gentle Rea*der) begun to satisfie thy greedye eyes with the freendly survey of the late confession of *Elizabeth Stile alias Rockingham,*[6] comprehending not a handful to the number of their devilish pageants played. So persever still I beseech thee with no lesse good will to peruse this true edition for thy sake and contentation only set foorth describing

2 Waies (ways).

3 A phrase taken from the preface to the other Windsor pamphlet, *A Rehearsall both straung and true*, A4v.

4 See the 'Life of Artaxerxes', *Plutarch's Lives*, vol. 11 (Loeb Classics edition [London: Heinemann; Cambridge, Mass: Harvard University Press, 1943], 135). Artaxerxes receives a gift of cold water gratefully because it represents all the donor has to give.

5 *Sic.* Empire.

6 i.e. *A Rehearsall both straung and true.*

the strange, cruell and diabolicall tiranny practised through the little regarde and great necligence[7] of Magistrates in these our dayes winking at ye faultes of the Offenders which neither regarded the pitteful plaints of the tormented, nor the continuall plagues of the Tormentor powred out day by day upon their honest and inocent Neighboures, some bereft of life, some of their wits and some of the naturall course of their lims.

Emongst which I being one of the least that suffered moste and oftnest went to ye pot,[8] thought it good to set foorth some parte bothe of mine owne troubles and of divers others for thy behoof, in revolving wherof, if from my hands thou expect for my philed phrase or lerned stile being but misled up in a homely cuntrie Cabbin where the practise of the flayle and whip more ri-{A3v}-per is then lernings lore, thou shalt greatly be deceived. But if a plain Shepherds tale neither prophane nor fained, oftner occupied in the tarbox and sheephook, Instruments more fit for me then either pen or inck may serve thy turn: receive thy desire.[9] Employe therfore thy paines in perusing the same, and if any thing thou find that either presently contenteth thy minde or that herafter proove to thy proffit: give thanks to them (and not to me) at whose instance I framed the same, which do on in[10] requitall of my paines: I have that which I doo expect. Thus farwel gentle Reader.

RG.

{A4} *The first attempt of Elizabeth Stile alias Mother Rockingam and her confederates* Witches executed for their offences the twentiesix day of February last past practised against the Author.

BEING AT DI-verse and sundry times greevouslye vexed, troubled and tormented aswell in Body as in Minde, some times in my raging fits detesting & abhorring all Company, eftsones again ernestly desiring the same, I often Imagined with my selfe what straunge disease and greef it should be that so should (beeing whole in Body and not overcharged with sicknesse, although exempt of perfect remembrance) abate my flesh and weaken my Body, and lying in my bed forworne with unquiet rest, heavy wt over much watching, & desirous to vanquish my pains by taking a little sleepe: suddainly about twelve a clock in the night a shodowe of a huge and mightie black Cat, appoered in my Chamber, which ye more as shee approched neer my bed side: so much the more began my here to stand upright, my hart to faint,

7 *Sic.*

8 Went to pot, was sacrificed or ruined.

9 Despite the confused syntax this is a uniquely ambitious display of gentlemanly mock-modesty, or *sprezzatura*, in witchcraft reporting of its day. Galis sets out to show that he is no publisher's hack-writer. In his portrayal of himself as a simple shepherd-artist, he is actually stressing his gentle status, his learning and his ability to use the favourite literary idioms of his day: here, pastoral and euphuism. John Lyly's *Euphues: The Anatomy of Wyt* was published in the same year, summing up and giving its name to the key elements of fashionable writing, many of which are used by Galis.

10 *Sic.*

and my paines more and more to encrease, in so much I was constrained to call for my Fathers Maid, to bring a Candle, whereby I might more clearly beholde mine Enemie which did so evelly intreat mee, which Maide, beeing entred into my Chamber: I willed to looke for ye Cat, but she was not to be found, neither could the light which shee brought continue burning, at which strange sight beeing amased: the Maide beeing gon to bed again, {A4v} And I left tumbling and tossing in my bed, more like to dye then any longer to live, my sheets wringing wet with sweat caused through this suddain feare, I called at the last to my remembrance a Brother of mine named James Galis who about the Age of fifteene yeeres falling out with one Mother Dutton one of the hellish broode, and at that time suspected to be in that indeed which afterward shee prooved was in like sorte taken in his bed, and bereft of his wits, which until this day are not his owne stil crying away with the Witch away with the Witch, I forewith conjectured that the same Cat which so amazed mee, was either some Witch or of some Witches sending and that my paines before and at that instaunce sustained was by some Witch practised upon mee. Wherupon knowing that prayer in all troubles and extremeties was the cheefest string wheron each true Christian ought for to strike, I tooke my prayer booke wherin was conteived aswel holsome and godly prayers as psalmes, and with the brackish teares distilling from the fountaines of my eyes, I sometimes red therin, and sometime againe singing Psalmes to the honor and glory of God which had vouchsafed of his meere mercie and goodnes to strengthen me in this my afflictions, utterly from the bottom of my hart detesting and having in defiaunce all the crue of devilish Enchaunters, wherof England at this day doth abounde.[11] Perswading myself that God beeing my helper, buckler and defence, neither any Witch nor all the Devils in hel (were they in number as many as the sands in the Sea could have once power to hurt mee, all this while not forgetting Job[12] whose faith no plague, no greef paine, nor vexation, that ever Sathan by Gods sufferaunce might over charge him with could not {B} any wise remoove, thus as I have said, spending & contriving weary and painful night in prayer, Aurora[13] began to shewe her self, whose cristall cleernes as it appeered: so began my paines to surcease, & I to be exonerated of the burden therof, which when I felt: I cause forwith the Bible to be brought mee, and incontinently I trurned to the before remembred history of that just man Job, of whose stedfast faith and milde patience when I had read and read againe, such strength in the Lorde did so abound in mee, that after that time all the plagues,

11 An idea also taken from *A Rehearsall both straung and true*, A2.

12 The models for Galis's construction of the perfect Protestant response to witchcraft are all biblical. He turns to sacred literature to find empathy with the persecuted psalmist (see also B3 for the most relevant psalms), and later to Job and Ephesians 6 in putting on 'the whole armour of God'. He shows himself shaping his experience using these models.

13 Dawn.

mischiefs and torments practised by the said hellish Hagges against mee could not afray mee.

How the Author occasioned to walke to Clueworth[14] *met with Mother Dutton whome he (least thinking on) brought to Windsore before the Magistrates which without any examination set her at libertie.*

REcovered of my greefs and by Gods devine providence restored by little and little to my former health, bearing yet in minde some parte of the said Mother Duttons dealing used upon my said Brother James, and after that upon my self, I determined hap what hap might, when convenient leysure might serve to bring the said Mother Dutton to Windesore, before the Magistrates there, to the intent if otherwise shee could not purge herself the better of that wherwith she should be charged: shee might receive such condign punishment as for such Offenders by the lawes of ye Realme was due and provided. Which determination as it was then remembred: so in processe of time it was forgotten, til it fortuned that walking one day after dinner to walk to Cluewoorth about certain my affaires which I had there to doo; shee met mee ful in the face, whose suddain meeting remooving my former intent then set in oblivion: caused mee furiously to lay holde upon her arme, by the which without many woords given I brought her to the hall a prison in Windesor desiring the keeper therof surely to keep her in his custody until commaundement were given him by the {Bv} Magistrates to the contrary which hee denyed to doo without some speciall warrant from ye Maior or the Justice for his discharge, wherupon I led her before Maister Richard Readforth at ye time Maior of Windesor desiring him as he was true Officer to God and to his Prince to give his warrant to the Jaylor for the better save keeping of this Witch heer brought by mee before him, who for her devilish Sorceries and enchauntments cruelly practised upon divers honest men deserveth not to live, affirming that if I could not proove her by sufficient tryall to be a weed woorthye of plucking up: I would receive such punishment as might be to all (attempting the like either against man or woman) a good ensample but he being belike as a great number be now a dayes ye more pittie, and I would to God it may be amended, mistrusting her devilish practises and fearing least some mischief might succeed his correction either to him or his, altogither forgetting his oth and dutie towards God and his Prince, for the due punishment of Offendors in ye case had & provided commaunded me yt without further delay I should let her go, which foorthwith I did no lesse bewailing her libertie then lamenting the lack of better Magistrates to weed out such Malefactors.

{B2} *How the said Mother Dutton after her delivery from the Authors hands by the Mayor, practised with her Associates his overthroowe.*

AFter this pestilent Witch was set at libertie, shee with her Confederates perceiving the little regard the Magistrates appointed to minister Justice, for

14 Clewer, an area bordering New Windsor.

the punishment of vice had of the complaintes made and put up against them and greatly encouraged therby, ceased not now to practise all kinde of meanes to vexe, trouble and molest mee which because of my stedfast faith in God they could not by them selves nor by their wicked spirits execute the same upon mee, they stirred up others to be their cruel ministers in the same.

First procuring my Freends whome Nature lincked in the league of loove and Freendship utterly to detest mee, shamefully to use mee and that which greeved mee moste maliciously to envie mee, in such sorte and so long that I often times wished exchaunge of my lyfe for a moste hasty and speedy death, thus living there in exile where reason would I should have been moste of all succoured, hated of all without cause, and looved of few, it chaunced that a Freend of mine Maister Robert Handley (before rehersed) who at that time for recreation sake making his aboade at a house of his in the cuntrie was likewise bewitched in his limmes so that he was not able to go,[15] who suspecting his greefes to come by witchcraft, caused mee to be sent for partely for Freendships sake which alwayes hath been equall betwixt us, and partely to use that by my meanes which hee him self by reason of his greefs could not put in practise, to whome when I was come after a little talke had, he told me that hee douted very much least he was bewitched, wherfore (quoth hee) good R. Galis, if any spark of Freendship hath ever been kindled betwixt us: I pray: thee to fetch mee a Witch, at whose sight, hope perswadeth mee I shall finde ease. At which woordes beeing indeed greatly mooved: inwardly (as one who looved his intire Freend) {B2v} bewailing my Freends troubles more then my owne, I went forth with out any woord speaking,[16] and amongst the crue of these helhounds I gat mee and within one half houre after God being my help: I brought foure before him, whose names ensue, **videllicet** Audrey the Mistresse, Elizabeth Stile **allias** Mother Rockingham, Mother Dutton and Mother Devil,[17] all which foure I caused to kneele downe before the said Maister Handley and one Maister Henry Bust Studient in Phisick (charging them holding a good cudgel over their backs) as ever they would passe thence a live, not only to tel what the said Maister Handley ayled: but also to ease him of his greef, to whome they replied using many excuses, that they neither could tel him his desease much lesse to help him therof.

Then going about to knowe how they spent their time in the service of God: I examined them in the Lordes prayer, the beleef and the ten

15 To walk.

16 Friendship and dramatic proofs of love are one of the staples of euphuistic romances, which again are one of Galis's stylistic models in constructing his story of witchcraft. The two genres now seem unlikely companions: but for Galis they work together to create a highly personal version of what witchcraft is. See *Witches Apprehended* (1613) for a later usage of a similar discourse.

17 See *A Rehearsall both straung and true* (1579).

Commaundements, wherin I founde them (to my great greef) as blinde as a beetle and as wise as a Calfe, then demaunding the cause of their negligence therin, they replied that since they were borne they were never taught them, neither could they finde any that would instruct them therin, and therfore it was to harde for them upon so short a warning to answere unto my objections, which replication when I heard, sorye for their time so ill imployed: I drue my purse and gave each of them a peny, charging them as they looved their owne soules helth: diligently to learn them least that they come to some ill end, for (said I) it can not other, wise[18] be but that for want of thone ye must loove the other and for the lack of the grace of God, the loove of his holy woord and commaundements: ye must needs serve the Devil your Lord and Maister, and there withall I bad them in God his name to departe, and in short space after my Freend Maister Handley came to his olde course I mean to his former health.

How the same foure Witches after their departure from Maister Handley his house wrought the Authors imprisonment and of his torments suffered during the time of his being in holde.

{B3} WHen these foure looving Sisters were departed from my Freends house, being of mee no other wise intreated or used then you have heard, misdeeming (and not without good cause) that I would woork their overthrow in time if I might be suffered, they sought by prison to a bridge my dayes, and because they them selves would be blamelesse and void of suspition, not contented with my paines passed beeing now hated, abhorred and as it were spitted at of all men, and especially of my owne Parents & naturall Bretheren and brought even to ye very brink of desperation (had not God of his infinit mercy and goodness with his mightie hand held me up giving me a great patience woorthy to suffer his crosse laid upon me for my offences) they caused their Familiars without the which they could not doo any thing, to stirre up and against mee to incence to Maior and Burgesses of the towne of Windesor (wherof my father whilst he lived was a cheef member)[19] who without any offence committed, any hurt pretended, or complaint made against mee, clapped mee up in Prison fast locked in a deep dungion, into the which I was let up and downe with a rope laden wt as many gyves and manacles as either my legges could cary or my hands be able to beare, there to remain without baile, until their further pleasure were therin had, a crueltie more woorthy for a traytor or a murderer then for any true subject to God & to his Prince. After I was thus inclosed in ye dark, deprived of all humain

18 *Sic.*

19 Richard Galis senior was not only three times mayor but also one of the town's Members of Parliament or Burgesses of Parliament, chosen by the Corporation as a townsman worthy to represent them. The Corporation (the mayor, aldermen, benchers and brethren) numbered twenty-eight to thirty men and were self-elected. They were a powerful body – hence their major role in this account (see C.H. Cooper and T. Cooper, eds, *Athenae Cantabrigiensis* [Cambridge, 1858], vol. 1, 561 for Galis).

company, refused to have any bed for my money, or libertie of the Prison upon good and sufficient bond, I then began to mistrust my self, and feared the sudain losse of my life, which easely then might have beene deprived and with some surmised tale easely aunswered to the worlde, though not hid from the face of the Lord, neverthelesse emboldened by the mightie help of God to cast away all feare and patiently to suffer my troubles: I ceased not according to my accustomed use and to my great comfort and consolation, to sing to the honor and prayse of God the fortie one the fortie two and the three and fortie Psalmes, begining **The man is blest that carefull is the needy consider. &c.** during thexecution of which crueltie: a pittieful sound of groning voice opened {B3v} the gates of mine eares, and presently my yrons which before by workemans cunning were rivetted on, making a wonderfull great noyse much like to a Smyth working of his mettall, fell of my legges, & I taken in so straunge a cace by the space of two houres, that I thought ye soule foorthwith would have left the chariot of my mortall body. But still persevering in my prayers, I ceased not to call upon the Lorde, not onely for my deliverance: but also that it would please him to turne the hartes of them which had so unjustly used their correction upon me. In the morning when it was daye, beeing not called to mine answere: I desired that I might be permitted to have some conference with Maister Doctor Day Deane of the Castell royall of Windsore, prebende men of great wisedome and learning,[20] to thentent I might (with their opinions) be fully resolved of that which gnawed my conscience, which by no meanes I could obtaine, but within two dayes after called to my answere before the Maior and his brethren, and examined of my yrons falling of, I tolde them as before is declared, who having nought els to charge me with, gave order for my deliverance, using with such extremetie their like power upon me more then a score of times, which here to expresse would be to long, and more tedious to the Reader, so that I was forced of my selfe to weave the webbe of mine owne banishement, rather desirous to live amiddes the desertes of **Lybia** among the Savadge and wilde beastes then in Windsore with my parentes and kinred.

How by the helpe of Syr Henry Nevell Knight, Maister Richard Warde Esquier, and other Gentlemen of worship,[21] *the author gat leave to passe the seas into Flaunders, where for a time he served under Captaine Morgaine.*

20 William Day, Dean of the Chapel Royal since 1572. A committed, well-known and extreme Protestant reformer and iconoclast, he was a natural godly choice as Galis's mentor (see *DNB*).

21 Sir Henry Nevell was high steward of the borough, and a prominent Protestant courtier. Knighted in 1549, he was a Member of Parliament like Galis senior (although for the county, Berkshire) and had been sheriff in 1570. Richard Warde (of Hurst, east of Windsor) was likewise eminent: the Royal Cofferer in four reigns, he died in 1578. See William Page and P.H. Ditchfield, eds, *Victoria County History: Berkshire*, 4 vols (1907; London: Institute of Historical Research, 1972), esp. vol. 3, 173–83, 193 (Nevell) and 176, 248–58 (Warde).

FInding here in native soyle no place of rest to shrowde my carefull[22] head but onely an ougly dungeon without light or comfort, no refuge succour or helpe, but that which straungers imparted unto me, I imagined daily with my selfe what were best for me {B4} to do to avoyde these troubles daily more & more encreasing. Sometimes musing upon this, sometime upon that, nowe devising one thing, then by and by an other, the lamentable estate and subversion of the lowe countrie in Flaunders, came to my minde, whereof a whyle considering, I determined to addresse my selfe towardes that coast, there to spend (if not the remainder of my dayes) yet at least some part of my youthfull yeares in the service of some one Gentleman or other. Nothing doubting, but that God knowing mine innocencie and the righteousnesse of my cause, would not onely prosper my attempt: but also give me happy successe to the ende of my travayles. Upon the which point being fully perswaded, loth without licence. First of my deare Father had and obtayned to depart (nevertheless his unkinde dealinges considered)[23] I bended my steppes to the worshipfull Sir Henry Nevell Knight, who with Maister Richard Warde Esquier, by waye of humble petition, I moved to talke with my father about the premisses, at whose importunate and earnest perswasions being overcome, graunted their requestes, whereof beeing advertised joyfull to see my desier take his effect, what haste I made to set all thinges in order for my travayle, let them judge that have tasted the like distresse. In fine armed at all assaies to countervayle my jorney before pretended, and ready prest to set forward on my waye, a double sorrowe began to combate within mee, and therewithall a doubtfull imagination. The one willing mee to cease travaile and enjoye the presence of my tender parentes, and loving companions no lesse carefull of my health then my selfe, the other encouraging mee to avoyde the dayly assaultes of my adversaries by chaunging the soyle to submitte my selfe into the handes of Lady Fortune. Thus traversing in doubtfull doubt, nowe musing on the one, then thinking on the other, and troubled beyond all measure, what were best to be doone: I pawsed me a while. At the last overcome with desier to proceade on my journey: I determined to put my self to ye mercy of **Aeolus** puffing blasts and to the merciless waves of Neptunes swelling Seaes.[24]

The next day bidding my Freends and Cuntrie farwel, I traviled toward London, and from thence I shipped my selfe {B4v} into Holland whether beeing safely arrived good hap so fel out on my side that before I had spent

22 Full of cares, anxious.

23 Galis's sentence structure disintegrates here – probably as a result of transcription or during typesetting, since if repunctuated the sentences are perfectly readable.

24 Gods of the wind and sea. In this section the pace of the narrative slows and it becomes a contemplative gentlemanly discussion of travel, with appropriate display of 'learned' references as in the preface. Again, this is a surprise when set beside the conventional early Elizabethan model of writing about witchcraft events and dramatically broadens our view of how witches might be constructed and represented.

a day or two in seeking best for my advantage, I found unlooked for of Maister William Morgan Gentleman such gentle intertainment that I imployed all my endvour to augment my credit with him, under whome I spent some time on the land, some times on the seas as occasion served as the Souldiers life desireth not rest in one place, halfe a yeeres service.

How his Captaine leaving the Cuntrie the Author was pricked with a loovely motion to his native Cuntrie to make returne to his Father, who upon his submission received him againe.

THe uprores a little before rife in Holand and in all the Cuntries there about, by valiant prowesse of martiall Knights suppressed: my Captain (leaving the Cuntrie) gave me occasion to think of my Freendes in England in the midst of all mine Enemies not forgotten, which for to see an earnest desire kindled my brest, and vanquished with loove and dutie had towards them, I made my return again to Windesor, more to reconsile my self to my deer father to whome before my departure I gave some occasion of displeasure, then for any affection I bare to the towne, before whose Fatherly aspect, when I was approched, my outwarde teares declaring my inward greefs: I fel prostrate on my knees and recognising my former follies, I craved meditation of forgivenes upon my speedy amendment. At the which submission pardoning that which was past upon performance of my promise moste like a looving Father received me again greatly joying my safe return. Neverthelesse desirous not to remain with him aboove three or foure dayes: I departed and made my repaire to London, and in Tower street became Covenant with Maister Stephen Heath a Vintner, til such time as my Father oppressed with infinit paines by meanes of the damnable sect did call me home cruelties and injuries doon and wrought against the braunch could not once stanch {C} their cruell myndes, thirsting after innocent bloud, without the life of my deare father, whose bitter paines diminishing his wonted strength by litle and litle caused him to yeeld unto the mercie of death, to the everlasting grief of all that loved him, but especially to mee and other his poore children, left as sheepe without a guide to the mercie of the Woulf. Alasse what should I say? to render him his due prayse, I wante sufficiencie, and to make long discourse of his milde and meeke pacience, wherein hee continued unto the last houre of his gasping breath, I can not for teares and grief, wherefore against my wil I am cut of from my purpose. But thus much you shall understande that no perswasions could prevayle with him that hee was bewitched, such was his strong belief in God, and yet diverse time sighingly complaining, would saye: O Lord, shall a man dye and bee not sicke? my harte is whole, and yet my inward paines consume me, and so meekely like a Lambe to the glorie of God, taking and suffering his troubles, passed the straightes of this mortall life, to lodge with **Lazarus** in **Abrahams** bosome.

Hhwe[25] *the Author after his fathers death abiding with his mother for her better*

25 *Sic.*

comfort, framing him selfe to live in the world, was prevented by the sayd witches to his utter undooing to this daye.

MY deare father by these helhoundes and Impes of the devell, thus bereft mee, and intiered in the ground (after whom we must all hie[26]) I determined to the comfort of my mother, sorrowing the want of her wedded make,[27] to abyde with her, framing my selfe like a subject to live, and as it became an honest man to do, so long as the time of his pilgrimage geveth him leave to abide, I went (with that litle which God and my father had left mee for my better maintenance) to buye sheepe and other cattell, whereby by due foresight and diligent taking heede: I might make retourne of my principall with some advantage,[28] but according to the proverbe, hee that reckoneth before his host must reckon twise, and so it fell to my lot. For after I had {Cv} stored my self with the said Cattaill more woorth at the time of their sale, then the money I paid for them, they began now one then an other and in fine almoste all to dye, and the rest living in such a case, lest that I was constrained to take half the money they cost mee gaining by them as Dickins did with his Dishes who bying five for twopence solde six for a peny, my cattail thus beeing consumed, and many other attempts enterprised by mee, turned topsie turvie, mine olde accustomed and raging fits began to set foot within my minde I to imagin that Sathans whelps were now setting a broch the vessel of their despite to seeke my utter spoyle and confusion. Wherfore I addressed my self to the woorshipfull Sir Henry Nevel Knight, who sufficiently before perswaded of my troubles, and greatly with my good Lady his bedfellowe, (with whome I had often conference) pitying myne estate.[29] I besought even in the bowels of our Lord Jesus Christe that either my Adversaries who hourely tormented mee might be cut of: or I my self to receive the like punishment if good and sufficient proof were not on my side against them.

How upon complaints made by the Author to Sir Henry Nevel they were commaunded to be brought before him, and not beeing able to answere him in the Articles of the Christian faith, they were publikly set under the Pulpit,

UPon which complaint after Sir Henry Nevel had advised him self, mooved with the pitteful aspect of my wildishe countenance, promise was made me that at a prefixed day he only for that purpose would come to Windesore,[30] and upon due examination had, seek redresse of my troubles. At which day appointed, I posted mee to the lodging of the said Sir Henry Nevel being in the Castel, there to renue the remembraunce of his promise, who knowing mine errand upon my first entrance into his Chamber commaunded me

26 Hurry, go.
27 Mate.
28 His original investment with some interest.
29 Elizabeth Gresham, Nevell's second wife, who died in 1573.
30 Nevell's seat was at Billingbear Park, in Waltham St Lawrence to the east of Windsor.

forthwith to bring them before him, at which commaundement, you may thinke I made no delay, but hasted mee about my busines, & brought {C2} before him as many as I suspected, which were, Audrey the Mistresse, Elizabeth Stile, Mother Dutton and Mother Nelson, saying, Sir I have executed your commaundement and brought them into your presence, which if by good and sufficient tryall, I can not proove to be Witches: let me receive the punishment due unto them, at which woordes quoth Sir Henry unto them, what say you to this? Then his Woorship further examined them in the presence of Maister Doctor Wickham Maister Wullard a Prebend of the Castel, Maister Morris, and Maister Stafferton Gentlemen,[31] how and after what sorte they lived, whome they served and how they had imployed their time, they aunswered, as every one would in his own case the best, saying, yt where they had been suspected to be Witches & woorkers of mischief against their neighbours, it was contrary and that the occasion put up against them was rather upon malice then otherwise. Then said I under your Woorships correction, if they be such good livers as they make them selves to be: I beseech you to examine them in the Articles of the Christian faith, and upon their aunswere judge of the rest. Then quoth Maister Wickham, can you say the Lordes prayer which he hath taught you? No forsooth quoth one, no forsooth quoth an other and likewise the rest, upon which replycation: Maister Wickham began with a moste godly protestation to perswade them not onely to forsake their damnable wayes afore & at that time used, and diligently to learne the Lordes prayer, the beleef, and the ten Commaundements, but also dayly for their better instructions to have recourse unto the Temple of God, to heare his devine service, and for th'xecution there of (because none durst wade so farre against them as I) I was appointed overseer, beeing charged that on the next Sunday following they should be brought to the Church, and publikly in the presence of all men to be set under the Pulpit during the time of Service.

{C2v} *How the said Witches were brought to the place apppointed and how Audrey the Mistresse and Mother Nelson within short time after died, upon whose death the Author felt moste greevous torments.*

COnceiving some good hope of future redresse upon thexamination had before the said Gentlemen of woorship if otherwise they were not converted from their follie: I hied me home to my Chamber, where locking the doore to mee I fel flat on the ground rendring thanks unto all mightie God for that it had pleased him of his infinit mercy to open the blinde eyes of the

31 William Wickham was chaplain to the Queen, Archdeacon of Surrey and, like John Wullard or Wolward, had been a Canon of Windsor since the early 1570s (S.L. Ollard, ed., *Fasti Wyndesoriensis: The Deans and Canons of Windsor* [Windsor: Dean and Canons of St George's Chapel, 1950]). Master Morris may be of the family of Great Coxwell, but if he were a recusant, as they were, he would hardly have been invited to establish correct religious practice. The Stafertons were a prominent local family with properties at Warfield, near Waltham St Lawrence, and Bray, north-east of Windsor (see *VCH*, vol. 3, 185, vol. 4, 487).

Magistrates at the last to looke upon such Offenders which before thorow their necligence, nusled up in all kinde of wickednes, ceased not day nor night to oppresse the Inocent, (my prayer ended) I went about my busines until the day was come wherin I should doo my dutie, at which day I armed my self in the Lord against the said Witches, whome gently intreating more to win their harts unto ye Lord, then for any feare I had of them: I conducted them to the Church and in the place appointed I set them downe, (my self not standing far of them) where after by the Preacher they had received their lesson, and schooled for their lewd behaviour and idle life spent to no profit, but to invent wickednes and mischief, they departed home. Afterwards whether it were for greef of the correction executed, or the inward gnawing of conscience, feeling them selves by the Preacher touched at the quick, (I cannot tel) but with in short space after, Audrey the Mistresse and Mother Nelson dyed, after whose death the sisters left behinde given over to their owne lusts and suffered to wallowe in their owne wickednes, made their assembly in the pits in Maister Dodges backside, a place where all their mischief was pretended, and there in generally agreed either to bring me unto my end, or living stil to feele a life a hundred times more sharpe then a present death, if other wise the sooner I sought not meanes to dislodge my self, and desirous not to use any delay in furthering their intents, about their accustomed {C3} houres of meeting in the night: my bed, ordained for my quiet rest became the augmentor of my greefs, and in stead of sleep I was fed with continuall watchings, caused through the extreame torturs and greevous paines sustained in the night. Thus having over passed many nights in paines, diverse and sundry times the aforesaid Cat or the devil him self in a Cats likenes: used to frequent and haunt my Chamber hurring and buzing about my bed, vexing and troubling mee beyond all measure, in such straunge and lamentable wise, that I was enforced with my weapon lying drawen uopon[32] my bed to keep my self waking in prayers least beeing over-come with sleepe: I should be strangled in my bed.

{C3v} *The Author being almost spent with grief, complaineth him the third time to Sir Henry Nevell, before whome hee brought the said Elizabeth Stile bound with a cart rope on the market daye.*

COnsumed with these infinite paines both in body and purse eche night assayled with a newe grief, lothing anie longer to live, seeing that in foure yeeres past, no reformation might bee had for all my complaintes. Leaving my carefull bedde, the witnes of my griefe and of my inwarde sorrowe: I made me ready and girding my Skeane[33] about my middle with a good cudgill in my hande, I gate me to Farneham to the house of father Roseman, whom furiously pulling out of his house by head and shoulders I charged (not using any daliaunce with me) to tell me my griefes. Who beeing agast

32 *Sic.*
33 A dagger.

at my dealinges, and fearing least that beeing not able to governe mee in my fury, I would strike of his head: Said, O Maister you are bewitched, you are bewitched, wherefore looke to your selfe, if not: in fine you wilbe distroyed, for you have many wicked women in Windsore, and such as doe much harme, and who practized the like on mee once, because I did displease them. Then I bad him tell mee what they were, who aunswered, that their names were Elizabeth Stile, Mother Dutton, and Mother Devell, at which wordes leaving him (not altogether recovered of the feare hee conceived by mee) I went to the sayde Elizabeth Stiles house, charging her to goe with mee unto Sir Henry Nevelles, which squatting downe upon her buttockes, shee denyed to doo. Then finding a Carte rope harde by, I bounde it about her myddle, and layde the rope on my shoulder, wherewith forceably I pulled her out of her house, drawing her a long the streate, beeing on the market daye (not one daring once to helpe mee) but a litle boye, which helde the rope by the ende) untill I came unto the lodging of Sir Henry Nevell, unto whome in the presence of a companie of Gentlemen at that time talking with him, I offered up my present, saying, be-{C4}-hold here rigth[34] worshipfull, I have brought you heer a monster, which because of her feebled lymmes, is not able to goe, I have taken paynes to drawe. Then shee began to curse, banne and sweare, foming at the mouth like a bore, to the great astonishement of all the beholders, which amased with that horrible sight (more for feare I thinke then for any good wyll) suffered her to escape, with the which departure (as I could not chuse beeing greatly greeved) seeing that for all my complaintes made, no hope of redresse was to bee looked for at the Magistrates handes: I thought nowe to use myne owne force uppon them. Wherefore dayly frequenting my selfe to have once a daye my recourse to their doores, I would nowe one, then an other, so Ribrost[35] with my cudgell (caried always about mee for the same purpose) that in the ende getting the upper hand, I had them in such awe, that the Scholer having offended, feared not so much his Maisters correction as they did my presence, as afterwardes it appeared by Mother Dutton, who so soone as shee had heard of my comming that waye: would have runne and locked her selfe into a Cheste for feare.

Howe the Author having occasion to be abroade one night at the houre of their meeting, hee sawe the Devell in a Carte sitting, and howe by the helpe of God he put him to flight, and other strange accidentes done by him.

MY courage nowe beeing augmented by the triumphant victorie gotten over myne enemies, and feeling no more taste of my passed grieffes, my businesse so falling foorth, it was my chance one night about xi. of the clocke in the night to ride by the place where these Impes acustomed use was to meete, to my house.

34 *Sic.*
35 Beat.

And in my waye as I was ryding, my horse beeyng {C4v} of a very good stomacke, sudainly stopped flinging and lashing out behinde, snorting and taking on out of all measure, neyther proceading further nor retorning back, wherewith all beeing litle amased because it was no straunge thing unto mee, I alighted and taking my sworde drawen in the one hand, and my buckler in the other, casting myne eye aside to see if I could perceive anie bodie stirring, I sudainly spied a most horrible sight and[36] oughly feende sitting in a poore mans cart, like one ryding to fetche in his harvest, with a payre of eies burning like the fiery flames, whose ougly shape when I behelde, falling on my knees in the middes of the dirt, I besought God to assist mee with his strength against this feende, and that through his mightie power I might get the victorie. Then rising, I went towardes the place where this good fellowe was watching for his praye. At whom (my faith stedfastly set in the Lord) I let flye with my sword, saying, avoide Sathan avoyde, and the name of God I charge thee to avoide, thou hast nought to do with mee,[37] wherefore go hunte after the Doe which hath caused thee here to sitte. At which wordes: a great light appeared round about the carte where he sat, and therewithall an horrible sent of brymstone was dispersed abroade, but hee was no more seene afterwarde, with the which sent Maister Aston of the Scalding house[38] comming that waye the self same present time, thought presently to have died, had not helpe come in the meane time.

This doone, I gate mee to my horse, upon whose back when I was amounted: I passed to my house as quietly as might be without harme, where not forgetting the goodnesse of God towardes them that put their trust in him, I spent an howre or two in prayer. The next day beeing come, no lesse desirous to be revenged of theim then they were to molest mee before: Hoping still to finde a meanes to cut theim off, and to weede theim cleane from the face of the earth, I practised many attemptes, and not so many as often executed to the entent I might bee brought to some further answere, for the extirpating and pulling up of the saide wicked weedes by the rootes. And because there was no Justice that would execute his office therein by the othe derected unto them. I determined to {D} proove what I could doo my selfe, wherefore I gat me a pounde of brimstone, and melted the same and dipped therein as it melted a great drie linnen cloth, and into a hovile of strawe of mother Duttons, I thrust it whereunto I put a great fier brande beeing of it selfe (the brimstone taken away) sufficient inough to have consumed a hundreth times as much, which burned unto ashes, ye strawe not once perished. An other time likewyse, one Richard Parker standing by, having bought a quarter of a pounde of gunne poulder, and as much of brimstone, I chose an arrowe from out of a sheafe, and thereunto I bounde the said poulder and

36 *Sic.*

37 Another biblical echo: Mark 5.7, Luke 8.28.

38 A place for preparing carcases by the scalding off of feathers or hair.

brimstone with stringes, making therein a litle touchhole whereby to give fier thereunto (when I thought it good) and thrust the same into an other hovile adjoyning to her house, fully determined to bring her togither with her house by fier to playe the last act of her tragedy, unto the which, with a matche set at the ende of a long sticke I gave fier, which arrowe albeit, it consumed to ashes, yet neverthelesse ye strawe still remained without any signe of hurt which straunge sight when I behelde, beeing a thing no lesse straunge to be tolde, then harde to be beleved: I sighing, sayde to my selfe. O Lord, what shall I doo unto this wicked impe, & to the rest of her confederates, whom neither fier or sworde may devoure, neither Gods thundering threates provoke to repentance. To suffer them longer to experiment life in their wickednesse, and to the overthrowe of their neighbours, my hart refuseth. And still to contrive and spende my time about it: is to my hinderance. If I complaine mee of their detestable dooings: the magistrates seame deafe, if I (as enemies to God and their Prince) molest or urge them: imprisonment laden with gyves falleth out to my share. If I crave helpe of the inferior sort (my correction so affrayes them) that albeit they would helpe, yet they dare not. Thus doo I see al hope of mans helpe taken from mee, and all comfort bereft mee: Wherefore I will henceforth cease and bridle my desires. And unto thee O Lorde, which knowing the secretes of all mens hartes, canst and wilt, when thou seest the time, roote out and pull up from thy good and chosen plantes such wicked graftes. To thee (I saie) will I remitte my cause, and seeke to lodge and settle {Dv} my selfe in some other soyle where justice may be ministered, vice corrected, & wronges redressed. And therewithal departed to my house, from whence within fewe daies, after I had set my affaires in good order: I departed to seeke my adventures, since which time of my departure, it hath pleased God at the last to strike these wicked and detestable livers with the rod of his correction. Who with the pot of their wickednesse so long powred the water of God his vengeance upon them that at the length they were apprehended and committed to the common gaile there to remaine untill by due proofe of their diabolicall livings be tried, & after triall had, receive the Guerdon answerable their demerites, where beeing founde giltie and convicted of the crime objected against them: they suffered at Abingdon the sixe and twentie daie of February last past for the same, as by the brief and summe of their confession here ensuing, thou maist more at large perceive.

The confession of Elizabeth Stile, alias Rockingham, a witch dwelling in Windsore in the Countie of Barke, declared in the gaile of Reading, in the said County in the xxi. yere of the raigne of our most dread soveraigne Lady Elizabeth. Queene of England, Fraunce and Ireland &c.

ELizabeth Stile, **alias** Rockingham apprehended for her witchcraft used in Windsore, and for the same brought before Sir Henry Nevel Knight, was by him examined, who for that he by manifest proofes of her unjust & unhonest behaviour, founde her an offendour unto the Queenes Majesties liedge people, committed her to the common gaile at Reading, where shee beeing examined, had (the feare of God pricking her thereunto as it seamed) some remorse of conscience, and confessed before Thomas Rowe, the Jaylour, John Knight, the Cunstable John Griffith an Inholder, & one William Pryntall, of divers as well men as women, that used to doo much harme, by Sorcery, witchecrafte, & enchantements, whose names hereafter ensue.

1 First that one father Rosiman **alias** Osborne, dwelling in Farneham in the Countie of Buckingham, and his daughter are witches, & that the said Rosiman can alter & chaunge {D2} him selfe into any kinde of beast that him listeth.

2 Item one mother Dutton, dwelling within Hodgkins in the parishe of Cleworth nere Windsore, can tell every mans errand assoone as shee seeth him, & worketh by a spirit in likenesse of a tode which shee nominateth Mawde, and she giveth him a drop of bloud in her flancke, and keepeth him alwayes in a garden in a border of grene herbes.[39]

3 Item one mother Devell dwelling in windsore by the pounde, keepeth a black Cat which shee nameth Jyll, & useth to carrie it in her lappe, and feedeth it with blood and milke, and Rosimans daughter hath a white Cat.[40]

4 Item one mother Margaret a lame woman, gooing with crutches, feedeth a kitling with crummes of bread and with some of her blood, and calleth it Jynne.

5 Item the said Elizabeth Stile, sayth that shee her self kept a Ratte, which shee named Philip, the which shee fedde with crummes of bread and blood of her right arme about the hand wrest, the place thereof not hidden, and saith, that further shee with the rest hath geven her right side to the Devill.[41]

6 Item this examinat further, saieth that father Rosimond and his daughter, mother Margarete, mother Dutton, and her selfe, were accustomed to make their meeting on the backside of Maister Dodges, where they used to conferre of such their enterprises as before they had determined of and practized.[42]

7 Item shee also confesseth that mother Devell was a poore woman, and used to go about begging of the almes of her honest neighbours, which if they did once deny her request, mischief alwayes ensued to them or to their cattel.[43]

39 *A Rehearsall both straung and true* named the owner of Mother Dutton's house 'Hoskins' but gave no name for her toad. Galis's editing of its texts presumably offers corrections and additions based on his local knowledge, but this does not mean that the *Rehearsall*'s version of events is invalidated – see below.

40 'Ponde' is changed to 'pounde', the assertion that the witch carried her cat in her lap is new, and Rosiman's daughter's white cat is an addition. Galis is presumably adding material from local gossip?

41 Item 6 from *A Rehearsall both straung and true* is omitted here. Thus it offers material which Galis has chosen to cut.

42 Formerly Item 7.

43 Formerly partly Item 3.

8 Item she further saieth, yt as concerning their craft & wicked practises, they have used it upon divers & sundry persons, of whom one Langford a Farmer, inhabiting in Windsore by the theames side was one, who died therby & whose maid shortly after drunk of ye same cup wherof the maister before had tasted.[44]

9 Item one maister Richard Galis Gent. (father of the author) who in times past, & ye thrise at ye least, aswel for his wisdome as for his pollitique & good government, had been Maior of windsore, was by their practise brought likewise to his end.[45]

10 Item one Switcher a Butcher, was served of ye same sauce.[46]

{D2v} 11 Item shee also saith that shee her self was the death of one Saddock by a clap shee gave him on the shoulder, because hee brake his promise in not giving her an olde cloke which hee promised to doo.[47]

12 Item that Mother Devel did over speake one William Foster a Fisher, and one Hil his wife a Baker.[48]

13 Item she also confesseth that they altogither with one consent over spake on[49] Humfrey Hesey and his wife, Richard Mils and John Mattingley, so that they lay every one long time sick before they could recover again their helth also and one Mastline a [Butcher].[50]

14 Item shee saith that on a time a Childe (beeing a mans Sonne in Windesore) hurled a stone on her house wherwith beeing mooved to anger shee tooke his pot from him, threatned to be even with him, wherwithall the Child went home wardes, and in the way meeting his Father he tolde him what had happened. To whome his Father said: ye hast doon some unhappinesse to her, come with mee and I will speak with her, and as they went togithers towards her house, the Childe sudainly began to cry out Oh my hand my hand, and his Father mervailing what he ailed looking upon his hand and beholding it turned clean out of course and that otherwise then Nature had framed it: tooke it in his hand and assayed to have turned it right again, but hee & an other man a neighbour of his (beeing with him at that present) could not doo it, the which was holpen afterwardes by Mother Dutton.[51]

44 This amalgamates Items 8 and 10 of *A Rehearsall both straung and true*. Galis begins his characteristic flowery language again here.

45 The praise of Galis senior is added to the former Item 9.

46 Previously Item 11.

47 Previously Item 15.

48 'Willies' is changed to 'Hil his'. Previously Item 17.

49 *Sic*.

50 'Hosie' becomes 'Hesey', and 'Mathynglise' becomes 'Mattingley'. A combination of *A Rehearsall both straung and true*, Items 12, 14 and 16.

51 Galis puts this story, which *A Rehearsall both straung and true* tells as an accuser's evidence from Elizabeth Stile's trial, into the witch's mouth as an examination story, entirely changing its context and thus its significance. He also alters the order of events so that the taking of the pitcher does not represent the 'being even' but the final injury more clearly does.

15 Item she saith that as woorking the death of th'afore named Lanckforde, Maister Galis Laukfoords Maide and Switcher the said Mother Dutton did make a picture of wax and did stick a hauthorn prick as it were against the hart of it that they died shortly after, and the said pictures they conveied in a hole made for the nonce[52] in the Chimney corner, before the which they set two bricks & as the wax melted so the man consumed unto death by which meanes shee saith they could kilany[53] of what degree soever.[54]
16 Item shee also saith that the said Mother Dutton did give a picture but whether it were of man or woman she dooth {D3} not remember & the man that had it of her, shee thinketh to be dead, and also yt one Gorge Whiting servant to Mathew Pain of Eaton had a picture of her self for one Foster, for that that same Gorge and Foster fel at woords and the picture, was made in Mother Duttons house, and Mother Devil said to her bun, spare not to plague him, thrusting a hauthorn prick against the hart of it, so yt he lay at the point of death, a long time but in the end Mother Dutton recovered him again, using their extremitie by kiling a Cowe of his.[55]
17 Item the said Elizabeth saith that the said Mother Dutton and Mother Devil were the first Inticers of her to all those afore said dooings, and that she and every of them did often times meet togither at Maister Dodges pits and sometime at the pound about eleven a clock at night, & that Mother Dutton and Mother Devil did alure her to doo and exercise ye craft which they them selves then and before used, and with them to forsake God and all his woorks and to give her selfe to the Devill.[56]
18 Item shee saith that on a time shee went to olde Rosimans house and found him stting at the root of an oke like an Ape and there talked with him long, and leaving him at her departure in the same shape, and at an other time she found him like an horse.[57]
19 Item shee saith that shee went on a time to olde Windesore to the bed-maker to beg milk which shee could not have because the maid was a milking but at her return shee said her Rat had provided bothe milk and creame.[58]

Both stories are valuable: they cannot both be accurate, but both are faithful to the same model of representing witchcraft – as a revenging of admitted wrong. The story shape seems the most important factor here, with detail coming a poor second. Accuracy is in any case a very elusive concept when dealing with supposed magical events hundreds of years old.

52 For the particular purpose.

53 *Sic.*

54 The details of the chimney corner are not in *A Rehearsall both straung and true* although they are described as part of Stile's confession – does Galis have personal knowledge of these very specific matters?

55 *A Rehearsall both straung and true* has 'Matthewe Glover' in its Item 19.

56 Previously Item 23.

57 The first half of *A Rehearsall both straung and true*'s Item 24 has been firmed up considerably here.

58 Previously Item 22.

20 Item shee confesseth that one Mother Audrey beeing one of the foure that sat under the Pulpit before shewed inhabiting in the Almes house was the cheef Mistresse of them all but shee is dead.[59]

21 Item shee saith that foure or five of the ablest men in Windesor (if shee had been so disposed) should not have brought her to the Gaile but that shee came of her owne accorde, for by the way as shee went with John Browne to the Gaile who was her Guide thither, her Bun came to her in the likenesse of a great black Cat and would have had her away, but {D3v} hoping for favour, she banished him againe.[60]

22 Item shee also saith that their woords of charme weare these, **come on let us go about it**, and presently they were changed into a new shape.[61]

To all which aforesaid Articles the said Elizabeth saied she would affirme, and unto her death truely stand to.[62]

This is not to be forgotten that the said Mother Stile albeit at the time of her apprehension and conduction to the Gaile shee was of perfect limme and joynt: yet neverthelesse was shee after the said confession made, so altered and changed, by the inchauntments of her owne Confederates: that she was ye moste odiblest[63] creature that ever man beheld, insomuch that shee was brought upon a barrowe to her arrainment before the Judges.[64]

This is to be remembred also that amongst the Offenders aforesaid, and at the time of their execution, Mother Margaret beeing upon the ladder and readye to playe the last act, of her life, and commiting her self to the merecie[65] of the law, by the which shee was adjudged for her desarts to suffer death: began to say the Lordes prayer in the which shee continued til shee came to these woords **and forgive us our trespasses &c.** at which place making a stay crying out against one Savoye Harvy of Windesor Ostler her accuser,[66] which then was comming towards the place of execution where they all suffered to see her end, saying art thou come to cast mee away? and speak to the People then standing by, mark the end of him before this time twelve-moonth, and waxing ougly to the terror of the Beholders shee impatiently ended her life.

Finis.

The Conclusion to the Reader.

THus hast thou heard heere moste looving Reader how much the foolish pittie and slacknes of the Magistrates of Windesore in executing their office,

59 Previously Item 26.
60 *A Rehearsall both straung and true* has 'Jhon Brome' in its final Item, 27.
61 This Item has no source in *A Rehearsall both straung and true.*
62 Originally part of Item 25.
63 Most odious.
64 *A Rehearsall both straung and true*, B2v.
65 *Sic.*
66 Perhaps the same ostler as *A Rehearsall both straung and true*, Bv, although the story of Mother Margaret's death has no source in the earlier pamphlet.

hath given occasion to these wicked Imps {D4} the Daughters of the Devill, to persist in their follye, thou hast heard also remembred unto thee what drifts of develish devises since the first time of mother Duttons apprehension and brought by mee before Maister Richard Redforth then Maior of Windesore, hath by them been practised to the great hurt of the Inhabitaunts, their neighbours, and to thy great admiracion, which if at that present had been as thorowely sifted out as it was but wincked at, and as to late (I may say) it hath been by some, (since those persons in the afore confession mentioned and by their enchauntments brought to their ends) not only had enjoyed their lives until this day: but I also a moste looving Father and they them selves an assured and stedfast rock in the time of their need, where now by their sufferance wee be deprived of bothe. But sith to call thinges long time past in oblivion to remembrance again, will but increace my greef and renue my sorowe: I therfore will with the vale of scilence cover that which my hart desired to expresse. Only I beseech the heavenly Father who is the giver of all goodnes that this ensample past and now to all men most apparaunt, may be so printed and rooted in the harts of all Magistrates appointed for the execution of true and upright Justice to the maintenaune of the good and pulling down of the wicked, that from hence foorth not only all poore mens causes may be pitied, their complaints accepted, and their wrongs redressed: but also that by their carefull industry and diligence employed, all Sorcerers, Witches and Charmerers may utterly be weeded out from the face of the earth to the commoditie of a common welth and to the honor & glory of God, to whome be all praise, laude, dominion and power for ever and ever Amen.

6

W.W., *A true and just Recorde* (1582)

At over one hundred pages, this is the longest witchcraft pamphlet since such publications began. The texts used here are from the British Library and Trinity College Cambridge, a combination of which gives the most legible version. The pamphlet seems to have been inspired by the self-publicising Brian Darcey or Darcy, JP, the magistrate who took the examinations of the witches involved. The events described are centred around the Essex village of St Osyth, in a region where the Darcy family were powerful – the head of the family being Baron Darcy of Chiche (St Osyth), the pamphlet's dedicatee.[1] Brian Darcy, a less important and older family member, had been a JP for two years when he questioned the witches, and became Sheriff of Essex in 1585, perhaps as a result of his obvious zeal and desire to shine.

Brian Darcy may be the author of the pamphlet, or he may have delegated this lengthy process to someone else – perhaps William Lowth, who, as Barbara Rosen discovered, dedicated a treatise to Darcy and a relative as his 'friends' in 1581.[2] There are stylistic similarities between Lowth's work and *A true and just Recorde*, as Rosen suggests, but Brian Darcy seems likely to have influenced the theme of the preface, an inhumane polemic advocating the burning of witches. The preface's reverential quotation from Jean Bodin, the French jurist and demonological author, seems likely to be linked to Darcy's probable reference to Bodin in questioning one of the witches, and we can be fairly sure that Darcy's is the mind behind the publishing project. Clearly, his records were carefully kept so that the pamphlet should be the fullest account yet given of the pre-trial legal process against witches, and should also include the informations of witnesses and victims. There is curiously little concentration on the outcome of the trial on 29 March: most of the convicted witches' sentences are gestured towards in the text with the single word 'condemned', but sometimes mistakes have been made even in this basic recording. The octavo pamphlet was licensed

1 See Cokayne, vol. 4, 78–9, and W.C. Metcalfe, ed., *The Visitations of Essex* (London, 1878), vol. 1, 44–6, for Darcy's family.

2 Bartholomew Batty, *The Christian mans Closet*, translated and with a preface by William Lowth (London, 1581). It was published, like *A true and just Recorde*, by Thomas Dawson.

to Thomas Dawson senior, a successful printer with a large business, on 6 April – perhaps it was prepared in a rush for topical publication, with resultant errors and omissions? One might otherwise have expected a careful recording of punishments. But instead we do not even know whether Brian Darcy attended the trial or not, although in the unique table at the end of the pamphlet it is said that he certified the documents to the assizes on 29 March. Surely nothing short of *rigor mortis* would have prevented him from enjoying his moment of glory before the judges, and Darcy did not die until Christmas Day 1587.

The table is a paradigm of the mood of the pamphlet, a wonderfully obsessive, almost loving, documentation of the statistics of the case, a fold-out extravaganza of detail attached to the back of the pamphlet. Each witch is numbered, and her crimes and spirits listed, in an attempt to control, classify and thus capture definitively the spattering of stories and accusatory suggestions laid out in the main text. Although it has omitted some of the cases where there was doubt as to which witch had attacked the victim, and abbreviated others, the list is very full and includes new material on some of the witches. Some of the sources of this sound gossipy ('as it is thought') and whilst the extra details might give information from documents not included in the pamphlet, there is very little to fill in the more obvious gaps. It seems likely that many of the key encounters between witnesses, suspects and magistrate went unrecorded, and that the table and the documents it summarises are in fact fragments of a far bigger matrix. Both are differently expressed attempts to make coherent and solid that which is essentially multiform, confused and ungraspable. If the main text is a mosaic mass of stories in which the reader is expected to discover a pattern, then the table is a neat linear diagram – whose ultimate failure is symbolised by the accidental omission from the list of the 'data' on Annis Glascocke and its insertion out of place as the pamphlet's final word. I have included a chronology of the events covered by the pamphlet as a third way for readers to find their way through *A true and just Recorde*.

Chronology of the St Osyth Documents

19 Feb.	Grace Thorlowe information against Ursley Kempe
19 Feb.	Annis Letherdall information against Ursley Kempe
20 Feb.	Ursley Kempe first examination
	confesses self, and accuses Ales Newman
21 Feb.	Ursley Kempe second examination
	confesses self, and accuses Ales Newman
21 Feb.	Ales Newman examination
22 Feb.	Elizabeth Bennett examination
	confesses self, and accuses 'Mother' Turner
23 Feb.	William Hook information against Ales Newman
24 Feb.	Ales Hunt information against Joan Pechey

24 Feb.	Elizabeth Bennett information against Ales Newman
24 Feb.	Ursley Kempe third examination confesses self, and accuses Elizabeth Bennett, Ales Hunt, Annis Glascock and Ales Newman
24 Feb.	William Bonner information against Elizabeth Bennett
24 Feb.	Annis Glascock examination
24 Feb.	Ales Hunt examination
25 Feb.	Margerie Sammon examination
25 Feb.	Margerie Sammon information against Joan Pechey
25 Feb.	Febey Hunt information against Ales Hunt (dating suspicious)
25 Feb.	Joan Pechey examination
25 Feb.	Thomas Rabbet information against Ursley Kempe and Ales Newman (dating could be suspicious)
26 Feb.	John Tendering information (no witch named, Elizabeth Bennett is suspected of causing the event he details)
1 Mar.	Richard Rosse information against Henry and Cysley Selles
1 Mar.	Henry and Cysley Selles examination
? 1 Mar.	Henry Selles junior information against Henry and Cysley Selles.
3 Mar.	John Selles information against Henry and Cysley Selles (dating suspicious)
3 Mar.	Joan Smith information against Cysley Selles

Some documents probably missing here (Richard Rosse and others' informations against Henry and Cysley Selles and their examination).

9 Mar.	Ursley Kempe information against Ales Newman
13 Mar.	John Sayer information against Ales Manfielde
13 Mar.	Joan Cheston information against Ales Manfielde
13 Mar.	Ales Manfielde examination confesses self, and accuses Margaret Grevell, Cysley Selles, Elizabeth Ewstace, Ursley Kempe, 'Mother' Turner, Ales Hunt, Margerie Sammon
14 Mar.	Robert Sannever information against Elizabeth Ewstace
14 Mar.	Elizabeth Ewstace examination
15 Mar.	Thomas and Mary Death informations against Cysley Selles
16 Mar.	John Wade, Thomas Cartwrite, Bennet Lane, Andrew and Anne West, Edmund and Godlife Osborne, Richard Harrison, John Pollin, 'Bret's wife' informations against Annis Herd
17 Mar.	Annis Herd examination
18 Mar.	Annis Dowsing information against Annis Herd (dating suspicious)
19 Mar.	Ales Baxter information (no witch named but probably Cysley Selles)
20 Mar.	John Carter, Nicholas Strickland informations against Margaret Grevell

20 Mar.	Felice Okey information against Elizabeth Ewstace
20 Mar.	Lawrence Kempe information against Ursley Kempe
24 Mar.	Margaret Grevell examination
25 Mar.	Edward Upcher, Ales Miles, Thomas Rice, Margery Carter, Ales Walter, Alan Duck, John Brasyer informations against Joan Robinson
25 Mar.	Joan Robinson examination
26 Mar.	Henry Durrant information against Ales Hunt.

{A2 (title page)[3]} **A true and just Recorde, of** *the Information, Examination* **and Confession of all the Witches, taken at** *S. Oses in the countie of Essex: whereof* **some were executed, and other some entreated according to the determination of lawe.**
Wherein all men may see what a pestilent *people Witches are, and how unworthy to lyve in a Christian Commonwealth.*
Written orderly, as the cases were tryed by evidence, **By W.W.**
Imprinted in London at the **three Cranes in the Vinetree by Thomas Dawson 1582.**
{A2v blank}
{A3} *To the right honourable and* **his singular good Lorde, the Lord Darcey,**[4] W. W. *wisheth a prosperous continuaunce in this lyfe to the glory of God, and a dayly preservation in Gods feare to his endlesse joye.*
IF THERE HATH BIN at any time (Right Honorable) any meanes used, to appease the wrath of God, to obtaine his blessing, to terrifie secreete offenders by open transgressors punishments, to withdraw honest natures from the corruption of evil company, to diminishe the great multitude of wicked people, to increase the small number of virtuous persons, and to reforme all the detestable abuses, which the perverse witte and will of man doth dayly devise, this doubtlesse is no lesse necessarye then the best, that Sorcerers, Wizzardes, or rather Dizzardes,[5] Witches, Wisewomen (for so they will be named) are rygorously punished. Rygorously sayd I? Why it is too milde and gentle a tearme for such a mercilesse generation; I should rather have sayd most cruelly executed; for that no punishment can be thought upon, be it never so high a degree of torment, which may be deemed sufficient for such a di-{A3v}-velish & damnable practise. And why? Because al the imaginations, al the consultations, al the conference, al the experimentes, finally the attemptes, proceedinges and conclusions of Sorcerers, Witches, and the rest of that hellishe liverie, are meere blasphemers against

3 The book begins with two A signatures, and A of the first is missing.
4 Thomas, Baron Darcy, a cousin of the same generation as Brian's grandchildren. He had become the third Baron in 1581.
5 Fools.

the person of the most high God;[6] and draw so neere to the nature of idolatrie (for they worshippe Sathan, unto whome they have sworne allegiaunce) that they are by no meanes to be exempted from the suspition of that most accursed defection, nay rather they are guiltie of apparaunte apostasie, which is more heynous (considering the circumstances of their ordinarie actions, then any trespasse against the seconde table, which ouglye sinnes of blasphemie, and grosse, or rather divelish idolatrie concurring in no malefactor so roundly, as in sorcerers, witches, Inchaunters &c. in whom the meete with a millian of enormities more; as it were in a centre; the magistrates of forren landes, noted so precisely, that weighing the qualitie of the cryme, they kept a due analogie and proportion of punishment, burning them with fire, whome the common lawe of Englande (with more measure of mercie then is to be wished) strangleth with a rope. An ordinary fellon, and a murtherer offending against the morall lawe of justice, is throtled: a Sorcerer, a Witch, (whome a learned Phisitian is not ashamed to avoch innocent, and the Judges, that[7] {A4} denounce sentence of death against them no better than hangmen) defying the Lorde God to his face; and trampling the pretious blood of that immaculate lambe Jesus Christ most despitfully under feete is stiffled: the one dyeth on the gallowes, and so doth the other: wherein

6 This passage is translated from Jean Bodin's *De la Demonomanie des Sorciers* (1580; Paris, 1587) fos 216–17. Bodin says: '*Or s'il y eut oncques moyen d'appaiser l'ire de Dieu, d'obtenir sa benediction, d'estonner les uns par le punition des autres, de conserver les uns de l'infection des autres, de diminuer le nombre des meschans, d'asseurer la vie des bons, & de punir les meschancetez les plus detestables que l'esprit humain peut imaginer, c'est de chastier a toute rigeur les Sorciers: combien que le mot de Rigeur est mal pris, attendu que il n'y a peine si cruelle qui peust suffire à punir les meschancetez des Sorciers, d'autant que toutes leurs meschancetez, blasphemes, & tous leurs desseings se dressent contre la Majesté de Dieu, pour le despiter & offenser par mille moyens*'. In modern English this reads: 'Now if there was ever a way to appease the wrath of God, to obtain his blessing, to frighten some by the punishment of others, to protect some from the contamination of others, to reduce the number of the wicked, to secure the life of the good, and to punish the most dreadful wickednesses that the human spirit can imagine, it is to punish, with utmost rigour, sorcerers: although the word 'rigour' is ill chosen, given that there is no punishment cruel enough to suffice to punish the wickednesses of sorcerers, all the more so since all their wickednesses, blasphemies, and all their designs are set up against the majesty of God, in order to defy and offend him in a thousand ways' (translation by Rebecca Selman and Marion Gibson). It can be seen that the prefacer's translation adds ideas to fit Bodin's theories into an English setting: for example, mentioning wisewomen, and suggesting the burning of witches on A3v. There are echoes of Bodin throughout the pamphlet.

7 A marginal note beginning on A3v and continuing on A4 reads '*Bodinus in confutatione futilis opinionis Wieri; Lamias, lamiarumq; Veneficia astruentis*'. Roughly translated, this cites 'Bodin, in confutation of the worthless opinion of Wier, supporting witches and the poisonings of witches'. Johannes Wier (Weyer, Wierus), in his *De praestigiis daemonum* of 1563, followed a similar semi-sceptical line to the later English writer Reginald Scot. His book has been translated into English as *Witches, Devils and Doctors in the Renaissance*, trans. John Shea, ed. George Mora (Binghampton, New York: Medieval and Renaissance Texts, 1991).

doubtlesse there is a great inequalitie of justice, considering the inequalitie of the trespasse, which deserveth a death so much the more horrible, by how much the honour of God is eclipsed, and the glorye due to his inviolable name most abhominably defaced, even to the uttermost villanie that they can put in practise.

This I speake (Right Honorable) upon a late viewe of tryall, taken against certaine Witches in the countie of Essex; the orderly processe in whose examinations, together with other accidents, I dilygently observing and considering their trecheries to be notable: undertooke briefly knit up in a fewe leaves of paper, their manifolde abuses: and obtaining the meanes to have them published in print, for that a number of memorable matters are here touched, to present the same unto your Lordship, of whose gentle acceptation though I dooe not doubt, yet will I not be over bolde thereupon to presume: but rather refer the same to your honours judgement and patronage by way of humilyation, that going abrode under coverte of your honourable name, the discourse maye seeme the {A4v} **more credible, your lordship knowing the grounds of this whole booke to be true and justifiable, and therefore the further off from feare of impugning. But supposing I have beene too tedious and sparing to trouble your Lordship with multitude of words, I build upon hope, & so put forth my booke, praying the Lord here to blesse your Honour, and all about you with the increase of his grace in this life, and with the presence of his divinitie in the lyfe to come. Amen.**

Your Honours to commaund W.W.

{2A} [**The xix. day of February** *the xxiiii yeere of the raigne of* **our Soveraigne Ladie Queene Elizabeth.**[8]

The information of Grace Thurlowe, the wife of John Thurlowe, taken before mee Brian Darcye the day and yeere above saide, against Ursley Kempe **alias** *Gray, as followeth.*

THE saide grace sayeth that about xii monethes past, or nere thereabouts, her Sone Davye Thurlowe, beeing strangely taken and greatly tormented, Ursley Kempe **alias** Grey came unto the said Grace to see how the childe did: At which time the childe lying upon a bed in the chimney corner, shee the said Ursley tooke it by the hande, saying, A good childe howe art thou loden: and so went thrise out of the doores, and every time when shee came in shee tooke the childe by the hande, and saide A good childe howe art thou loden. And so at her departure the said Grace prayed the saide Ursley to come againe unto {2Av} her at night to helpe her. And thereupon she the saide Ursley replied, and saide, I Warrant thee I thy Childe shall doe well enoughe, and yt[9] night it fell to rest the which it did not of a long time

8 Passages which are only semi-legible in the British Library copy used here are marked by square brackets and their deficiencies supplied from the Trinity College copy.

9 That.

before. And the next day the said Grace going to mille warde meeting the said Ursley, shee asked her howe her childe did, and shee said it tooke good rest this night God be thanked, I I saide the said Ursley,[10] I warrant thee it shall doe well. Note, that the palmes of the childes handes were turned wher the backes shoulde bee, and the backe in the place of the palmes.

The said Grace saith also, that about three quarters of a yeere ago she was delivered of a womanchild, and saith, that shortly after the birth thereof, the said Ursley fell out with her, for that shee woulde not suffer her to have the nursing of that childe, at suche times as she the said Grace continued in woorke at the Lorde Darceys place:[11] And saith, that shee the saide Grace nursing the said childe, within some short time after that falling out, the childe lying in the Cradle, and not above a quarter olde, fell out of the said Cradle, and brake her necke, and died. The which the said Ursley hearing to have happened, made answere, it maketh no matter. For shee might have suffe-{2A2}-red mee to have the keeping and nursing of it.

And the saide Grace saith, that when shee lay in, the saide Ursley came unto her, and seemed to bee very angrie for that shee had not the keeping in of the saide Grace, & for that she answered unto her that shee was provided: And thereupon they entred further into talke, the saide Grace saying, that if shee should continue lame as shee had doone before, shee woulde finde the meanes to knowe howe it came, and yt shee woulde creepe upon her knees to complaine of them to have justice done upon them: And to that shee the saide Ursley saide, it were a good turne: Take heed (said Grace) Ursley, thou hast a naughtie name. And to that Ursley made answere, though shee coulde unwitche shee coulde not witche, and so promised the saide Grace, that if shee did sende for her privily, and send her keeper away, that then shee woulde show the said Grace how shee shoulde unwitch herselfe or any other at any time.

And the said Grace further saith that about halfe a yeere past she began to have a lamenesse in her bones, & specially in her legges, at which time ye said Ursley came unto her unsent for and wtout request, and said she would helpe her of her lamenes, if she the said Grace woulde give {2A2v}her xii. pence, ye which the said Grace speaking her fayre, promised her so to doe, and thereupon for the space of v. weekes after, she was wel & in good case as shee was before. And then the said Ursley came unto the saide Grace, and asked her ye money she promised to her. Wherupon the saide Grace made answere: that shee was a poore and a needie woman, and had no money: & then the said Ursley requested of her cheese for it: but she said she had none. And shee the said Ursley, seeing nothing to be had of the saide Grace, fell out with her, and saide, that she woulde be even with her: and thereupon shee was taken lame, and from that day to this day hath so continued.

10 'Aye, aye'.
11 St Osyth Priory, home of the third Baron Darcy.

And she saith, that when she is any thinge well or beginneth to amend, then her childe is tormented, and so continueth for a time in a very strange case, and when he beginneth to amend: Then shee the saide Grace becometh so lame as without helpe shee is not able to arise, or to turne her in her bed.

The information of Annis Letherdall, wife of Richard Letherdall, taken by mee Brian Darcey Esquire, against Ursley Kempe, *alias* Grey the xix day of February.

{2A3} THe said Annis saith, that before Michaelmass last, she the said Ursley sent her sonne to the said Letherdals house, to have scouring sand, and sent word by the said boy, yt his mother would give her the dying of a payre of womens hose for the sand: But the said Annis knowing her to be a naughtie beast sent her none. And after she the said Ursley, seeing her gyrle to carry some to one of her neighbours houses murmured as the said childe said, & presently after her childe was taken as it lay very bigge, with a great swelling in the bottome of the belly, and other privie partes. And the saide Annis saith, yt about the tenth day of Februarie last shee went unto the said Ursley, and tolde her that shee had been foorth with a cunning body,[12] which saide, yt she the said Ursley had bewitched her childe: To yt the said Ursley answered, that shee knewe shee had not so been, and so talking further she said, that she would lay her life that she the said Annis had not been with any: whereupon shee requested a woman being in the house a spinning with the said Ursley, to beare witnesse what shee had said. And the next day the childe was in most piteous case to beholde, whereby shee thought it good to Carry the same unto mother Ratcliffe, for that shee had some experience of her skill. The which when the said mother {2A3v} Ratcliffe did see: shee saide to the saide Annis that shee doubted shee shoulde doe it any good, yet shee ministred unto it &c.

The enformation of Thomas Rabbet, of the age of viii yeres or thereabouts, base son[13] unto the said Ursley Kempe *alias* Grey, taken before me Brian Darcey esquire, one of her Majesties Justices, the xxv day of February, against his said mother.

THe saide Thomas Rabbet saith, that his said mother Ursley Kempe **alias** Grey hath foure severall spirites, the one called *Tyffin*, the other *Tittey*, the third *Pygine*, & the fourth *Jacke*: & being asked of what colours they were, saith, that *Tyttey* is like a little grey Cat, *Tyffin* is like a white lambe, *Pygine* is black like a Toad, and *Jacke* is black like a Cat. And hee saith, hee hath seen his mother at times to give them beere to drinke and of a white Lofe or Cake to eate, and saith that in the night time the said spirites will come to his mother, and sucke blood of her upon her armes, and other places of her body.

12 A wiseman or wisewoman.
13 Illegitimate.

This Examinat being asked, whether hee had seene Newmans wife to come unto his mother, saith that one morning he being in the cham-{2A4}-ber with his mother, his Godmother Newman came unto her, and saith, that then he heard her and his mother to chide, and to fall out. But saith before they parted they were friends: and that then his mother delivered an earthen pot unto her, in the which he thinketh her spirites were, the which she carried away with her under her aperne.

And this examinat saith, that within a fewe daies after the said Newmans wife came unto his mother, and yt he heard her to tel his mother that she had sent a spirit to plague Johnson to ye death, and an other to plague his wife.

The enformation of Ales Hunt, taken before mee Brian Darcey Esquire, the xxiiii. day of February, against Joan Pechey widdow.[14]

THis examinat Ales Hunt saith, that shee dwelleth in ye next house unto ye saide Joan Pechey, & yt she the said Joan two or three daies before Christmas last, went to ye house of Johnson ye Collector appointed for ye poore, whereas she ye said Joan received beefe & bread, the which the Examinat saith shee hearde to bee of the gift of ye said Brian Darcey). And this examinat saith that ye said Joan going homewardes, murmured & found great fault at Johnson, saying, he might have given that to a gyrle or another, {2A4v} and notte her, saying, the bread was to hard baked for her, and that shee then seemed to bee in a great anger therewithall. This examinat saith, shee was at that present in the house of the wydow Hunt, and that there was but a wall betweene them. The saide Joan comming to her house did unlocke her dore, the which this examinat did see her doe: And after shee was entred into her house, this examinat saith, she hard the said Joan to say, yea are you so sawsie: are you so bolde: you were not best to bee so bolde with mee: For if you will not bee ruled, you shall have Symonds sause,[15] yes saide the saide Joan, I perceive if I doe give you an inch, you you[16] will take an ell: and saith she is assured that there was no christian creature with her at that time, but that she used those speeches unto her Imps.

And this examinat saith, that she hath heard her mother say, that she the said Joan was skilfull and cunning in witcherie, and could do as much as the said mother Barnes: this examinats mother, or any other in this towne of St. Osees. And further saith she hath hard her mother to say yt the said Joan did know what was saide or done in any mans house in this towne.

14 This information, and the next (of Margery Sammon), are probably part of the examination of both these sisters for witchcraft. These informations don't reveal that the informants are in fact suspects – which affects our reading of them, suggesting that they are volunteered accusations rather than part of a confessional question and answer process. But later in the pamphlet examinations of the sisters are printed, and they are dated on the same day as these informations.

15 To go hungry (Rosen, 111, n. 10).

16 This word is repeated.

{2A5} **The information of Margerie Sammon sister to the saide Ales Hunt: taken before mee Brian Darcey Esquire, the xxv. day of Februarie against the said Joan Pechey as followeth.**

THe said Margerie sayth, that she hath hard the widowe Hunt to say, that the sayde Joan Pechey shoulde say that shee coulde tell what any man saide or did at any time in there houses, when & as often as shee listed:[17] and sayth, that the saide widowe Hunt did tell her that shee hath harde the saide Joan Pechey, being in her house, verie often to chide and vehemently speaking as though there had been some bodye present with her: And sayth, that shee went in to see to whome the saide Joan should speake, but shee founde no bodie but her selfe all alone: And sayeth, that shee the sayd Joan Pechey was with this examinates mother, mother Barnes, the day before shee departed, where this examinate left them together while shee went home to her mistris house, to doe her businesse and worke.

The enformation of John Tendering of Saint Osees, taken before me Brian Darcey esquire, the xxvi. of Februarie 1582.

{2A5v} THe said John sayth, that William Byette having occasion to come to this examinate, sayeth, that after they had conferred and talked, hee the saide William Byet did declare to this examinate, That, that morning he did tell him that he had a Cow wc[18] had lien two dayes or longer in a strange case, and had eaten nothing, and was not likly to live, & that he and his servants severall times had lifted at the said cowe to raise her upon her feet, but they could not make her to arise or stand: whereupon hee told this examinat, that he had caused his said servants to fetch straw, and to lay the same round about her: And that he himselfe tooke an Axe, minding to knocke her upon the head, and so to burne her: And said that the fire being kindled, the said Cowe of her selfe start up, and ran her way until it came to a wood stack and there stood still, and fell a byting of stickes, bigger then any mans finger, and after lived and did well.[19]

The enformation of Febey Hunt, daughter in lawe to Ales Hunt, of the age viii yeeres or thereabouts, taken before mee Brian Darcey esquire, the xv day of Februarie agaynst Ales Hunt her mother.

THe sayd Febey Hunt sayth, yt shee hath seen her mother to have two litle thinges like {2A6} horses, the one white, the other blacke, the which shee kept in a litle lowe earthen pot with woll, colour white and blacke: and that they stoode in her chamber by her bed side, and saith, that shee hath seene her mother to feede them with milke out of a blacke trening[20] dishe, and this examinat being caried after this confession by the Constables to her

17 Liked.

18 Which.

19 Tendering must be giving this information because Byet is dead. It is probably against Elizabeth Bennett. See note 34.

20 Wooden.

fathers house, shee shewed them the place were they stood and the borde that covered them: And this examinate chose out the dishe, out of which they were fedde, from amongst many other dishes. She this examinat did also confesse that her mother had charged her not to tell anything, what shee had seene: And if shee did those thinges woulde take her, and this examinate saith that her mother did send them to Hayward of Frowicke, but to what end shee can not tell, & shee being asked howe she knew the same, saieth, that shee hard her mother bid them to go.

The enformation of William Hooke Painter, taken before me Brian Darcey esquire, the xxiii of Februarie, against Ales Newman.

THis examinate William Hooke saith yt he dwelleth in the next house unto Ales Newman, & saith, that he hath hard William Newman, her husband to say unto ye said Ales his wife yt she {2A6v} was the cause of her husbands great miserie and wretched state, and sayeth, that when the saide Ales doeth give her husbande any meate to eate, then presently he the saide William saith to his wife, doest thou not see? doest thou see? whereunto this examinate sayth, that he hath hearde the saide Ales to say, if thou seest anything, give it some of thy meat. And saith further, that he hath hearde the saide William Newman bid the said Ales his wife to beate it away.

The enformation of Elizabeth Bennet, taken by me Brian Darsey esquire, the xxiiii. day of Februarie 1582, against Ales Newman.

THe sayde Elizabeth saith, that shee never sent any spirite to plague Johnson or his wife, neither knew shee mother Newman to have sent any of her spirits to plague him or his wife,[21] shee this examinate for her part sayth, shee was greatly beholding to the sayde Johnson and his wife. But denieth that ever shee sent any spirit to hurt him and his wife: or that shee knewe mother Newman to have hurt them. But this examinat saith that shee being at Johnsons to have wool to spinne, he being a clothmaker, of whom shee had many times worke, at that present mother Newman being come thither, she this exa-{2A7}-minate saith she hard the said mother Newman to desire Johnson to give her xii.d, saying yt her husbande lay sicke, whereunto shee heard him answere that hee woulde gladly helpe her husbande: but that hee had laide out a great deale more then he had received, saying, he was a pore man, and hee, his wife and familie, might not want for the helping of her husbande, saying that hee coulde not helpe her with any, untill he had collected more money, whereupon shee departed, and used some harde speeches unto him, and seemed to be much angrie.

21 An example of the blurred line between informations (against others) and examinations (of a suspect themself), and of the tendency of legal documents to oversimplify and categorise stories. Despite the questioner's title for her story, Elizabeth Bennett appears reluctant to incriminate any other, or even to confess anything herself, at this stage of her response to questioning. As she goes on, however, her narrative becomes what the document title prescribes: the conventionally shaped informant's story of the alleged victim angering the witch.

The examination and confession of Ursley Kemp alias Gray, taken at S: Osees, and brought before mee Brian Darsey esquire, one of her Majesties Justices of the peace, the xx. day of Februarie 1582.
Condemned.[22]

THe saide Ursley Kempe sayeth, that about tenne or eleven yeeres paste, shee this examinate was troubled with a lamenes in her bones and for ease thereof went to one Cockes wife of Weley,[23] nowe deceased, who telled this examinate that shee was bewitched, and at her entretie taught her to unwitche her selfe. And bad her take hogges dunge and charvell, {2A7v} and put them together and holde them in her left hand, and to takein the other hande a knife, and to pricke the medicine three times, & then to cast the same into the fire, and to take the said knife & to make three pricks under a table, and to let the knife sticke there: & after that to take three leves of sage, and as much of herbe John (**alias** herbe grace) and put them into ale: and drinke it last at night and first in the morning, & that shee taking the same had ease of her lamenesse.

The sayde examinate sayth, that one Pages wife, and one Grayes wife, beeing eyther of them lame and bewitched, shee beeing requested and sent for to come unto them, went unto them: And saieth, that shee knewe them to bee bewitched and at their desires did minister unto them the foresaid medicine, whereupon they had speedie amendement.

The saide Brian Darcey then promising to the saide Ursley, that if she would deale plainely and confesse the trueth, that shee should have favour & so by giving her faire speeches shee confessed as followeth.[24]

THe saide Ursley bursting out with weeping, fel upon her knees, and confessed that {2A8} shee had foure spirits, wherof two them were hees and the other two were shees: the two hee spirites were to punishe and kill unto death, and the other two shees were to punishe with lamenes, and other diseases of bodyly harme and also to destroy cattell.

And she this examinate, being asked by what name or names she called the saide spirites, and what maner of thinges, or colour they were of: confesseth

22 See note 41.

23 Weeley, a village about five miles north of St Osyth.

24 At this point, as the pamphlet reveals on 2A8v, the suspect begins confessing to Darcey 'privately'. What precisely this means is uncertain: perhaps the scribe or any onlookers were sent away. Clearly Darcey perceived this questioning, and the resultant document, to be different from the usual process of examination and he intends us to be aware of this – but only after we have read the information contained in it. He is probably promoting what he saw as the best foreign models of questioning (see the comment on offers of favour on B5) by showing the result and then revealing how it was obtained. If he recorded his wily eliciting of information in the original pre-trial documents, however, rather than adding it for the printed version, he laid himself open to challenges of unfairness which might have created judicial sympathy for the suspect. Possibly the examinations which he sent to the assizes were not so forthcoming about their origin. If they were, Darcey was at least declaring his trickery openly.

and saith: that the one is called *Tyttey*, being a hee, and is like a gray Cat, the seconde called Jacke, also a hee, and is like a blacke Cat, the thirde is called *Pigin*, being a she, and is like a blacke *Toad*, the fourth is called *Tyffin*, being a shee, and is like a white lambe.[25]

This examinate being further asked, whiche of the saide spirites shee sent to punishe Thorlowes wife, and Letherdalls childe, confessed and sayed, that shee sent *Tyttey* to punishe Thorlows wife, and *Pigin* Letherdalls Childe.

And this examinate, without any asking of her owne free will at that present, confessed and saide, yt shee was the death of her brother Kemps wife, and that she sent the spirite Jacke to plague her, for that her sister[26] had called her whore and witche.

And this examinate further confessed, {2A8v} that upon the falling out betweene Thorlowes wife and her, shee sent *Tyffin* the spirite unto her childe, which lay in the Cradle, and willed the same to rock the Cradle over, so as the childe might fall out thereof, and breake the necke of it.

These foresaide 5. last recited matters, being confessed by the saide Ursley privately to me the saide Brian Darcey, were afterwardes (supper being ended, and shee called agayne before mee, the saide Brian) recited and particularlie named unto her all which shee confessed as before in the presence of us, whose names bee hereunder subscribed.[27]

Also after this examinates aforesaide confession, the saide Thorlows wife, and Letherdalles wife being then in my house,[28] and shee the saide Letherdalls wife having her childe there also, were brought in my presence before this examinate: who, immediatly after some speeches had past betweene them, shee this examinate burst out in teares and fell upon her knees and asked forgivenesse of the saide Letherdalls wife, and likewise of Thorlows wife, and confessed that shee caused Newmans wife to sende a spirite to plague the childe, asking the saide Letherdalls wife, if shee were not afraide that night that the spirite came unto the childe, and telled her a-{B}-about the same houre,] and said that shee herselfe by reason thereof was in a great swete. And this examinate confesseth, that shee caused the same Newmans wife, to send a spirite to Thorlowes wife, to plague her where that thought good, &c.

25 This (20 February) appears to be the origin of eight-year-old Thomas Rabbet's story of his mother's familiars (25 February, 2A3v). However, further on in the pamphlet, child evidence seems to have been misdated to give the impression that it post-dated parental evidence (see especially the Selles children D–D2v and Annis Dowsing F4–F4v). Thus the evidence of spirit-keeping given by the children looks like mere confirmation of their parents' confessions, as here, instead of appearing to be the creation of wild stories which the adult suspect is then bullied into accepting and repeating. There is no guarantee that the same is not the case here.

26 Sister-in-law. See E4v–E5.

27 As Rosen says, rather plaintively, 'they are not here' (115). Possibly they were lost in the process of turning manuscript into print.

28 Presumably St Osyth Priory, rather than Brian Darcy's Tiptree residence.

The said Letherdals childe (being a woman childe) at the time of this examination, appeared to bee in most piteous sort consumed, and the privie and hinder partes thereof, to be in a most strange and wonderfull case, as it seemed to verye honest women of good judgement, and not likely to live and continue any long time.

Note also that it is specially to be considered, that the saide childe beeing an infante and not a yeere olde, the mother thereof carrying it in her armes, to one mother Ratcliffes a neighbour of hers, to have her to minister unto it, was to passe by Ursley this examinates house, and passing bye the wyndowe, the Infante cryed to the mother, wo, wo, and poynted with the finger to the wyndowe wardes: and likewise the chyld used the like as shee passed homewards by the said window, at which she confessed her conscience moved her, so as shee went shortly after and talked with the said Ursley, where {Bv} upon shee used suche speeches as mooved her to complaine.[29]

The seconde confession and examination of Ursley Kemp, taken the xxi. day of Februarie.

The said Ursley, being committed to the ward & keeping of the Constable that night, upon some speeches that shee had passed, said, that shee had forgotten to tell M. Darcey one thing, whereupon the next day she was brought before Brian Darcey, & the second time examined, who confessed and said.[30]

That about a quarter of a yeere last past, one Ales Neweman, her nere neighbour came unto this examinates house and fel out with her, and said shee was a witche, and that shee woulde take away her witcherie, and carrie the same unto M. Darcey: But this examinate saieth, shee thought shee did not meane it, but after they had chidden they became friendes, and so shee departed carying away with her, her spirites in a pot, as this examinate sayth. And shee further sayth, that about Christmas last, shee went to the said Ales Newman, and declared to her that Thorlows wife and shee were fallen out, and prayed the saide Newmans wife, {B2} to sende the spirite called *Tittey*, unto her to plague the sayde Thorlowes wife, where that thought good: The which this examinate saith, shee did, and at the returne of the saide spirite it tolde this examinate, that it had punished Thorlowes wife upon her knee, And then it had a reward by sucking blood of this examinate, and so returned as shee saith to the said Ales Neweman.

This examinate saith, that about three monethes past, shee and one John Stratton fel out, and the saide John called her whore & gave her other evill speeches, whereupon this examinate sayth, that shortly after shee sent her

29 To go to the justice.

30 This situating comment makes Ursley seem to be seeking the limelight which examination offered her – but in fact she uses her second confession to shift much of the blame for the alleged offences on to Ales Newman, and even on to the semi-autonomous spirits. This manipulation of apparent confession is the first of several examples in this pamphlet's narratives.

Boy for spices unto the wife of the said John: But shee sayeth, shee sent her none, wherupon this examinate sayeth, shee went unto the saide Newmans wife, and tolde her of the falling out between Stratton and her, and requested the saide Newmans wife, to sende *Jacke* the spirite unto Strattons wife to plague her, ye which the said Ales Newman promised this examinate to doe the nexte night, as this examinate saith shee did: And the spirite tolde this examinate when it returned, that it had plagued her in the backe even unto death: and the spirite did sucke of this examinate upon the left thigh, the which when she rubbeth (shee saith) it will at all times bleede.

{B2v} And shee sayeth that then the spirite did returne to the sayde Newemans wife agayne, and had the like rewarde of her as shee thynketh.

This examinate sayeth, that about Friday was sevennight[31] beeing about the nienth of Februarie, shee went unto the said Ales Newman, and did shewe her that one Letherdalls wife and shee were fallen out, and sayth, that shee prayed her to sende one of the spirites unto her younge chylde: whereunto shee the sayd Ales answered well she would: and this examinate saith, that at that time shee coulde have no longer talke with her, for that her husband was then present in the house: and this examinat saith that the said Ales sent the spirit *Pigin*, to plague ye said child where that thought good, and after that it had sucked of this examinate, shee saith it returned to the saide Newmans wife, and more at that time the saide examinate confessed not.

The third examination & confession of Ursley Kempe alias Gray, taken before me Brian Darsey esquire, one of her Majesties Justices of the peace, the xxiiii. day of Februarie.

THis examinate, being asked how she knew the said Elizabeth Bennet to have two spi-{B3}-rits[32] saith, that about a quarter of a yere past she went unto mother Bennets house for a messe of milke, the which shee had promised her: But at her comming this examinate saith shee knocked at her dore, and no bodie made her any answere, whereupon shee went to her chamber windowe and looked in therat, saying, ho, ho, mother Bennet are you at home? And casting her eyes aside, shee saw a spirit lift up a clothe lying over a pot, looking much like a Ferret. And it beeing asked of this examinate why the spirite did looke upon her, shee said it was hungrie.

This examinate, beeing asked howe shee knewe the names of mother Bennets spirites, sayth that *Tyffin* her spirite did tell this examinate that shee had two spirites, the one of them like a blacke Dogge, and the other redde like a Lyon, and that their names were *Suckin* and *Lyerd*, and sayeth that *Suckin* did plague Byettes wife unto death, and the other plagued three of his Beastes

31 A week ago last Friday.

32 An interesting opening: very clearly directing the examinate (who has now become an informant as well as a suspect), yet presumably based on information already given by her in an unrecorded context. The next section of her statement begins in the same way.

whereof two of them dyed, and the third leyer fire[33] or drooping, & not likly to live: Byette caused his folkes to make a fire about her: The Cow feeling the heate of the fire, starte up and came her way, and by that occasion was saved.[34]

{B3v} This examinate saith, that about the foureteene or fifteene day of Januarie last, shee went to the house of William Hunt to see howe his wife did and shee beeing from home, shee called at her chamber window and looked in, and then espied a spirite to looke out of a potcharde[35] from under a clothe, the nose thereof beeing browne like unto a Ferret. And sayeth, that the same night shee asked *Tyffin* her white spirite, what Huntes wives spirite had done:[36] And then it told this examinate, that it had killed Haywarde of Frowicke sixe beastes which were lately dressed of the gargette.[37] And sayeth, that her sayde spirite tolde her, that Huntes wives spirite had a droppe of her blood for a rewarde: but shee sayeth, that shee asked not her spirite upon what place of her body it was.

This examinate sayeth, that one Michell a shoomaker of Saint Osees did tell her, that he thought that Glascockes wife had bewitched his Chylde, whereof it dyed: Whereupon shee this examinate sayeth, that shee went home, and asked *Tyffin* her white spirite, whether the same were so: whiche tolde this examinate, that shee had bewitched the sayde chylde, and sent one of her spirites to plague it to the death.

{B4} And sayeth also, that the sayde Glascockes wife did bewitche the Base childe that Page and his wife have in keeping, and that her sayde spirite telled her so. And being demaunded, howe many spirits Glascockes wife had, and by what names shee called them, this examinate sayeth, that shee asked not her spirite *Tyffin* any such questions.

This examinate sayeth, that the sayde Elizabeth Bennette did sende her spirite *Suckin* to plague one Willingall, whereof hee languished and died: beeyng sicke of an impostume.[38]

33 Rosen suggests plausibly that this should read 'lay sick' and that 'probably the compositor picked up "a fire" from the succeeding sentence as he was setting "lay", since "fire" and "sick" would not be too unlike in Elizabethan handwriting' (Rosen, 118, n. 22).

34 This story is the one apparently repeated and enlarged upon by John Tendering on 26 February, which we have already read, inexplicably out of sequence and without the name of a suspect, on 2A5v.

35 Rosen suggests 'pot sherd', a shard or a broken piece of pot (118).

36 This story follows exactly the same shape as the previous one. Once a story shape had been offered by a suspect or witness and accepted, or at least recorded, by their questioner, it could sometimes be repeated *ad nauseam* in very unconvincing ways, and even retold by other people in their confessions. See Ales Manfielde's examination (D5v–D8, especially D7v for earthern pots and helpfully informed white spirits) for the best example of this repetition, recycling Ursley Kempe's statement.

37 Recently killed, because they had inflamed throats (see Rosen, 118, n. 23).

38 Abscess.

This examinate sayeth also, that the sayde Elizabeth sente the sayde spirite to William Willes his wife to plague her, whereof shee languished many yeeres and dyed.

This examinate sayeth, that the sayde Elizabeth (not above three weekes sithence) sent her spirite *Lyerd* to plague Fortunes wife and his chylde.

This examinate sayeth, that the sayde Elizabeth did sende her spirite *Lyerd* to Bonners wife to plague her, the whiche her sayde spirite, tolde this examinate to bee done upon the knee.

This examinate saith further, that Ales Newman went unto Johnson beeing Collectour {B4v} for the poore, and did require him to give her xii. d. for her husbande whiche was sicke. But hee answering her that he had disbursed more money then hee had collected, saying therefore hee coulde not then helpe her with any: The sayde Newemans wife fell out with him very angerly, and the next day after sent one of the spirites that shee had from this examinate to plague the saide Johnson and his wife unto the death: And that her spirite called *Tyffin* did tell the same unto her, and shee beeing asked what woordes the sayde Newemans wife used to Johnson upon the falling out, sayth, that shee asked not her said spirite.

This examinate sayeth, that Newmans wife beeing at Butlers, and asking a peece of meate, was denyed thereof: whereat shee went away mourmuring, And then shortely after sent one of her spirites to punishe him upon the backe: The whiche *Tyffin* her sayde spirite telleth this examinate was done, whereof hee languisheth and is greatly payned.

This examinate being asked, whether her white spirit called *Tyffin* did ever at any time tel her any untruths, or whether she had found it at a-{B5}-time[39] to tell any thing contrary to truth, saith, that the saide spirite did ever tell her true in any matter shee required of it, and saith, that shee never knewe it to tell her otherwise then truth.

This Exam. being asked, whether she sent any of her spirits to plague or punishe John Strattons childe, confesseth and saith, that the spirite which plagued Strattons wife to the death, did also punishe the saide Strattons childe, saying, that the saide childe shoulde not complaine thereof untill the mother were departed.

Note, it is to bee considered, that the saide Ursley Kempe in this her confession hath uttered many thinges well approved and confessed to bee most true: And that shee was brought thereunto by hope of favour.[40]

The Examination and confession of Ales Newman, taken before mee Brian Darcie Esquire, the xxi. of February.

Condemned.[41]

39 Should read 'any time' which is left out in the first line of B5.

40 See note 24.

41 One of several incompletenesses and errors in reporting outcome: Ales Newman was reprieved and imprisoned. She was released under a general pardon in 1588 (Ewen, *Witch*

THis examinat saith, that shee went unto the house where the saide Ursley Kempe **alias** Grey dwelt, and entred into communication with her, and that they fell out greatly and confesseth that shee saide unto the saide Ursley {B5v} that she knew her to be a witche, but denieth the residue of ye speeches alleadged by the said Ursley against this Examinat.

The said Brian Darcey finding this examinat to bee obstinate, and that shee coulde bee brought to confesse nothing, said to this Examinat, that hee woulde sever and part her and her spirites a sunder, nay sayth shee this examinat, that shal ye not, for I wil carry them with me, and hold being taken of her wordes, after some distance she added (if she have any).[42]

The enformation of William Bonner, taken before me Brian Darcey Esquire, the xxiii. day of February.

THe said William Bonner saith, that ye said Elizabeth Bennet and his wife were lovers[43] and familiar friendes, and did accompanie much together: and saith that since Candlemas[44] last his wife hath complained of a lamenesse in her knee, and that sithence also shee hath been much troubled. And saith also that not ten daies past the saide Elizabeth Bennet being with his wife, shee beeing sickely and sore troubled, the saide Elizabeth used speeches unto her, saying, a good woman how thou art loden, & then clasped her in her armes, and kissed her: Wherup-{B6}-on presently after her upper Lippe swelled & was very bigge, and her eyes much sunked into her head, and shee hath lien sithence in a very strange case.

Upon the saide enformation made by Ursley Kempe *alias* Grey, against Elizabeth Bennet, I Brian Darcey directed my warrant for her apprehension,[45] wherupon she was brought before me the said Brian, whose confession being taken the 22. day of February.

Condemned.[46]

THe said Elizabeth Bennet being charged with the foresaid information, denieth the same in generall, & after many and sundrie demands being asked, whether she had not a pot or pitcher of earth standing under a paire of

Hunting, 144–5; Cockburn, *Calendar: Essex: Elizabeth*, record 1300, and *Calendar: Introduction*, 199). Interestingly, she and Ursley Kempe were jointly charged (with killing Elizabeth, daughter of Richard Letherdall, Edena, wife of John Stratton, and Joan, daughter of John Thorlowe) but whilst both were found guilty of the offences, Kempe was hanged. Perhaps she was thought to be the stronger figure, leading Newman astray?

42 The 'distance' is greatly increased by framing the suspect's words in brackets.

43 Probably 'close friends'. The idea of lesbian witches is attractive to historians of persecution, but the term 'lovers' was used in describing a wide range of relationships.

44 2 February.

45 Either this is untrue or information is missing. In the records printed here, Ursley Kempe did not mention Elizabeth Bennett until 24 February. However, the opening of Kempe's 24 February examination does suggest missing or unrecorded material (see note 32) as does the opening questioning of Bennett here.

46 Elizabeth Bennett pleaded guilty (to killing William and Joan Byett) and was hanged (Ewen, 145; Cockburn, *Calendar: Essex: Elizabeth*, record 1316).

staires in her house & wool in the same, in the which usually the said two spirites did lie, denieth ye same with many othes, saying yt she was wel assured yt she had none such, wherupon it was said to her, if it be proved to your face, what will you say to al the other matters you have bin charged with, are they true? To that she made answere & said yea: Then was the pot brought before her, the which she then confessed to be her pot, but denied yt the wool therin was any of hers, then I calling her unto mee, saide, Elizabeth as thou {B6v} wilt have favour confesse the truth. For so it is, there is a man of great cunning and knoweledge come over lately unto our Queenes Majestie, which hath advertised her what a companie and number of Witches be within Englande: whereupon I and other of her Justices have received Commission for the apprehending of as many as are within these limites, and they which doe confesse the truth of their doeings, they shall have much favour: but the other they shall bee burnt and hanged.[47] At which speeches shee the saide Elizabeth falling upon her knees distilling teares confessed as heereafter followeth.

Saying, that one William Byet dwelt in the next house unto her three yeres, saying, yt the first yeere they did agree reasonably well, but ere the second yeare passed they fell out sundry and oftentimes, both with this examinat & her husbande, Byet calling her oftentimes olde trot and olde witche, and did banne and curse this examinat and her Cattell, to which this examinat saith, that shee called him knave saying, winde it up Byet for it wil light upon your selfe: and after this falling out this examinat saith, that Byet had three beastes dyed, whereof hee seeing one of them somewhat to droope, hee did beat the saide Cowe in such sorte (as this {B7} Examinat saith, that shee thought the said Cow did die thereof.

This examinat saith further, that Byets wife did beate her swine severall times with greate Gybets,[48] and did at an other time thrust a pitchforke through the side of one of this examinats swine, the which Durrant a Butcher did buie, and for that when he had dressed it, it prooved A messell,[49] this Examinat saith, shee had nothing for it but received it againe, &c.[50]

This examinat saith also, that above two yeeres past there came unto her two spirits, one called *Suckin*, being blacke like a Dogge, the other called *Lierd*, beeing red like a Lion, *Suckin* this examinat saith is a hee, and the other a

47 As Rosen suggests, this eminent man is Jean Bodin, whose visit to the Queen had only just ended. Darcy is, nevertheless, lying about the promise of favour, and neither did he have a special commission for his activities (Rosen, 121–2, nn. 24, 25). His assertion of a connection with the court would not have seemed implausible to the suspect, however – John, second Baron Darcy, had played host to the Queen in St Osyth's Priory in 1561 (Cokayne, 78).

48 Staves, cudgels, pieces of wood.

49 Rosen suggests 'a measled' or with tapeworms (122, n. 28).

50 It is noticeable that after this break, Elizabeth Bennett suddenly starts to tell stories of spirits. Again, something has changed subtextually.

shee. And saith, on a time as this examinat was comming from mill, the spirite called *Suckin* came unto her and did take her by the coate, and helde her that shee coulde not goe forwarde nor remoove by the space of two houres, at the which (this examinat saith) she was much amased, and shee saith, that the spirite did aske her if she this examinat woulde goe with it: Whereat shee this examinat saide, In the name of God, what art thou? Thou wilt not hurt mee, at the which speeche it said no, & this Examinat saith, that shee then prayed devoutly to Almightie God to deliver her from it: at which time the[51] {B7v} did depart from her untill shee had gone a good way, and being come within xxx. or xl. rodes[52] of her house, this examinat saith, that the said spirite came againe unto her and tooke her by the coates behind, & held her fast, whereat this examinat saith, that she desired God to deliver her from that evill spirite, and then that did depart to the Wel. And this examinat saith, yt within one houre after, the same same[53] spirite came againe unto her she being a sifting of her meale, & saith, the same remained with her untill she had laied her leaven,[54] and then departed.

The saide examinat saith, that the next day shee being a kneading of her bread, the saide spirite came againe unto her, and brought the other spirite with it called **Lierd**, and that one of them did aske her why she was so snappish yesterday, to that this examinat saith, that shee made answere, I trust I am in the faith of God, and you shall have no power over mee, at which wordes this Examinat saith, the saide spirites departed.

Then shee this examinat saith, that shee beeing a making of a fire in her Oven, the said spirites came againe unto her, and tooke her by the legge, this examinat feeling it to take her by the leg saith she said, God and the holy Ghost deliver me from the evill spirites, at which words {B8} this examinat saith, that the said spirites did depart to her thinking.

But this examinat saith, that within halfe an houre after she having a fier fork in her hand, and beeing a stirring of the fire in the Oven,[55] the spirit (called **Suckin**) came unto her & tooke this examinat by the hippes, and saide, seeing thou wilt not be ruled, thou shalt have a cause, & would have thrust this examinat into ye burning Oven, & so had (as this examinat saith) but for the foresaide forke, but this examinat striving and dooing what shee coulde to her uttermost, the saide spirite burnt her arme, the which burning

51 Should read 'spirite', which is left out in the first line of B7v.
52 Roods/rods (a rod is 6–8 yards).
53 This word is repeated.
54 She had added yeast to her bread mixture.
55 Each stage of the story is based on a stage in the domestic process of making bread. The story is not a conventional witch's confession of the keeping of spirits – it is more like a temptation or series of attacks by spirits, as usually told by a victim of possession (or obsession, where spirits outside the body control their victim). This pattern, and the concentration on the teller's everyday tasks, suggests that the suspect is determinedly resisting the telling of self-incriminating stories and interpreting her narrative quite differently from her questioner.

is apparaunt and evidently too bee seene, and when it had thus doone it did depart.

And this Examinat saith, that about a moneth after or more, shee beeing a walking in a croft[56] neere unto a Barne called Heywoods Barne, the spirite called **Suckin** came and followed this examinat, she spying the same as she looked backe, at the sight thereof this examinat saith, yt her eies wer like to start out of her heade then she saith yt she did beseech God to governe and guide her from the evill spirites, whereupon shee saith they did depart.

But the same evening she this examinat being set a milking of a red Cowe with a white face, {B8v} [saith that *Suckin* and *Lierd* came againe unto her, and saith that *Suckin* appeared at that time in the likenesse of a blacke dogge, and *Lierd* in the likenesse of a Hare, the one beeing on the one side of her, the other on the other side of her within lesse then two yardes: And saith, that the Cowe shee was then a milking of, snorted and ranne away, and brake her paile and spilt al her milke, neither coulde she get the said Cow any more that night to stand still, and saith, that for the losse thereof her husband did much chide her, but shee woulde not tell what was the cause: and she praying to the father, the sonne, & the holy ghost, saith that they did depart, and that shee sawe them not a quarter of a yeere after, not above three times since Midsommer last.[57]

The said exam. saith, that about that time they appeared againe unto her, and saith that a little before there was a falling out betweene her and the saide Byet, whereupon and for that Byet had oftentimes misused her this examinat and her Cattell, shee saith, that shee caused *Lyard* in ye likenes of a Lion to goe & to plague the saide Byets beastes unto death, and the spirite returning tolde this examinat that it had plagued two of his beastes, the one a red Cow, the other a blacke. And saith that the spirite] {C} tolde her, that hee plagued the blacke Cowe in the backe, and the read Cowe in the head.

This Examinate saieth further, that aboute Whitsontyde last past, the spirit called *Suckin*, did come againe at that tyme unto her, sayeing to this Examinate, that hee had mette Byettes wife two severall tymes, tellyng this Examynate, that it mette her once in this Examinates yarde, and the next day after it sayde, that it met her at the style, going into her grounde: And saieth it tolde this Examinate, it had plagued ye said Byets wife to the death. She this Examinate saying it was done by the spirite, but not by the sending of this Examinate. The sayde spirite sayeing, I knowe that Byet and his wife have wronged thee greatly, and doone thee severall hurtes, and beaten thy swyne, and thrust a pytchforke in one of them, the which the spirite sayde to have doone, to winne credit with this Examinate.[58]

56 Arable enclosure.

57 There is a sense that this was meant to be the end of the suspect's story, but that the examination went on, demanding more material. As before, there is a break in narration and suddenly Elizabeth Bennett begins (for whatever reason) to tell self-incriminating anecdotes.

And this Examinate saieth further, that aboute Lammas last past: For that the sayde William Byet had abused her, in calling her olde trot, old whore, and other lewde speaches, shee this Examinate, caused the spirite, called *Suckin*, to goe and plague the sayde Willyam Byette where that woulde: The which the sayd spyrite did, and at the retourne of it, it {Cv} tolde this Examinate, that it met Byet in the barne yarde, and that it plagued him in the hippes, even unto death: And saith she gave it a rewarde of mylke: and saith, that many tymes they drinke of her milke bowle. And being asked how shee came by the sayde spirites, she confessed and sayde, that one Mother Turner did sende them unto her to her house (as shee thinketh) for that she had denyed the sayde Mother Turner of mylke:[59] And when, and as often as they did drinke of the mylke: This Examynate saith they went into the sayd earthen pot, and lay in the wooll.

The Examynation and Confession of Annis Glascocke, wife of John Glascocke, sawyer, taken before me Bryan Darcey Esquyre, the xxiii. of February.

This Examinate beeing charged by Mychel the shoomaker, that a woman, Fortunes fellowe with her in the house, should reporte her to bee a naughtie woman, and a dealer in witchcrafte, denyeth that she knewe anye such woman, or that any such speaches were used unto her.[60]

This Examinat being charged that one sparrowe being lodged in her house, shoulde heare a straunge noise or rumbling since Christmas {C2} last, saith, that she made a noyse by removing of boards one night for that she woulde have him to lye in an other chamber.

This Examinate saith also, that long sithence she dwelt by the space of one quarter or more with her brother Edward Wood, and that at several tymes in that time certain ledden weights and great stones were cast into the house, and divers straunge noyses of rumblinges hearde: the which weights & stones

58 A very interesting retelling of the usual story. The suspect distances herself from the spirit – it acted autonomously, absolving her of guilt, and the *maleficium* which it says it did is presented as part of a wider temptation of the suspect to get her to 'credit', or believe in, the spirit. Demonologically this is a completely logical story: a writer such as George Gifford would interpret it without hesitation as a series of temptations in which the devil cajoles and threatens his victim, and at last tells her (falsely) that he has done a kind action in punishing her enemy. In return, he expects gratitude and possible worship, after which he will perform more false *maleficium* at the witch's request, and finally engineer her arrest and condemnation. However, Bennett's story was clearly not read in this critical way.

59 As Rosen says, the spirits are clearly seen as an affliction, not a blessing (Rosen, 125, n. 30), and this is the usual possession victim's story of angering a witch and then being haunted by her imps. However, the suspect has now also made the crucial admission in the other, expected, story of witchcraft: that she herself then kept the spirits and sent them to harm her neighbours.

60 A confusing passage. It seems to say that the examinate was charged by Mychel that an unnamed woman, in the presence of Fortune's servant, had reported Annis to be a naughty woman.

came alwayes neerest one Arnolds head, being then a boorder in that house, and saith that Arnoldes wife was accompted a witch: And was suspected to cause the same stones to be cast, to the intent to dryve her husband from boording there being in Jelosie of this Examinate: She being at that tyme not above the age of xx. yeares.[61]

This Examinate saith, that by many yeares past she was much troubled with straung aches in her bones, and otherwise: wherof she consumed by the space of two or three yeares: And saith, yt she was told, that about Sudbery[62] there dwelt one Herring (named to bee a Cawker[63]) to whome she went, who declared to this Examinate, yt she was haunted with a witch (naming Arnolds wife) And that she should not escape death wtout she had some remedy, wherupon this examinat saith, yt she praied ye said Herring to helpe[64] {C2v} And that hee then delivered unto her a little lynnen bagge of the breadth of a groate, full of small thinges like seedes, and willed her to put the same where her payne was most, the which shee proved by sowing it uppon her garmente, neare the place where her greefe was: And after a while this Examinate saieth, she recovered, and was well.

This Examinate denyeth that ever she hurt the base Childe, which Pages his wife kept, or that there was anye falling out betweene this Examinate and her: And sayeth, that shee knoweth not, whether the sayde Childe bee a base Childe or not.

This Examinate beeing charged, that shee sent a spirite to plague Michell, the shoomakers Childe, or that shee had bewitched the said Childe, denyed that shee had doone eyther of both.[65] And she being asked, whether she ever fell out with one Fortune or his wife, or whether shee hurt any of their children, saieth, that there was no falling out betweene them, or that shee hurt any of his Children.

Annys Letherdall and Margaret Sympson women appoynted, to see and view the body of this Examinate: sayde, and affyrme uppon their credites, that upon the left side of the thighe of this Examinate, there be some spots, {C3} and upon the left shoulder likewise one or two: Which spottes bee like the sucked spots, that Ursley Kempe hath uppon her bodie.[66]

This Examinate and the sayde Ursley Kempe **alias** Greye, being brought before mee face to face, the sayde Ursley then charged this Examinate to have plagued and punyshed Mychelles Childe, whereof it dyed: And also Fortunes wives Childe, whereof it languyshed. At which speaches this Examinate used outragious wordes, calling the sayde Ursley whore, saying,

61 See *A World of Wonders* (1595).

62 Sudbury in Suffolk, some twenty-five miles north-west of St Osyth.

63 Caulker – one who works with oakum and pitch sealing joints, usually on ships.

64 Should read 'her', which is left out of the first line of C2v; wtout – without.

65 *Sic.*

66 More evidence of unrecorded examination events surrounding Kempe.

shee would scratch her: for shee was a Witch, and that shee was sure shee had bewitched her: For that shee coulde not nowe weepe.[67]

The Confession and Examynation of Ales Hunt, the Wife of Willyam Hunt, taken before me Bryan Darcey Esquyre, the xxiiii. day of February.

THe sayd Ales Hunt beeing asked, whether there was anye falling out beetwene this Examinate, and Haywarde of Frowycke, or his Wyfe: saieth, there was none: But rather shee had cause to be beeholding unto them saying, that Haywardes wife did christen her a Childe.[68] And she being charged to have a spirit {C3v} in a potsharde, which Ursley Kempe had seene,[69] denyed that shee had anye such, or that shee had plagued Haywardes Cattell with that or with any other spirite.

This Examinate being asked, if she never did feede her spirits with mylke out of a lyttle trenyng dishe, sayde no: the which dyshe was brought by the Constable from her house, and then shewed to this Examynate, the which shee denyed to bee her dyshe, or that she had any such in her house.[70]

This Examinates warrant beeing made, and to her read, and shee committed to the Counstable to be carryed to the Gaile, desired to speake alone with mee the saide Bryan Darcey: whereupon I wente into my Garden, and this Examinate followed mee, shee then falling uppon her knees with weeping teares, confessed and sayde, that shes[71] had within vi. dayes before this examination, two spirits, like unto little Coltes, the one blacke, and the other white: And saith she called them by the names of *Jacke* and *Robbin*: And that they tolde her, that the sayde Ursleye Kempe would bewray her this Examinate, and willed her therefore to shift for her selfe. And so they went from her, and sithence this Examinate saith shee sawe them not.

{C4} This Examinate saith, that her sister (named Margerie Sammon) hath also two spirites like Toades, the one called *Tom*, and the other *Robbyn*: And saith further, her sayde Syster and shee had the sayd spyrites of their Mother, Mother Barnes: who departed out of this world within xii. dayes before the taking of this examination.[72]

67 Inability to weep was a traditional proof that the tearless one was a witch, rather than a victim. But Annis intends to scratch Ursley to draw blood on her and cure herself of this affliction. Both statements seem to be recorded as proof of mutual guilt, however. There is no record of Glascocke's trial: she was found guilty of killing Martha, daughter of Michael Stevens, Abraham Hedg, and Charity, daughter of William Page. She was reprieved, but died in gaol (Cockburn, *Calendar: Essex: Elizabeth*, record 1304, and *Introduction*, 146).

68 This obscure phrase might mean that Haywarde's wife had 'christened' one of Ales's children, which was sometimes done if the baby appeared sickly and likely to die unbaptised.

69 See B3v.

70 This dish was identified by the suspect's stepdaughter, Febey Hunt, in an information dated 25 February (2A6) – the day *after* Ales Hunt's examination. The use of the dish here, on the 24th, makes the date of the 25th for Febey's statement highly dubious.

71 *Sic.*

72 There is no mention of Hunt's trial verdict here: she was acquitted of bewitching William Hayward's cattle, and killing Rebecca, daughter of Henry Durrant (Cockburn, *Calendar: Essex: Elizabeth*, record 1301). See B7 and D4v–D5.

The Examination and confession of Margery Sammon, taken before mee Brian Darcie Esquire, the xxv. of February.

THe sayde Margerie Sammon, sister to the sayde Ales Hunt, daughter to one mother Barnes lately deceased, (which mother Barns was accompted to bee a notorious Witche) saith, that shee remayned at home with her mother by the space of halfe a yeare, and saith shee was with her mother several times, when shee laye sicke, and also at the houre of her death: But denyeth the having of any spirites of her sayd Mother, or that her mother had any to her knowledge.

The said Margery yt night being committed to ye ward & keeping of ye cunstable, and the nexte daye brought before mee the saide Bryan in the presence of her sister Ales Hunte, And beeing charged by her sayde Syster to have {C4v} two spirites like toades, given her by her mother at her death, utterlye denyed the same saying, I defie thee, though thou art my sister, saying she never sawe anye such: At which speaches her sister taking her aside by the arme, whyspred her in the eare: And then presentlye after this Examinate with great submission and many teares, confessed that she had two spirites delyvered her by her mother, the same day shee departed. And that shee this Examinate caryed them awaye with her in the evening, they beeing in a wicker basket, more then half full of white and blacke wooll: And that she asking her mother what shee should doe with them, she bad her keepe them and feede them: This Examinate asking wherewithall: her mother answered, if thou doest not give them mylke, they will sucke of thy blood: And sayeth, she called them by the names of *Tom* and *Robbin*. And this Examinate beeing asked how often she had given them meate sithence shee had them, saieth and confesseth, that she fed them twise out of a dyshe with mylke: And beeing asked when shee fed them last, this Examinate sayde, uppon Twesday last past before this examination, and that with mylke.

This Examinate sayeth also, that when shee tooke them of her mother, shee sayde unto her, {C5} if thou wilte not keepe the said spirits, then send them to mother Pechey, for I know she is a Witch, and will bee glad of them.[73] And saith further, that shee hearing, that Ursleye Kempe was apprehended, and fearing that shee shoulde bee called in question, saieth thereupon shee tooke the saide spirites beeing in a basket, and in the evening wente unto the grounde of her Master, and so into Reads grounde, and bad them goe to the sayde mother Pechey: And which wordes they skypped out of the said basket, and wente before this Examinate, shee this Examinate sayeing, all evill goe with you, and the Lorde in heaven blesse mee from yee: And sayeth,

73 This careful transfer of suspicion to Joan Pechey is linked to the informations given against her by Hunt and Sammon (2A4–2A5). They may possibly be extracts from this document, or records of follow-up questioning. Sammon's examination shows her accepting some of the necessary confessional discourse but changing it to accusatorial as soon as possible – culminating in the gift of her incriminating inheritance to Pechey.

shee myghte see the sayde spyrites goeing towarde a barred style, goeing over into Howe lane: And when they came at the style, shee saieth, they skypped over the same style and wente the readye waye to mother Pecheyes house: And saieth shee verilye thinketh the sayde mother Pechey hath them.[74]

The Examination and confession of Joane Pechey widdowe, taken before mee Brian Darcie Esquire, the xxv. of February.

{C5v} This Examinate Joan Pechey beeing asked how olde shee was, saith, shee is threescore yeares and upwardes: And saith that shee hath dwelt in the Towne of S. Oseys above xl. yeares: And saith she knew Mother Barnes, and she knewe her to bee no witch, or that she ever heard her to bee accompted, or to have skill in any witchery. And she being asked whether shee was with her when she lay upon her death bed, saith that she was not. This Examinate also denyeth, that she hath or ever had any Puppettes, Spyrites or Maumettes: Or that shee had any Spirites, which she bought, or were conveyed unto her by Margerie Barnes, or sent by any other sithence the death of Mother Barnes.

This Examinate also denyeth, that ever shee sayde to any of her neighbours, or to any other person in secrete sorte or meerely, that she knew or could tell what any man in the Towne at a any[75] time dyd or sayed, when she her selfe listed or would know.

This Examinate saith, that she never used any of those speaches, which Ales Hunte hath enformed against her, As yea art thou so sawsie? art thou so boulde? thou were not best to bee so bould, for if thou beist, thou shalt have Simonds sauce.

{C6} This examinate being asked, what she thought of the sodaine death of Johnson the Collector, saith, he was a very honest man, and dyed very sodainely: And saith she heard, that one Lurkin shoulde saye, that hee heard Johnson to saye, that Mother Newman had beewitched him. And beeing asked of whome shee heard it, shee aunswered shee coulde not tell. And sayth that shee her selfe never used anye harde speaches against the sayde Johnson.

This Examinate beeing charged to have willed her Sonne Phillip Barrenger, beeing of the age of xxiii. yeares to lye in bedde with her, denyeth that shee had so doone, other then shee had willed him at some tymes to lye uppon the bedde at her backe.

74 Rosen suggests that Margery Sammon may have fled, only to appear at the assizes of March 1583/4 under the name of Margery Barnes of St Osyth (Rosen, 156, n. 45). Sammon is referred to as 'Margerie Barnes' on C5v. Unusually, Margery Barnes was charged with the keeping of spirits with the intention of using them for bewitchment, as well as with actual maleficium. Links with Margery Sammon include Barnes's St Osyth residence, and the fact that one of her spirits is recorded as being called 'Pygine' like Ursley Kempe's. She was acquitted (Ewen, 150–1; Cockburn, *Calendar: Essex: Elizabeth*, record 1432).

75 *Sic.*

But the saide Phyllyppe beeing examined, confesseth and saith, that manye times and of late hee hath layne in naked bed with his owne mother, being willed and commaunded to doe of her.[76]

This Examinate beeing asked, whether she had any Cat in her house, sayth that shee hath a Kyttyn, and a little Dogge. And beeing asked, what coulour the Kyttyn was of, shee this Examinate sayed she could not tell, saying yee maye goe and see.[77]

{C6v} **The Information of John Sayer one of the Constables of Thorpe,[78] taken before mee Bryan Darcey Esquyre, one of her majesties Justices against Als Manfielde, the xiii. daye of March.[79]**

THe saide John saieth, that above one yeare sithence hee had a Thetcher, which was a thetching of a barne of his, neere Mother Manfieldes house, and that then shee the sayde Ales came unto the Thetcher, and would have had him to thetche over an oven of hers, wherunto this Thetcher made aunswer and sayde, hee woulde doe it, if his mayster woulde let him, but els hee woulde not doe it, whereunto shee sayde, hee had beene as good as to have willed you to doe it. For I will bee even with him. And hee saieth, that within a while after, hee had occasion to come by the house of the sayde Ales Manfielde with his carte, well neere three quarters loaden, and beeing before her doore uppon the harde grounde: saieth, his carte stoode, that hee coulde not make it goe forwarde nor backwarde, by the space of one howre and more: The which he saieth, hee thought to bee doone by some witcherie, which the sayde Ales Manfielde then used.[80]

{C7} **The Information of Robert Sannever, taken before mee Brian Darcey Esquire, one of her M. Justices the xiiii. of March.**

THe sayde Robert saieth, that aboute xv. yeeres past, ther dwelt with him the daughter of Elizabeth Ewstace, and that for some lewde dealynges, and behaviour by her doone, hee saieth, hee used some threatning speeches unto her, beeing his servaunt: And that shortlye after shee wente home to her sayde mother, and telled her of her maysters using of her: and the nexte daye hee saieth, as hee was a sitting by his fire side, his mouth was drawne awrye, well neere uppe to the upper parte of his cheeke: whereuppon hee sayeth, hee sent presentlye to one of skill to come unto him, who came unto him, And that hee seing him in that case, tooke a lynnen cloath, and covered his eyes, and stroake him on the same side with a stronge blowe, and then

76 There is no separate information from Barrenger. The questions asked of Pechey seem unusually circumspect, until the idea of incest is raised – perhaps to jolt her into confession.

77 Pechey was not tried, but discharged by proclamation, only to die in gaol (Cockburn, *Calendar: Essex: Elizabeth*, record 1325, and *Introduction*, 146).

78 Presumably Thorpe-le-Soken, a village about five miles north-east of St Osyth.

79 The material from other villages is later than that for St Osyth town, suggesting a gradual spread of accusations and stories towards the north-east.

80 See D7.

his mouth came into the right course: and hee sayeth that hee willed this Examinate to put awaye his servaunt, and that out of hand: the which he saieth he did.

This Examinat saith, that iii. yeres sithence his brother Crosse[81] was taken verye sickly, and at tymes was without any remembrance, & that he sent for this Examinat, & when he came unto {C7v} him, hee tolde him that Margaret Ewstace had bewitched him, and brought him into that weak state hee then was at: Wherto this Examinate saith, that if that bee so, hee then wished a spyt red hotte and in her buttocks, which speaches of his, hee sayth was carryed by one then in the house unto the saide Mother Ewstace, and this Examinate saith, that shee seeing a neighbour of his going towardes this Examinates house, asked her whether shee was going, and she answered unto this Examinates house: Whereunto she the sayd Mother Ewstace should say, naye goe not thyther, for he saith I am a witch: And sayed, his wife is with Childe and lustie, but it will bee otherwise with her then hee looketh for: Whereuppon this Examinate saith, that his wife had a most straunge sicknes, and was delivered of childe, which within short time after dyed.

This Examinate saith, that the Sommer after he milked vii. milche beasts, and that al that sommer many and very often tymes, his sayde beasts did give downe blood in steede of milke and that hee had little, or no profit by them: And hee saith that about iiii. monethes after many of his hogges did skippe and leape aboute the yarde in a straunge sorte: And some of them dyed.

{C8} **The Information of Ursley Kemp alias Grey, taken at Colchester by Thomas Tey[82] and Brian Darcey Esquires, two of her M. Justices the ix. of March.**

THis Examinate beeing charged that shee shoulde reporte to severall persons that have comen unto her, sithence her imprysonment, that Ales Newman shoulde send a spirit to plague the late Lorde Darcey, whereof hee dyed:[83] And shee being asked, whether shee saied so, saith shee sayed, that Tyffyn her white spirit tolde her that Ales Newman had sent a spyrite to plague a noble man, of whome we (meaning the poore) had all reliefe: The which she saith she tooke to be the said Lord Darcey, And other wise she sayed not.

The Information of Rychard Rosse of little Clapton,[84] taken before mee Bryan Darcey Esquyre, agaynst Henry Cilles and Cysley his wife, the i. day of March.

THe sayd Richard saith, that about vi. years past, the sayd Henry Cilles wrought with this Examinate in husbandry many and several times, & saith

81 See E4.

82 The Teys were an extensive Essex family based at Marks Tey, twelve miles north-west of St Osyth.

83 John, second Baron Darcy, had died at St Osyth on 3 March 1580/1 and was buried there.

84 Little Clacton, a village about two miles north-east of St Osyth.

yt at one time he the said Henry being at plough in ye said Richardes ground with his plowgh of horses, they being as well and as likely to any mans judgement, as any mens {C8v} horse myght be when they beganne to worke: yet before they had gone twise or thrise aboute the lande, two of his lykest horses fell downe in moste straunge wise, and dyed.

This Examinate sayeth, that a little before he had denyed the sayde Cillys of two bushels of maulte, which she would have had for three shillings, but he helde it at tenne groates.[85] And sayeth further, that within a whyle after the sayde Cysleye Cyllis did come unto this examinates wife, brynging with her a poke, and desired to buye a bushell, or a bushell and a halfe of maulte of her, or as much as her bag would hould: But for that shee the sayd Cysley would not give her her price, shee departed without having anye, using many harde speaches at that time: whereupon they fell out.

This Examinate saieth also, that his wife finding Cylles his cattell in his grounde, bid hunt them out therof, which Cylles his wife seeing, was thereat in a great anger, and gave her lewd speeches, & saith that presently after, many of his beaste were in a most straung taking: the which he doth say, to be wrought by some witchcraft, or sorcery by ye said Henry or Cisly his wife.

This Examinate saieth, that about xii. months & more past, a barn of his standing in his ground, a good way of from his dwelling house wt {D} much corne therin, was in a most sodeine sorte fired and burnt: But (hee saieth) hee cannot charge the said Henry or Cysley his wife, to bee the doers thereof, other then the youngest sonne of the saide Henrie and Cisley, should say heere is a goodly deale of corne, and a man unknowen shoulde answere there was the divels store.[86]

The enformation of Henrie Sellys, sonne of the saide Henrie, taken before mee Brian Darcey Esquire, the saide day and yeere.

THe saide Henrie saith, that hee is of the age of ix. yeeres, and that sithence Candlemas last, one night about midnight, there came to his brother John

85 There seems to be some confusion in the pamphlet between Henry and Cysley Selles here – the account of the malt refers to both 'the sayde Cillys' (Henry) and 'she' (Cysley).

86 In the March assizes of 1582, Cysley Selles (Cilles) and Ales Manfielde were charged with burning down Rosse's corn-house with its grain (Ewen, 144–5; Cockburn, *Calendar: Essex: Elizabeth*, record 1302). Both were acquitted but Cysley Selles was found guilty of bewitching to death a child of Thomas Death (see D8v) and remanded. Henry Selles appears on the list of discharged bailees (Cockburn, *Calendar: Essex: Elizabeth*, record 1327). But in the August assizes of 1582 Henry and Cysley Selles (Sylls) and their son Robert, were charged with two separate arson attacks on buildings belonging to Richard Rosse (Rose) – one of which was the original incident mentioned in *A true and just Recorde* (Cockburn, *Calendar: Essex: Elizabeth*, record 1343). One of these incidents is, however, after the trial, when Cysley ought still to have been in gaol. All three were acquitted. However, they were still not released, for both Cysley and Henry died in gaol in early 1583 (Cockburn, *Introduction*, 146). All the adult witnesses against the Selles family are connected to Richard Rosse, and one suspects a continued campaign by him against them. Joan Smith's apparent reluctance to accuse them (see D3) is interesting in this light.

a spirite, and tooke him by the left legge, and also by the litle Toe, which was like his sister, but that it was al blacke: at which time his brother cryed out and said, Father, Father, come helpe mee, there is a blacke thing yt hath me by ye legge, as big as my sister: whereat his father said to his mother, why thou whore cannot you keepe your impes from my children? whereat shee presently called it away from her sonne, saying, come away, come away, At which speech it did depart.

This examinat saith, that the next day hee {Dv} tolde his mother hee was so afraid of the thing that had his brother by the legge that he swett for feare, and that he coulde scarse get his shirt from his backe: his mother answering thou lyest, thou lyest whoresonne. This Examinat being asked, wherewith hee had seene his mother to feede her Imps and wherein, hee saith, yt she fed them out of a blacke dish, ech other day with milke: and saith, that he hath seene her to carry it unto a heape of wood and brome standing under a crab tree by the house, and being asked what their names were, he saith, that one of them is called by two names which is **Herculus**, sothe **hons**, or **Jacke**,[87] & that is a blacke one, & is a hee, and the other is called **Mercurie**, and is white, and is a shee: and that their eyes bee like unto goose eyes, and saith, that he hath seen his mother to remoove foure Brome fagots, and so to creepe into the crabtree roote, whereas they stand and lye upon a fleese of wooll. And this Examinant saith further, yt the same night Rosse his maide was taken:[88] when his father came home, his mother told him her husbande, that she had sent **Herculus** to Rosse his maide: and he answered, yee are a trim foole. This examinat saith, that as hee and his mother were comming (they being in Rosse his Bromefield) she said unto him, take heed ye say nothing.

{D2} **The information of John Selles the youngest sonne of Henry and Cysley, taken before mee Brian Darcey Esquire, the third day of March.**

THe said John Selles saith, that he is about the age of vi. yeeres iii. quarters, & saith, yt one night there was a blacke thing like his sister, that tooke him by the legge and that hee cried out, saying, father, father, come helpe me and defende mee, for there is a blacke thing that hath me by the legge: at which he saith, his father said to his mother, ye stinking whore what meane yee? can yee not keepe your imps from my children? & beeing asked what colour they were of, & what they were called, he saith, that one is black, & another is white, & yt he hath hard his mther to call them Imps, & that they have eyes as big as himselfe: and he saith, yt his father bad his mother put them away or els kill them. And saith, yt a while sithence his mother delivered them to one of Colchester[89] (he thinketh his name is Wedon

87 Rosen suggests 'Herculus, other John or Jack' (133, n. 35).

88 Probably Ales Baxter. See D4.

89 Colchester is ten miles north-west of Little Clacton.

or Glascocke) and saith yt Wedons wife had a cap to dresse[90] of his mothers, and saith, that they were carried away in a basket at that time. And beeing asked, whether his father or mother bade him that hee shoulde saye nothing, hee saieth, that his {D2v} mother said unto him that hee should goe before: a gentleman, and willed him to take heed he telled no tales nor lyes.

He saith, that his father called one of them, which is the blacke **one, John**, which he said his father mocked him because his name was so: And his mother called ye white one an **Impe**. He saith he hath seene his father to feede them out of a blacke dish with a woodden spone, and yt he knoweth the same dishe, & the last time he fed them it was behinde the Bromestacke at ye crabtree. And hee saith, that the man which carried them away gave his mother a pennie, and that when she should goe to him she should have another pennie, hee saith at that time his brother was from home at one Gardeners house.

And being asked, whether ever hee sawe his mother to feede them, he saith, that he hath seene his mother to feed them twise, and that out of a dish with a spone with thinne milke.

Note also, it is to be considered, that there is a scarre to be seene of this examinats legge where it was taken, and also the naile of his little Toe is yet unperfect.

The information of Joan Smith wife of Robert Smith,[91] taken before mee Brian Darcey Esquire, the said day and yeere.

{D3} THe said Joan saith, that one holy day in the after noone sithence Michaelmas last, shee had made her selfe readie to goe to Church, and tooke in her armes her young childe & opening her dore, her mother (grandmother to the child) one redworths wife, and Selles his wife were at the said dore readie to draw the latch, shee this examinat telling her mother she was comming out of dores to Churchward: whereat the grand mother to the child, tooke it by the hand & shoke it, saying, a mother pugs art thou comming to Church? And Redworthes wife loking on it, said, here is a jolie & likely childe God blesse it? after which speeches, Selles his wife saide, shee hath never the more children for that, but a little babe to play wtall[92] for a time. And she saith within a short time after her said childe sickned and died: But she saith yt her conscience wil not serve her, to charge the said Cysley or her husband to be the causers of any suche matter, but prayeth God to forgive them if they have dealt in any such sort. &c.

The examination and confession of Henrie Selles and Cysley his wife, taken before mee Brian Darcey Esquire, the first day of Marche.

THe said Henry saith, that he hath wrought in husbandry by some long time past with {D3v} Richard Rosse of litle Clapton, and yt one time he

90 Decorate.

91 See D4v.

92 Withall.

being at plough, two of his horses upon a sodaine fell downe and were in a most strange taking, but what the occasion should be thereof (he saith) he knew not. And saith, yt he doth not remember yt he would have had any mault of the saide Rosse at his price, or yt there was any falling out betweene them: and denieth yt his childe cried out unto him, saying, father, come helpe me, or that he called his wife stinking whore: and denieth all the residue of the matters in general enformed against him, &c.

Condemned.

The said Cysley his wife saith, that she doth not remember yt Rosse his wife did at any tyme hunt her catell being in her ground, or yt shee used any hard speeches to his wife thereupon, or yt shee fel out for yt she could not have any mault at her price: but she saith at one time she met Rosse his wife, & that there was some talke betweene them, the which shee doeth not remember more then the saide Rosses wife saide, I shall see at your ende what you are. And being asked if shee knewe not mother Tredsall, shee saith shee knew her, but she denieth, yt she saide if she were a witche, she learned the same of the saide mother Tredsall:[93] and denieth that her childe cry-{D4}-ed out in the night to his father, and all the residue of ye matters in general enformed against her.

Ales Gilney, Joan Smith, and Margaret Simson women of credite, appointed by mee Brian Darcey, to view and see the body of the saide Cysley, say, that shee hath upon her body many spots very suspitious, and the said Margaret saith, that they bee much like the sucked spots, that shee hath seene upon the body of Ursley Kempe and severall other.

The enformation of Ales Baxter servant with Richarde Rosse, taken by mee Brian Darcey Esquire, one of her Majesties Justices of the peace, the xix. day of Marche.

THE saide Ales saith, that about Hallamas[94] last past about foure of the clocke in the after noone, shee went a milking into her masters grounde two closes[95] of from the house, and she had eight or niene beastes to milke, and saith yt after she had milked all but one, and as shee was a milking all but one, before shee had halfe done, the Cow start and stroke downe her paile, and that shee saw all the rest to make a staring and a looking about: And shee {D4v} saith as shee was a making an ende of milking of that Cowe, shee felt a thing to pricke her under the right side, as if she had been striken with ones hande, and she saith that after, as shee was going homewardes with her milke neere the style in the same closse, there came a thinge all white like a Cat, and stroke her at the hart, in such sort as shee could not stand, goe, nor speake, and so she remained untill her said master & two of his workmen did carry her home in a chaire: she saith, she saw the

93 More missing evidence.
94 Hallowmass or All Saints' Day – 1 November.
95 Enclosed fields or yards.

said thing to go into a bush by the style, & that she knew not her master when he came unto her.

Robert Smith saith, that about Hallamas last past he wrought wt Richard Rosse, and that about v. a clocke was called by the said Rosse to helpe him to fetch home his maid, & going then with him they found the said Ales his maide sitting leaning against the stile, & in yt case as she could not stand, go, nor speake, and yt he and one other with their masters helpe tooke her up and brought her home in a chaire.

The information of Henrie Durrant, taken by mee Brian Darcey Esquire, one of her Majesties Justices of peace, the 26. day of March, against Ales Hunt.

THe said Henry Durrant saith, yt about the second day of this present month, he went to {D5} chester[96] to appeare before the Justices there to bee bounde from killing of fleshe,[97] and after that hee had so done he saith, that he went with several of his neighbours unto the Castle, to see the witches that were committed thyther, at which time he saith, he talked with Ursley Kemp **alias** Gray, who then tolde him after some demaunds which hee used unto her, that Ales Hunt and her mother (the widow Barnes) had bewitched his daughter, whereof she dyed, saying, that because they were denied of a peece of Porke at suche time as they came for it, therefore they were offended with you: and saieth further, that hee doth remember that they came unto him, and woulde have had a peece of Porke, the which for that it was newly dressed, and somewhat whot,[98] he made them answere that he woulde not cut it out.

The enformation of Richard Rosse and others together, with the confession of Henrie Selles and Cisley his wife.[99]

The examination and confession of Ales Manfield, taken at Thorpe, and brought before me Brian Darcey esquire, one of her Majesties Justices, the xiii. day of Marche.

{D5v} *Condemned.*[100]

THe saide Ales Manfielde saieth, that shee is of the age of threescore and three yeeres or there aboutes, and that about xii. yeeres sithence one margaret Grevell came unto this examinat and saide, that shee shoulde goe out of her house yt shee dwelt in unto another house in the towne: And then telled her that she had foure Impes or spirites the whiche shee woulde not carrie with her to that house, for feare they shoulde be espied or seene, and prayed her this examinate that shee woulde keepe them, and also telled her what

96 Should read 'Colchester' – 'Col' is omitted from the end of D4v.

97 Durrant was a butcher (B7). See D4v–D5.

98 *Sic.* Hot.

99 It is unclear whether there are documents missing here, or whether the subheading has been misplaced.

100 Completely inaccurate – see note 86. Manfield was apparently not charged with witchcraft at all.

they woulde doe for her (saying shee should have them upon condition that shee the sayde Margaret might have them at her pleasure, otherwise shee should not have them) and with what, and howe shee shoulde feede them, and at her desire and request shee sayth that shee was contented to keepe them: And thereupon shee sayeth it was concluded and agreed betweene her and this examinate, that shee the sayde Margaret shoulde have them as often and as many times as shee would at her pleasure, and that then shee received them.

This examinate being asked, what names they were called by, and of what likenes, saieth that one of them was called *Robin*, an other *Jack*, the thirde *William*, the fourth *Puppet* **alias** *Ma*-{D6}-*met*, & that two of them were hees and the other two were shees, & were like unto blacke Cats, and sayth that she kept them in a boxe with woll therein: And yt they did stand upon a shelfe by her bed where she lay. This examinate saith also, yt ye said Margaret Gravel hath commen unto her many & often times sithence ye saide agreement betweene them made, & according to ye said condition hath received of this examinat ye said imps or spirits: shee this examinat being telled of her some times wherfore she would have them, & that some times she knew by asking ye said imps or spirits where they had bin, & what they had done when they returned againe unto her. And being asked how often & when to her remembrance, she this examinat saith, about 7 yeres since ye said mother Gravel came unto this examinate & told her yt Chestons wife & she were fallen out, & had chidden very much: & that she gave her evill speeches, whereupon shee requested to have ye spirit *Robin* to go to plague his beasts: & then sent it, which said when it returned, yt Cheston being at plow & leaving worke, Yt it had plagued a bullocke of his yt was well liking & lustie, wherof it should pine and die.

This examinate saith, that the saide Margaret Grevell, well neere two yeres after, sent her spirite *Jacke* to goe plague Cheston, upon the great Toe unto the death.

{D6v} This Examinate saieth, that when it returned it tolde her that it had plagued the saide Cheston upon the Toe even unto death, and that it had sucked blood of the saide Margrettes bodie, and that besides it had of her Beere and Breade for the labour: and saith, that shee this examinate gave it Beare and Breed[101] then also for telling of her.

This examinate saith also, that five yeeres past or there aboutes, her spirit *Robin* tolde her that Margarette Grevell had sent the saide spirite unto her husband to plague him, where of he pined above halfe a yeere and more, having by that meanes many and severall straunge sores, and thereof died. And this Examinate saith that, that hee woulde eate as much or more then two men woulde doe, and that it sucked blood upon the bodye of the saide

101 *Sic.*

Margaret for the labour: she this examinate being asked upon what place, saith the saide spirite did not tell her.[102]

This examinat saith, that on a time she went unto the house of Joan Cheston widow, and desired of her to give her some Curdes: but shee sayeth shee gave her none, whereupon she saith, that shee sent Impe *Puppet* **alias** *Mamet* to plague her Beastes, where that woulde, and so it did: And that when the saide Impe returned, it tolde this examinate that it had plagued {D7} foure of her Beastes with lamenesse, and that it did sucke blood upon this Examinates body for a rewarde.

This examinate sayth, that about two yeres past, one John Sayer did fetch doung out of an Orchard, from a pittes banke, neere this examinates house, and did by reason thereof, gulle a greene place before her doore, whereupon shee saieth, shee sent her Impe called *Puppet* **alias** *Mamet* to stay the Carte being before the dore, the which it dyd, and shee saieth that shee sawe him and others to lift at the wheeles, and to set his hauser rope, the which did litle good, and that the same hauser rope and other of his horse harnesse burst a sunder, and shee saieth, shee gave her said Impe Beere for the labour.[103]

This examinate saieth, that litle before Michaelmas[104] last, her saide foure Impes saide unto her, saying, I pray you Dame give us leave to goe unto little Clapton to Celles, saying, they woulde burne Barnes, and also kill Cattell, and shee saith, that after their returne they tolde her that they had burnt a barne of Rosses with corne,[105] and also tolde her that Celles his wife knewe of it, and that all they foure were fedde at Cels house by her al ye time they were away from this examinate, wc shee sayeth was about a sevennight: And that *Puppet* sucked upon this exami-{D7v}-aminates[106] left shoulder at their returne unto her: And the rest had beere.

This examinate saith, that *William*, one of her Impes not above a sevennight before her apprehension, tolde her that shee shoulde be called in question, and bad her shift for her self:[107] saying, they woulde nowe depart from her and goe unto saint Osees unto mother Gray, mother Torner, or mother Barnes two daughters, but to which of them it was that they would goe shee doth not nowe remember: but they told her yt they to whom they went had hurt men & women to death, & several mens cattel and other thinges.

This examinate saith, yt about a quarter of a yere since, she went unto ye house of mother Ewstace to speake wt her, at wc time she saith, shee saw three imps wc she had standing in a yearthen pot in ye one side of her house nere ye hearth, & saith that one of them was white, ye other gray, & the

102 Up to this point this document is more like an information – here it changes and Manfielde confesses willingly about 'her', rather than Grevell's, familiars.

103 See C6v.

104 29 September.

105 See note 86.

106 *Sic.*

107 This echoes a phrase used in Ales Hunt's examination on C3v.

third blacke, & saith they were like cats. This examinat saith also, that her white spirit told her,[108] yt mother Ewstace their dame, sent her impes to hurt a childe, whereof it shoulde pine and become lame, but whose childe shee remembreth not.

Also this examinate saith, yt upon some conference between mother Ewstace & her, shee this examinate told mother Ewstace, yt mother Grevel did plague her husband, wherof he died, which {D8} was done by her spirit *Robin*: & she saith that she also told mother Ewstace, yt mother Grevel sent her spirite *Jacke* to plague Cheston to the death: but what answere she the said mother Ewstace then made, shee nowe remembreth not.

This examinate saith, that about a yere since the said mother Gravel told her, that she had caused her impes to destroy severall brewinges of beere, & batches of bread, being asked where, she saith a brewen at Reades, a brewen at Carters,[109] and a brewen of three or foure bushelles of malte at Brewses.

The said confession being made by the saide Ales in maner and forme aforesaid, I the same Brian in the presence of they cunstables & other the Townesmen of Thorpe, sayde as I had severall tymes before unto the sayde Ales, what a danger it was, and howe highly shee should offende God if shee shoulde charge any person with any thing untrue, and also telled her that her saide confession should bee read agayne unto her, willing her that if shee hearde any thinge read that she knew was not true, that she should speake, and it shoulde be amended, the which being done, shee sayde her confession was true, and the sayde Margaret and Elizabeth beeing then also called before mee, shee affirmed her confession to their faces.[110]

{D8v} **The enformation of Thomas Death & Marie his daughter, taken by me Brian Darcey esquire, one of her Majesties Justices, the xv. day of March.**

THe sayde Thomas Death saith, that about two yeeres sithence, there was a great falling out betweene this examinates wife and the sayde Cisly Celles, for that one George Battell having put a child of his to the nursing and keeping of the saide Cisley, and after he taking the saide childe away from her, and put the same to this examinates wife to be nursed & kept, whereupon at the next meeting of the sayde wives, the saide Celles his wife chid

108 Ales Manfielde had said that all her spirits were black (D6) but here echoes a phrase of Ursley Kempe's and Kempe's story shape (B3–B3v) about her white spirit confirming sightings of other witches' familiars. Kempe and Hunt were examined on 24 February and it seems unlikely that Manfield was present then, but somehow their stories are recycled here – by Manfield, her questioner, or her recorder?

109 See E2–E2v.

110 This carefully described attempt to get the suspect/informant to withdraw her confession suggests that Darcey was unsure of its worth (perhaps because of the repeat pattern and inconsistencies highlighted above) and wanted his account to display his care to protect the innocent, as well as his trapping of the guilty. Such recorded unease about a confession is very unusual. 'Elizabeth' is 'Mother Ewstace'.

and rayled at her, and saide, thou shalt loose more by the having of it then thou shalt have for the keeping of it, & within one moneth after (as he now remembreth) he saith that a child of his, of the age of foure yeres, being in good liking and well, went but out of the doores into the yarde, who presently fell downe dead, and after by helpe being brought to life, the saide childe was in a pitious case, and so died presently.[111]

This examinate saith, that hee had presently after severall Swine the which did skippe and leape about the yarde, in a most straunge sorte, and then died. And he saith that over night he had {E} [a Calfe which was very fat, and the next morning he found the same dead.

This examinate saith, that hee having bin at sea and newely arrived at Ipeswitch,[112] a messenger which was newely come from his wife, by chaunce mette him, who told this examinate that his daughter Marie was taken very strangely, and lay in a most pitious case, saying he had brought her water to carry unto a Phisitian to have his opinion thereof. Whereupon this examinate saieth, that hee and the messenger went therewith unto one Berte dwelling in that Towne, and shewed him the same, hee saieth he asked him if that his daughter were not bewitched? But hee saide that hee woulde not deale so farre to tell him, whereupon hee not satisfied to his minde, met after with an acquaintance of his, and asked him where hee might goe to a cunning man, telling him in what case his daughter lay in: who then sent him to a man whome he knewe not, nor his name hee nowe remembreth not, with whome after hee had conferred and shewed his daughters saide water: This examinate sayeth, hee tolde hym if hee had not commen with some great haste to seeke helpe, hee had come too late: And this exa-{Ev}-minate sayeth, that hee toulde him that within two nyghtes after the parties that had hurte his daughter shoulde appeare unto her, and remedie her: And hee sayeth, that hee him selfe did not then come home, but went to sea: But hee sayeth hee sent his messenger home with thinges that were to bee ministred unto his said daughter.

This examinate sayeth, that when he came home, his wife tolde him that the next nyght after his daughter had receyved the thinges ministred unto her, that shee heard a noyse like a groning, and that shee did arise and went unto her daughter, and asked her howe shee did: whereunto her daughter made answere and sayed, ah mother that you had commen a little sooner, you shoulde have seene Celles wife and Barkers wife her standing before mee.

Marie Death, daughter of the sayd Thomas Death, sayeth, that about two yeeres sithence upon a Sunday, shee was taken with an ache or numnes from her necke down her backe all over: And shee sayeth, that after her mother had ministred thinges unto her sente from a Phisition: The nexte nyght after shee say-{E2}-eth shee hearde a voyce, saying unto her, looke up at which

111 See note 86.

112 Ipswich, a port twenty miles north of Little Clacton.

shee lifted up her eyes, and then did see Celles wife and Barkers wife standing before her in the same apparell that they did usually weare. And shee this examinat sayeth, shee thought they saide unto her bee not afraide, and that they vanished away, as shee thinketh it was about midnight. And the nexte day after, this examinate saieth, shee amended, and was in case to arise without help, where afore two or three coulde scarce turne her in her bed as shee lay.

The enformation of Joan Cheston widowe, John Carter and other the inhabitantes of the Towne of Thorpe, taken before mee Brian Darcey Esquire, one of her Majesties Justices of the peace, the xiii. day of March against Ales Manfielde.[113]

THe sayde Joan saieth, that in sommer last, mother Manfielde came unto her house and requested her to give her Curdes, shee saith that answere was made that there was none, and so shee departed. And within a while after some of her cattell were taken lame & could not travell to gather their meat, so that her servants were constrained to mow down grasse for them by {E2v} the space of eyght dayes, shee sayeth, that afterwardes the saide mother Manfielde came agayne unto her, and demaunded Curdes, and shee sayeth, that shee then telled the saide mother Manfielde, that shee had bewitched her Cattell, and that shee then sayde unto her, that if her cattell did not amend and become well, shee woulde burne her. Whereupon shee sayeth, that her cattell did amende, and within a very shorte while after were as well as before.

Lyndes wife sayeth, that the sayde Mother Manfielde came unto her, and asked her a mease of Mylke, who answered that shee had but a little, not so muche as woulde suckle her calfe, whereat shee departed: and shee sayeth, that that nyght her Calfe dyed, being verye lustie, and xx. dayes olde.

The enformation of John Carter & others of Thorpe, taken by mee Brian Darcey esquire, one of her Majesties Justices, the xx. day of March agaynst Margarette Grevell.

Continued in prison.[114]

THe saide John sayeth, that on a tyme Margaret Grevell came unto this examinates {E3} house, desiring her to have Godesgood,[115] whiche was denied

113 Carter's information is actually in the next section, against Margaret Grevell. It is unclear why informations are sometimes grouped together in the pamphlet – especially when the subheading of a grouping is inaccurate. It has been suggested by Clive Holmes ('Women, Witnesses and Witches', *Past and Present* 140 (1993), 54) that some of the informants organised others to bring accusations. There is no evidence of this here, although it might be true of Richard Rosse's case against the Selles'. It is unclear whether the actual documents would have contained multiple informations, or whether the pamphleteer/s are responsible for these groupings. Perhaps it is simply a space-saving device in an already over-long pamphlet?

114 Actually Grevell was acquitted (of killing Robert Cheston – Cockburn, *Calendar: Essex: Elizabeth*, record 1303).

115 God's good, suggests Rosen: perhaps alms or yeast (142, n. 40). It is unclear precisely what Grevell is said to have wanted – but the story is, as usual, one of charity denied.

her, and sayeth that within a fewe dayes after his folkes went in hande with brewing: But of two brewinges after they coulde make no beere, but was fayne to put the same to the swill Tobbe, whiche was halfe a Seame[116] at a brewing, & sayth, yt the third tyme they went to Brewing, with the like quantitie, and that his sonne beeing a tall and lustie man of the age of xxxvi. yeeres, was wished to take his Bowe and an arrowe, and to shoote to make his shaft or arrowe to sticke in the Brewing Fatte,[117] and that he shotte twise and coulde not make the same to sticke, but at the thirde time that hee shotte, hee made the same to sticke in the brewinge Fatte, and after hee sayth they coulde brewe as well as before.

Nicholas Stricklande Butcher, sayeth, that Margaret Grevell sent her sonne unto him for a Racke of Mutton, hee having newely killed a Mutton, saying, the same was whot and that he coulde not cutte it out, and sayeth that hee bad him come agayne in the after noone, and the Munday after his wife seething Mylke for the breakefaste of his woorkfolkes, the same stancke and was bytter: And sayeth within fewe dayes {E3v} after his wife went to chearne her Creame that shee had gathered, and that shee was from the morning untill tenne of the clocke in the night a Chearning, and coulde have no butter: the whiche this examinate seeing, hee sayeth hee caused his wife to powre the saide Creame into a Kettle, and to set it upon the fire, the whiche was done: And making a great fire under it, this examinate sayeth, they coulde not make it to seeth over: Then this Examinate sayeth, that hee seeeing[118] it woulde not doe, hee sayeth hee tooke the kettell off the fire, and powred the one halfe thereof into the fire, and the other halfe hee let stande on the Kettle, the whiche hee sayeth stancke in suche exceeding sorte, as they coulde not abyde in the house. And this examinate sayeth, that the seconde time that his wife went to chearne her Creame, shee continued a chearning and coulde have no butter, but that it was as the other, the which hee sayeth, his wife was constrayned to put it into ye swill Tub. And after yt this Examinate saith, that the head and master Cowe at five beastes did also cast her Calfe, and presentlye after fell a haultynge, the whiche hee fearyng that it woulde have dyed, saying, that he fed it and killed it.

{E4} **The enformation of Felice Okey widowe, taken by mee Brian Darcey esquire, one of her Majesties Justices of the peace, the xx. day of March against Elizabeth Ewstace.**

THe saide Felice sayeth, that shee was the late wife of Thomas Crosse, and that shee on a time finding the geese of Elizabeth Ewstace in her grounde, did drive them out, and that by mischaunce one of her geese was hurt: whereat the sayde Elizabeth fell out exceedinglye with this Examinate, and gave her harde speeches, saying, that thy husbande shall not have his health,

116 A seame is one horse-load; swill is pigs' food.
117 Vat.
118 *Sic.*

nor that whiche hee hath shall not prosper so well as it hath done, and that shee also sayde, thou haste not so good lucke with thy gooslings, but thou shalt have as badde: And shee sayeth that never after that shee coulde have any of them geese whiche shee her selfe kept: and also the same night shee sayeth, that one of her Kine gave downe blood insteede of mylke, and after for the space of viii. dayes.

THis examinate saith, that her late husbande T Crosse, was taken in a strange sort, & ther-[119]{E4v} pyned, and sayeth, that on a time as her said husbande was a walking in his grounde, hee was cast amongst Bushes, and was in that case that hee coulde neyther see, heare, nor speake, and his face all to beescratched: and shee sayeth, that hee beeing in that strange case, when hee came to his memorie, hee woulde alwayes crye out upon the sayde Elizabeth even unto his dying day, and woulde say that sithence shee the sayd Elizabeth had threatned him he was consumed, and that shee had bewitched him.[120]

The examination of Lawrence kempe taken before mee Brian Darcey esquire, one of her Majesties Justices, the xx. day of March, against Ursley kempe.

THe sayde Lawrence sayeth, that his late wife was taken in her backe, and in the privie partes of her bodye, in a very extreame and most straunge sorte, and so it continued about three quarters of a yeere, and then shee died, and hee sayeth, that his saide wife did tell him severall times that Ursley kempe, his sister, had forspoke her, and that shee was the onely cause of that her sicknesse.

{E5} This examinat saith, that his saide wife did tell him that two yeeres before, shee mette the said Ursley his sister upon Eliotsheath, & that she fell uppon her, & then tooke up her clothes and did beat her upon the hippes, and otherwise in wordes did misuse her greatly.

This examinat saith that when his wife lay a drawing home, and continued so a day and a night, all the partes of her body were colde like a dead creatures, and yet at her mouth did appeare her breath to goe and come: and that she so continued in that case until the said Ursley came unto her without sending for, and then lifted up the clothes and tooke her by the arme, the which shee had not so soone doone, but presently after she gasped, and never after drew her breath and so dyed.[121]

The examination and confession of Margaret Grevell, taken before mee Brian Darcey Esquire, one of her Majesties justices of the peace, the 24. day of March.

Continued in prison.[122]

THis examinat saith, that she is of the age of lv. yeeres or there abouts, & being charged with the foresaide enformation and confession {E5v} made by

119 Should read 'ther-of' – 'of' is omitted from E4v.
120 See also C7–C7v.
121 See also 2A8.
122 See note 114.

the said Ales Manfield against her, denieth the same in generall, and saith, that shee her selfe hath lost severall bruings, and bakings of bread, and also swine, but she never did complaine thereof: saying, that shee wished her gere[123] were at a stay, and then shee cared not whether shee were hanged or burnt, or what did become of her.

This examinat beeing asked, what falling out was or hath beene between Cheston & her, saith, on a time shee went to the saide Joan Ceston[124] to buie a pennie worth of Rie meale, but shee woulde let her have none, and saith, she said that it was pitie to doe her any good, saying, that she this examinat had told master Barnish yt shrifes[125] dogge did kill a Doe of his by the parke pale, and saith, that there was none other falling out as shee remembreth.

This examinat beeing viewed and seene by women, say, that they cannot judge her to have any sucked spots uppon her body.

This examinat and the saide Ales Manfield beeing brought before Brian Darcey, the saide Ales did affirme her confession made by her to her face to be true.

{E6} **The Examination and confession of Elizabeth Eustace, taken before mee Brian Darcey Esquire, the xiiii. day of marche.**

Continued in prison.[126]

THe said Elizabeth Eustace saith, shee is of the age of liii. yeeres or thereabouts, and denyeth the enformation and confession made by the sayd Ales Manfield in generall: Or that ever shee had any Impes or Mamettes saying, out upon her hath shee tolde anye thing of mee? and shee beeing asked, what conference had been betweene her the & sayd[127] Ales Manfielde saith, that there was none to her remembrance, other then once she went unto her, and carried her ointment to annoynt her lamenesse that shee was troubled with, and that then there was no conference which she remembreth.

The saide Ales Manfielde in my presence did affirme her confession made against the said Elizabeth to and before her face to face.

The enformation of John Wadde, Thomas Cartwrite, Richard Harrison with several others the parishioners of little Okeley,[128] taken by mee Brian Darcey Esquire one of her Majesties justices the 16. day of march.

{E6v} JOhn Wade saith, that about two moneth sithence Annis Heard, saide unto him, that shee was presented unto the spirituall Courte for a witch,[129]

123 Doings, affairs – also refers to talk, especially nonsense.

124 *Sic.*

125 This is a confusing passage: Rosen glosses 'shrifes' as 'Sheriff's' (145).

126 Ewstace was not tried, but discharged by proclamation (Cockburn, *Calendar: Essex: Elizabeth*, record 1325).

127 *Sic.*

128 Little Oakley is about ten miles north-east of St Osyth.

129 She had been accused of witchcraft and had to appear before a church court. An Anne Heard of Little Oakley was similarly accused in 1592, and might be the same person (Macfarlane, 291, record 1084).

and prayed him to be a meanes to helpe her, that she might answere the same when the dayes were longer: whereunto he said, that hee told her that the Regester dwelt at Colchester, saying, it must be hee that therein may pleasure thee: whereto she saide, that shee woulde goe to John Aldust of Ramsey[130] to speake unto him, for that he goeth to Colchester that he might speak to the officers for her, and so she departed: this examinat saith, that since that time he drove fortie sheepe and thirtie lambes to a pasture yt he had at Tendring,[131] beeing thereof well neere fourescore Acres, the which hee had spared by some long time, and knew the same to be a good sheepes pasture, and saith, that after they had bin there viii. or ix. dayes, hee went to see them (having neverthelesse appointed one to looke to them): And at his comming he found one to bee dead, another, to bee lame, another to sit drowping, and a lambe in the same case by it, whiche all died, and he founde one other with the necke awry, which is in that case to this day, and one other whiche was so weake that it coulde not arise, & this examinat saith, that sithence he with others that presented her, and sithence shee the {E7} saide Annis talked with him, he hath had not so fewe as twentie sheepe and lambes that have died, and be lame and like to die: & hee saith, that hee hath lost of his beasts & other cattell, which have dyed in a strange sort.

Thomas Cartwrite saith, that after a great winde & snowe wel neere three yeeres sithence, there was an arme or boughe of a tree of his that was blowen downe, whereof Annis Herd had removed a peece and laid the same over a wet or durtie place to goe over, which being to this examinat unknowen, hee tooke the same & the rest and carried it home: the which the saide Annis knowing, that hee had carried the same away, she said, that the churle (meaning this examinat) to a neighbour of hers had carried away the peece of the bough that she had laied to go over, saying, that shee woulde bee even with him for it. After which this Examinat saith, within three nights after, there then beeing a snowe two of his beasts went from all the rest, where as they lay as he might well perceive by the snowe, and the head Cowe fell over a great bancke into a ditch on the other side, and there lay with the necke double under her, and the head under the shoulder, but alive, and he saith, he gate it home by good helpe and laied it in his barne, and saith, that it lay fourteene dayes in a {E7v} groning and piteous sort, but of all that time woulde eate nothing, whereupon hee saith hee tooke an axe & knocked it on the head. And also the other Cowe that was with the said Cow being a calving in a most strane sorte died, the which this examinat saith, yt hee verily thinketh to be done by some witchery by the saide Annis Herd.

Bennet Lane wife of William Lane, saith, yt when she was a widdow, Annis Herd beeing at her house she gave her a pint of milke & also lent her a

130 A village about a mile north-west of Little Oakley.
131 A village about six miles south-west of Little Oakley.

dish to beare it home, the which dishe she kept a fortnight or 3. weekes, & then ye girle of the said Annis Herds came to her house on a message: & she asked the girle for the dish, & said though I gave thy mother milk to make her a posset I gave her not my dish, she this examinat being then a spinning: & so ye girle went home, & as it seemed told her mother, who by her sent her dish home to her, ye which girle having done her arrand, & being but a while gone: shee this examinat saith, she could no longer spin nor make a thread to hold, whereat she was so greeved yt she could not spin, she saith, she tooke her spindle and went to the grindstone therewith once or twise, & grownd it as smoth as she coulde, thinking it might be by some ruggednesse of ye spindle that did cause her thread to breake, and so {E8} when she had grownd it as wel as she could she went againe to worke therewith, thinking that then it would have done, but it would not do no better then it did before: then she saith, yt shee remembred her self and tooke her spindle and put it into ye fire, & made it red hot, & then cooled it gaine[132] and went to worke, and then it wrought as well as ever it did at any time before.

This examinat saith, that an other time the saide Annis Herd owed her two pence, and the time came that shee shoulde pay the Lordes rent,[133] and she beeing a poore woman was constrained to aske her the two pence, and to borow besides (as shee said): whereto she the saide Annis answered, that shee had paied eight or nine shillings that weeke, and shee had it not nowe: saying she should have it the next weeke, whereto shee this Examinat saide, you must needes helpe me with it now, for this day I must paye the Lordes rent, then shee saide shee must goe borrowe it and so went and fetched it, saying, there is your money, whereunto shee this examinat answered, and said, now I owe you a pint of milke, come for it when you will & you shall have it: the which she came for ye next day & had it with ye better,[134] this examinat saith, yt ye next day she would have flete[135] hir milke bowle, but it wold not abide ye fleeting, but would rop & role as it {E8v}[136] the white of an egg, also the milk being on the fier it did not so soone seath but it woulde quaile, burne by and stincke, the which shee saide shee thought might be long of[137] ye feeding of her beasts, or els that her vessels were not sweete, whereupon she saith, she scalded her vessels, and scoured them with salt, thinking that might helpe, but it was never the better but as before: then she saith, shee was full of care, that shee shoulde loose both milke and creame, then shee saith it came into her minde to approove another way, which was,

132 Again.
133 Tithe, money due to the church.
134 Butter? (Rosen 148.)
135 Skimmed.
136 Should read 'were', which is omitted from the end of E8.
137 'Along of', because of.

shee tooke a horse shue and made it redde hote, and put it into the milke in the vessals, and so into her creame: and then she saith, shee coulde seath her milke, fleete her creame, and make her butter in good sort as she had before.

Andrewe West and Anne saith, that on a time the said Annis Herd came unto his house, saying, she had been at mill, and that she coulde get neither meale nor bread, at which her speeches hee knowing her neede, saith, hee caused his wife to give her a peece of a lofe, and that then he said unto her, Annis, thou art ill thought of for witchcraft, the which she then utterly denyed yt she coulde or did any such thing: whereunto he saith, his wife saide wee have a sort[138] of pigges I wott not what we shall doe with them] {F} saying, I woulde some body had one or two of them, to that the said Annis said, that if a poore body should have one of them and bestow cost, & that then if they should die it would halfe undoe them, and said if her Landlord would give her leave to keepe one, she then wished that she would give her one of them, whereunto this examinat said, shee should have one: But for that she came not for it, this examinat saith, that he did thinke that she cared not for it, and after a while one of her neighbours bought two of them, and within ii. or iii. dayes after the said Annis came for one: to whom this examinat said, for yt they had not hard no more of her, that he thought she would have none, and told her that he had sold two of them, and so the said Annis departed and went home.

This examinat saith, yt his wife the next day sent unto the said Annis a pound of wooll to be spun: and that she said to the boy that brought it, saying, can she not have her weeders[139] to spin the same? and that she then said to ye boy, your Aunt might as well give me one of her pigges, as to Penly and this examinat saith, that within two houres after, one of the best pigs that he had set upon a crying as they stood all together before the dore in the yard, and the rest of the pigs went away from yt at the length the pig that cried folowed stackering as though it were lame in the hinder partes, and yt then he called his weeders {Fv} to see in what strange case the pig was in, and asked them what was best to doe therewith, to which some of them said, burne it, other said, cut of the eares & burn them, and so they did, & then the pig amended by & by. and within two daies after this examinats wife met with the said Annis Herd, and shee then burdened her with that she had said to her boy: To which ye said Annis made answere, yt she did say so: and then this examinats wife told the said Annis in what case her pig was, saying, thou saidest the other day thou hast no skill in witcherie, his saide wife then said, I will say thou hast an unhappie tongue. After which, this examinats wife could not brewe to have any drinke yt was good, so as she was full of care, saying, yt somtimes she put one thing into her brewing

138 A great number.

139 Those whom she employed to weed the crops.

fat, sometimes an other thing to see if it could doe it any good, but shee saith, it did none: then she saith one gave her counsell to put a hot yron into her mesh[140] fat, the which she did, and then shee could brewe as well as she did before.

Edmond Osborne and Godlife his wife, said that a litle before Christmas last past, he bought at Manitree[141] mault, and brought it home, and said to his wife, good wife, let us have good drinke made of it. And the next day shee went in hand to brew the same, and when she had meshed her first worte[142] and did let it goe, that did verye {F2} well: Then his said wife having occasion to send her lad to their ground, she bade the lad call at Annis Herds for iii. d. the which shee owed her for a pecke of Aples, and that the lad so did: And she answered him very short, and saide, shee had it not now, saying, she shold have it as soone as ye Wooll man came: and the lad came home, & tolde his dame what she had said. And at yt time, she this examinat was readie to meshe ye seconde time, & when she had done, her mesh fat wrought up[143] as the fat doth when it was set a worke with good beere, and bare up a hand breadth above ye fat, and as they thrust in a sticke or any other thing, it would blow up and then sinked againe, then she saith, yt she did heat an yron redde hot, and put ye same into it, & it rose up no more. And then she let goe, and then shee did seath the wort, and when it was sodden it stancke in suche sorte, as that they were compelled to put ye same in the swill tubbe.

Richard Harrison Clerk, person of Beamond[144] saith, that he and his late wife did dwell at little Okely, in a house of his said wife, & that hee the said Richard Harrison had also the personage of Okely in farme, and about Sommer was twelvemonth, he being at London his wife had a Ducke sitting on certaine egges under a Cherrie tree in a hedge, and when the saide {F2v} Duck had hatched, his said wife did suspect one Annis Herd a light woman, and a common harlot to have stolen her duckelins, & that his said wife went unto the said Annis Herd & rated her and all too chid her, but she could get no knowledge of her ducklins, and so came home & was very angry against the said Annis. & within a short time after, the said Richard Harrison went into a chamber, and there did reade on his bookes for the space of 2. or 3. houres bidding his said wife to goe to bed wt the children, and yt he would come to her, and she so did: and being a while laid downe in her bed, his wife did crie out: Oh Lord Lorde, helpe me & keepe me, and he running to her, asked her what she ailed? and she said, Oh Lord I am sore afraid, and have bin divers times, but that I would not tell you, and said, I am in doubt husband, that

140 Mash – malt mixed with hot water to form wort.
141 Manningtree, a town eight miles west of Little Oakley.
142 Infused malt.
143 Rose, became agitated.
144 Parson of Beaumont, a village four miles south-west of Little Oakley.

yonder wicked harlot Annis Herd doth bewitch me and ye said Richard, said to his wife, I pray you be content and thinke not so, but trust in God and put your trust in him onely, and he will defend you from her, and from the Divell himselfe also: and said moreover, what will the people say, that I beeing a Preacher shoulde have my wife so weake in faith.

This examinat saith, yt within two moneths after his said wife said unto him, I pray you as ever there was love betweene us, (as I hope {F3} there hath been for I have v. pretie children by you I thanke God) seeke som remedie for me against yonder wicked beast (meaning the saide Annis Herd). And if you will not I will complaine to my father, and I thinke he wil see som remedie for me, for (said she) if I have no remedie, she will utterly consume me, whereupon this examinat did exhort his said wife as hee had before, & desired her to pray to God, and yt he wold hang her the said Annis Herd if he could prove any such matter and after he went to the personage, and there he saith he gathered plummes: and the said Annis Herd then came to the hedge side and Anwicks wife with her, and said unto him, I pray you give me som plummes sir: and this examinat said unto her, I am glad you are here you vield strumpet, saying, I do think you have bewitched my wife, and as truly as God doth live, if I can perceive she be troubled any more as she hath been, I will not leave a whole bone about thee, & besides I will seeke to have thee hanged: and saith, he saide unto her that his wife would make her father privie unto it, and that then I warrant thee he will have you hanged, for he will make good friends, & is a stout man of himselfe. and saith, yt then he did rehearse divers things to her yt were thought she had bewitched, as Geese & hogges, & as he was comming downe out of the tree, shee the said Annis {F3v} did sodenly depart from him without having any plummes.

This examinat saith, after which speeches so by him used unto her, and before Christmas, his said wife was taken sore sick, & was at many times afraid both sleeping and waking, & did call this examinat her husbande unto her not above two dayes before her death, and saide unto him, husband, God blesse you and you children, and God send you good friends, for I must depart from you, for I am nowe utterly consumed with yonder wicked Creature, naming the saide Annis Herd, which wordes hee saith were spoken by her in ye presence of John Pollin, & mother Poppe, and within two daies after his said wife departed out of this world in a perfect faith, she divers times in her sicknesse and before, repeating these wordes, Oh Annis Herd, Annis Herd shee hath consumed me.

John Pollin saith he was at master Harrisons when his wife lay sicke, & neere ye departing out of this world, & that her husband gave her good counsell for her salvation, and that she then said, O Annis Herd, Annis Herd.

Brets wife saith, shee heard mistres harrison say, that the said Annis Herd had consumed her even to the death, & that she cryed out upon her to the houre of her death.

{F4} The enformation of Annis Dowsing base daughter of Annis Herd, taken before mee Brian Darcey Esquire, one of her Majesties Justices, the xviii. day of March.

THe said Annis saith, that shee is of the age of vii. yeeres the Saturday before our Lady day next,[145] and shee being asked whether her mother had any little things, or any little imps, she saith, that she hath in one boxe sixe Avices[146] or Blackbirds: being asked of what colour, shee saith, they be white speckled, and all blacke, and she saith, that she hath in another boxe, vi. spirits like Cowes (being asked howe big) shee saith, they be as big as Rattes, & that they have little short hornes, & they lie in the boxes upon white and blacke wooll: and she saith, that her mother gave unto her one of the saide Cowes, whiche was called by the name of Crowe, which is of colour black & white. and she saith, yt her mother gave to her brother one of them, which she called Donne, & that is of colour red & white. And she being asked wherewithall she had seene her mother to feed the Avices & black-birdes, she saith, she hath seene her feed them somtimes wt wheat, barley, somtimes wt otes, & with bread & cheese, & the Cowes yt were like beasts, somtime wt wheat straw, somtime wt barley straw, ote straw, and wt hay, & being asked what she gave them to {F4v} drinke, she saith, sometimes water & sometimes beere, such drinke as they drunke.

She this examinat saith, yt her brother somtimes seeing them the Avices and blackbirdes, to come about him, saith, that he saith they keepe a tuitling and tetling, and that then hee taketh them and put them into the boxes.

She being asked if she saw them sucke upon her mother, saith, that the Avices & blackbirdes have sucked upon her hands, and upon her brothers legges: being willed to shew the place, she said, here sucked Aves, & here sucked Aves, and heere sucked Blackbird. And being asked how one spot upon the backe of her hands came so somewhat like the other, she saith the same was burnt.

The examination and confession of Annis Herd of little Okeley, taken by me Brian Darcey Esquire, one of her Majesties Justices of the peace, the xvii. day of March.

Continued in prison.[147]

THe said Annis Herd saith, that she told one of her neighbors that the churle (meaning Cartwrite) had carried away a bough which she had laid over a flowe in the high way, and saide that she was faine to goe up to the anckle every steppe, and that shee said hee had beene as good hee had not caried it away, for she would fetch as much wood out of his hedges as that doeth

145 25 March – very soon.

146 A word not in the *OED*.

147 Actually Herd was acquitted, having only been charged with bewitching John Wadde's sheep (Cockburn, *Calendar: Essex: Elizabeth*, record 1312).

{F5[148]} come unto. And she saith also that she remembreth she came unto goodman Wad, & telled him that she was presented into the spiritiuall court for a witch, & that then she desired yt she might answere the same when the dayes were longer.
Also she confesseth yt Lannes wife gave her a pinte of milk & lent her a dish to carie it home in, & that she kept the dishe a fortnight or longer, & then sent it home by her girle, & also that Lannes wife came to her for ii. d. which shee ought her.
Also she confesseth that she came to the house of her neighbour West, & telled him that she had bin at mille, but she could get no meale, nor yet no bread, & that he gave her a piece of a loafe: and she confesseth the speeches that then were of the pigs: And that she saide to ye boy that brought woll, yt his Aunt might aswell have let her have one as Penley. She saith also, yt shee remembreth yt she came to goodwife Osborne, & bought of her 3. peckes of aples,[149] & confesseth yt shee ought unto her iii.d. but denieth that the boye or ladde came to her for any money.
Also she remembreth that mistres Harison charged her to have stollen her ducklings, & that she called her harlot & witch, & confesseth yt she came unto M. Harison, he being at ye parsonage a gathering of plumms, & that shee prayed him to give her some plumms: But denieth that she hath any imps *Aveses* or blackebirds, or any kine called {F5v} *Crowe* or *Donne*: And all and every other thing in generall, or that shee is a witch or have any skill therein.

The enformation of Edward Upcher, Thomas Rice, and several others of the inhabitants of Walton, taken by me Brian Darcey esquire, the xxv. day of Marche.

THe said Edward saith, yt he & wife being at Colchester, this last weeke, they went together unto the Castle, to speake wt Ursley Kemp, & then entring into talke wt her, saieth, he asked her if she could tell what sicknes or diseases his wife had, wherunto ye said Ursley then told him, yt his wife was forspoken or bewitched, he then asked her by whom, she told him it was by a woman yt dwelt in their town, saying, that ye party hath one of her eares lesse then ye other, & hath also a moole under one of her armes, and hath also in her yard a great woodstacke.
Ales Miles saith, that shee went to the house of Joan Robinson for a pound of sope, at which time shee the saide Joan was gone from home, And saith that her maide Joan Hewet told her, that her Dame made her nose bleed, and then called her Catte to eate ye same, saying she did marvell why her dame shoulde call the Catte to eate her blood.
Thomas Rice saith, that about xiiii. dayes past, {F6} Joan Robinson came unto the house of this examinate, and desired to borrowe a Hayer,[150] the

148 Signature reads G5 here.
149 A peck is a quarter of a bushel. These measures vary depending on locality and period.
150 A mysterious item – as it is March, it cannot be needed for haymaking, though it could

which his wife denyed her, saying, that she was to use it her selfe, whereat shee departed, and presently after there arose a great winde, whiche was like to have blowen downe their house. And the next day after one of his Kine could not calve without helpe, it being drawen from her died, and the Cowe was in danger and did hardly escape.

And sayeth also, that his wife hath a broode Goose a sitting, that hath been as good for the bringing foorth of her broode as any goose in Walton, and sayeth, that sithence the said Joan was denied of the hayer, the goose in the night will goe from her neste, and will not suffer his wife nor none of his folk to come neare her but shee will flie away, so as shee hath lost two of her egges.

And sayeth also, that he thinketh the same to be done by the said Joan by some witchcraft.

Margery Carter saith that about ten yeeres past, the husbande of the sayde Joan came unto this Examinates house, and requested this Examinates husbande to hyre a pasture for a Cowe, the whiche shee sayeth was denied him, with aunswere that hee coulde not forbeare it for feare hee might want for his owne beastes. {F6v} and that presently after two of his best & likliest beasts in a strange sort brake their neckes: & saith also yt presently after this mischance Joans husband came unto this examinats husband W. Carter, & said, God restore you your losse, nowe you may pastor me a cowe, the which then he did, and then his beasts left breaking of their necks. And saith also, yt about 2. yeeres since, the said Joans husband would have bought a house and an acre of ground of W. Carter her husband, the wc hee would not sell unto him, for yt he would not have him his neighbour. And ye next day he had a faire ambling mare, for ye which he might have had 5. L.[151] often times: The wc mare of her selfe came in to ye stable, & presently was in a great sweat, & did hold her tongue out of her head, & shooke & quaked in a strange sort, & presently died, the wc when it was fleed,[152] a neighbours dog came & fed of it, and thereof presently died.

Also she saith, not above 14. daies past, the said Joan Robinson came unto this examinate, & requested to borrow a Heyer, to whom she made answere yt she had vowed not to lend the same: And saith, that wtin 3. daies after, shee had one of her best beasts drowned in a ditche where there was but a litle water.

Ales Walter saith, yt well nere 4 yeeres past, the said Joan came unto her, & requested to bie a pig of her: wherto she saith she woulde lende her {F7} one, but sell her any she would not: whereto the said Joan said yt she would have none except she did bye it, & so they parted. And presently after ye

be a haymaking tool such as a rake which would have had other uses. The most likely meanings from the *OED*'s list are: a rabbit snare or a hedging tool.

151 Five pounds.

152 Flayed, skinned.

sowe would not let her pigs sucke, but did bite & flye at them, as though shee had bin madde, when they had sucked above 7. dayes very well: & shee saith yt she sold of the pigs, the which Joan Robinson hearing, came unto her, and requested to bie one of them, which she had for 3.d. and telled her that her sowe did the like, & bad her give them milke as it came from the Cowe and they woulde drinke, which shee approved,[153] and they dranke.

This examinate saith, that two yeeres since, she going to the house of Joan Robinson, found her and her husband sitting by the fire, with whom after she had talked, Joan Robinson required to bye two pigs of her sowe that then was to pige. whereto shee said shee woulde see first what shee should have her self, and would not then promise her any. And the same night her Sowe piged two piges in the cote where shee lay, and for the more safetie of them, she tooke a broome faggot and laid it close over wharte the dore, because the pigs should not come out, & saith the same night all the farey[154] of pigs being ten came out over the broome sheafe, and stoode one before an other in a tract place lieke horses in a teem, beinge al dead to the number of nine, & the tenth was drowned by the pond side being about a rod from ye cote.

{F7v} Allen Ducke saith, that about five or sixe yeeres past the saide Joan came unto this examinate, and requested to bye a Cheese of his wife, but shee made her answere, that shee coulde sell none, yet neverthelesse shee was very desirous to have one, the whiche shee sayeth, shee denyed her, and that shee went away in a great anger. And this examinate sayeth, that the next day he went with his Cart & foure horses therein to fetch a lode of corne, & that his wife & two of her children rid in the Cart. And saith, that as he went towardes the fielde he watered his horses at a ware[155] called the Vicarage ware, whiche horses when they had drunke, he could not gette them out of the water, but was faine to wade to the forhorse head, it beeing about a yarde deepe, and to take him by the head and to lead him out. This examinate saith, that the said Joan came unto this examinates wife at two severall times to bie two pigges, whereof hee saith she was denied, & presently after he had two pigs that died. And saith, that he assuredly thinketh yt the saide pigs died of some witchcraft which she the saide Joan used, and the like for the staying of his horses being in the water.

John Brasyer saith, yt about two yeres since the said Joan Robinson came unto this examinates house, and requested to bie a sow pigge to weane, the which was a moneth old, whereunto he told {F8} her he ment to weane it him selfe, and that hee woulde not let her have it, the which being a fat and a well liking pigge above all the rest, the next day died.

Also this examinate saith, yt sithence Christmas last past, this examinates wife went unto the sayde Joan Robinson, to pay her money shee ought unto

153 Tried.
154 Farrow.
155 Weir.

her for wares which shee had beeing due upon scores: And for that she his wife would not pay her her owne reckoning, shee fell out with his wife: And presenely[156] after he had a cow that was drowned in a ditche not a foote deepe with water: Al which he supposeth was done by some witchcraft by the saide Joan.

The enformation and confession of Joan Robinson, taken by me Brian Darcey esquire, one of her Majesties Justices of peace, the xxv. day of March.

THe saide Joan saith, shee went to the house of T. Rice to borrowe a Heyer two dayes before a flawe of winde which was denied her: but denieth that she hath any impes or caused his calfe to die, or that she hurt her brood goose.

Also shee remembreth that her husband went to W. carter to bie a house & an acre of ground, & to hire a cow pastor, & to borrow a Hayer of goodwife Carter. But denieth yt she sent any impes to hurt any of his beasts, or his ambling mare, or caused any cow of his to be drowned.

{F8v} Also this examinate saith, that shee went to bye a pigge of Ales Walter, but denieth that she requested to bye any that was not pigged of her or of any other at any time, & denieth that shee sent any Impes or spirites to kill any of her pigges, and all the other matters against her enformed shee denieth in generall.[157]

Imprinted in London at the *tree*[158] *Cranes in the Vine***tree, by Thomas Dawson. 1582.**

{fold out table}

The names of xiii. Witches, and those that have beene bewitched by them.

The Names of those persons that have beene bewitched and thereof **have dyed, and by whome, and of them that have receyved bodyly harme &c. As appeareth upon** sundrye Enformations, Examinations and Confessions, taken by the worshipfull Bryan Darcey Esquire: And by him certified at large unto the Queenes Majesties Justices, of Assise of the Countie of Essex, the xxix. of Marche. 1582.

S. Osythes	The Witches.		
1	Ursley Kempe alias Grey	bewitched to death	Kempes Wife. Thorlowes Childe. Strattons wife.
2	Ales Newman and Ursley Kempe	bewitched to death	Letherdalles Childe and Strattons wife.

156 *Sic.*
157 There is no record of Joan Robinson in legal documents at all.
158 *Sic.*

Confessed by Ursley and Elizabeth.		The sayde Ales and Ursley Kempe	bewitched	Strattons Childe, Grace Thorlowe,	whereof they did languish
	3	Elizabeth Bennet	bewitched to death	William Byet and Joan[159] his wife, and iii. of his beasts. The Wife of William Willes and William Willingalle.	
		Elizabeth Bennet	bewitched	William Bonners Wife, John Butler,[160] Fortunes Childe, whereof they did languish.	
		Ales Newman	bewitched to death	John Johnson and his Wife, and her owne husband, as it is thought.[161]	
Confessed the Cattell.	4	Ales Hunt	bewitched to death	Rebecca[162] Durrant, and vi. beasts of one Haywardes.	
	5	Cysley Celles	bewitched to death	Thomas Deathes Childe.	
Little Clapton.		Cysley Celles	bewitched	Rosses mayde, Mary Death Wherof they did languish	
Thorpe.	6	Cysley Celles and Ales Manfielde	bewitched Richard Rosses horse and beasts, and caused their Impes to burne a barne with much corne.		
Confessed by Ales Manfield	7	Ales Manfielde and Margaret Grevell	bewitched to death	Robert Cheston and Grevell husband to Margaret.	
		Ales Manfield and Margaret Grevell	bewitched the widdow Cheston and her husband v. beasts, and one bullocke, and severall brewinges of beere, and batches of bread.		
Thorpe.	8	Elizabeth Ewstace	bewitched to death	Robert Stannivettes[163] Childe and Thomas Crosse.	
		[Eli]zabeth Ewstace	bewitched Robert Sannevet vii. milch beasts, which gave blood in steede of milke, and severall of his Swine dyed.		

159 A new detail, confirmed by the indictment.

160 See B4v for the only mention of Butler, in connection with Ales Newman.

161 This was not alleged in the informations themselves, hence the tentative tone of its suggestion here. William Newman's death gives context to William Hooke's information against Ales, 2A6–2A6v.

162 A new detail, confirmed by the indictment.

163 Previously 'Sannever'.

Little Okley.	9	Annys Herd	bewitched to death	Richard Harrisons wife, and two wives of William Dowsinge, as it is supposed.[164]
		Annys Herde	bewitched Cartwright two beasts, wade, sheepe and lambs xx. West, swine and pigs, Osborne a brewing of beere, and severall other losses of milke and creame.	
Walton.	10	Joan Robynson	bewitched beastes, horses, swine and pigs of severall mens.	

[T]he sayd Ursley Kemp had foure spyrites viz. their names Tettey a hee like a gray Cat, Jack a hee like a [bl]ack Catt Pygin a she, like a black Toad, & Tyffyn a she, like a white Lambe. The hees were to plague to death, & the shees to punish with bodily harme, & to destroy cattell. Tyffyn, Ursleys white spirit did tell her alwayes (when she asked) what the other witches had done: And by her the most part were appelled,[165] which spirit telled her alwayes true. As is well approved by the other Witches confession.

The sayd Ales Newman had the said Ursley Kemps spirits to use at her pleasure.

Elizabeth Bennet had two spirits, viz. their names Suckyn, a hee like a blacke Dog: and Lyard red [lyke a Lyon a shee].

Ales Hunt had two spirits lyke Coltes, the one blacke, the other white.

11 Margery Sammon had two spirits like Toads, their names Tom and Robyn.

Cysly Celles had two spirits by severall names viz. Sotheons Herculus, Jack or Mercury.

Ales Manfield and Margaret Grevell had in common by agreement iiii spirits, viz. their names Robin, Jack, Will, Puppet, alias Mamet, whereof two were hees, and two shees, lyke unto black Cats.

Elizabeth Ewstace had iii. Impes or spirits, of coulour white, grey and black.

Annis Herd had vi. Impes or spirites like avises and black byrdes. And vi. other like Kine, of the [bignes of Rats, with short hornes, the] Avises shee fed with wheat, barly, Otes and bread, the Kine with strew and hey.

	Annys Glascocke[166]		
12	Joan Pechey	These have not confessed any thing touching the having of spirits.	
13	Joan Robinson		
	Annis Glascoke	bewitched to death	Mychell Stevens Childe.[167] The base Childe at Pages. William Pages Childe.

164 Again, an unofficial note is struck. The report (F4) that Annis Herd's 'base child' was surnamed Dowsing perhaps illuminates this addition to her story, and Richard Harrison's representation of her as a harlot.

165 A legalism – accused.

166 Unnumbered and presumably added after having been omitted.

167 Presumably 'Michell' the shoemaker (B3v, C2v), unexpectedly surnamed and confirmed by the indictment.

7

The severall factes of Witch-crafte (1585)

This octavo pamphlet has lost its title page and is thus known by the heading on the first page of its narrative. There is only one known copy of this pamphlet, in the College of Wooster Library, Ohio. Other accounts of Harkett, such as *An Account of Margaret Hackett, a notorious Witch, who consumed a young man to death, rotted his Bowells and backbone asunder, who was executed at Tiborn 19 February 1585* are presumably lost – although this may be the original title of this work and thus the same pamphlet. It has no entry in the Stationers' Register, but is attributed by the *STC*[1] to John Charlewood. He was a book-seller from the 1550s to 1570s and a printer thereafter. There are no surviving trial records of the case, but the account of Harkett's committal to Newgate and her trial suggests that she was treated as was usual for Middlesex felons. London and Middlesex were linked administratively and had no 'assize' system. The sessions of gaol delivery were a near equivalent and, as a prisoner from Middlesex, Harkett would have been sent to London for the gaol delivery of Newgate held at the Old Bailey.

The pamphlet appears to be made from paraphrases of informations, since each anecdote begins with the name of a victim or witness being given. All the stories are presented as revenges for specific, usually economic, injuries. The pamphlet is thus a relatively traditional account with a little padding and some comment by the pamphleteer – a great contrast in its brevity to the recent *A true and just Recorde*. The pamphleteer tells his stories simply and vividly, and tends to stress the witch's turpitude and the horror of the revenges which she inflicted on her innocent neighbours – a trend which will become more apparent in later pamphlets.

1 A.W. Pollard and G.R. Redgrave, with Katherine Pantzer, *A Short-title Catalogue of Books Printed in England, Scotland and Ireland 1475–1640*. 2nd edn, 3 vols (London: Bibliographical Society, 1986–91).

{A3} **The severall factes of** *Witch-crafte, approoved* **and laid to the charge of** *Margaret Harkett, of the Towne of* **Stanmore, in the Countie of Middlesex, for the** *which she was arraigned and condemned* **at the Sessions house, before her Majesties Justices the 17. of February, and executed for the same at Tyborne[2] this 19. of February. 1585.**

On Wensday beeing the seventh day of **February** last past **Anno. 1585 Margaret Harket** of the Towne of Stanmore, in the Countie of Middlesex widdowe about threescore yeeres of age, was arraigned, examined, found guiltie and {A3v} condemned at the Sessions of Gaole delivery, for the Cittye of London and Middlesex: at the Sessions house in the olde Bailie, where by the severall othes of sundrie honest persons, these matters were prooved, videlizet. That she came to a Close in the same Towne of **Stanmore**, belonging to one **Joane Frynde**, whose Pease beeing ripe and readie to gather, she (without the consent of the said **Joane Frind** or any other household) did gather a Basket full, and filled her Aporne also with the sayd Pease,[3] and when she was ready to depart, this **Joane Frind** who ought[4] the Close came, and demaunded why shee dyd gather those pease without leave, wherefore she willed her to deliver her the pease that were in her basket, and those that were in her lappe she would give her.

But this ungodly woman[5] did flynge the pease downe on the ground, saiynge, if you make so muche a doo for a fewe pease, take them al, the next yeere I will have enoughe of my owne, and you shal have fewe enoughe. So she curssed the {A4} same ground and stamped on it & went her wayes, & never since that tyme, that the women could have any pease growe in her ground or any other Corne wold growe in the same place.

William Fryndes wife[6] of the sayd Towne of **Stanmore**, brought home a Childe to Nurse from **Westminster** where the Parents dwelt: who brought the Child and shewed it to her husband, but hee sayd unlesse hee knewe the Parentes of the Childe, hee would not suffer her to keepe it: this Witche beeing at her house the same time, owinge her a grudge, sayd, what will you doo with a Nurse Childe, you will but sterve it, sure I will warrant you the Child shall not prosper: and the Childe shortly after did fall sicke, and consumed to the death in most straunge manner, so that in three weekes followinge the Childe dyed, and was consumed and parched lyke a greene leafe that had beene hanged to drye in a Chimney.

She came to the house of one **William Goodwinne** of the same Towne {A4v} for yeast, the Servauntes denyed that there was any in the house: notwith-

2 The place of execution for London felons.

3 This large-scale theft might suggest that Harkett intended to sell the peas on – Middlesex was the traditional market garden of London.

4 Owned.

5 The pamphleteer intervenes to attack the witch.

6 Three of Harkett's accusers, probably represented here by edited informations, are apparently members of the same family – see also A5.

standinge, the Stande[7] was newe filled, and the servauntes were lothe to take of the yeast. Whereat this Witch said you shall have lesse, and so went her wayes, and the next day following, though none of the house did drawe out any drinke out of the same Stande, yet was it found dry without drinke or yeast, except a fewe hard dryed dregges.

She came thether also another time for Oatemeale, and they would give her none: And foorthwith a Lambe (which was kept in the same house) beeinge in the roome where the Witch was: fell downe and dyed presently.

She came into a Gentlemans ground called Maister **Mashe** of **Stanmore**, where shee was stealinge of Wood, and the Baily takinge her with the manour,[8] made her to leave it behinde her: and gave her two or three small blowes over the Backe not hurtinge her:[9] whereat shee sayd hee should repent it, and so she went her wayes. Shortly after this {A5} Bailie fell into a franzinesse, so that hee became starcke madde, beeing bound and chayned in his bedde: could get no remedie, untill it pleased God that this witch came home to his house, and at his beds side shee kneeled downe and asked him forgivenesse: whereat hee cryed, away with the Witch, breake her necke downe staiers, for she hath bewitcht me, and God be thanked was afterward restored to his health and wits, and it now very well.

She came to one of her neighbours to borrowe a Horse, knowinge him to have foure very good indifferent Geldinges, the worst worth foure markes: and he denyed her thereof, but she sayd, she would bee even with him, and shortlie after all his foure Geldinges were dead, and dyed sodainely one after an other.

She came to one **John Frynde** of the age of twenty yeeres, the sonne of **Thomas Frynd** beeing of the same Towne, and offered him a payer of shooes to sell, her price was ten pence, and he offered {A5v} her 6. pence and would give her no more. Whereat she was sore vexed, because at that time she had need of money: this was in the latter ende of Summer, so the fellowe thinkinge nothing, went to gathering of Peares from of the Tree, and upon a suddaine fell downe to the ground, and did hurte his Coddes[10] with the said fall, so that he was constrained to keepe in the house. But this Witch did openly make reporte in the Towne, that he was burned with a Whore, and that hee came to her and desired to have his pleasure of her: which speeches came to the fellowes eare, who a quarter of a yeare after he was recovered, did meete this Witch in the Towne: where hee asked why she gave out such lewde speeches of him, beeing most unjust, demaunding of her, if ever hee spake to her in any such sort, but she aunswered that he knew best: then

7 An open tub, usually a barrel set on end.

8 *Sic.* Perhaps should read 'within the manor'.

9 The pamphleteer protects the witch's victim from our censure here, in accordance with his earlier comment on her.

10 Testicles.

he charged her that hee thought his harme came by her meanes, I said she, I have not doone with thee yet: so hee went about his businesse and beeinge come home, he complained of {A6} his backe and his belley, saying assuredly that hee thought she had bewitched him: so his paine encreased more and more, and hee began to growe into a consumption, and wasted away like as the Childe before mencioned, like a parched or wethered leafe, hanged up in the smoke of a Chimney, and dyed three monthes after, and before he dyed his side did burst, and his guttes and backe bone was rotted in sunder, so that his guttes and bowels beeing rotten did issue foorth of his belley: and dyed hereof in most pitifull and greevous manner, the sayd partie taking it upon his death, that her witch-craft and sorcery was the cause of his death. After whose death the Townes men made complaint of her dealinge to the Justice,[11] who commaunded one Maister **Norwood** a Gentleman in the Towne to goe search her house: this Gentleman went thether and did searche her house, yet desired the Justice not to apprehend her, until there were some further triall made of her. But she promised for theyr searching, she would requite them short-{A6v}-lie: and forthwith, the next morninge one of the Gentlemans best milch Kyne, which was worth foure marke beeinge well over night, was found dead. The Gentleman fearing some greater injurie by her, dyd then commaunde his servauntes that they should give her nothinge, if she came thether to crave any thinge, so within two days after shee came for butter milke, but they denyed her thereof: and after that they could never make Cheese or Butter since.

Then was shee apprehended and brought before the Justice, by whome she was examined, and by him committed to the Gaole of **Newgate**, where she remained untill the Sessions, helde for Gaole deliverie of London and Middlesex: And then by twelve honest substanciall men for the causes aforesayd, was found guiltie and woorthie of death: where shee had Judgement and was executed accordingly.

FINIS.

11 The JP is unnamed, which suggests that if the pamphleteer did have access to informations, he used them in an abbreviated form.

8

The Apprehension and confession of three notorious Witches (1589)

The Apprehension and confession of three notorious Witches was entered in the Stationers' Register on 16 July 1589, to its publisher Thomas Lawe, and the quarto was printed for him by Edward Allde. The publication details have been cropped from the only surviving copy, in Lambeth Palace library. After a sharply condemnatory but stylistically fuzzy preface, which seems to refer only obliquely to witchcraft, it provides accounts of three witches probably based on their examinations. Finally, there is an account of their execution. The text used here is in Lambeth Palace library.

After the first examination, that of Joan Cunny, there is inserted without comment a scurrilous little piece of reportage from someone who apparently attended the trial of Cunny and her daughters. This voice has also added notes to Cunny's examination, and his influence on the portrait we are given of her seems likely to be extensive. For example, her name is given in legal records as Cony, and since 'cunny' meant vagina, perhaps the reporter has even altered the witch's name in pursuit of an extra joke. His interest in Cunny is – appropriately – as a lewd woman with 'naughty' daughters and illegitimate grandchildren, and his commentary thus stands out from the dryer legal constructions of witches which surround it. In the examinations, Cunny and Joan Upney (the next witch to be dealt with by the pamphlet) appear more conventionally as old, wicked women unskilfully using their familiars to kill and hurt their neighbours.

The final examination is a little different: we are given a detailed and oddly literary account of the encounters between Joan Prentice and her familiar, a ferret. The ferret is a good deal more like traditional representations of Satan, tempting and betraying, than most familiars in the pamphlets, although there are some similarities with the story of Elizabeth Bennett (*A true and just Recorde*, 1582) and the familiar is called Satan, like Elizabeth Frauncis's cat (*The Examination and Confession of certaine Wytches at Chensforde*, 1566). Satan's wooing of Joan Prentice is the main focus of her examination – later *maleficium* is presented as simply another element in their ultimately disastrous relationship.

The pamphlet ends with a return to gossipy reportage, perhaps by the same observer as before. The mixing of legal records with third-person comment is an interesting foretaste of the move away from the use of pre-trial documents and towards narrative accounts in later Elizabethan and Jacobean accounts of witch-trials. All three represented witches were hanged, whilst the examinations of Cony's daughters (who were, respectively, imprisoned, and reprieved because of pregnancy) are omitted. This may be as a result of a deliberate decision, or a chance occurrence.

{A (title page)} **The Apprehension and confession of three notorious Witches.** *Arreigned and by Justice condemned and* **executed at** *Chelmes-forde,* **in the Countye of Essex,** *the 5. day of Julye, last past. 1589.* **With the manner of their divelish practices and keeping of their spirits, whose fourmes are heerein truelye proportioned.**[1]

{Av blank}

{A2} **To the Reader.**

If we would call to remembrance the manifolde mercies and innumerable benefites which the Almighty hath and daily bestoweth upon us, in consideration therof, we are bound to with-draw our filthy affections and naughty dispositions, from the use of such detestable dealinges, as both are detested of God, whose almighty commaundements forbiddeth them, and unto man, whose lawes are constituted to punish them as odious before the sight of God, wheron our earthly lawes groundeth and consisteth, and therfore used to punish or cut of such lewde or filthye offenders as by breaking the devine decrees of the Almightie, by the lawes of man deserves to be condemned: But such is the blindenes of our estate, the naughtines of our affections, and the desire of our divelish appetites, that neither the commaundements of God, the lawes of our Realme, the love of our neighbours, our owne welfare, or the fall of others can or may move us to consider how profitable it were for us to examine our lives, and to blemish[2] such vices in us as both the lawes of God and man forbiddeth: For what can be more odious or abhominable unto God then the deprivation of his divine power, by yeelding our selves serviles unto sathan for a little worldly wealth, or hatred we have to our neighbours, where we might rest the servantes, nay the Sonnes of Al-{A2v}-mighty God, who sent his only Sonne to redeeme us from the servitude of bondage, and to bring us unto his blisse and eternall felicitie, which shall evermore remain perfect, which if we would consider, what christian is so blinded with ignorance or overcome with the illusions of Sathan, but he would tremble to think upon the judgments of the Almightie pronounced against such offenders, or the lawes of the Realme, which by justice decydeth[3] them from their devilish

1 Publication details are missing from here.

2 Probably should read 'banish'. Typesetting errors might explain the somewhat wandering logic of the whole piece.

3 Dissuadeth?

practises and abhominations? the glory wherof, although it be secretly concealed and used, yet can it not long continue, because the Almighty will be no partaker of any such dealinges, nor the hart of any faithfull Christian conceale the secrets therof: which for example I have heere published unto you the discourse of such divelish practises as have been used by notorious Witches, whose names and actions I have severally touched in the treatise following: with the manner of their accusations, taken and approved before both honorable and woorshipfull her Majesties Justices, at the last Assises holden at Chelmesford in the County of Essex, according to the coppies both of the offendours confession by examination: and their accusations regestred.[4]

{A3} **The araignement and execution of** *Joan Cunny of* **Stysted**[5] *in the Countye* **of Essex widowe, of the age of fourescore yeeres, or ther-abouts, who was brought before** *Anthony Mildemay*[6] **Esquire, the last day of March.** *1589.*

IN primis,[7] this examinate saith and confesseth, that she hath knowledge and can doo the most detestable Arte of Witchecraft, and that she learned this her knowledge in the same, of one mother Humfrye of **Maplested,**[8] who told her that she must kneele down upon her knees, and make a Circle on the ground, and pray unto Sathan the cheefe of the Devills, the forme of which praier that she then taught her, this examinate hath now forgotten, and that then the Spirits would come unto her,[9] the which she put in practise about twenty yeeres since, in the Feelde of **John Wiseman** of **Stysted** Gentleman, called Cowfenne feelde, and there making a Circle as she was

4 Presumably by this the pamphleteer means that he has seen both pre-trial examinations and actual trial documentation, such as indictments. He may, however, simply be referring to the reading out of the indictments (see B2v). The judges at the trial (3 July according to records) were Robert, Baron Clarke and Serjeant John Puckering, although it is likely that only one of them attended the criminal trials. Usually the other judge would be hearing civil cases simultaneously. Clarke had several Essex estates and was a well-known local figure; Puckering, Serjeant at Law since 1580, had been Speaker of the House of Commons and was a favourite with the Queen.

5 Stisted, a village ten miles north-east of Chelmsford.

6 Probably Anthony, son of Sir Walter Mildmay (the former Chancellor of the Exchequer, who died in 1589, *DNB*). His estate was at Moulsham, near Chelmsford. Anthony was later knighted and became ambassador to France. Curiously, he is not listed as a justice of peace, which means that the name given here may be a mistake – other Mildmay JPs of the period include Thomas, Sir Thomas, Henry and Anthony's brother Humphrey (Emmison, *Elizabethan Life: Wills of Essex Gentry and Merchants, passim*).

7 A marginal note reads: **This witch had nine Spirits 2. of them were like unto a black dog, having the faces of a Toade.** The source of the sensational information and comment contained in the notes is unclear: perhaps it was gossip at the trial, or material from another examination of Cunny or the child witnesses against her. It is clearly in a totally different vein from the examination printed here, although we are meant to find the two sources complementary. The note writer probably attended the trial – see A4.

8 Maplestead, five miles north of Stisted.

9 Marginal note: **These spirits belonging to this witch, did sucke commonly upon a sore leg which this mother Cunny had.**

taught, and kneeling on her knees, said the praier now forgotten, and invocating upon Sathan: Two Sprites did appeere unto her within the said Circle, in the similitude and likenes of two black Frogges, and there demaunded of her what she would have,[10] beeing readye to doo for her what she would desire, so yt she would promise to give them her soule for their travaile, for otherwise: they would doo nothing for her. Wher-upon she did promise them her soule, and then they concluded with her so to doo for her, what she would require, and gave themselves severall names, that is to say, the one Jack, and ye other Jyll, by the which names she did alwaies after call them. And then taking them up, she caried {A3v} them home in her lap and put them in a Box and gave them white bread and milke.[11]

And within one moneth after she sent them to milke Hurrelles Beastes, which they did, and they would bring milke for their owne eating and not for her. And further, she saith that her sprites never changed their colour since they first came unto her, and that they would familiarly talke with her, when she had any thing to say or doo with them in her owne language.[12]

And likewise she confesseth that she sent her saide spirits to hurt the wife of John Sparrowe the elder, of **Stysted**, which they did, and also that where Maister John Glascock of **Stysted**, aforesaide: had a great stack of Logges in his yarde, she by her said Spirits did overthrowe them.

And further, saith that she hath hurt divers persons within this sixteene or twenty yeeres, but how many she now knoweth not.

Furthermore, she confesseth that she sent her sprites unto William Unglee of **Stysted** Miller, and because they could not hurt him, she sent them to hurt one Barnabie Griffyn his man, which they did.

Likewise she confesseth, that she sent her saide sprites, to hurt Maister Kitchin Minister of the saide towne,[13] and also unto one George Coe of the saide towne shoomaker, to hurt him likewise: but they could not, and the cause why they could not, as the saide sprites tolde her, was because they had at their comming a strong faith in God, and had invocated and called upon him, that they could doo them no harme.

And further she saith, that Margaret Cunny her Daughter, did fall out with Father Hurrill, and gave {A4} him cucsed[14] speeches, and ther-upon, she thinketh she sent her spirits to her.[15]

10 Marginal note: **She had fower principall spirits. The first was Jack. The second was Jyll. The third was Nicholas. The fourth was Ned.**

11 Marginal note: **Jack killed mankinde. Jyll killed womenkinde. Nicholas killed horses. Ned killed Cattell.**

12 Marginal note (set too high up the page, see below): **Note how Gods spirit confoundeth the impes of wickednes.**

13 Richard Kitchin, Rector of Stisted (Patrick Collinson, *The Elizabethan Puritan Movement* [London: Jonathan Cape, 1967], 37).

14 *Sic.*

15 Margaret Cunny (also spelt Cony) was convicted of bewitching John Gwian, and, with

Also she dooth utterlye denye that she sent her saide spirits to Finches wife, Devenishes wife, and Renold Ferror or any of them to hurt them.

And beeing further examined, she confesseth that although her said spirits at some time can have no power to hurt men, yet they may have power to hurt their Cattell.[16]

This Joane Cunny, living very lewdly, having two lewde Daughters, no better than naughty packs, had two Bastard Children: beeing both boyes, these two Children were cheefe witnesses, and gave in great evidence against their Grandam and Mothers, the eldest being about 10. or 12. yeeres of age.

Against this Mother Cunny the elder Boye gave in this evideoce[17] which she her selfe after confessed, that she going to **Braintye**[18] Market, came to one Harry Finches house, to demaund some drink, his wife being busie and a brewing, tolde her she had no leysure to give her any. Then Joane Cunnye went away discontented: and at night Finches wife was greevously taken in her head, and the next day in her side, and so continued in most horrible paine for the space of a week, and then dyed.

Mother Cunnye confessed that she sent her spirite Jill to torment her.[19]

The same boy confessed that he was commaunded by his Grandmother to fetch a burden of wood, which he gathered, but another boye stole it from him, and he came home without: and tolde his Grandam: and she commaunded her sprite to prick the same boy in the foote, which was doone, and the same boy came to the {A4v} barre lame and gave evidence against her.[20]

Againe the same boy confessed that his Grandam when he had lost his wood, saide she would have wood enough: and bad him goe into Sir Edward Huddlestones ground beeing high Sheriffe of the Sheere, and to take with him Jack the sprite, and so he did, who went unseene to any body but to

Avis Cony (Cuney), of bewitching Jeremiah Browne. She would have been sentenced to a year's imprisonment with four appearances at pillories in local market towns. Avis was convicted of killing Richard Francke, son of William, and sentenced to death, but reprieved because she was found to be pregnant (Cockburn, *Calendar: Essex: Elizabeth*, records 2008 and 2029). Both were still in prison a year later (record 2096).

16 This seems to be the end of Joan Cunny's examination. The rest of the material about her is in a different tone, comparable to that of the marginal notes surrounding her examination, and portrays the witch quite differently. It is informal and gossipy, and it appears from the information given that its author attended Cunny's trial. This is a good example of how source can affect content and tone, giving contrasting images of witchcraft.

17 *Sic.*

18 Braintree, a town about a mile south-west of Stisted.

19 Joan Cunny's examination shows her denying this crime, so her alleged confession of it may have been in prison, in court or at her execution – either way, the two pieces of text are further set apart by this difference of information. Cunny (Cony) was found guilty of killing Elizabeth Finch, wife of Henry, and bewitching Joan Danishe, Barnard Gryffyn and Elizabeth Sparowe (Cockburn, *Calendar: Essex: Elizabeth*, record 2009).

20 This suggests that the writer saw the boy, reinforcing the belief that he was at the trial gathering extra material.

the boy, and when they came to a mighty Oke tree, the spirit went about it, and presently the Tree blew up by the roots: and no winde at all stirring at this time: which Master high Sheriffe acknowledged to be blown down in a great calme.[21]

The confession of Joan Upney of Dagenham,[22] in the Countye of Essex, who was brought before Sir Henrye Gray Knight,[23] the third of May. 1589.[24]

THis examinate saith, that one Fustian Kirtle, otherwise called White-cote, a witch of **Barking,**[25] came to her house about seaven or eight yeeres agoe and gave her a thing like a Moule, and tolde her if she ought any body any ill will, if she did bid it, it would goe clap them.[26]

She saith that Moule taryed not above a yeere with her, but it consumed away, and then she gave her another Moule and a Toad, which she kept a great while, and was never without some Toades since till her last going away, because she heard John Harrolde and Richard Foster say she was a witch, and urch[27] other woordes.[28]

She saith that one day she left a Toade under the groundsill at Harrolds house, and it pinched his wife {B} and sucked her til she dyed, but it never came to her the saide Joan Upney againe.

She saith, that one day another Toade went over her threshold as Richard Fosters wife was coming that way, and it went and pinched her, and never returned againe.

Other two Toades she left at home, when she ran away, but they consumed away.

She saith that her eldest Daughter would never abide to meddle with her Toades, but her youngest daughter would handle them, and use them as well as her selfe.[29]

21 Edward Huddlestone ('Edmund Huddleson' in the assize records) was present in court in his official capacity – the sheriff was appointed annually and his duty was to organise the twice-yearly assizes in accordance with the precepts issued by the judges of assize.

22 A village twenty miles south-west of Chelmsford.

23 Henry Grey of Pirgo, near Romford (two miles from Dagenham, Emmison, *Elizabethan Life: Wills of Essex Gentry and Merchants, passim*). He was knighted in 1587/8.

24 In May 1589 a woman named Upney, of Dagenham, was imprisoned after appearing at the archdeaconry court of Essex – this may be the same person, or one of her daughters (Macfarlane, 282, record 924).

25 Barking is three miles west of Dagenham. See also *A World of Wonders* (1595) for this woman.

26 Strike or attack them – with magical overtones.

27 *Sic.*

28 Upney was convicted of killing Joan Harwood and Alice Foster (Cockburn, *Calendar: Essex: Elizabeth*, record 2022).

29 One Alice Upney was discharged by proclamation at the end of the trial (Cockburn, *Calendar: Essex: Elizabeth*, record 2030). A Francisca Upney appeared in the Star Chamber court in 1597 – Macfarlane suggests she is a witch and Joan Upney's daughter (Macfarlane, 302, record 1190).

The examination of Joan Prentice, one of the women of the Almes house of Hinningham Sibble,[30] within the saide County: beeing taken the 29 of March, in the 31 yeere of the raigne of our Soveraigne Lady Elizabeth.

IN Primis, this saide examinate saith and confesseth, that about sixe yeeres last past, betweene the feastes of all Saintes, and the birth of our Lord God,[31] the devill appeared unto her in the Almes house aforesaide: about ten of the Clock in the night time, beeing in the shape and proportion of a dunnish culloured Ferrit, having fiery eyes, and the saide Examinate beeing alone {Bv} in her Chamber, and sitting upon a low stoole, preparing her selfe to bedward: the Ferrit standing with his hinder legs upon the ground, and his fore legs setled upon her lappe, and setling his fiery eyes upon her eyes, spake and pronounced unto her these woords following, namelye: Joan Prentice give me thy soule, to whome this Examinate being greatly amazed, answered and said: In the name of god what art thou The Ferrit answered, I am satan, feare me not my comming unto thee is to doo thee no hurt but to obtaine thy soule, which I must and wil have before I departe from thee to whome the saide examinate answered and said, that he demaunded that of her which is none of hers to give, saying: that her soule appertained onely unto Jesus Christ, by whose precious blood shedding, it was bought and purchased. To whome the saide Ferret replyed and saide, I must then have some of thy blood, which she willingly graunting, offered him the forefinger of her left hand, the which the Ferrit tooke into his mouth, and setting his former feete upon that hand, suckt blood therout, in so much that her finger did smart exceedingye:[32] and the saide examinate demaunding againe of the Ferrit what his name was: It answered Bidd. and then presently the said Ferrit vanished out of her sight sodainly.

{B2} Item, the saide examinate saith further, that about one moneth after, the saide Ferrit came againe unto her in the night time as she was sitting upon a little stoole, preparing her selfe to bed-ward, as is above saide: Joan wilt thou goe to bed, to whome she answered yea that I will by Gods grace, then presently the Ferret leapt up upon her lap, and from thence up to her bosome, and laying his former feete upon her lefte shoulder, sucked blood out of her lefte cheeke, and then he saide unto her, Joan if thou will have me doo any thing for thee, I am and wilbe alwaies ready at thy commaundement, and ther-upon she beeing a little before fallen out with William Adams his wife of **Hinningham Sibble** aforesaide: willed the Ferret to spoile her drinke which was then in brewing, which he did accordingly.[33]

30 Sible Hedingham, a village about sixteen miles north of Chelmsford, close to Maplestead.

31 Between 1 November and 25 December.

32 *Sic.*

33 Despite its conventional acts of maleficium, this examination has a literary quality beyond the usual flat legalisms of such documents. Its detailed scene-setting and suspenseful, dramatic dialogue, as well as the chivalric, almost romantic, relationship between spirit and

Item, the saide examinate furthermore saith and confesseth, that the saide Ferret divers times after appeered unto her alwaies at the time when she was going to bed, and the last time he appeered unto her was about seaven weekes last past, at which time she going to bed, the Ferrit leapt upon her left shoulder, and sucked blood out of her lefte cheeke, and that doone: he demaunded of her what she had for him to doo? To whom she answered, goe unto Maister Glascocks house, and nippe one of his children a little, named Sara, but hurt it not, and the next night he resorted unto her againe, and told her that he had doon as she willed him: namely, that he had nipt Sara Glascock, and that she should dye therof, to whome she answered and saide, thou villaine what hast thou doon, I bid thee to nip it but a little and not to hurt it, and hast thou killed the {B2v} childe? which speech being uttered, the Ferrit vanished away suddenly, and never came to her sithence. Item, she affirmeth, that the occasion why she did will her Ferret to nippe the saide childe, was for that she beeing the daye before at the house of the saide Maister Glascok, to begge his almes, answere was made to her by one of his maiden servantes, that both her Maister and Mistres were from home, and therfore desired her to be contented for that time, and therupon the examinate departed greatlye discontented, and that night sent her Ferret to nip the childe as is abovesaide.[34]

Item, she saith and affirmeth, that at what time soever she would have her Ferret doo any thing for her, she used these woordes, Bidd, Bidd, Bidd, come Bidd, come bidd, come bidd, come suck, come suck, come suck, and that presently he would appeere as is aforesaide: and suckt blood out of her left cheeke, and then perfourmed any mischeefe she willed or wished him to doo for her unto or against any of her neighbours.

Lastly the said examinate saith, and confesseth, that one Elizabeth Whale, the wife of Michaell Whale of Henningham Sibble aforesaide labourer, and Elizabeth Mott, the wife of John Mot of the saide Towne Cobler, are as well acquainted with her Bidd as her selfe is, but knoweth not what hurt they or any of them have doone to any of their neighbours.[35]

When their inditements were read, and their examinations also, they stoode upon their tearmes, to prolong life: yet to make the matters more apparant, sundry witnesses were produced to give evidence {B3} against them and firste the Judge of the circuite very wisely with a great foresight, called in the two Basterd Children before mentioned, and comended them greatlye for telling

witch, are unusual and give yet another view of what witchcraft was thought to be. Whether this is due to the examinate, her recorder or the pamphleteer is debatable, but again sourcing the story is an important part of understanding it.

34 Prentice was convicted of killing Sara Glascock (Cockburn, *Calendar: Essex: Elizabeth*, record 1998).

35 Elizabeth Whale is listed among discharged bailees at the trial's end (Cockburn, *Calendar: Essex: Elizabeth*, record 2031) whilst Elizabeth Mott was discharged by proclamation (record 2030).

the trueth of that which he should aske them, concerning their Grandam and their mothers, which they did, and having saide what they could, together with the depositions of sundrye other witnesses, they having confessed sufficient matter to prove the inditements. The Jury found these bad women guiltie and that they had slaine Men, women and Children, And committed very wicked and horrible actions, divers and sundrye times, and ther-upon the Judge proceeded, and pronounced the sentence of death against them, as worthely they had deserved.[36]

After they had received their judgments, they were convayed from the Barre backe againe to Prison, where they had not stayed above two howers, but the officers prepared them-selves to conduct them to the place of execution: to which place they led them, and being come thether, one Maister Ward a learned devine, being desired by the Justices, did exhorte these wicked women to repentance, And perswaded them that they would shewe unto the people the trueth of their wickednes, and to call upon God for mercy with penitent hartes. And to aske pardon at his hands for the same: some fewe prayers they saide after the precher, but little els: more then this, that they had deserved to dye, in committing those wicked sinnes: and so tooke their deathes patiently.

Note, that Mother Upney being inwardlye pricked and having some inward feeling in conscience cryed out saying: that she had greevously sinned, that the de-{B3v}-vill had deceived her, the devill had deceived her, and that she had twice given her soule to the Devill, yet by the meanes of Gods spirite woorking in her, and the paines which Maister ward tooke with her, she seemed very sorry for ye same, and died very penitent, asking God & the world forgivenes, even to ye last gaspe, for her wicked and detestable life.

FSNIS.[37]

36 This account of procedure, whilst a reasonable summary of the main elements of a felony trial, sugggests that all three women were tried together. In fact, each was tried by a separate jury (Cockburn, *Calendar: Essex: Elizabeth*, records 1997, 2006 and 2015). Also, it is likely that the convicted witches had to wait for sentencing – it usually happened on the last day of the assizes. Here the pamphleteer makes events neater for the purposes of closure.

37 *Sic.*

9

A Most Wicked worke of a wretched Witch (1592)

This is an unusual pamphlet in several ways, and it also marks the definitive divergence of two ways in writing about witchcraft in popular literature.

The account is the first pamphlet on English witchcraft to be wholly composed of third-person narrative since Richard Galis's *A Brief Treatise* (1579). Like Galis's account, it uses no documents and presents itself instead as a story told by a respectable narrator – with equally limited success. *Newes from Scotland*, a pamphlet concerning witches at North Berwick, had been published only a few months before *A Most Wicked worke* (1592) and is also a narrative account, so G.B., a Master of Arts whose identity is not known, had a more recent model for telling his story.[1] In this case, there may have been no trial from which to draw documents. Since many legal records for London and Middlesex in this period are missing, we cannot know whether this Middlesex case resulted in a trial or not. But whatever the reason, narrative was the pamphleteer's preferred generic model, and the pamphlet thus marks a move towards storytelling and away from documentary reproduction. Like Galis and the author of *Newes*, G.B. is a reasonably cultivated writer: his pamphlet is prefaced by a poem and a biblical quotation, and expressed in language which at times is flowery and elegant, euphuistic and entertaining. He may have been involved with the study of law, for legal terminology repeatedly flavours the pamphlet despite the absence of actual legal documents. The preface shows a growing interest in the demonological, listing Satan's names and 'explaining' their significance. Thus the stress is on elegant and accessible narration, not on stilted hopping from one examination to another.

Another noticeable trend is evident in that the protagonist, a working man, is presented by the cultured author as being slightly amusing, like Galis's cudgelled Father Roseman and the captured Elizabeth Stile. This too suggests the shape of things to come – that witchcraft pamphlets were moving upmarket in their discourse on the subject, and focusing more on 'the better sort'. Finally, the protagonist is presented as entirely innocent: the witch became irritated with him for reasons beyond his control, and there was no denial of charity by him or infliction

1 There is evidence that *Newes* might feed into Richard Burt's account of his aerial abduction in other ways, including rumours of flying as a result of witch attack (see Rosen, 204).

of injury upon her. The witch is thus presented as malicious without just cause: a marked change from the traditional representation in pamphlets based on documents, which tend to specify what the victim had done to the witch to incur his or her wrath. However, this representation of the victim as the hapless butt of the witch's wickedness recalls Galis's account. It seems to me that in returning to the Galis model, G.B. helps us see the emergence of differing trends in writing about witchcraft: documentary pamphlets which present traditional stories of injury to and revenge by witches, and aim at a less learned style, set against narrative accounts which stress the innocence of the victim, the learning of the author and socially stratified factors in the story of witchcraft. These latter traits became more common in the pamphlets of the next few decades, although Thomas Potts's 1612 *Wonderfull Discoverie* is a notably exceptional hybrid.

A Most Wicked worke's printing details do not match those in official records – quite a common occurrence at the time, when rights were often traded among publishers, but worth noting. Entered in the Stationers' Register on 7 April 1592, to John Kydde, the pamphlet's text was presumably then passed to William Barley, a rather convoluted transmission of this supposedly true story, and to a somewhat maverick figure. Barley, a draper, printer and bookseller, had been questioned several times about his publications and his opposition to the monopoly system operated by the Stationers' Company, and he had been imprisoned for contempt at their instigation in 1591. Similarly, Robert Bourne, who printed the quarto for Barley, was banned from printing in the 1580s for breaking a Star Chamber decree. He resurfaces as a printer for the first time here, clearly unabashed. Both men were thus publishers who were not averse to ignoring Company rules on ownership and probity of texts. The text used here is in Lambeth Palace library.

Finally, there is a problem with the alleged truth of the pamphlet's subject matter – 'newly recognised', as the pamphlet alleges. Given the careful description of the story's source, it is a surprise to discover that some of the magical incidents recounted as documentary reports bear a very close resemblance to happenings in a play performed in the same year, Robert Greene's *Friar Bacon and Friar Bungay*. Whilst there was certainly a Master Richard Edlin of Woodhall in Pinner in 1592, it is possible that events surrounding his servant have been transformed by contact with writers in the capital. G.B., at least allegedly an M.A., might be expected to have access to literary culture, and may have rewritten, for Kydde or for Barley, the story he received. Perhaps the entire incident is a fabrication – indeed, unless we accept the possibility of magical flight, then delusion or fiction must be at the root of the account. The pamphlet thus serves as a sharp warning against accepting events narrated in witchcraft pamphlets as transparently easy to analyse, and it introduces further complications of genre into an already difficult interpretative field.[2]

2 See my note 'Greene's *Friar Bacon and Friar Bungay* and *A Most Wicked Worke of a Wretched Witch*: A Link', *Notes and Queries* (March 1997), 36–7 for further details.

{A (title page)} **A MOST WICKED** *worke of a wretched Witch, (the* **like whereof none can record these manie yeares in England.)** *Wrought on the Person of one Richard Burt,* **Servant to Maister** *Edling* **of Woodhall in the Parrish of** *Pinner* **in the Coun***tie of Myddlesex, a myle be***yond Harrow.**
Latelie committed in March last An. **1592 and newly recognised according to the truth,**[3] *by* **G.B.** *maister of Arts.*
Printed by R.B. for William Barley, and are to be sold at his shop in Gratious streat.
{Av} **Hexasticon.**[4]

Of wrathfull witches this same pamphlet tels,
How most of all on simple folke they worke.
What woonders to they may atchive by spels,
God weede them out in every cell they lurke,
God weeds them out, but satan stil doth hatch,
fresh Impes, whereby of al sorte he may catch.

Levit. 20. 6.
If any turne after such as worke with spirits, and after soothsaiers, to goe a whoring after them, then will I set my face against that person, and will cutte him off from among his people.
{A2} **A most wicked worke of a wret***ched Witch, wrought on the Person of one Richard Burt.*

SO long (right Gentle and courteous Reader) as wee live heere in this wretched vale of miserie, and myserable estate of our Probationership, we are all even the best of us all, to account no better of our selves, then that we live in a perpetuall warrefare, and most dangerous and deadlie combat.

Our Enimies that we are to fight against are in number three: The world, the Flesh, and the Dyvell: two wherof notwithstanding (such is our blinde perseverance) the moste parte esteeme their entire friends, whereas indeed they are the hande-mynisters of our Archenimie, all under colourable frendship deceiving their familiars,[5] and seeking their death both of bodie and soule.

Our graund foeman Sathan Architect of all mischiefe, in scripture hath many proper names, to explaine his malitious nature: Of his crueltie hee is called **Abaddon**, a Destroier, bicause that not like a common enimie hee is contented with the death and downefall of our bodies, but imagineth utter destruction of the soule also, and intollerable tormentes joyntlie to them both: Of his

3 This implication that false stories have been circulated is not borne out by any surviving accounts, but it does suggest that the pamphlet is conscious of its place in a developing narrative.

4 A six-line poem, with a pun on 'hex'.

5 Those who are familiar with the world and the flesh, their friends.

crafte hee is tearmed a Theefe, bicause he inventeth by what meanes he may slile and unwittinglie set upon the godlie. Of his malice he is called **Diabolus**, an accuser, bicause evermore day and night he is busie, accusing the consciences of the righteous.

He is named a Dragon of his pollicie, bicause that since {A2v} the time of **Adam**, among so many thousands, in so many yeares, there hath been founde none so wise or warie, that could withstand his stratagems, but he hath wounded and poisoned them well nighe unto death.

He hight[6] a Lion also of his power, bicause that as the solide bodie of the Lion is powerfull: so especiallie consisteth great strengthe and power in his taile.

We doubt not but this adversarie, or **Apollyon** of ours of himselfe is mightie, puissant, & strong enough againste such faintie cowards, and wilfull flo-backs as we are, yet to make his victorie more sure, and not to faile of his purpose, he useth also the force of his tayle: that is, his inthraled bondslaves, whom he hath sealed to execute his wil and pleasure uppon the harmelesse, which is perfourmed many times divers and sundry waies: neyther dooth he so usually shew his pollicie, puissance and power by anye his oficers, as he dooth by subtle seedemen of false doctrine, and inchanting sorcerers: the one in stead of instruments to inveigle the mind and soule, the other to assaile the mortall bodie, and beguile and intrappe the sences.[7]

I speake nothing of those pseudosedmen, but I purpose (God willing) to treat of damnable Wytches, of their spight and spelles, odious in the sight of God, detested of the good, and moste hurtfull to themselves, manifesting what power and preminence through Gods permission, that Father of sinne Sathan hath over sinfull worldlings.

About Shrovetide last, one **Richard Burt**, servant to a Gentleman, named M. **Edling**, dwelling at **Woodhall** in the parishe of **Pinner** in **Middlesex**,[8] a myle beyond **Harrow** on the **Hill**, going to his maysters Barne, standing at the Townes ende, accompanied with a great mastive dogge, suddenly espied an Hare start before him, and thinking to have set his dogge at her, missed of his purpose: for the dogge not onely refused to follow, but in stead of following began to faint,[9] and runne rounde about his maister, {A3} and to whine pittifully, as who shoulde say that kinde of game was not for them: The man taking heartie grace himselfe, followed so nighe, that he saw her take in at one Mother **Atkyns** house, whome before that time he knew to

6 Is called.

7 The convoluted syntax makes this difficult to interpret – presumably the seed men are Catholics, often linked with sorcerers (see *The Examination of John Walsh* [1566])?

8 Richard Edlin leased Woodhall in 1553 and again in 1609/10. The Edlins were a substantial local family. See Diane K. Bolton, 'Harrow including Pinner' in *The Victoria History of the Counties of England. Middlesex*, ed. R.B. Pugh (Oxford: Oxford University Press, 1971), vol. 4, 169–271.

9 To lose courage.

be a notorious witch: Whereupon, blessing himselfe, & mindful of the name of God, he boldly said, avant witch.

This was the first occasion (namely the tearming of hir a with[10]) of al poore **Richard Burts** future tragedie: but to go forward. It hapned the said **Richard Burt** a month after, meeting hir neere to his maisters barne, and given hir the time of the daye, like a perverse woman, like a perillous waspe, like a pestiferous witch, incensed with hate at the sight of him held downe hir head, not daigning to speake.[11]

The next day which was on wednesday the 8. of march going againe to his maisters barne to thrash,[12] & serve certaine beasts, bicause he would not trudge too and fro for letting his work, carried his dinner with him, which was bread, butter, cheese and applepy, & a bottle of the best beer: being come to the barne he laide his provision, and setled close to his busines, labouring hard til twelve of the clock, at which time hunger assailing and custome prevailing, he went to dinner, wherin he had not long continued, but ther was opposite to his view a monstrous blacke Cat among the straw, which began to shake the strawe, and to make a wad thereof. The fellow being agast start up with his applepie in his hande (for it had byn pittie a poore hungrie thresher should have lost so good a repast) suddenly hearing a voice that commanded him, come away: Away quod he, whither shal I come? The spirit answering againe, sayde: Come and leave thy vittels behind thee and thy knife also. Poore simplicity keeping his applepy stil in his hand, came to the barne dore, where suddenly hee was hoised up into the aire, and carried over many fields, by the way espyeng his mai.[13] plow a plowing, but not able to cal unto them, although he seemed to have his memorie most perfect:[14] thence passing over to Harrow, where on the side of the hill there {A3v} is a greate ponde was drawne through it, & ther left his hat (which was a token of that torture) because he could stay in no place, but was violentlie rapt up the hiil,[15] and over the tops of the trees at Harrow Church, so farre he absolutelie remembreth, but being haled further, he was taken (as he seemeth) into a place which was all fire, where was heard such lamentable howling and dolefull crieng, as if all the damned fiends of hell had beene tortured, and tormenten in that Limbo.

10 *Sic.*

11 A marginal note reads: **Unspeakable is the malice of a wicked woman**.

12 Thresh – to separate grain from husks with a flail.

13 Master's.

14 Here is the first similarity to Robert Greene's play, *Friar Bacon and Friar Bungay*. In the play, the hostess of an inn at Henley is tempted outside by spirits belonging to the magician Bacon – she too is 'hoised' up into the air carrying food with her. Greene's play was performed at the Rose Theatre in February and March 1591/2 (Robert Greene, *Friar Bacon and Friar Bungay*, ed. Daniel Seltzer [1594; London: Edward Arnold, 1964], Scene 2, lines 116–31; W.W. Greg, ed., *Henslowe's Diary*, 2 vols (London: Bullen, 1904), vol. 1, F7–9). See my note on 'Greene's *Friar Bacon*'.

15 *Sic.*

You heare into how strange and passionate a place this **Richard Burt** was translated, now it remaineth to shewe with what Symtomes the place was furnished.

First therefore (he affirmeth) it was exceeding hot, replenished with more than Cymmerian[16] darkenesse, plentiful in filthy odors and stinches, ful of noise and clamours, insomuch that hee seemed to heare infinite millions of discrepant noises, but saw nothing save onelie the fire which caused such an unquenchable drouth in his stomache, that presentlye minding a pennie hee had in his purse: looked round about for an Alehouse where he might spend it.[17]

Hearing therefore these foresaid voices, and thinking some of them had spake unto him, he answerd sayeng, heer is no worke for me to doo: immediatlie it was reanswered, coast away with him, but with this proviso thou passest that thou be secret, and say nothing when thou commest home: but he replied, and said, my maister will aske me where I have beene: with that he was not suffered to speak any further, but his toong was doubled in his mouth, his legs burnt, hands and armes scorched, his coat pincht of his backe, and throwne into the fire, immediatly soring over hedges and ditches, sowsed in mire and durt, scratched with thornes and briers, so singed and disfigured, that it is both lamentable and terrible to behold him.

Being brought againe to **Pinner** where his Mayster doth dwell, he first repaired to a ditch to drinke, and after-{A4}-wards in this pickle visited one of his acquaintance, whoe sometime served **M. Edling** also: but whether hee sorted thither for that his friends house was nighest, or would not go home for shame that hee had beene absent foure whole daies togither, I cannot shew you: Onlie this, being sunday morning his maister chanced (as his custome was to passe by that way to Church at the same instant, whoe not knowing poore **Richard Burt** his lost sheepe, demanded of his quondam servant if he had gotten him a man: a man sir quod he, why it is your man **Richard**: my man quoth the Gentleman, that cannot bee, and therewithall beeing halfe amazed made a pause and earnestlie beheld him, at length willing him in the name of God to tel where he had bin though he could not speake, yet having memory made signes and evermore pointed toward the house where mother **Atkins** did dwell, looking so grislie and fiercelie that waie, that he tore and rent al that came in his hands.

16 A Crimean people, believed to live entirely in the dark.

17 This unlikely detail is the second similarity with *Friar Bacon and Friar Bungay*. In it, the comic servant Miles talks with a devil, and inquires about both the tippling houses and the lusty fires of hell. When he asks for an office which he can perform there, the devil promises him that he shall be a rich tapster (inn keeper) there, because hell is hot and so its inhabitants are continually thirsty (Scene 15, lines 30–45). A few lines further down A3v, Richard Burt is also concerned to find work in this fiery place.

In the meane while it was thought requisite, that the Parson of the towne named **M. Smith,**[18] and mai. **Burbridge** of Pinner parke[19] gentleman should be sent for,[20] whoe comming to the dumbe man and pittieng his plight, the Parson charitably and like himselfe laboured about him, wrinched open his teeth got open his mouth, indented his finger under his toong, and with much adoo got it unfoulded, the first wordes he spake were these: Woe worth mother **Atkins**, woe worth mother **Atkins**, for she hath bewitched me: whereupon he would not be quiet, but ever requested that he might speak with hir.

Maister **Burbidge** and M. **Smith** caused hir to bee sent for, who being present, he never ceased til he had scratched and drawne bloud on hir, perswading himselfe that was a remedy sufficient under God, that would make him well: neither was it or is it any Capital error, experience testyfies: for since that he hath mended reasonablie, and nowe goeth to the Church.

{A4v} Thus have you heard briefly the cares and crosses, that poore **Richard Burt** sustained (as they say)[21] in **summo gradu**, the eighth, the ninth, tenth and eleventh daies of march last past, what time hee was absent from his maister the foresaid whole daies, and used (as ye have heard) after the foresaid manner.

Thus then leave we **Richard Burt**, but with mother **Atkins** we must prosecute a little further.

It is credibly reported in **Pinner,**[22] that the saide mother **Atkins** on a time resorting to the house of M. **Burbidge** for milke (at what time the maids were busie at the dairy) and not obtaining hir desire, immediatly upon hir departure out of doores, the Creame beganne to swel and rise in the cherne, that it burst open the top of the Cherne, and runne about the kitchen and forth at the sinke-hole, and all their huswiferie for that day went to wracke,[23] that al was quite lost, and nothing could possiblie be well ordered: O rebels towards God: enemies to mankinde: catterpillers of a common wealth, the fire is too good to consume them.

Many and sundry like actions of extreame rage and crueltie are imputed to her, only we will conclude, and shut up these clauses, with this that followeth. Not long since the forenamed witch entring the ground of one **Gregorie Coulson**, to crave some releefe (for she lyveth of almes and good peoples charitie) she found him busilie imploied about some countrie affaires, Radling hys lambs[24] (I thinke it was) and framing hir petition to him, because he did not straight waie leave al and accomplish it she flung forth in a fume:

18 Perhaps Thomas Smith, Vicar of Ruislip 1565–1615.

19 Pinner Park is half a mile from Pinner, near Hatch End.

20 A marginal note reads: **The dutie of a good minister.**

21 Lawyers – a summing-up phrase meaning in total, step by step.

22 The source for this story sounds like local gossip.

23 A marginal note adds: **Witches ar the moste unprofitable crraturs in the world** (*sic*).

24 Marking them with colour.

But it was not longe after her departure, but he had finished his labour also, and letting forth two Lambs into a yard, suddenly they began so nimbly to skip and friske to and fro, that they never ceased after til they died.[25]

FINIS

25 The narrator appears to be constructing this story as he tells it – citified disdain for country affairs gives way to a certainty about the nature of the work damaged by witchcraft with surprising speed.

10

'A memoriall of certaine most notorious witches' (1595)

This extract is a version of the lost pamphlet *The Examination and Confession of a notorious Witch named Mother Arnold* from *A World of Wonders. A Masse of Murthers. A Covie of Cosonages* (1595).

In 1574 or 1575 a pamphlet entitled *The Examination and Confession of a notorious Witch named Mother Arnold, alias Whitecote, alias Glastonbury at the Assize of Burnt wood in July 1574; who was hanged for Witchcraft at Barking*, was published. It was a topical account of Cecilia (or Cecily) Glasenberye, who has already been mentioned in *A true and just Recorde* (1582) and *The Apprehension and confession of three notorious Witches* (1589). She was tried at Brentwood on 19 July 1574. We know that she was 'mother Arnold' because on her indictments the name 'Arnolde' has been written and then scratched out. Some documentation of her trial survives, but it only mentions one of the cases described in the pamphlet, that of William Newman. The original pamphlet may have been compiled from informations, or paraphrases of them, about events which never came to trial. Clearly gossip might also play a part in constructing Mother Arnold's story. Over the subsequent centuries, the original account of the case was lost completely and remains so – presumably all copies of it were destroyed.

This pamphlet's account is most likely a truncation, made in 1595, of the 1574–5 work. It is the only version of the lost pamphlet which we have, and is printed here as such. We can measure to some extent how much survives because the 1595 pamphleteer also used material from *A Most Wicked worke of a wretched Witch* (1592) which can be compared with its original to check the extent of the later pamphleteer's editing. In fact, whilst he cut the 1592 account quite severely, omitting prefatory material and the concluding stories, paraphrasing and simplifying its style, and leaving out data such as the name of the farm and of the minister, he maintained the overall structure of the main story reasonably intact. The same is probably true of the account of Mother Arnold. Much is lost, but interesting material remains.

A World of Wonders is a classic compilation pamphlet, in old-fashioned black-letter, with snippets of a wide variety of 'true' stories. The quarto was printed for William Barley, probably by Valentine Simmes, and written by T.I. (according to the *STC*). It is not mentioned in the Stationers' Register. The text used here is in Trinity College Library, Cambridge. We do not know the publication details of the lost pamphlet. Its partial survival is a matter of chance, and gives a fascinating insight into the reuse of stories and pamphlets in the period. For a brief account of the pamphlet's re-emergence see Marion Gibson, 'Mother Arnold: A Lost Witchcraft Pamphlet Rediscovered', *Notes and Queries*, vol. 243, no. 3 (September 1998), 296–300.

{E2v} A memoriall of certaine most notorious witches, and of their dealings

There dwelled not so long since, but that of some it may be remembred. In **Barking** in **Essex** seven miles distaunt from London a Witch named mother white-coate **alias** mother **Arnold alias** mother **Glassenbury** who committed many execrable factes, as may appeare.

There was dwelling in **Barking** one Thomas Clark a fisher who having angred this witch, went foorth in mackerel {E3} time to catch flounders, and he and two boyes sayling downe almost as farre as Lee[1] where they cast out his nets, in the same place was such an neddy[2] that he could by no meanes woork, neither his nets come in order, as they should do, but upon a sodaine this **Clarke** cryed out and sayd that he sawe mother **Arnolde** the witch walking in the water, and withall cryed the spirit entred into him and mooved him to kill him selfe so that hee tooke a hatchet, a hooke and a knife and threw them overbourd, and after tyed he himselfe about the middle with a rope and so fell mad, so that the boyes cryed unto other fishermen, who seeking to help him, there was a whirlepoole that had almost cast them away so that none durst come neer them, at length a boat of **Green wich**[3] perceiving the whirlepoole threw a roape unto them and so plucked him into his boate and so brought him home to **Barking** where he remained mad, and lying still bound cryed out of mother **Arnold**, and in the end dyed thus tormented.[4]

The said mother **Arnold** going in precession with other her neighbours in gangweek[5] and **William Daulbie** seeing her very lively came unawares behind her and strooke up her heeles giving her a fall, and after thrust him selfe

1 Upriver from Barking, some seven miles south-west on the south bank of the Thames.

2 Eddy.

3 About five miles south-west of Barking, on the south bank.

4 Each anecdote is a neat tale of cause and effect related to a particular victim, suggesting that the original pamphlet may have been based on informations. The traditional format and concerns presumably result from the pamphlet's origin in the period when documents were more common than narrative in pamphlets. However, this seemingly straightforward story also contains more than a hint of the sirens and the classical witch Circe from Homer's *Odyssey*.

5 Rogation week, the time of public procession and beating of parish bounds leading up to Ascension Day.

into the prease of the people to the intent she might not know who did it, but she arysing came immediatly to him taking him by the hand thanked him for her fall, and sayd she would be even with him.

They[6] went to one **Malles** house a mile and a half from **Barking** where she complained of the young man and after some victualls given her by the good-wife went homeward againe.

Malles wife and *D*a**ulbie** going to **Barking** togither a good pace but could set no eye of her, till they came by **Barking**, where she sat a praying under a tree, and so passed by her, and so went home, where beeing not a quarter of an houre, but **Daulbie** was so miserably vexed, that he sought to kill himself, thrust his hedde into the swilling tub full of swines meat,[7] where he had smothered him self if help had not prevented it.

Then would he have runne into a hotte oven to the burning fire brands with his teeth that hee burned his mouth and lippes very sore: when night came his freinds had him to bed, but his vexation growing wursse and wursse and he feeling his bowels burne within him (as a pot seething on the fire) could not indure {E3v} the bed but lay for the most part all the night out of a windowe which hee so byted with his teeth that it may be perceived still, so long as the window endureth, and in these miserable cases continued. At last helped by an other witch, was at the Assises bound to appeare at Burntwood[8] where hee gave evidence against mother **Arnold** in the hearing of her owne daughter, who after came to him and saide you have given shrode[9] evidence against my mother but you will be little better for it. And the next night following, rysing to make water was stroken in the neck that hee fell sick and was faine to be brought from Burntwood to Rainford[10] in a Cart, and so from thence home, beeing pitiously vexed till he gave up the ghost.

When Master **Clement Sisley** Esquire had examined this witch and tolde her she should goe to prsson[11] the wiech[12] desired that shee might not goe to prison, for the spirit would be revenged as it hapned when hee tooke paper in his hand to make his warrant suddainely both his feete were taken from him by reason wherof, he fell on a plaine[13] pavement of free stone in his owne house at Tastbury hall and strook out the huckle bone of his thigh

6 It is not clear who is referred to here – the next paragraph makes even less sense. If the pamphlet is a version of the 1574 one, it may be confusing *because* it is a contraction of the earlier pamphlet. The giant breathless sentences, erratic grammar and very fast pace may result from the summarising of stories originally in a more measured framework.

7 Food *for* pigs.

8 Cecily Glasenberye was tried at Brentwood on 19 July 1574 and convicted of several murders and other offences (Cockburn, *Calendar: Essex: Elizabeth*, record 724). Brentwood is twelve miles north-east of Barking.

9 Shrewd: meaning here pointed, effective.

10 Romford? On the road from Brentwood to Barking, this is five miles north-east of Barking.

11 *Sic.* This section has several mistakes in composition.

12 *Sic.*

13 Flat (thus his fall is the more remarkable).

out of the joynt, so that for three weekes space he could not goe, nor stand along time after her execution but used stilts[14] for necessities sake.[15]
But before he committed her to the Jaiole, he caused her to be searched by honest wives who betweene her kercheif and her hat found wrapped in a linned cloth swines dung, the herb cherwell dill, red fenell and saint Johns woort, the right hand or forefoote of a Moulewarp,[16] which upon the opening so stanck that no person could abyde it.
After the finding of this shee kneeled downe uppon her knees, desiring them if she might not have the whole, yet to let her have some part therof, but the same by the commaundement of the Justice was burned.
IF I should write at full the manifolde mischeifes of this most detestable practicioner, they would fill a great volume, as how she lamed *N*ewman of **Stratforde**[17] a tanner, how shee stole {E4} an handchercher from his wife and after five dayes keeping it sent it backe againe by one of her neighbours, who delivering it, faire, and white, to **Newmans** mayd, presently there fell three dropps of bloud upon it one after another, and the mayd amazed giving it to her mistris it became all over red as bloud most wonderfull.
Also how shee vexed one **Harison** beeing a Dutch man meeting him at **Mile-end**[18] and stroke him so lame that he was faine to hire a horse, to carry him home, and bewitched him dumbe, that he could not speake: and made his horse to shake, and dance, for the space of one whole yeare.
Also how she threatned **George Male** at the Grayhound at **Barking** that for so much as he thrust her and her daughter out of his doores and would give them nothing, this witch threatned that shee would set a Bee in his tayle the next time. Yea and that a singer sayd the daughter. So not long after he determining te[19] ride, put on a new payre of hose with a double rugge[20] in them prysed fortie shillings, the first day of his riding he was so tickled in the buttocke, that he scratched through all, both hose and lynings and such a hole in his flesh, that it was not whole a moneth after.
Many other mischeifs might be heere numbred, but I meane not to stand long uppon these detestable actions only this to be noted, that beeing often examined, when she was to answere suddainely there rose in her throate a swelling as bigge as a mans fist, black as pitch, and then she seemed to have

14 Crutches.

15 The *nomina ministrorum* for the summer assizes of 1574 shows that Clement Sisley was indeed excused attendance because of illness (Cockburn, *Calendar: Essex: Elizabeth*, record 717).

16 See also Ursley Kempe's bone-ache remedy, *A true and just Recorde* (1582), 2A7.

17 Four miles west of Barking. In the indictment (Cockburn, *Calendar: Essex: Elizabeth*, record 724), William Newman is described as a yeoman who lost the use of his limbs from 6 June 1574 to 20 June because of Cecily Glasenberye's witchcraft.

18 Seven miles south-west of Barking.

19 *Sic.*

20 A coarse woollen material, here used as lining.

the hitchcough,[21] as though she would speake but could not, and in this case the examiners would strike her on the brest but she required them not to doe so: And when she was executed such a stincking vapour issued foorth of her mouth that the behoulders were scantlye able to endure it. All which is moste wounderfull.[22]

21 Hiccups.

22 The pamphlet then prints its edited version of *A Most Wicked worke* (1592) and mentions 'the tirannie of the witches of **Warboys**', presumably from *A Most strange and admirable discoverie* (1593). It also speaks of 'the cruell devises of mother **Bumby** the witch of **Rochester**' but if there is a lost pamphlet behind this reference, we are given no further information on it.

11

'The severall practises of Johane Harrison and her daughter' (1606)

This extract is from *The Most Cruell and Bloody Murther committed by an Inkeepers Wife, called Annis Dell . . . With the severall Witchcrafts, and most damnable practises of one Johane Harrison and her Daughter.*

The pamphlet containing this selection of stories deals primarily with the murder of a three-year-old child and the cutting out of his sister's tongue by Annis Dell and George Dell, who were tried and executed at Hertford assizes in August 1606. There are two pamphlets of the same year dealing with the case: the other is titled *The Horrible Murther of a young Boy of three yeres of age, whose sister had her tongue cut out; and how it pleased God to reveale the offendors, by giving speech to the tongueles Childe.* As with most murder pamphlets, the horrific story is told in a third-person narrative which conjures up in vivid and compelling detail the 'cruell and bloody' killing of the victim, and the providential discovery of the perpetrators. The Dells, with a gang of others, allegedly killed the boy for his money – which they had been given by a thief and his wife who had already murdered the childrens' parents. The surviving child, we are told, was mutilated and left to die in a hollow tree. After her escape she presents a picture of terrifying trauma and destitution, from which she is delivered when her speech is miraculously restored after four years of itinerant begging. The names of witnesses and an account of events at the trial are given, and the story is thus authenticated far more carefully than the account of witchcraft which follows it. The harrowing tale of toddler murder, torture and abuse in the midst of a civilised community is also in striking contrast to the entertaining account of witchcraft, which is brief, patched together in apparent haste, and, after some unpleasant tales of *maleficium*, finally and surprisingly represents the witch as a figure of fun. This striking use of comedy recalls elements in *A Most Wicked worke* (1592) and points to the fact that witchcraft need not be discussed purely in a solemn, legalistic context.

The lack of specificity and the gossipy tone of the story of Johane Harrison suggest that it was based on observation and overhearings at the assizes. The two witches executed at the assizes in summer 1606 were in fact named Alice and Christian Stokes, a discrepancy of name which may be reflected in the changing first initial of the elder 'Harrison' here. Similarly, no magistrate's or witnesses' names are given, although the latter are preserved on the surviving indictments. This lack of interest in documented detail is again in contrast with the far more painstaking Dell account. There is, however, an unusual and totally uncomprehending description of physical evidence, which was presumably displayed at the trial? The account is more interested in amusing its readers than in making incisive comment about witchcraft, suggesting the further development of the genre of pamphlets which rely on authorial interaction with the reader rather than the use of documents for their literary effect.

This quarto was entered in the Stationers' Register by bookseller William Firebrand on 25 September 1606 and printed by Thomas Purfoot for Firebrand and John Wright. Purfoot and Wright both worked in father–son partnerships, producing ballads, broadsides and pamphlets on omens, wonders and political events. The other account of the Dell murder was also published by Firebrand, and printed by Edward Allde. The text used here is in the British Library.

{C2v} The severall practises of *Johane Harrison*, and her daughter, condemned and executed at *Hartford* for Witch-craft, the 4 of August last, 1606.

AT the Assizes held in the beginning of August last in the County of **Hartford**, in the Kings Majesties behalfe for Gaole deliverie, there were by the verdict of the Countrey, Foure onely Offenders found worthy to have deserved death, of which 2 (as have been spoken of, the Mother & the Son) for murther,[1] and one **Johane Harrison** & her daughter for damnable Witch-craft, wrayed[2] time that offences shold come thus prodigious, that the Offspring borne to be a comfort to the Parents, and the parents as much delighted in the Children, should be cause of one anothers untimely death and fatal overthrow.[3]

This **J.H.** dwelling at **Royston**[4] in the sayd County of **Hartford**, of long time having been suspected for witchcraft; now (upon just cause) was apprehended, and her house according to the true course of Justice, being searcht, there was found in a chest of hers, such sufficient instruments, (which she after confest were helpes to her in her practises) that could there have beene no other proofe nor evidence against her, they only had been sufficient to judge her unworthy of long life. This Chest being opened, there was first taken out by the Offic[ers] all the bones due to the Anatomy of man & woman, and under them haire of all colours that is customarily worne, in the bottome was found a parchment lapt up in a compas no bigger than a groat, but being open, was in breadth every way 2 spans; in ye midst of this {C3} parchment was coloured (in the purest colours) a heart proportionable

1 The Dells, whose story occupies the entire pamphlet to C2. The pamphlet correctly reports that only four people were executed.

2 Bewrayed: betrayed. The pamphleteer presumably means that the times are being exposed in their true, evil, character.

3 An attempt to link the stories thematically.

4 Royston is a town some sixteen miles north of Hertford.

to the hart of a man; and round about fitting even to the very brim of the parchment, were coloured in severall colours very curiously divided braunches, on which hung dangling things like ashen keys, and at the ends of them in some places figured, and others proportioned a mouth, in briefe the whole joynts and artiers of a man.[5]

This **J.H.** being upon her examination, and finding such apparant witnes induct against her of her severall fellonies & murthers, neglected not to confesse her utmost secret therin, that she had power (by the helpe of that parchment, man & womans bones, and man and womans haire) to inflict (by the helpe of her spirits, which she reported to have 2 attending on her, one for men, another for cattell) in any joynt, synnow,[6] or place of the body, by only but pricking the point of a needle in that place of the parchment, where in his or her body she would have them tortured, which torture of hers once begun in them, their paine should continue so restlesse, that a present death had bin more happier, than so lingring a calamity; and those whome she intended to kill had the same in effect. If she gave a pricke in the middle of ye parchment, where she had placed the heart, which relation of her may certainely be beleeved by the severall consequents that she was condemned upon.[7] First a good countrey Yeoman (a neighbor of hers) & she falling at some words together, he calling her old Hagge, or some such like name of reproofe: She made him this answere, I will say little to thee, but thou shalt feele more from me hereafter. The honest man had scarse been departed from her halfe an houre, but hee felt himselfe, as if he had been set into your scotch-boote, or spanish strappado, or your **Morbus Gallicus**, was nothing to it,[8] sometimes in a pestiferous heat, & others, a chill cold, but at al times in continual aches, & wracking of his limbs as if the Divell had set him on his Tentors to make broad-cloth of him.[9] In this perplexitie he continued consuming himselfe, not being able neither to goe nor stand, nor Phisicke could not helpe him, nor no meanes bee had to ease him.

{C3v} When one of his neighbors comming in neighborly love to visit him, he began to open his mind to him, that he perswaded himselfe, by such a

5 As Rosen suggests, this is probably an anatomical diagram from an illuminated book. The pamphleteer's apparent ignorance and lack of curiosity about this is interesting – this literate person can offer no more incisive description of the diagram than the simple similes of ash keys and mouths. Even if these are the similes of his source rather than himself, one would expect a glossing explanation from anyone who had any medical or bibliographical knowledge at all.

6 Sinew.

7 This sentence is presumably intended to run on from the last, without break. The pamphlet is full of syntactical and grammatical errors.

8 Forms of torture, and the 'French' pox, syphilis. The boots were inflicted upon Dr Fian in the Scottish witchcraft pamphlet *Newes from Scotland* of 1591/2, which may suggest a link here. The syntax becomes confused as the pamphleteer waxes more confiding and colloquial in his narration and more sympathetic to the witch's victims.

9 Tenter-hooks were used for stretching cloth.

one she[10] was bewitched, and hee was as faithfully perswaded, that if he could have but 2 or 3 good scratches at her face, wherby he might draw blood of her, he should recover presently, his neighbour advised him by some wile to send for her home, yet (yt between them both held unconvenient, for that either suspecting her selfe, or for not being friends she would not come) that in the night following his neighbor would have this sicke man caried in a chaire, & lodged in his house, and in the morning his wife, (whom he knew she was good friends withal) should by some wile or other draw her theher,[11] whan if he of himself were not strong inough to scratch her, he (as he held charily) wold help him.[12] This the next morning was done accordingly, the Witch comes, & is well scratcht, upon which within 3 or 4 daies (as fast as the man could recover strength) he is up, & goes abroad: which this **A.H.**[13] perceiving, arrests him & by a triall in law for this battry had 5 s[14] damages, and her costs of suit given her, the man (according as he was condemnd) paid her, which no sooner by her received, but ye honest man fell into his former passion, languishing a while & died: in the same maner she served another, who meeting her out of the towne in a lane, tooke the like revenge upon her, & recovered. Both which blowne over (only a little murmurd against by a neighbor of hers) a yong woman being washing clothes in an outer rowme next ye street where in a wanscot[15] cradle her child lay a sleep; when this **A.H.** daughter chanced to come by just in the instant as she was throwing out a little wrinsing water, and by chaunce some of which unawares sprinkled upon her, which ye wench seeming mooved at, called to her with these words. Do you throw your water upon me gossip, before it be long Ile be revenged for it. The woman (sorry for the offence) had done,[16] followed her busines, & thought no further of

10 Should presumably read 'he'.

11 *Sic.*

12 Whilst the general sense of this passage is clear enough, the syntax and sentence length indicate a lack of direction in the material. The attempt to see events empathetically through the eyes of the victim's friend might suggest that his account is a source here.

13 The change in the witch's name again suggests confusion over story and chosen representation: perhaps it is a reflection of the name of one of the witches at Hertford assizes in 1606, Alice Stokes (J.S. Cockburn, *Calendar: Hertfordshire: James I* [London: HMSO, 1975], record 162). She and another woman, Christian Stokes (record 161), were tried by the same jury as the Dells and are generally believed to be the witches described here. But the relationship between actual events and this narration is clouded by carelessness and by the prioritising of adjectival comment over the more traditional bare description.

14 Five shillings: this exchange, whether an accurate record or not, suggests that the witch's blood was no longer a magical cure if it had been 'paid for'. There is no assize record of this action for battery.

15 Panelled oak.

16 *Sic.* This could mean that the woman 'had done' with the matter (i.e. she dismissed it from her mind) or may be intended to read 'she had done', which would indicate further textual hiccups here.

it, when on the sudden (while she was but stept into a next rowm to hang up some clothes) the cradle wherein her child lay, was throwne over shatte-{C4}-red all to peeces, the child upon the face whelmed under it, & killed. Thus we see the Divell hath such power on these his damnable servants, that neither men nor infants are to be pitied by them. Not long after she had all bewitched a wealthy mans daughter in the towne, who having a good substantiall Yeoman to her brother,[17] in pitie of his Sisters griefe, rode to **Cambridge**,[18] and there acquainting a friend of his with his sisters affliction: the scholler told him she was bewitched, yet in regard they two had beene of an ancient friendship, & that himselfe had some acquaintance with his sister, in spite of her **Incubi**,[19] her spirits, & the divell, & al heed[20] help: which according to promise he performed, and by that time her brother was returned, his sister was recovered, in revenge of (for that her sorcery was crost, & the mayd reduct[21] to helth by her brothers carefulnes) she caused such a plague upon all his cattell, that they all immediatly perisht, & consumed, not one of that great store he had being left, to be a remembrance of the rest: himselfe shortly after did[22] these, & a number more at her triall were inferd against,[23] onely one more amongst the rest, though but a homely tale, for that it made al the Bench to laugh, Ile record of her, & conclude.[24]

How the Witch served a Fellow in an Alehouse.

THere was an honest Fellow, and as boone[25] a companion dwelling in **Royston**, one that loved the pot with the long necke almost as well as his prayers; for (quoth he) as I know one is medicinable for the soule, I am sure

17 As her brother.

18 Cambridge is ten miles north-east of Royston.

19 An unusually learned term: it most often referred to male demons who preyed sexually on humans, although there are connections with the idea of the Night-mare and the sense of being suffocated in one's sleep.

20 He'd – see also C4v.

21 Restored.

22 Died? The sense collapses completely here.

23 Alice Stokes was convicted of bewitching Richard Bland on 2 December 1605 so that he died on 25 April 1606, and also accused of bewitching John Rumbold in 1603 but acquitted. Witnesses John Rumbold and John Bland are recorded (Cockburn, *Calendar: Hertfordshire: James*, record 162, and Ewen, records 476 and 477). Christian Stokes was convicted of bewitching Roger Gybbons on 22 January 1606 so that he died on 9 June, and bewitching John Peirse alias Hogg in 1593 so that he died in 1594. She was acquitted of bewitching Jane Wakefeild in 1599. Witnesses were Jane Wakefeild, Judith Gybbons, Elizabeth Farron and James Youlden (Cockburn, *Calendar: Hertfordshire: James*, record 161, Ewen, records 478–80).

24 This story might possibly reflect a real event, but if so it is greatly elaborated into a typical jest. More likely, the introduction of a comic story as filler may suggest that the writer is bored with the material, or that it peters out at this point. There may also be compositors' errors here, with missing words.

25 Good, jolly.

the other's phisick for ye bodie.[26] It was this Fuddle caps chance with 3 or 4 as good Malt-wormes as himselfe, and as sure, where the best lap[27] was to be found, together as 4 Knaves in a payre[28] of cards, to be drinking, where this Witch came in, & stood gloting[29] upon them. Now this Good-fellow (not enduring to looke upon a bad face, but his owne, especially when he is Cup-shot[30]) called aloude to her, Doe you heare Witch, looke tother waies, I cannot abide a nose of that fashion, or else turne your face ye wrong side outward, it may look like raw flesh for flyes to blow maggots in. Stil as the {C4v} Witch was ready to reply, he would crosse her with one scurvy Jest, & between every Jest drinke to her, yet sweare, God dam him: she should starve ere she should have a drop on't, since the pot was sweet hee'd keepe it so, for should but her lips once looke into the lid on't, her breath's so strong, & would so stick in the cup, that all the water yt runs by **Ware**[31] would not wash it out again. At last the witch got so much time to cal to him, Doest thou heare good friend (quoth she) that thou throwst in thy drink apace, but shall not find it so easie comming out. Nay, as for the comming out (answerd the fellow) I throwd it in above, & it shal come out beneath, & then thou shalt have some of it, if thou wilt, because I am in hope it will poyson thee. Then with this greeting away goes the Witch in a chafe, & the fellow sits down to follow his drink, but as the end of all drunkards, is either to ming[32] or to sleepe. So out goes this fellow, & drawing his Gentleman Usher against a pale side,[33] finds me a top of his nose[34] a red lump as big as a cherry, & in his belly felt such a rumbling, as if the Tower of **Babell** had falne about his eares: oh the sight thereof drave his hart to an ague, & his tongue to an alarum and out he cries, the Witch, the Witch, I am undone, I am undone: O God, women of **Royston**, helpe, helpe, the Witch, the Wicth,[35] I am a man spoyld, helpe, I am undone. At that word help, the Wich,[36] in comes one of his fellowes runs in hast, & asked him

26 The change of tone to irreligious and bawdy joking, the colloquialisms and slang terms, suggest a snippet from another genre becoming part of an otherwise reasonably solemn account. The comic potential of witchcraft is interesting: it follows the horrific murder account as a kind of lighthearted conclusion of the 'and finally' variety still common in news broadcasts. As such it suggests further flexibility in writing about witchcraft and how we might read it.

27 Drink, liquor.

28 Pack.

29 Looking sullenly or furtively, frowning.

30 Drunk – with an interesting verbal link to 'elf-shot', meaning that the sufferer is afflicted by fairies and sometimes therefore by witches.

31 A town two miles east of Hertford, on the River Mimram.

32 Urinate.

33 Fence.

34 Clearly a euphemism for penis.

35 *Sic.*

36 *Sic.*

what they should helpe the Witch? Oh (quoth he) to the gallowes, for I am undone by her.[37] Well, yet out he runs, wherefor that night she would not be found, but the next morning meeting her in a lane, his pain rather increased, than lesned, & there fasts[38] his ten commandements[39] upon her, he almost scratcht out her eyes: nay, left her not till he brought her to ye towne, where for this and the rest, she was apprehended, and she and her daughter, with **George Dell** and his Mother, worthily suffered death the 4 of August.[40]

FINIS.

37 This is a standard joke: 'help! the witch' is mistaken for 'help the witch' and answered accordingly by the straight man here.

38 An archaic form of 'fastens'.

39 Fingers.

40 The assizes began on 1 August 1606 and this is a likely execution date.

12

The Witches of Northamptonshire (1612)

This pamphlet is the meeting point of a number of different discourses in writing about witchcraft. It is, for example, clearly related to contemporary accounts of possession. *The Most strange and admirable discoverie* (1593), one such account, deals with the supposed witchcraft attack made on the Throckmorton family of Warboys (in Huntingdonshire) by mother, father and daughter of the Samuel family. 'Mother' Alice Samuel was employed by the victims, and their children first accused her of causing their fits and trances, before widening their denunciations to include her husband and daughter. *The Witches of Northamptonshire* picks up some of the themes of the Warboys pamphlet: motiveless attack on virtuous victims, bewitchment/possession of wealthy people by their social inferiors, inter-familial conflict, witchcraft as an inherited crime, order and godliness versus disorder and vice. Gilbert Pickering, the witch-hunting uncle of the victims of Warboys, makes a reappearance. He attempted diagnostic experiments with the suspected witches and the children in the early 1590s, and these are echoed here, twenty years later, in his attempt to try the Bill family by the swimming test. The reporting of events is similar in each work too: narrative accounts of events interspersed with comment, and without much recourse to documentary proofs. Whilst *The Most strange and admirable discoverie* is much longer and more thorough than the later pamphlet, *The Witches of Northamptonshire* shares the concerns, the godly frame of reference and the form of the earlier work.

The pamphlet is connected to several sources in similar ways: a manuscript account of the case tells a parallel although interestingly different story, whilst John Cotta, the Northamptonshire physician and writer on witchcraft, probably mentions the case in his *Triall of Witchcraft.*[1] Just as Cotta was concerned with trial and experiment to establish the truth of witchcraft and possession, so the author of this pamphlet sometimes adopts an inquiring scientific tone. He balances

1 BL Sloane 972, fo. 7 (in the British Library) and John Cotta, *The Triall of Witchcraft* (London, 1616), 67. The relationship between this pamphlet and the MS is discussed in greater depth in Marion Gibson, 'Devilish Sin and Desperate Death: Northamptonshire Witches in Print and Manuscript', in *Northamptonshire Past and Present* 51 (1998), 15–21.

godly inquiry into the nature of witches with natural philosophy and historical references, and also quotes (without attribution) from George Gifford and King James on demonology. He is thus a minor demonologist in his own right, interpreting the theories of the great and good to fit his own knowledge of local circumstance, popular report and individual stories about witches. Like the Warboys pamphleteers and other writers of narrative accounts of witchcraft, he has a lively sense of social difference, and the chaos brought about by its breakdown in witchcraft attack. And like the author of the manuscript account, he is interested in stories from the trial and gossip surrounding it, but not in pre-trial documents. Discourses about witchcraft interest him more than recorded historical specifics such as dates, charges and courtroom procedure. The pamphlet thus focuses attention on some of the changes which have occurred in the reporting of witchcraft events since 1566. Both in its preface and main text, it also suggests growing tension over demonological beliefs, disbelief in witchcraft, and questioning of the judiciary and other authority (a trend which continues in *The Wonderful Discovery of the Witchcrafts of Margaret and Phillip Flower* (1619) and Henry Goodcole's *The wonderfull discoverie of Elizabeth Sawyer* (1621)). The author mounts a vigorous attack on 'Oppositors' of the *status quo*, as part of a genuinely thoughtful engagement with debate about witchcraft – as also does the 1619 pamphleteer. As accounts of witchcraft become personal narratives rather than edited reproductions of legal records, educated individuals are seen grappling with the problems presented by their subject and public reaction to it.

The quarto was licensed on 16 October 1612 to Arthur Johnson of St Paul's Churchyard and printed by Thomas Purfoot of Newgate and his son, who were involved in producing the account of Joan Harrison in 1606. The text used here is in the Bodleian Library. Trial records no longer exist, but it seems likely that the pamphleteer picked up information from the margins of the trial and wove it, together with gossip (apparently distorted as in Chinese whispers), into a semi-coherent account. He seems well read and confident of his rhetorical skills, but there is no evidence to point to his identity.

{A2 (title page)} THE WITCHES *OF* NORTHAMPTONSHIRE.
Agnes Browne. Arthur Bill.
Joane Vaughan. Hellen Jenkenson Witches
Mary Barber.
Who were all executed at *Northampton* the 22. of *July last.* 1612.
LONDON, Printed by *Tho. Purfoot,* for *Arthur Johnson.* 1612.
{A2v blank}
{A3} **THE ARRAIGNMENT, Conviction and execu***tion of certaine Witches at* **Northampton,** *the* 22. *of* **July last past.**

AMongest the rest of sinnes where-with the perfection of God is most of all displeased in the corruption of man, There is none (I suppose) more distastfull or detestable to his Purity, then this damnable and Devillish sinne of

Witchcraft; For that it seemes to make an eternall seperation, and an irreconciliable divorce betwixt the pure Mercies of God, and the tainted soules of such miserable people: Who for the most part, as they are of the meanest, and the basest sort both in birth and breeding, so they are the most uncapable of any instruction to the contrary, and of all good meanes to reclaime them.

{A3v} But as there are many, that remaine yet in doubt whether there be any Witches, or no, or any such spirits, who offer their service unto them, or rather who by fained service do tyrannize over them: So to answere their doubts, would aske a greater labour, and perhaps more art, and better experience then I intend, or happily can shew. Onely this, that if neither those confutations that are already learnedly set forth, Nor ancient records of the Witches called **Druides**, in old time confinde into the Isle of **Man**, nor the ordinary reportes of the strange mischiefes done by the Witches of **Norway** might seeme sufficient proofes of this matter:[2] Yet mee thinkes that the common experience, which our learned and Reverend Judges of the Land, finde daily in their yeerely Circuites by the convictions of such offendors, and the plaine and manifest Evidences brought in against them, who being in this this[3] kinde dangerously infected, have from time to time stood foorth upon their Arraignement, and as their lives have beene held to bee the most detestable, so their deathes have beene observed to prove the most desperate, might put it out of question, that some such there be abroad in the world, who by the damnable practise of Witch-craft have sold themselves to the Devils servies. In regard whereof I may conclude, that either it must be granted that there are Witches both in name, and nature, or else the **Oppositors**, that being (I suppose) more precise then wise, standing rather upon the singularity of their owne opinions, then the certainty of Reason or Judgement, must needs doe palpable wrong and open Injury to the discretions, or consci-{A4}-ences of our learned Judges, and the power and vertue of our Lawes, in the execution of Justice, making that hated, and unheard off[4] Tyranny, which is done by the lawfull power and vertue both of the **Soveraigne**, and Subordinate authority.

2 The conflation of witches with druids presumably implies shared paganism, magical priestcraft and bloodthirstiness – Celtic human sacrifice had been routinely deplored since Roman times. But it also implies a connection in the writer's mind between an 'old religion' and a modern crime – a matter of hot debate in recent times (see for example Carlo Ginzburg, *Ecstasies*, trans. Raymond Rosenthal [London: Hutchinson Radius, 1990]). As in England, witchcraft became a matter of increasing concern in Norway in the late sixteenth century. For Norwegian cases see Hans Eyvind Naess, 'Norway: The Criminological Context' in Bengt Ankarloo and Gustav Henningsen, eds, *Early Modern European Witchcraft* (1990; Oxford: Clarendon Press, 1993), 367–82. The writer's concern as a demonologist is unusual: the history and geography of witchcraft.

3 *Sic.*

4 *Sic.*

Some doe maintaine (but how wisely let the wiser judge) that all Witchcraft spoken of either by holy writers, or testified by other writers to have beene among the heathen or in later daies, hath beene and is no more but either meere Cousinage, or Collusion, so that in the opinion of those men, the Devill hath never done, nor can do any thing by Witches. It may be, some will say, what hurt can grow from this opinion? The hurt that may ensue and grow thereof, none can tell that hath not first seene somewhat by experience. Wee all see that one kernell of Wheat being sowne, a whole eare growes up, and sometimes brings forth an hundreth kernils in it. If an error be planted, who can tell what increase it may yeild in time? The ground doth not bring forth the corne with such increase as the heart of Man doth errors. If we draw in one linke of a Chaine, another followes, and is by and by in sight, which draweth wee knowe not how many after it, untill we see the last. There is no Error that goeth alone, or that is not linked unto another. That holy Wrytte therefore (which makes the Man of God perfect and perfectly instructed unto every good worke) must judge and decide the controversie in this case. Let us then sticke unto the same for testimony and proofe.

{A4v} **What a Witch is, and the Antiquity of Witchcraft.**

TO know things aright and perfectly, is to know the causes thereof. A **Definition** doth consist of those causes which give the whole Essence, and containe the perfect nature of the thing defined: where that is therefore found out, there appeares the very cleere light. If it be perfect, it is much the greater, though it be not fully perfect, yet it giveth some good light.

For which respect though I dare not say, I can give a perfect Definition in this matter, which is hard to doe even in knowne things, because the Essentiall forme is hard to be found, yet I doe give a Definition, which may at the least give notice, and make knowne what manner of Persons they be, of whom I am to speake. A Witch is one that worketh by the Devill, or by some Devillish or Curious Art, either hurting or healing, revealing things secret, or foretelling things to come, which the Devill hath devised to entangle, and snare mens soules withall, unto damnation.[5] The **Conjurer**, the **Enchaunter**, the **Sorcerer**, the **Deviner**, and whatsoever other sort there is, are indeed compassed within this circle. The Devill doth (no doubt) after divers sorts, and divers formes deale in these: But no man is able to shew an Essentiall difference in each of them from the rest.

{B} I hold it no wisedome, or labour well spent to travell much therein: One Artificer hath devised them all. They are all to one end and purpose, howsoever they much differ in outward Rules for practise of them, that is little or nothing besides meere delusion. Every Man will confesse that the father of lies is not to be trusted. Every man knowes that all his dooings are hidden under coulorable shewes. Shall wee then seeke for stedfastnes in his wayes?

5 This is George Gifford's definition from *A Discourse of the Subtill Practises of Devilles by Witches and Sorcerers* (1587), B2.

shall wee be so foolish as to imagine that things are effected by the vertue of words, gestures, figures, or such like? All those are doubtlesse but to deceive, and draw men forward, and so plung them more deepely into sinnes, and errors.

Touching the Antiquity of Witchcraft, wee must needs confesse that it hath beene of very ancient time, because the Scriptures doe testifie so much, for in the time of **Moses** it was very rife in **Egipt**, Neither was it then newly sprong up, beeing common, and growne unto such ripenes among the Nations, that the Lord reckoning up divers kinds, saith that the Gentiles did commit such abhominations, for which hee would cast them out before the Children of **Israel**. How long it was before that time cannot for certainty be discussed: Saving that (as is sayd) it was not young in those daies when **Moses** wrote. If wee mainetaine that it was before the flood, there is great reason to justify the Assertion. Wee know that the Devill was exceeding crafty from the beginning, alwaies laboring to seduce, and deceive after the worst manner. If he fayled of his desire, it was because Men had not procured Gods displeasure to {Bv} come upon them, to deliver them over unto strange delusions, but God complaineth, that men had wonderfully corrupted their waies, long before the Flood:[6] God beeing then provoked by the wickednesse of the world, what should make us doubt but that through his Just judgement the Devill had power given him and was let loose, that he might seduce, and lead the prophane Nations into the depth and gulfe of all abhominable sinnes? Thus much concerning the certainety of Witches, and the Antiquity of Witchcraft, This that followes shall in some sort shew their Divillish practises.

{B2} **The Arraignement and Execution of** *Agnes Browne*, **and** *Joane Vaughan* **or** *Varnham* **his**[7] **daughter, who were both executed at Northampton the 22. of July last.**

THis **Agnes Browne** led her life at **Gilsborough**[8] in the county of **Northampton**, of poore parentage and poorer education, one that as shee was borne to no good, was for want of grace never in the way to receive any, ever noted to bee of an ill nature and wicked disposition, spightfull and malitious, and many yeeres before shee died both hated, and feared among her neighbours: Beeing long suspected in the Towne where she dwelt of that crime, which afterwards proved true. This **Agnes Browne** had a daughter whose name was **Joane Vaughan** *or* **Varnham** a maide (or at least unmaried) as gratious as the mother, and both of them as farre from grace as Heaven from hell.

This **Joane** was so well brought up under her mothers elbow, that shee hangd with her for company under her mothers nose.[9] But to the purpose. This

6 Genesis 6.5.

7 The daughter of Varnham.

8 A town eight miles north-west of Northampton.

9 Is this vicious sentence really written by the thoughtful prefacer? We clearly need to see

Joane one day happening into the company {B2v} of one Mistris **Belcher**, a vertuous and godly Gentlewoman of the same towne of **Gilsborough.**[10] This **Joane Vaughan**, whether of purpose to give occasion of anger to the said Mistris **Belcher**, or but to continue her vilde, and ordinary custome of behaviour, committed something either in speech, or gesture, so unfitting, and unseeming the nature of woman-hood, that it displeased the most that were there present: But especially it touched the modesty of this Gentlewoman, who was so much mooved with her bold, and impudent demeanor, that shee could not containe her selfe, but sodainely rose up and strooke her, howbeit hurt her not, but forced her to avoide the company: which this Chicken of her Dammes hatching, taking disdainefully and beeing also enraged (as they that in this kind having power to harme, have never patience to beare) at her going out told the Gentlewoman that shee would remember this injury, and revenge it: To whom Mistris **Belcher** answered, that shee neither feared her nor her mother: but bad her doe her worst.

This trull[11] holding her selfe much disgraced, hies home in all hast to her mother, and telles her the wrong, which shee suggested Mistris **Belcher** had done unto her: Now was the fire, and the tow met, all was enflamed: Nothing but rage and destruction: Had they an hundred Spirits at command, the worst, and the most hurtfull had beene called to this counsell, and imployed about this businesse. Howbeit upon advise (if such a sinne may take or give advise) they staied three or foure daies before they practised any thing, to avoide {B3} suspition, whether the mother advised the daughter, or the daughter the mother I know not, but I am sure the devill never gives advise to any man or woman in any act to be wary.[12]

The matter thus sleeping (but rage and revenge doe never rest) within a while was awaked, which Mistris **Belcher** to her intollerable paine too soone felt: For being alone in her house, she was sodainely taken with such a griping, and gnawing in her body, that shee cried out, and could scarce bee held by such as came unto her, And being carried to her bed her face was

belief in witchcraft, and discussion of it, as a complex of ideas and rhetorical moves which could easily encompass such diverse expressions as crude jokes, empirical inquiry and pious exegesis.

10 Elizabeth Belcher was the wife of Dabriscourt Belcher or Belchier (?1580–1621), gentleman dramatist and traveller to the Low Countries where he settled in the early seventeenth century (*DNB*). His absence from this account is striking – his wife relies on her brother for help when she becomes ill.

11 Trollop, strumpet.

12 It is passages such as this – imaginative 'reconstructions', whimsical speculation and moral reflection – which set later Elizabethan and Jacobean pamphlets apart from earlier ones before 1590. In particular, they characterise the third-person narrative accounts which largely replace pamphlets using legal documents – but even Potts, a 'traditional' pamphleteer in the later era, relies on them. It is as if the preface has leaked into the main text, and witchcraft must now be commented on ceaselessly to contain it, frame it artfully and ensure right interpretation.

many times so disfigured by beeing drawn awrie that it bred both feare, and astonishment to all the beholders, and ever as shee had breath, she cried, **Heere comes** *Joane Vaughan*, **away with** *Joane Vaughan*.

This Gentlewoman beeing a long time thus strangely handled, to the great griefe of her friends, it happened that her brother one Master **Avery**, hearing of his Sisters sicknesse and extremity came to see her, and beeing a sorrowfull beholder, of that which before hee had heard, was much mooved in his minde at his Sisters pittifull condition, and the rather for that as hee knew not the nature of her disease, so hee was utterly ignorant of any direct way to minister cure or helpe to the same. Hee often heard her cry out against **Joane Vaughan** alias **Varnham**, and her mother, and heard by report of the neighbours that which before had happened betwixt his Sister, and the said **Joane**: In so much as having confirmed his suspition that it was nothing else but Witch-craft that thus {B3v} tormented his Sister, following Rage rather then Reason, ranne sodainely towards the house of the said **Agnes Browne** with purpose to draw both the mother and the daughter to his Sister for her to draw bloud on:[13] But still as hee came neere the house, hee was sodainely stopped, and could not enter, whether it was an astonishment thorough his feare, or that the Spirits had that power to stay him I cannot judge, but hee reported at his comming backe that hee was forcibly staied, and could not for his life goe any further forward, and they report in the Country that hee is a Gentleman of a stoute courage: Hee tried twice or thrice after to goe to the house, but in the same place where hee was staied at first, hee was still staied: Belike the devill stood there Centinell, kept his station well.

Upon this Master **Avery** beeing sory and much agrieved that hee could not helpe his Sister in this tormenting distresse, and finding also that no physicke could doe her any good or easement, tooke a sorrowfull leave and heavily departed home to his owne house.

The Impe of this Damme, and both Impes of the Devill, beeing glad that they were both out of his reach, shewed presently that they had longer armes then he, for he felt within a short time after his comming home that hee was not out of their reach, beeing by the devillish practises of these two helhounds sodenly & grievously tormented in the like kind & with the like fits of his sister, which continued untill these two witches either by the procurement of {B4} Maister **Avery** and his friends (or for some other Divillish practise they had committed in the countrey) were apprehended, and brought to **Northampton** Gaole by Sir **William Saunders** of **Codesbrooke**[14] knight.[15]

13 The traditional remedy for witchcraft attack. See B4 for a discussion of its efficacy.

14 The Saunders were a Protestant family living at Cottesbrooke, a few miles east of Guilsborough.

15 Such precision following such vagueness is unusual and suggests a variety of sources for this account, probably including committal documents and gossip.

To which place the Brother and the Sister were brought still desirous to scratch the Witches. Which Art whether it be but superstitiously observed by some, or that experience hath found any power for helpe in this kind of Action by others, I list not to enquire, onely this I understand that many have attempted the practising thereof, how successively[16] I know not. But this Gentleman and his Sister beeing brought to the gaole where the Witches were detained, having once gotten sight of them, in their fits the Witches being held, by scratching they drew blood of them, and were sodainely delivered of their paine. Howbeit they were no sooner out of sight, but they fell againe into their old traunces, and were more violently tormented then before: for when Mischiefe is once a foote, she growes in short time so headstrong, that she is hardly curbed.

Not long after Maister **Avery** and his Sister having beene both in **Northampton** and having drawne blood of the Witches, Ryding both homewards in one Coach, there appeared to their view a man and a woman ryding both upon a blacke horse, M. **Avery** having spyed them a farre off, and noting many strange gestures from them, sodainely spake to them that were by, and (as it were Prophetically) cryed out in these words, That either they or their Horses should presently miscarry, And imediately the horses {B4v} fell downe dead.[17] Whereupon Maister **Avery** rose up praysing ye grace and mercies of God, that he had so powerfully delivered them, and had not suffered the foule spirits to worke the uttermost of their mischiefe upon men made after his image, but had turned their fury against Beasts. Upon this, they both hyed them home, still praysing God for their escape, and were never troubled after.

I had almost forgotten to tell you before,[18] that M. **Avery** was by the Judges themselves in ye Castle yard of **Northampton**, seene in the middest of his fits, and that he strangely continued in them untill this **Joane Vaughan** was brought unto him.[19]

But now to draw neere unto their ends, this **Agnes Browne** and her daughter **Joane Vaughan**, or **Varneham** beeing brought to their Arraignement, were there indighted for that they had bewitched the bodies of Maister **Avery** and his sister Mistris **Belcher** in manner and forme aforesayd, Together with the

16 Successfully.

17 This confusing episode is constructed differently, and with more and clearer detail, in the MS account. In the MS, Master Avery fears for his safety and at that moment another man's horse falls down dead on the highway ahead of the party. The other man's wife also becomes ill with fits.

18 This indication of hasty or confused construction suggests (together with the admission further down B4v that one story did not come into the writer's hands) a collection of variously sourced stories about the case, put together with little interest in chronology. The last few anecdotes – from this point onwards – seem likely to be culled from gossip.

19 The MS gives a much fuller account of Avery and Belcher in their fits at the assizes. This suggests that the MS author may have been present, whilst the pamphleteer is relying on fragments of hearsay for his account.

body of a young Child to the death (the true relation whereof came not to my hands) To all which they pleaded not guilty, and putting themselves upon the couutrey[20] were found guilty. And when they were asked what they could say for themselves, why ye sentence of death should not be pronounced against them, they stood stiffely upon their Innocence. Whereupon Judgement beeing given, they were carried backe unto the Gaole, where they were never heard to pray, or to call uppon God, but with bitter curses and execrations spent that little time they had to live, untill the day of their Execution, when never asking pardon for their offences either of God, or the world, in this {C} their daungerous, and desperate resolution, dyed.

It was credibly reported that some fortnight before their apprehension, this **Agnes Browne**, one **Ratherine**[21] **Gardiner**, and one **Joane Lucas**, all birds of a winge, and all abyding in the Towne of **Gilsborough** did ride one night to a place (not above a mile off) called **Ravenstrop**,[22] all upon a Sowes backe, to see one mother **Rhoades**, an old Witch that dwelt there, but before they came to her house the old Witch died, and in her last cast cried out, that there were three of her old friends comming to see her, but they came too late. Howbeit shee would meete with them in another place within a month after. And thus much concerning **Agnes Browne**, and her daughter **Joane Varnham**.[23]

{Cv} **The Arraignement, Conviction and Execution of one** *Arthur Bill* **of** *Raundes* **in the County of Northampton.**

THis **Arthur Bill**, a wretched poore Man, both in state and mind, remained in a towne called **Raunds**[24] in the County aforesayd, begotten and borne of parents that were both Witches, and he (like a gratious Child) would not degenerate, nor suffer himselfe to stray from his fathers wicked Counsels, but carefully trode the steps that hee had divillishly taught him.

This **Arthur Bill** was accused that he should bewitch the body of one **Martha Aspine** alias **Jeames**, the daughter of one **Edward Aspine** of the same towne, to death. But this matter remaining doubtfull that it could not be cleerely tryed upon him, hee beeing strongly suspected before, by bewitching of di-{C2}-vers kinds of cattle, to be guilty of that crime, And beeing also publiquely knowne to bee of an evill life and reputation, together with his father and mother. The Justices and other officers (thereby purposing to trie the said

20 *Sic.* The compositor quite often uses letters upside down and this is probably an example.

21 *Sic.*

22 Ravensthorpe, two miles south of Guilsborough.

23 This episode is described in the MS as a *vision* of Master Avery's, not a real event, and the witches involved were Alce Abbott, Catherine Gardiner and Alce Harrys. All these witches are discussed in the MS. Browne and Vaughan were, it says, jointly indicted for the attack on Avery and Belcher, with Gardiner, Joane or Jane Lucas, Harrys, and Abbott. Some other accusations are reported against the last three. An indictment (for killing animals) against three women named Wilson is also reported. But the MS does not deal with the three other witches which the pamphlet now goes on to discuss.

24 About eighteen miles north-east of Northampton.

Arthur by an experiment that (many thinke) never failes) caused them all to bee bound, and their Thumbes and great Toes to bee tied acrosse, and so threw the father, mother and sonne, and none of them sunke, but all floated upon the water.

And hereby the way, it is a speciall thing worthy generall noting and observation, that there are two signes or tokens which are tokens as more certaine, then others, to detect and find out Witches by. The one is the marke where the Spirits sucke, and the trying of the insensiblenesse thereof. The other is their fleeting on the water. Concerning which though I dare affirme nothing for certainty, there beeing (for ought I know) neither evident proofe in nature, nor revelation from heaven to assure us thereof: yet mee thinkes I may say the like of this, as is held of the bleeding of a slaine body in presence of the mutherer.[25] For as in a secret murther, if the dead Carkase bee at any time either seene or handled by the murtherer, it doth streitway gush out of blood, as if the blood should by issuing foorth in such strange manner cry unto heaven for revenge of the murtherer, God having as may seeme appointed, that secret supernaturall signe for triall of that secret unnaturall crime, that the blood left in the body should thus appeare, {C2v} and as it were challenge the murtherer, for that blood which hee before had felloniously stollen from the body: so it may bee, that God hath appointed (for a supernaturall signe of the monstrous impiety of Witches) that the Element of water should refuse to receive them in her bosome, that have shaken from them the sacred water of Baptisme, and wilfully refused the benefit thereof by making that breach and fall from God in participating thus vildly with the Spirits of **Beliall**: By whom and in the exercise of which sinne, their hearts are so hardened, that not so much as their eyes are able to shead teares, threaten or torture them as you please: God not permitting them as may bee thought to dissemble their obstinacy in so horrible a crime; No not the women, though that sex bee ready to shead teares upon every light occasion: But to returne to our matter.[26]

These three, the Father, Mother and Sonne, beeing thus seene floating upon the water, the suspition that was before not well grounded, was now confirmed: Whereupon the said **Arthur Bill** beeing the principall or (I thinke) the onely Actor in this Tragedy, was apprehended and sent to **Northampton** gaole the nine and twentith[27] day of May last by Sir **Gilbert Pickering** of **Tichmash** alias **Tichmase**[28] in the same County knight,[29] and presently after

25 *Sic.*

26 This section is full of quotations from King James's *Daemonologie* (Edinburgh, 1597), 80–1.

27 *Sic.*

28 Titchmarsh, a village five miles north of Raunds. Gilbert Pickering, related by marriage to the Throckmortons of Warboys, was a gentleman of Puritan leanings – see *The most strange and admirable discoverie* (1593).

29 Again this suggests access to a committal record, whilst the rest of the account is much less specific, and must often be based on speculation and imaginative storytelling. This pattern continues through the final two cases reported here.

his commitment fearing that his old father would relent, and so happily[30] confesse that which might bee prejudiciall unto him, sent for his mother to come unto him, to whom bewraying his {C3} minde, they both joyned together, and bewitched a round ball into the Throat of his Father, where it continued a great while, his Father not beeing able to speake a word. Howbeit the ball was afterwards had out, and his Father prooved the principall witnesse against him.

His Mother for feare of hanging, (not any hatred, or detestation shee bare unto the sinne) many times fainted, and would often pitifully complaine unto her Spirit, that the power of the Law would bee stronger then the power of her art, and that she saw no other likelihood, but that shee should be hanged as her Sonne was like to bee: to whom her Spirit answered, giving this sorry comfort, that shee should not bee hanged, but to prevent that, shee should cut her owne throate: Shee hearing this sentence, and holding it definitive, in great agony, and horror of minde and conscience fell a raving, crying out that the irrevocable Judgement of her death was given and that shee was damned perpetually, cursing and banning the time wherein shee was borne, and the houre wherein she was conceived.

Her Neighbours often hearing her bitter execrations bad her call upon God, and to be sorry for the sinnes which shee had committed, But shee could in no case endure to heare it: And having thus for 3. or 4. daies tormented her selfe in this Agony, at last she made good the Devils word, and to prevent the Justice of the Law, and to save the hangman a labour, cut her owne throat.

Her Sonne beeing all this while in prison, and {C3v} hearing of his Mothers death, and that his Father was become a witnesse against him, was much perplexed in his minde, that his Mother was dead, in whom he most trusted, and his Father living, whom he most feared, Howbeit hee stiffly stood still in the deniall of every thing, pleading nothing but his innoceney,[31] Notwithstanding that hee had before at unawares confest, that he had certaine Spirits at commaund, which being imployed, would doe any mischiefe to any man, woman or child that hee would appointe.

It is said that hee had three Spirits to whom hee gave three speciall names, the Divell himselfe sure was godfather to them all., The first hee called **Grissill**, The other was named **Ball**, and the laste **Jacke**, but in what at[32] shapes they appeered unto him I cannot learne. For Divels can appeere both in a bodily shape, and use speech and conference with men. Our Saviour saith, **That a Spirit hath neither flesh nor bones**:[33] A Spirit hath a substance, but yet such as is invisible, whereupon it must needes bee granted, that

30 Perhaps (haply).
31 *Sic.*
32 *Sic.*
33 Luke 24.39.

Devils in their owne nature have no bodily shape nor visible forme, it is moreover against the Truth and against Piety to beleeve, that Devils can create, or make bodies or change one body into another, for those things are proper to God.
It followeth therefore that whensoever they appeare in a visible form, it is no more but an apparition and counterfeit shew of a body, unlesse a body be at any time lent them. And when they make one body {C4} to beare the likenes of another, it is but a colour. Some man will say, what reason is there to shew they can doe so much, beeing of an essence invisible? Wee may not stay heere within the limits of our owne reason, which is not able to comprehend, what way Devills should be able to worke such operations. Wee may not (I say) measure their power, and subtilties in working for our owne capacity and understanding: But wee must looke what the Cannon of Scripture doth testify in this behalfe. Wee have manifest proofe that the Devill can take a bodily shape. For when **Aaron** had cast downe his staffe, and it was turned into a Serpent, The enchaunters of **Egypt** cast downe their staves, and they became Serpents,[34] which was indeed but in shew, and appearance, which the Devill made, For he deluded the Sences both in hiding the forme of the Staves, which indeed were not any way changed: As also in making a shew of such bodies, as were not. This was done openly, otherwise it might be thought to be a meere illusion. For wee see that men in extreame sickenes, thinke they heare a voice, and see a shape, which none other in presence either heareth or seeth, some are so melancholy that they imagine they heare and see that which they doe not: For Sathan doth so delude the fantasie, that the party supposeth that his very outward sences doe perceive the matter: But heere was no such thing. All that were with **Pharao** did thinke there were very Serpents in deede, Saving that **Moses** and **Aaron** did know it the jugling of the Devill.
But to returne to this **Arthur Bill**: Hee (mise-{C4v}-rable man) lying in prison from the 29 day of May to the 22 of July following, many resorted to him, willing him to leave off all colour and dissimulation, and not to suffer his Conscience to double with his Tongue, But to cleere his heart and his thoughts before the Majestie of him, to whome no secrets are hid, That the world might be witnesse of his confession and contrition to pray with him and for him, For although hee had wandred and gone astray, hee might by his true contrition and their hearty prayers bee brought unto the fold againe.
But his Conscience beeing feared, and his heart steeld, could receive no impression, but stood like an Image of Adamant, more easy to be broken in peeces, then bee peirced. In this obduracie of mind and Spirit hee continued untill the Assises where beeing Arraigned for severall crimes committed, but especially for the Murther of the sayd **Martha Aspine**, contrary to the peace of our

34 Exodus 7.

Soveraigne Lord the King, his Crowne, and dygnity, hee pleaded to them all not guilty, and putting himselfe upon the Countrey, was by them found guilty. Uppon the verdict whereof, his countenance changed, and he cried out, that he had now found the Law to have a Power above Justice, for that it had condemned an Innocent.[35]

It seemes to me that these vilde Spirits, which these Witches have at commaund, and by their imployment are suffred to have power to hurt the bodyes of others, have a greater Power over them that set them a worke, For they doe not onely feed uppon them participating with the blood of humane {D} flesh for the redemption wherof Christ shed his owne precious blood, But it appeares that they have also power even over their Soules, leading them into wandring by-waies, and such erroneous Laberinths, that in the wilfull obstinacie and perverse sufferance of their owne minds to stray in this daungerous desart of obduracie, they are lost for ever.

But to conclude with this **Arthur Bill**, that so ill concluded with the world, He beeing brought to the place of Execution, and standing uppon that fatall stage for offenders, pleaded still his innocencie, that Authority was turned into Tyranny, and Justice into extreame Injury, to the great wonder, and disdaine of all the lookers on.

Thus with a dissembling Tongue and a corrupted Conscience, hee ended his course in this world, with little hope or respect (as it seemd) of the world to come.

{Dv} **The Arraignement, and Execution of** *Hellen Jenkenson.*

THis **Helen Jenkenson** dwelling at a Towne called **Thrapston**[36] in the County of **Northampton**, was noted a long time to be of an evill life and much suspected of this crime before her apprehension, for bewitching of Cattle and other mischiefes, which before time she had done.

This **Helen** was apprehended for bewitching of a Child to death, and committed to **Northampton** Gaole the 11 of May last by Sir **Thomas Brooke** of **Okely**[37] Knight. A little before whose apprehension, one Mistris **Moulsho** of the same Towne (after she was so strongly suspected) getting her by a wyle into a place convenient would needs have her searched, to see if they could find that insensible marke which commonly all Witches have in some privy place or other of their bodies.[38] And this Mistris **Moulsho** was one of the chiefe that did search her, and found at the last that which they sought

35 This pamphleteer seems unusually tolerant of the conflict that surrounds witchcraft. He does not censor or unthinkingly condemn the views of 'Oppositors' (even the convicted), but reports and answers them in a way which is unlike anything else we have seen in accounts of trials. As a writer with some pretensions to being a demonologist, he is perhaps more open to debate about the abstract principles of witchcraft than a hack pamphleteer would have been, despite his crude sketches of the witches themselves.

36 A village four miles north of Raunds.

37 Oakley, a village ten miles north-west of Thrapston.

38 This is a variant on the search for a teat.

for to their great amazement: at that time this Mistris **Moulsho** had a Bucke[39] of clothes to be washt out. The next morning the Mayd, when shee came to hang {D2} them forth to dry, spyed the Cloathes, but especially Mistris **Moulshoes** Smocke to be all bespotted with the pictures of Toades, Snakes, and other ougly Creatures, which making her agast, she went presently and told her Mistris, who looking on them, smild, saying nothing else but this; Heere are fine Hobgoblins indeed: And beeing a Gentlewoman of a stout courage, went immediately to the house of the sayd **Helen Jenkenson**, and with an angry countenance told her of this matter, threatning her that if her Linnen were not shortly cleered from those foule spots, she would scratch out both her eyes: and so not staying for any answere went home, and found her linnen as white as it was at first. This **Helen** being brought to the barre, and beeing indicted of the murther of the Child, pleaded thereunto not guilty, but the verdict beeing given up against her, shee cryed out, woe is mee, I now cast away, But (like the rest) did stoutly deny the accusations, and sayd that she was to die an Innocent, I thinke as Innocent as the rest: And at the place of Execution made no other confession but this, That she was guiltlesse, and never shewd signe of Contrition for what was past, nor any sorrow at all, more then did accompany the feare of death. Thus ended this woman her miserable life, after she had lived many yeares poore, wretched, scorned, and forsaken of the world.

{D2v} [**The Arraignement and Execution of** *Mary Barber.*

THis **Mary Barber** of **Stanwicke**[40] in the said County of **Northampton** was one in whom the licentiousnesse of her passions grew to bee the Master of her Reason, and did so conquer in her strength and power of all vertue, that shee fell to the Apostasy of goodnesse, and became diverted, and abased[41] unto most vilde actions, cloathing her desperate soule, in the most ugly habiliments, that either Malice, Envy, or Cruelty could produce from the blindnesse of her degenerate, and devillish desires. As shee was of meane Parents, so was she monstrous and hideous, both in her life, and actions. Her education and barbarous nature never promising to the world any thing, but what was rude, violent, and without any hope of proportion, more then only in the square of viciousnesse. For out of the oblyvion, and blindnesse of her seduced sences, shee gave way to all the passionate, and earthly faculties of the flesh, and followed all the **Fantazmas** vanities, and **Chimeras** of her polluted and unreasonable delights, forsaking the Society of Grace, and growing enamored upon all the evil that Malice or Frenzy could minister to her vicious desires & intendments.

{D3} As appeared by her bewitching a man to death, and doing much other hurt and harme to divers sorts of cattle in the Country. For which shee was

39 A quantity of clothes, usually a basket, which are being bleached.

40 A village a mile south-west of Raunds.

41 Rosen reads 'abused' – either word is plausible (Rosen, 354).

committed to **Northampton** gaole the 6 day of May last by Sir **Thomas Tresham**,[42] and the same and many other matters beeing plainely and evidently manifest and proved against her by good evidence, shee had the sentence of death, worthily pronounced against her. In the time of her imprisonment she was not noted to have any remembrance or feeling of the haynousnesse of her offences or any remorsefull tongue of the dissolute and devillish course of her life.

The prison which makes men bee fellowes and chambermates with theeves, and murtherers (the common guests of such despised Innes) and should cause the imprisoned party, like a **Christian Arithmetician** to number and cast up the account of his whole life, never put her in minde of the hatefull transgressions she had committed, or to consider the filth and leprosie of her soule, or intreat heavens mercy for the release thereof. Prison put her not in minde of her grave, nor the grates and lockes put her in remembrance of hell, which deprived her of the joy of liberty, which she saw others possesse: The jangling of irons did not put her in minde of the chaines where with she should bee bound in eternall torments, unlesse heavens mercy unloosed them, nor of the howling terrors and gnashing of teeth, which in hel every soule shal receive for the particular offences committed in this life, without unfained & hearty contrition. She never remembred or thought] {D3v} she must die, or trembled for feare of what should come to her after death. But as her life was alwaies known to be devillish, so her death was at last found to be desperate. For she (& the rest before named) beeing brought from the common gaole of **Northampton** to **Northampton Castle**, where the Assises are usually held, were severally arraigned and indited for the offences they had formerly committed, but to the inditements they pleaded not guilty: Putting therefore their causes to the triall of the Country, they were found guilty and deserved death by the verdit[43] of a credible Jury returned. So without any confession or contrition, like birds of a feather, they all held and hanged together for company, at **Abington** gallowes hard by **Northampton**, the two and twintith[44] day of July last past: Leaving behinde them in prison many others tainted with the same corruption, who without much mercy and repentance are like to follow them in the same tract of Precedencie.[45]

FINIS.

42 Evidently the writer knows nothing else about Mary Barber. The Treshams were a large Catholic family, whose main seat was at Rushton. This they lost in 1614 through debt caused by involvement in the Gunpowder Plot (see Mary E. Finch, *The Wealth of Five Northamptonshire Families* [Oxford: Northamptonshire Record Society, 1956]).

43 *Sic.*

44 *Sic.*

45 These may be the witches dealt with in the manuscript.

13

Thomas Potts, *The Wonderfull Discoverie of Witches* (1612)

Thomas Potts's enormous quarto is probably the most famous account of English witches ever written, a fact reflected in the number of publications based on it, and the organising of a conference in April 1999, at St Martin's College, Lancaster, entirely devoted to it and the events it describes. This very long account, printed by William Stansby for John Barnes, exists in two editions: the one used here is the second, with its additional page of *errata* and Potts's full name (originally T.P. Esquier). A copy of the first edition, as well as the edition used here, is in the Bodleian Library. Entered in the Stationers' Register on 7 November 1612, the pamphlet is a unique recreation of the process of a witch-trial, and an instructive glimpse of the anxiety of the legal authorities to publish and justify their actions against these particular witches. It reverts firmly to the model of writing about witchcraft which involves the reproduction of legal documents.

There is no sense in other pamphlets of the urgency, and official sanction, which this pamphlet clearly shows was accorded to Potts's compilation of pre-trial and assize documents. Other witch-cases seem to be written up and printed by a combination of chance circumstances – an eager magistrate, vociferous victims, the acquisition of a report from a trial, or an incomplete set of examinations or informations, by a publisher. *The Wonderfull Discoverie of Witches* is different in that it appears to have been carefully planned, and effort made to collect and situate material to give the reader the most comprehensive possible account. This seems likely to be linked to the fact that the alleged plot by the Pendle witches to blow up Lancaster Castle was seen as a close parallel with the Catholic Gunpowder Plot of 1605.

In the care with which information was gathered and grouped, Potts makes *A true and just Recorde*, Brian Darcy/W.W.'s monumental account of pre-trial procedures, appear both skimpy and badly organised: no mean feat. The 1612 pamphlet blends traditional use of legal documents with a wholly modern desire to comment on the material presented, and to put a continual spin on it by interjections, in a way which Darcy's pamphlet did not do. It is also carefully ordered so that readers can follow the trial of each witch as if they had been present, adding suspense and building up the reader's sense of each witch's character and performance at the trial. Legal phrases are garnished with fancy fonts and trumpeted, with obsessive repetition, in gigantic lettering reminiscent of modern tabloid headlines. Thus the pamphlet has elements of demonology, propaganda and deliberate soap-opera drama as well as simple reportage.

However, although the reader may be impressed by the sense of historical re-enactment exuded by the pamphlet, she or he must also be wary of the devices used to create this effect. Substantial chunks of procedure, such as the grand jury stage, are omitted, and Potts routinely presents written pre-trial documents as an account of what went on verbally at the trial itself, which is clearly inaccurate. He frequently edits and pastes together material within examinations and informations, which destroys their internal coherence and logic and conceals patterns of questioning and storytelling – most obviously in the oft-repeated statements by Elizabeth, James and Jennet Device. Whole documents and parts of statements are missing, and evidence is sometimes oddly chosen, suggesting lost documents or wilfully concealed elements. Such omissions as are obliquely acknowledged should make us aware of those which are not. Despite the judge's assurances that the author's insertions are minimal and objective, this is also untrue – inserted comments demonise the witches ferociously, whilst the Salmesbury section of the pamphlet is pure anti-Catholic propaganda. The patron of the pamphlet was the erstwhile Sir Thomas Knyvet, who helped foil Guy Fawkes's intent to blow up Parliament. Thus the pamphlet is far from being a transparent 'record' of events in 1612.

Neither is the pamphlet a unified whole. The Pendle and Salmesbury cases are clearly separate, and cases at Padiham and Windle are also added – whilst the material on Yorkshire witch Jennet Preston may be by another author altogether. This section is tacked on after Potts's carefully planned peroration, its tone is far more assertive that Potts's, and it has a more explicit focus on claims of injustice in the north of England than does the main body of the text. Puzzlingly, the pamphleteer clearly only had access to documents from the Lancaster assizes, and not from York. This makes the Preston account an enigmatic conclusion to a pamphlet already stuffed with matters for textual debate.

There are a great number of books, booklets, articles and theses dealing with aspects of the events described by Potts. Many are short, accessible summaries written for readers interested in local history, and curious tourists. They are sometimes more reliant on myth rather than on researched account, although each approach has something to offer the reader – often a unique retelling of events. Walter Bennett's *The Pendle Witches* (1957; Preston: Lancashire County Books, 1993) blames Elizabeth Chattox (briefly mentioned by Potts) for sparking off the persecution by 'spiteful accusations' (7). Richard Catlow's *The Pendle Witches* (Nelson: Hendon Publishing, 1976) is illustrated with a photograph of 'Demdike and Chattox – Satan's consorts'. Taken from a 1970's BBC film, they are looking sinister on a bridge, with a dead goose. Robert Neill's entertaining novel *Mist over Pendle* has Roger Nowell as its hearty hero and explains what might have happened by reference to Puritanism, papistry and poisoning (London: Hutchinson, 1951). However, there are also solid scholarly studies of the events. The first modern account was James Crossley's introduction to his 1845 edition of *The Wonderfull Discoverie*, published by the Chetham Society (Old Series, vol. 6). It contains most of the historical discoveries to be made about the case, and records some of the unverifiable stories with scholarly Victorian firmness. The best account of the Lancashire witchcraft trials is Edgar Peel and Pat Southern's incisive, accurate and sensible *The Trials of the Lancashire Witches*, now in its fourth edition (1969; Nelson: Hendon Publishing, 1994). Readers are referred to this throughout the notes where a reference is considered helpful, for although many accounts of the case contain similar material there is no synthesis so well researched and written. The best account of the Yorkshire events is Jonathan Lumby, *The Lancashire Witch-craze: Jennet Preston and the Lancashire Witches 1612* (Preston: Carnegie Publishing, 1995). Despite its pleasantly dramatic imagination and its conspiracy theory surrounding Jennet Preston and the Listers, this is an intelligent and well-researched account full of thought-provoking ideas.

Chronology of the Pendle, Salmesbury, Windle, Padiham and Gisborne documents

Potts's persistent editing and reworking of documents hampers any attempt to reconstruct what was said, when, and by whom. The pamphlet also has a tendency to omit dates or date documents as 'the day and year aforesaid', even when this is clearly wrong. Presumably this is because documents have been reordered, and probably fragmented and transcribed for convenience, without redating. What follows is a reconstruction which does not attempt to conceal the problems but offers a summary of accusations and confessions together with an account of documents left undated or omitted.

Pendle

13 Mar. Alizon Device misdated examination (probably 30 Mar.)
accuses Demdike

30 Mar. Elizabeth Device examination
accuses Demdike

30 Mar. Alizon Device examination
incriminates self, accuses Demdike and Chattox

30 Mar. James Device examination
accuses Alizon Device

30 Mar. information of Abraham Law
accuses Alizon Device

2 Apr. Elizabeth Demdike examination
incriminates self, accuses Anne Chattox and Anne Redferne

2 Apr. Anne Chattox examination
incriminates self

Potts says that Roger Nowell then committed Demdike, Chattox, Alizon Device, and 'Redferne old and young' (?) but apparently not Elizabeth or James Device.

Salmesbury

15 Apr. William Alker information
accuses Jane Southworth

Pendle

27 Apr. James Device examination
incriminates self and accuses Demdike, Alizon, Anne Chattox, Elizabeth Device, Alice Nutter, Katherine Hewit, Alice Graye, Jennet Preston, John Bulcock, Jane Bulcock

27 Apr. Elizabeth Device examination
incriminates self and accuses Demdike, Alice Nutter, Anne Crounckshey and concurs with James Device's naming of those at the meeting

5 May Henry Hargreives information
accuses Jennet Preston

19 May Anne Chattox gaol examination
incriminates self and accuses Demdike, Widow Lomeshaw

Windle

12 July Peter Chaddock information
accuses Isabel Robey

The next three informations seem likely to be truly 'the day and place aforesaid'.

12 July Jane Wilkinson information
accuses Isabel Robey

12 July Margaret Lyon information
accuses Isabel Robey

12 July Margaret Parre information
accuses Isabel Robey

Salmesbury

7 Aug. John Singleton information
accuses Jane Southworth

Padiham

9 Aug. Jennet Booth information
accuses Margaret Pearson

Missing

Pendle

Anne Redferne examination
Katherine Hewit examination

Padiham

Margaret Pearson examination

Windle

Isabel Robey examination

Gisborne

Jennet Preston examination

Informations of Anne Robinson, Thomas Lister and other witnesses against Jennet Preston are given as (undated) paraphrases.

Undated documents

Pendle

James Robinson information
  accuses Chattox and Redferne
Demdike examination
  accuses Chattox and Anne Redferne
Anne Chattox examination
  incriminates self and accuses Widow Lomeshaw and Jane Boothman
James Device gaol examination
  incriminates self

Salmesbury

Grace Sowerbutts information
  accuses Jennet Bierley, Ellen Bierley, Jane Southworth, Old Doewife probably shortly after 4 April
Thomas Walshman information – no accusation

Pendle

Margaret Crooke information
  accuses Anne Redferne

John Nutter information
accuses Anne Chattox and Anne Redferne
James Device information
accuses Anne Redferne, Thomas Redferne, Marie Redferne

James Device was also taken to view Jennet Preston and confirm his identification of her – no date is given for this particular piece of evidence but it is part of one of the versions of the examination on 27 April.

Other documents are dated as being given in court and have no pre-trial date.

Pendle

Jennet Device accuses Demdike, James Device, Elizabeth Device, Alizon Device, Hugh Hargraves's wife, Christopher Howgate, Elizabeth Howgate, Alice Nutter, Christopher Jackes and his wife.

James Device produces a similar list (accuses Hugh Hargrieves's wife, Jane Bulcock, John Bulcock, Alice Nutter, Elizabeth Hargrieves, Christopher Howgate, Elizabeth Howgate, Alice Graye, Katherine Hewit–Mouldheeles, Jennet Preston). Later versions of James's list, edited for use against other witches, show that he gave it on 27 April. Elizabeth Device confirms his list on 27 April. Her accusation of Katherine Hewit, Alice Graye, John and Jane Bulcock, and Jennet Preston is probably on the same day.

Salmesbury

Thomas Sowerbutts and others' informations accusing the Salmesbury women

Pendle

John Law information accusing Alizon Device

Pendle/Padiham

Anne Chattox information accusing Margaret Pearson

Documents actually produced at the assizes

Salmesbury

19 Aug. Grace Sowerbutts assize examination
19 Aug. Jennet Bierley, Ellen Bierley and Jane Southworth assize examinations.

{a (title page)[1]} THE WONDERFULL DISCOVERIE OF WITCHES IN THE COUNTIE OF LANCASTER.
With the Arraignement and Triall of Nineteene notorious WITCHES, at the Assizes and generall Gaole deliverie, holden at the Castle of LANCASTER, *upon Munday, the seventeenth of August last,* 1612.
Before Sir JAMES ALTHAM, and Sir EDWARD BROMLEY, Knights, BARONS of his Majesties Court of EXCHEQUER: And Justices *of Assize,* Oyer *and* Terminor, *and generall* Gaole deliverie in the circuit of the *North Parts.*
Together with the Arraignement and Triall of JENNET PRESTON, *at the Assizes holden at the Castle of Yorke, the seven and twentieth day of Julie last past,* with her Execution for the murther of Master LISTER *by Witchcraft.*
Published and set forth by commandement of his Majesties Justices of Assize in the North Parts.
By THOMAS POTTS *Esquier.*
LONDON.
Printed by *W. Stansby* for *John Barnes,* and are to be sold at his shop neare Holborne Conduit. 1613.
{av blank}
{a2} TO THE RIGHT HONORABLE, *THOMAS*, LORD KNYVET, BARON OF ESCRICK in the Countie of Yorke, my very honorable *good Lord and Master.* AND TO THE RIGHT HONORABLE *AND VERTUOUS LADIE, THE Ladie* ELIZABETH KNYVET *his Wife, my* honorable good Ladie and MISTRIS.[2]
RIGHT HONORABLE,
Let it stand (I beseech you) with your favours whom profession of the same true Religion towards God, and so great love hath united together in one, Jointly {a2v} *to accept the Protection and Patronage of these my labours, which not their owne worth hath encouraged, but your Worthinesse hath enforced me to consecrate unto your Honours.*
To you (Right Honourable my very good Lord) of Right doe they belong: for to whom shall I rather present the first fruits of my learning then to your Lordship: who nourished then both mee and them, when there was scarce any being to mee or them? And whose just and uprght[3] *carriage of causes, whose zeale to Justice and Honourable curtesie to all men, have purchased you a Reverend and worthie Respect of all men in all partes of this Kingdome, where you are knowne. And to your good Ladiship* {a3} *they doe of great right belong likewise;*

1 The book begins with an unmarked section, which I have labelled signature 'a', followed by the A signature. There are a lot of blank pages in A, and these two sections may have been reset – perhaps to accommodate extra prefatory and authorising material.
2 Thomas Knyvet was a gentleman of the Privy Chamber in high favour with James I. He had arrested Guy Fawkes and heard his confession, and was created Baron Escrick in 1607. He had married Elizabeth Hayward in 1597 (*DNB*).
3 *Sic.*

Whose Religion, Justice, and Honourable admittance of my Unworthie Service to your Ladiship doe challenge at my handes the uttermost of what ever I may bee able to performe.

Here is nothing of my own act worthie to bee commended to your Honours, it is the worke, of those Reverend Magistrates, His Majesties Justices of Assizes in the North partes, and no more then a Particular Declaration of the proceedings of Justice in those partes. Here shall you behold the Justice of this Land, truely administered, **Proemium & Poenam**, *Mercie and Judgement,*[4] *freely and indifferently bestowed and inflicted; And above all* {a3v} *thinges to bee remembred, the excellent care of these Judges in the Triall of offendors.*

It hath pleased them out of their respect to mee to impose this worke upon mee, and according to my understanding, I have taken paines to finish, and now confirmed by their Judgement to publish the same, for the benefit of my Countrie. That the example of these convicted upon their owne Examinations, Confessions, and Evidence at the Barre, may worke good in others, Rather by with-holding them from, then imboldening them to, the Atcheiving such desperate actes as these or the like.

These are some part of the fruits of my time spent in the Service of my Coun-{A}*-trie, Since by your Grave and Reverend Counsell (my Good Lord) I reduced my wavering and wandring thoughts to a more quiet harbour of repose.*

If it please your Honours to give them your Honourable respect, the world may judge them the more worthie of acceptance, to whose various censures they are now exposed.

God of Heaven whose eies are on them that feare him, to bee their Protector and guide, behold your Honours with the eye of favor, be evermore your strong hold, and your great reward, and blesse you with blessings in this life, Externall and Internall, Temporall and Spirituall, and with Eternall happines in the World to come: to which I commend you Ho-{Av}*-nours; And rest both now and ever, From my Lodging in Chancerie Lane, the sixteenth of November* **1612.**

Your Honours
humbly devoted
Servant,
Thomas Potts.

{A2 blank}

{A2v} **UPon the Arraignement and triall of these Witches at the last Assizes and Generall Gaole-deliverie, holden at Lancaster, wee found such apparent matters against them, that we thought it necessarie to publish them to the World, and thereupon imposed the labour of this Worke upon this Gentleman, by reason of his place, being a Clerke at that time in Court, imploied in the arraignement and triall of them.**

Ja. Altham.
Edw. Bromley.

4 More literally, reward (praemium) and punishment.

{A3 blank}
{A3v} *AFter he had taken great paines to finish it, I tooke upon mee to revise and correct it, that nothing might passe but matter of Fact, apparant against them by record. It is very little he hath inserted, and that necessarie, to shew what their offences were, what people, and of what condition they were: The whole proceedings and Evidence against them, I finde upon examination carefully set forth, and truely reported, and judge the worke fit and worthie to be published.*
Edward Bromley.
{A4[5]} Faults escaped in the Printing.
Page, C3: M. *Bavester*, for *Bannester*, brough, for brought.
Page, E2 This people, for these. Page, H Here they parted, for there. page, K2 these, for this hellish. page, S3 In the Verdict of Life and Death, Not guiltie, for guiltie. page, S3 one Horse or Mare, for one Mare in the Indictment. page eadem, for the Triall of her life, reade for the triall of her offence. page, T their view, for your view.[6]
Gentle Reader, although the care of this Gentleman the Author, was great to examine and publish this his worke perfect according to the Honorable testimonie of the Judges, yet some faults are committed by me in the Printing, and yet not many, being a worke done in such great haste, at the end of a Tearme, which I pray you, with your favour to excuse.
{A4v illustrated}
{B} A particular Declaration of the most barberous and damnable Practises, Murthers, wicked and divelish Conspiracies, practized *and executed by the most dangerous and malitious* Witch *Elizabeth Sowthernes* alias *Demdike*, of the Forrest of *Pendle* in the Countie of *Lancaster* Widdow, who died in the Castle at *Lancaster* before she came to receive her tryall.
THough publique Justice hath passed at these Assises upon the Capitall offendours, and after the Arraignement & tryall of them, Judgement being given, due and timely Execution succeeded; which doth import and give the greatest satisfaction that can be, to all men; yet because upon the caryage, and event of this businesse, the Eyes of all partes of *Lancashire*, and other Counties in the North partes thereunto adjoyning were bent: And so infinite a multitude came to the Arraignement & tryall of these Witches at *Lancaster*, the number of them being knowen to exceed all others at any time heretofore, at one time to be indicted, arraigned, and to receive their tryall, especially for so many Murders, Conspiracies, Charmes, Meetinges, hellish and damnable practises, so apparant upon their owne examinations & confessions. These my honourable & worthy Lords, the Judges of Assise, upon {Bv} great consideration, thought it necessarie & profitable, to publish

5 After this point, the entire text is in Roman font, unless otherwise specified.
6 Actually there is no such mistake. The printer may refer to the perfectly correct use of the phrase on Vv.

to the whole world, their most barbarous and damnable practises, with the direct proceedinges of the Court against them, aswell for that there doe passe divers uncertaine reportes and relations of such Evidences, as was publiquely given against them at their Arraignement. As for that divers came to prosecute against many of them that were not found guiltie, and so rest very discontented, and not satisfied. As also for that it is necessary for men to know and understande the meanes whereby they worke their mischiefe, the hidden misteries of their divelish and wicked Inchauntmentes, Charmes, and Sorceries, the better to prevent and avoyde the danger that may ensue. And lastly, who were the principall authors and actors in this late woefull and lamentable *Tragedie*, wherein so much Blood was spilt.

Therefore I pray you give me leave, (with your patience and favour,) before I proceed to the Indictment, Arraignment, and Tryall of such as were Prisoners in the Castle, to lay open the life and death of this damnable and malicious Witch, of so long continuance (old *Demdike*) of whom our whole businesse hath such dependence, that without the particular Declaration and Record of her Evidence, with the circumstaunces, wee shall never bring any thing to good perfection: for from this Sincke of villanie and mischiefe, have all the rest proceeded; as you shall have them in order.

She was a very old woman, about the age of Fourescore yeares, and had been a Witch for fiftie yeares. She dwelt in the Forrest of *Pendle*, a vaste place, fitte for her profession:[7] What shee committed in her time, no man knowes. Thus lived shee securely for many yeares, brought up {B2} her owne Children, instructed her Graund-children, and tooke great care and paines to bring them to be Witches. Shee was a generall agent for the Devill in all these partes: no man escaped her, or her Furies, that ever gave them any occasion of offence, or denyed them any thing they stood need of: And certaine it is, no man neere them, was secure or free from danger.

But God, who had in his divine providence provided to cut them off, and roote them out of the Commonwealth, so disposed above, that the Justices of those partes, understanding by a generall charme[8] and muttering, the great and universall resort to *Maulking Tower*,[9] the common opinion, with the report of these suspected people, the complaint of the Kinges subjectes for the losse of their Children, Friendes, Goodes, and cattle, (as there could not be so great Fire without some Smoake,) sent for some of the Countrey, and tooke great paynes to enquire after their proceedinges, and courses of life.

In the end, *Roger Nowell* Esquire, one of his Majesties Justices in these partes, a very religious honest Gentleman, painefull in the service of his Countrey:

7 Pendle Forest, and Trawden Forest, are moorland areas near Burnley – called 'forest' because they were designated as hunting areas. Pendle Hill is the best-known landmark in what was in Potts's eyes clearly a wilderness. Lancaster is about twenty miles north-west of Pendle.

8 A chattering of many voices.

9 Generally believed to be at Blacko, about three miles east of Pendle Hill.

whose fame for this great service to his Countrey, shall live after him, tooke upon him to enter into the particular examination of these suspected persons:[10] And to the honour of God, and the great comfort of all his Countrey, made such a discovery of them in order, as the like hath not been heard of: which for your better satisfaction, I have heere placed in order against her, as they are upon Record, amongst the Recordes of the *Crowne* at *Lancaster*, certified[11] by M. *Nowell*, and others.

{B2v} The voluntarie Confession and Examination of *Elizabeth Sowtherns* alias *Demdike*, taken at the Fence[12] in the Forrest of *Pendle* in the Countie of *Lancaster*.

The second day of Aprill, *Annoq: Regni Regis Jacobi Angliae. &c. Decimo, et Scotiae Quadragesimo quinto*;[13] Before *Roger Nowell* of *Reade* Esquire,[14] one of his Majesties Justices of the peace within the sayd Countie. *Viz.*

THe said *Elizabeth Sowtherns* confesseth, and sayth; That about twentie yeares past, as she was comming homeward from begging, there met her this Examinate neere unto a Stonepit in *Gouldshey*,[15] in the sayd Forrest of *Pendle*, A spirit or Devill in the shape of a Boy, the one halfe of his Coate blacke, and the other browne, who bade this Examinate stay, saying unto her, that if she would give him her Soule, she should have any thing that she would request. Whereupon this Examinat demaunded his name? and the Spirit answered, his name was *Tibb*: and so this Examinate in hope of such gaine as was promised by the sayd Devill or *Tibb*, was contented to give her Soule to the said Spirit: And for the space of five or sixe yeares next after, the sayd Spirit or Devill appeared at sundry times unto her this Examinate about *Day-light* Gate,[16] alwayes bidding her stay, and asking her this examinate what she would {B3} have or doe? To whom this Examinate replyed, Nay nothing: for she this Examinate said, she wanted nothing yet. And so about

10 Roger Nowell of Read, sheriff in 1610. The relation of eminent Protestant divines, he was also connected by his mother's first marriage to the Starkie family whose possessed children had caused a sensation in the late 1590s. A conjuror (Edmund Hartley, hired to heal them) had been executed for witchcraft, and John Darrell and George More, later notorious, had been called in as exorcists. See Jonathan Lumby, *The Lancashire Witch-craze: Jennet Preston and the Lancashire Witches, 1612* (Preston: Carnegie, 1995) for the fullest biographical details of all the families involved in the Pendle, Salmesbury and Gisburne cases, and John Darrell, *A True Narration of the Strange and grevous vexation of the devil, of 7. persons in Lancashire* (1600), George More, *A True Discourse concerning the Certaine Possession and Dispossession of 7. Persons in one familie in Lancashire* (1600) and Samuel Harsnett, *A Discovery of the Fraudulent Practices of John Darrel* (1599) for the Starkie case.

11 Brought to court and authenticated there.

12 Fence is a village three miles south-east of Pendle Hill.

13 The regnal years are used as dates: King James has been King of England for ten years, and of Scotland forty-five years. James ascended the Scottish throne on 24 July 1567 and the English on 24 March 1603/4.

14 Read Hall is about four miles south-west of Pendle Hill.

15 Goldshaw is an area south-west of Pendle Hill.

16 See note 32.

the end of the said sixe yeares, upon a Sabboth day in the morning, this Examinate having a litle Child upon her knee, and she being in a slumber, the sayd Spirit appeared unto her in the likenes of a browne Dogg, forcing himselfe to her knee, to get blood under her left Arme: and she being without and apparrel saving her Smocke, the said Devill did get blood under her left arme. And this Examinate awaking, sayd, *Jesus save my Child*; but had no power, nor could not say, *Jesus save her selfe*: whereupon the Browne Dogg vanished out of this Examinats sight: after which, this Examinate was almost starke madd for the space of eight weekes.[17]

And upon her examination, she further confesseth, and saith. That a little before Christmas last, this Examinates Daughter having been to helpe *Richard Baldwyns* Folkes at the Mill: This Examinates Daughter did bid her this Examinate goe to the said *Baldwyns* house, and aske him something for her helping of his Folkes at the Mill, (as aforesaid:) and in this Examinates going to the said *Baldwyns* house, and neere to the saide house, she mette with the said *Richard Baldwyn*; Which *Baldwyn* sayd to this Examinate, and the said *Alizon Device*[18] (who at that time ledde this Examinate, being blinde) get out of my ground Whores and Witches, I will burne the one of you, and hang the other. To whom this Examinate answered: I care not for thee, hang thy selfe: Presently whereupon, at this Examinates going over the next hedge, the said Spirit or Divell called *Tibb*, appeared unto this Examinat, and sayd, *Revenge thee of him.* To whom, this Examinate sayd againe to the sayd Spirit. *Revenge thee eyther of him, or his.* And so the said Spirit vanished out of her sight, and she {B3v} never saw him since.

And further this Examinate confesseth, and sayth, that the speediest way to take a mans life away by Witchcraft, is to make a Picture of Clay, like unto the shape of the person whom they meane to kill, & dry it thorowly: and when they would have them to be ill in any one place more then an other: then take a Thorne or Pinne, and pricke it in that part of the Picture you would so have to be ill: and when they would have any part of the Body to consume away, then take that part of the Picture, and burne it. And when they would have the whole body to consume away, then take the remnant of the sayd Picture, and burne it: and so thereupon by that meanes, the body shall die.

{B4} The Confession and Examination of Anne Whittle *alias* Chattox, being Prisoner at *Lancaster*; taken the 19. day of May, *Annoq; Regni Regis Jacobi Angliae Decimo: ac Scotiae Quadragesimo quinto*; Before *William Sandes* Maior of the Borough towne of *Lancaster*.

17 Elizabeth Demdike's account of her initiation differs in date from Potts's glossing version on Bv (why?), and is reminiscent, in its finally aggressive familiar, of the story told by Elizabeth Bennett in 1582. In another hint at the dynamics of questioning affecting confession, none of Demdike's *maleficium* in this examination pre-dates her arrest by more than a year despite her alleged long continuance as a witch.

18 Actually, Alizon has not been mentioned – possible evidence of Potts's rearrangement and cutting of his documentary sources.

James Anderton of *Clayton*, one of his Majesties Justices of Peace within the same County, and *Thomas Cowell* one of his Majesties Coroners in the sayd Countie of Lancaster. *Viz.*[19]

FIrst, the sayd *Anne Whittle*, alias *Chattox*, sayth, that about foureteene yeares past she entered, through the wicked perswasions and counsell of *Elizabeth Southerns*, alias *Demdike*, and was seduced to condescent & agree to become subject unto that divelish abhominable profession of Witchcraft:[20] Soone after which, the Devill appeared unto her in the likenes of a Man, about midnight, at the house of the sayd *Demdike*: and thereupon the sayd *Demdike* and shee, went foorth of the said house unto him; whereupon the said wicked Spirit mooved this Examinate, that she would become his Subject, and give her Soule unto him: the which at first, she refused to assent unto; but after, by the great perswasions made by the sayd *Demdike*, shee yeelded to be at his commaundement and appoyntment: whereupon the sayd wicked Spirit then sayd unto her, that hee must have one part of her body for him to sucke upon; the which shee denyed then to graunt unto him; and withall asked {B4v} him, what part of her body hee would have for that use; who said, hee would have a place of her right side neere to her ribbes, for him to sucke upon: whereunto shee assented.

And she further sayth, that at the same time, there was a thing in the likenes of a spotted Bitch, that came with the sayd Spirit unto the sayd *Demdike*, which then did speake unto her in this Examinates hearing, and sayd, that she should have Gould, Silver, and worldly Wealth, at her will. And at the same time she saith, there was victuals, *viz.* Flesh, Butter, Cheese, Bread, and Drinke, and bidde them eate enough. And after their eating, the Devill called *Fancie*, and the other Spirit calling himselfe *Tibbe*, carried the remnant away: And she sayeth, that although they did eate, they were never the fuller, nor better for the same; and that at their said Banquet, the said Spirits gave them light to see what they did, although they neyther had fire nor Candle light; and that they were both shee Spirites, and Divels.[21]

And being further examined how many sundry Persons have been bewitched to death, and by whom they were so bewitched: She sayth, that one *Robert Nutter*, late of the *Greene-head* in *Pendle*,[22] was bewitched by this Examinate, the said *Demdike*, and Widdow *Lomshawe*, (late of *Burneley*)[23] now deceased. And she further sayth, that the said *Demdike* shewed her, that she had bewitched to death, *Richard Ashton*, Sonne of *Richard Ashton* of *Downeham*[24] Esquire.

19 This is a gaol examination of Anne Chattox, not her first examination as one might expect.
20 The vocabulary of this opening suggests how filtered the examinate's own ideas and words might be by her educated examiners (and by pamphleteers).
21 The spirits' confused number and sex suggests the incoherence of this account.
22 Green Head is a farm near Fence.
23 Burnley is a town about six miles south-east of Pendle Hill.
24 Downham is a village two miles north-west of Pendle Hill.

{C} The Examination of Alizon Device, of the Forrest of Pendle, in the County of *Lancaster* Spinster, taken at *Reade* in the said Countie of *Lancaster*, the xiii.[25] day of March, *Anno Regni Jacobi Angliae. &c. Nono:*[26] *et Scotiae xlv.*

Before *Roger Nowell* of *Reade* aforesayd Esquire, one of his Majesties Justices of the Peace within the sayd Countie, against *Elizabeth Sowtherns*, alias *Demdike* her Graund-mother. *Viz.*

THe sayd *Alizon Device* sayth, that about two yeares agon, her Graund-mother (called *Elizabeth Sowtherns*, alias old *Demdike*) did sundry times in going or walking togeather as they went begging, perswade and advise this Examinate to let a Devill of Familiar appeare unto her; and that shee this Examinate, would let him sucke at some part of her, and shee might have, and doe what shee would.

And she further sayth, that one *John Nutter* of the *Bulhole*[27] in *Pendle* aforesaid, had a Cow which was sicke, & requested this examinats Grand-mother to amend the said Cow; and her said Graund-mother said she would, and so her said Graund-mother about ten of the clocke in the night, desired this examinate to lead her foorth; which this Examinate did, being then blind: and her Graund-mother did remaine about halfe an houre foorth: and this Examinates sister did fetch her in againe; but what she did when she was so foorth, this Examinate cannot tell. But the next {Cv} morning this Examinate heard that the sayd Cow was dead. And this Examinate verily thinketh, that her sayd Graund-mother did bewitch the sayd Cow to death.

And further, this Examinate sayth, that about two yeares agon, this Examinate having gotten a Piggin[28] full of blew Milke by begging, brought it into the house of her Graund-mother, where (this Examinate going foorth presently, and staying about halfe an houre) there was Butter to the quantity of a quarterne of a pound in the said milke, and the quantitie of the said milke still remayning; and her Graund-mother had no Butter in the house when this Examinate went foorth: duering which time, this Examinates Graund-mother still lay in her bed.

And further this Examinate sayth, that *Richard Baldwin* of *Weethead*[29] within the Forrest of *Pendle*, about 2. yeeres agoe, fell out with this Examinates Graund-mother, & so would not let her come upon his Land: and about foure or five dayes then next after, her said Graund-mother did request this Examinate to lead her foorth about ten of the clocke in the night: which this Examinate accordingly did, and she stayed foorth then about an houre, and this examinates sister fetched her in againe. And this Examinate heard

25 A mistake: this should read the 30th – see R4 and note 180.

26 See note 13.

27 Bull Hole is a farm near Newchurch, a village two miles south-east of Pendle Hill.

28 Small pail.

29 A farm near Roughlee, about three miles east of Pendle Hill.

the next morning, that a woman Child of the sayd *Richard Baldwins* was fallen sicke; and as this Examinate then did heare, the sayd Child did languish afterwards by the space of a yeare, or thereaboutes, and dyed: And this Examinate verily thinketh, that her said Graund-mother did bewitch the sayd Child to death.

And further, this examinate sayth, that she heard her says Graund-mother say presently after her falling out with the sayd *Baldwin*, shee would pray for the sayd *Baldwin* both still[30] and loude: and this Examinate heard her cursse the sayd *Baldwin* sundry times.

{C2} The Examination of *James Device* of the Forrest of *Pendle*, in the Countie of *Lancaster* Labourer, taken the 27. day of April, *Annoq Regni Regis Jacobi, Angliae, &c. Decimo: as Scotiae Quadragesimo quinto*: Before *Roger Nowell*, and *Nicholas Banister Esq.*[31] two of his Majesties Justices of Peace within the sayd Countie.

THE sayd Examinate *James Device* sayth, that about a month agoe, as this Examinate was comming towards his Mothers house, and at day-gate of the same night,[32] this Examinate mette a browne Dogge comming from his Graund-mothers house, about tenne Roodes distant from the same house: and about two or three nights after, that this Examinate heard a voyce of a great number of Children screiking and crying pittifully, about day-light gate; and likewise, about ten Roodes distant of this Examinates sayd Graund-mothers house. And about five nights then next following, presently after daylight, within 20. Roodes of the sayd *Elizabeth Sowtherns* house, he heard a foule yelling like unto a great number of Cattes: but what they were, this Examinate cannot tell. And he further sayth, that about three nights after that, about midnight of the same, there came a thing, and lay upon him very heavily about an houre, and went then from him out of his Chamber window, coloured blacke, and about the bignesse of a Hare or Catte. And he further sayth, that about S. *Peters* day last,[33] one *Henry Bullocke* came to the sayd *Elizabeth Sowtherns* house, and sayd, that her Graund-child *Alizon Device* had bewitched a Child of his, and desired her that she would goe with him to his house; which accordingly she did: And thereupon she the said *Alizon* fell downe on her knees, & asked the said *Bullocke* forgivenes, and confessed to him, that she had bewitched the said child, as this Examinate heard his said sister confesse unto him this Examinate.

{C2v} The Examination of Elizabeth Device, Daughter of old Demdike, taken at *Read* before *Roger Nowell* Esquire, one of his Majesties Justices of Peace within the Countie of *Lancaster* the xxx. day of March, *Annoq Regni Jacobi Decimo, ac Scotiae xlv.*

30 Silently.

31 Nicholas Bannister of Altham, near Reade.

32 A marginal note glosses '*Evening.*'

33 29 June.

THe sayd *Elizabeth Device* the Examinate, sayth, that the sayd *Elizabeth Sowtherns*, alias *Demdike*, hath had a place on her left side by the space of fourty yeares, in such sort, as was to be seene at this Examinates Examination taking, at this present time.

Heere this worthy Justice M. *Nowell*, out of these particular Examinations, or rather Accusations,[34] finding matter to proceed: and having now before him old *Demdike*, old *Chattox*, *Alizon Device*, and *Redferne* both old and young,[35] *Reos confitentes, et Accusantes Invicem*.[36] About the second of Aprill last past, committed and sent them away to the Castle at *Lancaster*, there to remaine untill the comming of the Kinges Majesties Justices of Assise, then to receive their tryall.

{C3} But heere they had not stayed a weeke, when their Children and Friendes being abroad at libertie, laboured a speciall meeting at *Malking Tower* in the Forrest of *Pendle*, upon Good-fryday, within a weeke after they were committed, of all the most dangerous, wicked, and damnable witches in the County farre and neere. Upon Good-fryday they met, according to solemne appoyntment, solemnized this great Feastival day according to their former order, with great cheare, merry company, and much conference.[37]

In the end, in this great Assemblie, it was decreed M. *Covell* by reason of his Office, shall be slaine before the next Assises: The Castle of *Lancaster* to be blowen up, and ayde and assistance to be sent to kill M. *Lister*, with his old Enemie and wicked Neighbour *Jennet Preston*; with some other such like practises: as upon their Arraignement and Tryall, are particularly set foorth, and given in evidence against them.

This was not so secret, but some notice of it came to M. *Nowell*, and by his great paines taken in the Examination of *Jennet Device*, al their practises are now made knowen. Their purpose to kill M. *Covell*, and blow up the Castle, is prevented. All their Murders, Witchcraftes, Inchauntments, Charmes, & Sorceries, are discovered; and even in the middest of their Consultations, they are all confounded, and arrested by Gods Justice: brough[38] before M. *Nowell*, and M. *Bavester*,[39] upon their voluntary confessions, Examinations, and other Evidence accused, and so by them committed to the Castle: So as now both old and young, have taken up their lodgings with

34 Potts is right: technically these documents are both examinations and informations.

35 It's not quite clear whom Potts means here: Anne Redferne is described as Anne Chattox's daughter but who is the other Redferne?

36 '*Reos confitentes*' is the first echo of speeches from the trial of the Gunpowder plotters, one of several. This conventional short phrase (referring to the prisoners' confession and mutual accusation) would not be noticeable without the others, but see William Cobbett, *Complete Collection of State Trials and Proceedings for High Treason* (London, 1809), vol. 2, 185.

37 The idea of feast is of course an inversion of the solemnities of the Christian Good Friday, a traditional fast.

38 *Sic.* See *errata*, as also for note 39.

39 *Sic.*

M. *Covell*, untill the next Assises, expecting their tryall and deliveraunce, according to the Lawes provided for such like.

{C3v} In the meane time, M. *Nowell* having knowledge by this discovery of their meeting at *Malkeing Tower*, and their resolution to execute mischiefe, takes great paines to apprehend such as were at libertie, and prepared Evidence against all such as were in question for Witches.

Afterwardes sendes some of their Examinations, to the Assises at Yorke, to be given in Evidence against *Jennet Preston*, who for the murder of M. *Lister*, is condemned and executed.[40]

The Circuite of the North partes being now almost ended.

The 16. of August.

Upon Sunday in the after noone, my honorable Lords the Judges of Assise, came from *Kendall*[41] to *Lancaster*.

Whereupon M. *Covell* presented unto their Lordships a Calender, conteyning the Names of the Prisoners committed to his charge, which were to receive their Tryall at the Assises: Out of which, we are onely to deale with the proceedings against Witches, which were as followeth. *Viz.*

{C4} The Names of the Witches committed to the Castle of *Lancaster*.

Elizabeth Sowtherns.	Who dyed before
alias	shee
Old Demdike.	came to her tryall.

Anne Whittle, alias *Chattox*.
Elizabeth Device, Daughter of old *Demdike*.
James Device, Sonne of *Elizabeth Device*.
Anne Readfearne, Daughter of *Anne Chattox*.
Alice Nutter.
Katherine Hewytte.
John Bulcocke.
Jane Bulcocke.
Alizon Device, Daughter of *Elizabeth Device*.
Isabell Robey.
Margaret Pearson.

The Witches of Salmesbury.

Jennet Bierley.	*Elizabeth Astley.*
Elen Bierley.[42]	*Alice Gray.*
Jane Southworth.	*Isabell Sidegraves.*
John Ramesden.	*Lawrence Haye.*

The next day, being Monday, the 17. of August, were the Assises holden in the Castle of *Lancaster*, as followeth.

{C4v} PLACITA CORONAE

40 Note the present-tense creation of drama.
41 Kendal, the previous assize town, is eighteen miles north of Lancaster.
42 *Sic.*

Apud Lancasterium.
Deliberatio Gaole Domini Regis Castri sui Lancastrii ac Prisonariorum in eadem existent. Tenta apud Lancasterium in com. Lancasterii. Die Lunae, Decimo septimo die Augusti, Anno Regni Domini nostri Jacobi dei gratia Angliae, Franciae, et Hiberniae, Regis fidei defensoris; Decimo: et Scotiae Quadragesimo sexto;[43] *Coram Jacobo Altham Milit. uno Baronum Scaccarii Domini Regis, et Edwardo Bromley Milit. altero Barono, eiusdem Scaccarii Domini Regis: ac Justic. Domini Regis apud Lancastr.*[44]

UPon the Tewesday in the after noone, the Judges according to the course and order, devided them selves, whereupon my Lord *Bromley*, one of his Majesties Judges of Assise comming into the Hall to proceede with the Pleaes of the Crowne, & the Arraignement and Tryall of Prisoners, commaunded a generall Proclamation, that all Justices of Peace that had taken any Recognisaunces, or Examinations of Prisoners, should make Returne of them: And all such as were bound to prosecute Indictmentes, and give Evidence against Witches, should proceede, and give attendance: For hee now intended to proceed to the Arraignement and Tryall of Witches.

After which, the Court being set, M. Sherieffe was commaunded to present his Prisoners before his Lordship, and prepare a sufficient Jurie of Gentlemen for life and death.[45] But heere we want old *Demdike*, who dyed in the Castle before she came to her Tryall.

{D} Heere you may not expect the exact order of the Assises, with the Proclamations, and other solemnities belonging to so great a Court of Justice; but the proceedinges against the Witches, who are now upon their deliverance here in order as they came to the Barre, with the particular poyntes of Evidence against them: which is the labour and worke we now intend (by Gods grace) to performe as we may, to your generall contentment.

Whereupon, the first of all these, *Anne Whittle*, alias *Chattox*, was brought to the Barre: against whom wee are now ready to proceed.

{Dv} The Arraignement and Tryall of Anne Whittle, *alias* Chattox, of the Forrest of *Pendle*, in the Countie of *Lancaster*, Widdow; about the age of Fourescore yeares, or thereaboutes.

Anne Whittle, alias *Chattox.*

IF in this damnable course of life, and offences, more horrible and odious, then any man is able to expresse: any man lyving could lament the estate of any such like upon earth: The example of this poore creature, would have

43 See note 13.

44 Delivery of the gaol of the lord king of his castle of Lancaster, and of the prisoners existing in the same. Held at Lancaster in the county of Lancashire on Monday the seventeenth day of August in the tenth year of the reign of our lord James, by the grace of God king of England, France and Ireland, defender of the faith; and of Scotland the forty-sixth year; before Sir James Altham, baron of the exchequer of the lord king, and Sir Edward Bromley, another baron of the same exchequer of the lord king and justices of the lord king at Lancaster.

45 It was the sheriff's duty to organise the assizes.

moved pittie, in respect of her great contrition and repentance, after she was committed to the Castle at *Lancaster*, untill the comming of his Majesties Judges of Assise. But such was the nature of her offences, & the multitude of her crying sinnes, as it tooke away all sense of humanity. And the repetition of her hellish practices, and Revenge; being the chiefest thinges wherein she alwayes tooke great delight, togeather with a particular declaration of the Murders shee had committed, layde open to the world, and given in Evidence against her at the time of her Arraignement and {D2} Tryall; as certainely it did beget contempt in the Audience, and such as she never offended.

This *Anne Whittle*, alias *Chattox*, was a very old withered spent & decreped creature, her sight almost gone: A dangerous Witch, of very long continuance; alwayes opposite to old *Demdike*: For whom the one favoured, the other hated deadly: and how they envie and accuse one an other, in their Examinations, may appeare.[46]

In her Witchcraft, alwayes more ready to doe mischiefe to mens goods, then themselves. Her lippes ever chattering and walking: but no man knew what. She lived in the Forrest of *Pendle*, amongst this wicked company of dangerous Witches. Yet in her Examination and Confession, she dealt alwayes very plainely and truely: for upon a speciall occasion being oftentimes examined in open Court, shee was never found to vary, but alwayes to agree in one, and the selfe same thing.

I place her in order, next to that wicked fire-brand of mischiefe, old *Demdike*, because from these two, sprung all the rest in order: and were the Children and Friendes, of these two notorious Witches.

Many thinges in the discovery of them, shall be very worthy of your observation. As the times and occasions to execute their mischiefe. And this in generall: the Spirit could never hurt, till they gave consent.

And, but that it is my charge, to set foorth a particular Declaration of the Evidence against them, upon their Arraignement and Tryall; with their Divelish practises, consultations, meetings, and murders committed by them, {D2v} in such sort, as they were given in Evidence against them; for the which, I shall have matter upon Record. I could make a large Comentarie of them: But it is my humble duety, to observe the Charge and Commaundement of these my Honorable good Lordes the Judges of Assise, and not to exceed the limits of my Commission. Wherefore I shall now bring this auncient Witch, to the due course of her Tryall, in order. *viz.*

46 A marginal note reads: '*Her owne examination*'. It's not clear whether this refers to an edited-out part of Chattox's examination in which she described her feud with Elizabeth Demdike, or if Potts is pointing us to the end of the paragraph and 'their Examinations'. The former seems likely, with Potts giving the source of his account of enmity between the two women. The idea of a feud has long been associated with this case, and was presumably based on the quarrel over theft (see E4) but there is actually surprisingly little evidence of it in the reproduced documents, apart from E3. One wonders if Potts removed any sections referring to feud?

Indictment.

THis *Anne Whittle*, alias *Chattox*, of the Forrest of *Pendle* in the Countie of *Lancaster* Widdow, being Indicted, for that shee feloniously had practised, used, and exercised divers wicked and divelish Artes called Witchcraftes, Inchauntmentes, Charmes, and Sorceries, in and upon one *Robert Nutter* of *Greenehead*, in the Forrest of *Pendle*, in the Countie of *Lanc*: and by force of the same Witchcraft, feloniously the sayd *Robert Nutter* had killed, *Contra Pacem, &c.*[47] Being at the Barre, was arraigned.[48]

To this Indictment, upon her Arraignement, shee pleaded, Not guiltie: and for the tryall of her life, put her selfe upon God and her Country.

Whereupon my Lord *Bromley* commaunded M. Sheriffe of the County of *Lancaster* in open Court, to returne a Jurie of worthy sufficient Gentlemen of understanding, to passe betweene our soveraigne Lord the Kinges Majestie, and her, and others the Prisoners, upon their lives and deathes; as hereafter follow in order: who were afterwardes sworne, according to the forme and order of {D3} the Court, the Prisoners being admitted to their lawfull challenges.[49]

Which being done, and the Prisoner at the Barre readie to receive her Tryall: M. *Nowell*, being the best instructed of any man, of all the particular poyntes of Evidence against her, and her fellowes, having taken great paynes in the proceedinges against her and her fellowes; Humbly prayed, her owne voluntary Confession and Examination taken before him, when she was apprehended and committed to the Castle of *Lancaster* for Witchcraft; might openly be published against her: which hereafter followeth. *Viz.*

The voluntary Confession and Examination of *Anne Whittle*, alias *Chattox*, taken at the *Fence* in the Forrest of *Pendle*, in the Countie of *Lancaster*; Before *Roger Nowell Esq*, one of the Kinges Majesties Justices of Peace in the Countie of Lancaster. Viz.

THe sayd *Anne Whittle*, alias *Chattox*, upon her Examination, voluntarily confesseth, and sayth, That about foureteene or fifteene yeares agoe, a thing like a Christian man for foure yeares togeather, did sundry times come to this Examinate, and requested this Examinate to give him her Soule: And in the end, this Examinate was contented to give him her sayd Soule, shee being then in her owne house, in the Forrest of *Pendle*; whereupon the Devill then in the shape of a Man, sayd to this Examinate: Thou shalt want nothing; and be revenged of whom thou list. And the Devill then further com-{D3v}-maunded this Examinate, to call him by the name of *Fancie*; and when she wanted any thing, or would be revenged of any, call on *Fancie*, and he would be ready. And the sayd Spirit or Devill, did appeare unto her not long after,

47 Against the peace (of the King).

48 Anne Chattox was presumably jointly charged with Anne Redferne (N3v–N4).

49 The accused were allowed to object to any members of the jury whom they felt would be prejudiced against them – although this right was seldom exercised.

in mans likenesse, and would have had this Examinate to have consented, that he might hurt the wife of *Richard Baldwin* of *Pendle*; But this Examinate would not then consent unto him: For which cause, the sayd Devill would then have bitten her by the arme; and so vanished away, for that time.

And this Examinate further sayth, that *Robert Nutter* did desire her Daughter one *Redfearns* wife, to have his pleasure of her, being then in *Redfearns* house: but the sayd *Redfearns* wife denyed the sayd *Robert*; whereupon the sayd *Robert* seeming to be greatly displeased therewith, in a great anger tooke his Horse, and went away, saying in a great rage, that if ever the Ground came to him, shee should never dwell upon his Land. Whereupon this Examinate called *Fancie* to her; who came to her in the likenesse of a Man in a parcell of Ground called, *The Laund*;[50] asking this Examinate, what shee would have him to doe? And this Examinate bade him goe revenge her of the sayd *Robert Nutter*. After which time, the sayd *Robert Nutter* lived about a quarter of a yeare, and then dyed.

And this Examinate further sayth, that *Elizabeth Nutter*, wife to old *Robert Nutter*, did request this Examinate, and *Loomeshaws* wife of *Burley*, and one *Jane Boothman*, of the same, who are now both dead, (which time of request was before that *Robert Nutter* desired the company of *Redfearns* wife) to get young *Robert Nutter* his death, if {D4} they could; all being togeather then at that time, to that end, that if *Robert* were dead, then the Women their Coosens might have the Land: By whose perswasion, they all consented unto it. After which time, this Examinates Sonne in law *Thomas Redfearne*, did perswade this Examinate, not to kill or hurt the sayd *Robert Nutter*; for which perswasion, the sayd *Loomeshaws* Wife, had like to have killed the sayd *Redfearne*, but that one M. *Baldwyn* (the late Schoole-maister at *Coulne*)[51] did by his learning, stay the sayd *Loomeshaws* wife, and therefore had a Capon from *Redfearne*.

And this Examinate further sayth, that she thinketh the sayd *Loomeshaws* wife, and *Jane Boothman*, did what they could to kill the sayd *Robert Nutter*, as well as this Examinate did.

{D4v blank}

{E} *The Examination of* ELIZABETH SOTHERNES, alias OLD DEMBDIKE: *taken at the Fence in the Forrest of Pendle in the Countie of Lancaster, the day and yeare aforesaid.*

Before, ROGER NOWEL *Esquire, one of the Kings Majesties Justices of Peace in the said Countie, against* ANNE WHITTLE, alias CHATTOX.

THe said *Elizabeth Southernes* saith upon her Examination, that about halfe a yeare before *Robert Nutter* died, as this Examinate thinketh, this Examinate

50 The Laund is an area near Fence.

51 Colne is the nearest town to Blacko, about five miles east of Pendle Hill. Walter Bennett names the schoolmaster as Nicholas Baldwin of Greenfield who died in 1610 (*The Pendle Witches* [1957; Preston: Lancashire County Books 1993], 15).

went to the house of *Thomas Redfearne*, which was about Mid-sommer, as this Examinate remembreth it. And there within three yards of the East end of the said house, shee saw the said *Anne Whittle*, alias *Chattox*, and *Anne Redferne* wife of the said *Thomas Redferne*, and Daughter of the said *Anne Whittle*, alias *Chattox*: the one on the one side of the Ditch, and the other on the other: and two Pictures of Clay or Marle lying by them: and the third Picture the said *Anne Whittle*, alias *Chattox*, was making: and the said *Anne Redferne* her said Daughter, wrought[52] her Clay or Marle to make the third picture withall. And this Examinate passing by them, the said Spirit, called *Tibb*, in the shape of a black Cat, appeared unto her this Examinate, and said, turne back againe, and doe as they doe: To whom this Examinate said, what are they doing? whereunto the said Spirit said; they are making three Pictures: whereupon she asked whose pictures they were? whereunto the said Spirit said; they {Ev} are the pictures of *Christopher Nutter*, *Robert Nutter*, and *Marie*, wife of the said *Robert Nutter*: But this Examinate denying to goe back to helpe them to make the Pictures aforesaid; the said Spirit seeming to be angrie, therefore shove or pushed this Examinate into the ditch, and so shed the Milke which this Examinate had in a Can or Kit:[53] and so thereupon the Spirit at that time *vanished* out of this Examinates sight: But presently after that, the said Spirit appeared to this Examinate againe in the shape of a Hare, and so went with her about a quarter of a mile, but said nothing to this Examinate, nor shee to it.

The Examination and evidence of JAMES ROBINSON, *taken the day and yeare aforesaid.*

Before ROGER NOWEL *Esquire aforesaid, against* ANNE WHITTLE, alias CHATTOX, *Prisoner at the Barre as followeth.* viz.[54]

THe said Examinate saith, that about sixe yeares agoe, *Anne Whittle*, alias *Chattox*, was hired by this Examinates wife to card[55] wooll: and so upon a Friday and Saturday, shee came and carded wooll with this Examinates wife, and so the Munday then next after shee came likewise to card: and this Examinates wife having newly tunned[56] drinke into Stands,[57] which stood by the said *Anne Whittle*, alias *Chattox*: and the said *Anne Whittle* taking a Dish or Cup, and drawing drinke severall times: {E2} and so never after that time, for some eight or nine weekes, they could have any drinke, but spoiled, and as this Examinate thinketh was by the meanes of the said *Chattox*. And further he saith, that the said *Anne Whittle*, alias *Chattox*, and *Anne Redferne* her said Daughter, are commonly reputed and reported to bee Witches. And

52 Worked, kneaded.
53 A small open tub.
54 This description suggests that Robinson's evidence is here being given in court, although it reads like a normal written information.
55 Comb out wool for spinning.
56 Stored away, barrelled.
57 Barrels.

hee also saith, that about some eighteene yeares agoe, he dwelled with one *Robert Nutter* the elder, of Pendle aforesaid. And that yong *Robert Nutter*, who dwelled with his Grand-father, in the Sommer time, he fell sicke, and in his said sicknesse hee did severall times complaine, that hee had harme by them: and this Examinate asking him what hee meant by that word *Them*, He said, that he verily thought that the said *Anne Whittle*, alias *Chattox*, and the said *Redfernes* wife, had bewitched him: and the said *Robert Nutter* shortly after, being to goe with his then Master, called Sir *Richard Shuttleworth*,[58] into Wales, this Examinate heard him say before his then going, unto the said *Thomas Redferne*, that if ever he came againe he would get his Father to put the said *Redferne* out of his house, or he himselfe would pull it downe; to whom the said *Redferne* replyed, saying; when you come back againe you will be in a better minde: but he never came back againe, but died before Candlemas[59] in Cheshire, as he was comming homeward.

Since the voluntarie confession and examination of a Witch, doth exceede all other evidence, I spare to trouble you with a multitude of Examinations, or Depositions of any other witnesses, by reason this bloudie fact, for the murder of *Robert Nutter*, upon so small an occasion, as to threaten to take away {E2v} his owne land from such as were not worthie to inhabite or dwell upon it, is now made by that which you have alreadie heard, so apparant, as no indifferent man will question it, or rest unsatisfied: I shall now proceede to set forth unto you the rest of her actions, remaining upon Record. And how dangerous it was for any man to live neere this people,[60] to give them any occasion of offence, I leave it to your good consideration.

The Examination and voluntarie Confession of ANNE WHITTLE, alias CHATTOX, *taken at the Fence in the Forrest of Pendle, in the Countie of Lancaster, the second day of Aprill*, Anno Regni Regis JACOBI Angliae, Franciae, & Hiberniae, decimo, & Scotiae xlv.

Before ROGER NOWEL, *Esquire, one of his Majesties Justices of Peace within the Countie of Lancaster.*

SHe the said Examinate saith,[61] That shee was sent for by the wife of *John Moore*, to helpe drinke that was forspoken or bewitched: at which time shee used this Prayer for the amending of it, *viz.*

A Charme.

Three Biters hast thou bitten,
The Hart, ill Eye, ill Tonge:

58 The chief justice of Chester from 1589, Shuttleworth lived at Gawthorpe (Lumby, 185) near Padiham, five miles south of Pendle Hill.

59 2 February.

60 This is corrected to 'these people' by the printer.

61 This account lacks the usual introductory repetition of names, and probably thus begins some way into the examination.

{E3} *Three bitter shall be thy Boote,*
Father, Sonne, and Holy Ghost
a Gods name
Five Pater-nosters, five Avies,
and a Creede,
In worship of the five wounds
of our Lord.

After which time this Examinate had used these prayers, and amended her drinke, the said *Moores* wife did chide this Examinate, and was grieved at her. And thereupon this Examinate called for her Devill *Fancie*, and bad him goe bite a browne Cow of the said *Moores* by the head, and make the Cow goe madde: and the Devill then, in the likenesse of a browne Dogge, went to the said Cow, and bit her: which Cow went madde accordingly, and died within six weekes next after, or thereabouts.

Also this Examinate saith, That shee perceiving *Anthonie Nutter* of Pendle to favour *Elizabeth Sothernes*, alias *Dembdike*, she, this Examinate, called *Fancie* to her, (who appeared like a man) and bad him goe kill a Cow of the said *Anthonies*; which the said Devill did, and the Cow died also.

And further this Examinate saith, That the Devill, or *Fancie*, hath taken most of her sight away from her. And further this Examinate saith, That in Summer last, save one, the said Devill, or *Fancie*, came upon this Examinate in the night time: and at diverse and sundry times in the likenesse of a Beare, gaping as though he would have wearied[62] this Examinate. and the last time of all shee, this Examinate, saw him, was upon {E3v} Thursday last yeare but one, next before Midsummer day, in the evening,[63] like a Beare, and this Examinate would not then speake unto him, for the which the said Devill pulled this Examinate downe.

The Examination of JAMES DEVICE, *sonne of* ELIZABETH DEVICE, *taken the seven and twentieth day of Aprill,* Annoq; Reg. Regis JACOBI Angliae, &c. Decimo ac Scotiae xlv.

Before ROGER NOWEL and NICHOLAS BANISTER, *Esquires, two of his Majesties Justices of the Peace within the said Countie.* viz.

ANd further saith,[64] That twelve yeares agoe, the said *Anne Chattox* at a Buriall at the new Church in Pendle,[65] did take three scalpes[66] of people, which had been buried, and then cast out of a grave, as she the said *Chattox* told this Examinate; and tooke eight teeth out of the said Scalpes, whereof she kept foure to her selfe, and gave the other foure to the said *Demdike*,

62 Worried?
63 Midsummer Eve, 23 June.
64 This account definitely begins midway through the examination.
65 Newchurch is two miles south-east of Pendle Hill.
66 Skulls.

this Examinates Grand-mother: which foure teeth now shewed to this Examinate, are the foure teeth that the said *Chattox* gave to his said Grand-mother, as aforesaid; which said teeth have ever since beene kept, untill now found by the said *Henry Hargreives*[67] & this Examinate, at the West-end of this Examinates Grand-mothers house, and there buried in the earth, and a Picture of Clay there likewise found by them, about halfe a yard over in the {E4} earth, where the said teeth lay, which said picture so found, was almost withered away, and was the Picture of *Anne, Anthony Nutters* daughter; as this Examinates Grand-mother told him.

The Examination of ALLIZON DEVICE *daughter of* ELIZABETH DEVICE*: Taken at Reade, in the Countie of Lancaster, the thirtieth day of March,* Annoq; Reg. Regis JACOBI nunc Angliae, &c. Decimo, & Scotiae Quadragesimo quinto.

Before ROGER NOWEL *of Reade aforesaid, Esquire, one of his Majesties Justices of the Peace, within the said Countie.*

THis Examinate saith, That about eleven yeares agoe, this Examinate and her mother had their fire-house broken, and all, or most part of their linnen clothes & halfe a peck of cut oat-meale, and a quantitie of meale gone, all which was worth twentie shillings or above: and upon a Sunday then next after, this Examinate did take a band and a coif, parcell of the goods aforesaid,[68] upon the daughter of *Anne Whittle, alias Chattox*, and claimed them to be parcell of the goods stolne, as aforesaid.

And this Examinate further saith, That her father, called *John Device*, being afraid, that the said *Anne Chattox* should doe him or his goods any hurt by Witch-{E4v}-craft; did covenant with the said *Anne*, that if she would hurt neither of them, she should yearely have one Aghen-dole[69] of meale; which meale was yearely paid, untill the yeare which her father died in, which was about eleven yeares since: Her father upon his then-death-bed, taking it that the said *Anne Whittle*, alias *Chattox*, did bewitch him to death, because the said meale was not paid the last yeare.

And she also saith, That about two yeares agone, this Examinate being in the house of *Anthony Nutter* of Pendle aforesaid, and being then in company with *Anne Nutter*, daughter of the said *Anthony*: the said *Anne Whittle*, alias *Chattox*, came into the said *Anthony Nutters* house, and seeing this Examinate, and the said *Anne Nutter* laughing and saying, that they laughed at her the said *Chattox*: well said then (sayes *Anne Chattox*) I will be meet with the one of you. And upon the next day after, she the said *Anne Nutter* fell sicke, and within three weekes after died. And further, this Examinate saith, That about two yeares

67 See Y4–Y4v for Hargreives. An unusual description of the use of physical evidence of witchcraft in examining a suspect/informant.

68 A head-band and a skull-cap worn in the house, part of the goods.

69 A measure, possibly about 8 pounds (Edgar Peel and Pat Southern, *The Trials of the Lancashire Witches* [1969; Nelson: Hendon Publishing, 1994], 18).

agoe, she, this Examinate, hath heard, That the said *Anne Whittle*, alias *Chattox*, was suspected for bewitching the drinke of *John Moore* of Higham[70] Gentleman: and not long after, shee this Examinate heard the said *Chattox* say, that she would meet with the said *John Moore*, or his. Whereupon a child of the said *John Moores*, called *John*, fell sicke, and languished about halfe a yeare, and then died: during which languishing, this Examinate saw the said *Chattox* sitting in her owne garden, and a picture of Clay like unto a child in her Apron; which this Examinate espying, the said *Anne Chattox* would have hidde with her Apron: and this Examinate declaring the same to her mother, her {F} mother thought that it was the picture of the said *John Moores* childe.

And she this Examinate further saith, That about sixe or seven yeares agoe, the said *Chattox* did fall out with one *Hugh Moore* of Pendle, as aforesaid, about certaine cattell of the said *Moores*, which the said *Moore* did charge the said *Chattox* to have bewitched: for which the said *Chattox* did curse and worry the said *Moore*, and said she would be Revenged of the said *Moore*: whereupon the said *Moore* presently fell sicke, and languished about halfe a yeare, and then died. Which *Moore* upon his death-bed said, that the said *Chattox* had bewitched him to death. And she further saith, That about sixe yeares agoe, a daughter of the said *Anne Chattox*, called *Elizabeth*, having been at the house of *John Nutter* of the Bull-hole, to begge or get a dishe of milke, which she had, and brought to her mother, who was about a fields breadth of the said *Nutters* house, which her said mother *Anne Chattox* tooke and put into a Kan; and did charne[71] the same with two stickes acrosse in the same field: whereupon the said *John Nutters* sonne came unto her, the said *Chattox*, and misliking her doings, put the said Kan and milke over with his foot; and the morning next after, a Cow of the said *John Nutters* fell sicke, and so languished three or foure dayes, and then died.

In the end being openly charged with all this in open Court; with weeping teares she humbly acknowledged them to be true, and cried out unto God for Mercy and forgiveness of her sinnes and humbly prayed my Lord to be mercifull unto *Anne Redfearne* her daughter, of whose life and condition you shall heare more upon {Fv} her Arraignement and Triall: whereupon shee being taken away, *Elizabeth Device* comes now to receive her Triall being the next in order, of whom you shall heare at large.

{F2} THE ARRAIGNMENT *and Triall of* ELIZABETH DEVICE (*Daughter of* ELIZABETH SOTHERNES, alias OLD DEMBDIKE) *late wife of* JO. DEVICE, *of the Forrest of Pendle, in the Countie of Lancaster, widow, for Witchcraft; Upon Tuesday the eighteenth of August, at the Assises and generall Gaole-Deliverie holden at Lancaster*

Before *Sir* EDWARD BROMLEY *Knight, one of his Majesties Justices of Assise at Lancaster.*

70 Higham is a village three miles south of Pendle Hill, near Fence.

71 Charm? Churn seems unlikely.

Elizabeth Device.

O Barbarous and inhumane Monster, beyond example; so farre from sensible understanding of thy owne miserie, as to bring thy owne naturall children into mischiefe and bondage; and thy selfe to be a witnesse upon the Gallowes, to see thy owne children, by thy devilish instructions hatcht up in Villanie and Witchcraft, to suffer with thee, even in the beginning of their time, a shamefull and untimely Death. Too much (so it be true) cannot be said or written of her. Such was her life and condition: that even at the Barre, when shee came to receive her Triall (where the {F2v} least sparke of Grace or modestie would have procured favour, or moved pitie) she was not able to containe her selfe within the limits of any order or government: but exclaiming, in a very outragious manner crying out against her owne children, and such as came to prosecute Indictments & Evidence for the Kings Majestie against her, for the death of their Children, Friends, and Kinsfolkes, whome cruelly and bloudily, by her Enchauntments, Charmes, and Sorceries she had murthered and cut off; sparing no man with fearefull execrable curses and banning: Such in generall was the common opinion of the Countrey where she dwelt, in the Forrest of Pendle (a place fit for people of such condition) that no man neere her, neither his wife, children, goods, or cattell should be secure or free from danger.

This *Elizabeth Device* was the daughter of *Elizabeth Sothernes*, old *Dembdike*, a malicious, wicked, and dangerous Witch for fiftie yeares, as appeareth by Record: and how much longer, the Devill and shee knew best, with whome shee made her covenant.

It is very certaine, that amongst all these Witches there was not a more dangerous and devilish Witch to execute mischiefe, having old *Dembdike*, her mother, to assist her; *James Device* and *Alizon Device*, her owne naturall children, all provided with Spirits, upon any occasion of offence readie to assist her.

Upon her Examination, although Master *Nowel* was very circumspect, and exceeding carefull in dealing with her, yet she would confesse nothing, untill it pleased God to raise up a yong maid *Jennet Device*, her owne daughter, about the age of nine yeares (a witnesse unexpected,) to discover all their Practises, Meetings, Con-{F3}-sultations, Murthers, Charmes, and Villanies: such, and in such sort, as I may justly say of them, as a reverend and learned Judge of this Kingdome speaketh of the greatest Treason that ever was in this Kingdome, *Quis haec posteris sic narrare poterit, ut facta non ficta este videantur?* That when these things shall be related to Posteritie, they will be reputed matters fained, not done.[72]

And then knowing, that both *Jennet Device*, her daughter, *James Device*, her sonne, and *Alizon Device*, with others, had accused her and layd open all

72 Potts acknowledges his inspiration and, to some extent, model here: Sir Edward Coke's magisterial description of the Gunpowder Plot. Coke was the Attorney General (Cobbett, 166).

things, in their Examinations taken before Master *Nowel*, and although she were their owne naturall mother, yet they did not spare to accuse her of every particular fact, which in her time she had committed, to their knowledge; she made a very liberall and voluntarie Confession, as hereafter shall be given in evidence against her, upon her Arraignement and Triall.

This *Elizabeth Device* being at libertie, after Old *Dembdike* her mother, *Alizon Device*, her daughter, and old *Chattocks* were committed to the Castle of Lancaster for Witchcraft; laboured not a little to procure a solemne meeting at Malkyn-Tower of the Graund Witches of the Counties of Lancaster and Yorke, being yet unsuspected and untaken, to consult of some speedie course for the deliverance of their friends, the Witches at Lancaster, and for putting in execution of some other devillish practises of Murther and Mischiefe: as upon the Arraignement and Triall of *James Device*, her sonne, shall hereafter in every particular point appeare at large against her.

{F3v} The first Indictment.[73]

THis *Elizabeth Device*, late the wife of *John Device*, of the Forrest of Pendle, in the Countie of Lancaster Widdow, being indicted, for that shee felloniously had practized, used, and exercised divers wicked and devilish Arts, called *Witch-crafts, Inchauntments, Charmes*, and *Sorceries*, in, and upon one *John Robinson*, alias *Swyer*: and by force of the same felloniously, the said *John Robinson*, alias *Swyer*, had killed. *Contra pacem, &c.* being at the Barre was arraigned.

2. Indictment.

The said *Elizabeth Device* was the second time indicted in the same manner and forme, for the death of *James Robinson*, by Witch-craft. *Contra pacem, &c.*

3. Indictment.

The said *Elizabeth Device*, was the third time with others, *viz. Alice Nutter*, and *Elizabeth Sothernes*, alias *Old Dembdike*, her Grand-mother,[74] Indicted in the same manner and forme, for the death of *Henry Mytton. Contra pacem, &c.*

To these three severall Indictments upon her Arraignement, shee pleaded not guiltie; and for the tryall of her life, put her selfe upon God and her Countrie. So as now the Gentlemen of the Jurie of life and death, stand charged to finde, whether shee bee guiltie of them, or any of them.

{F4} Whereupon there was openly read, and given in evidence against her, for the Kings Majestie, her owne voluntarie Confession and Examination, when shee was apprehended, taken, and committed to the Castle of Lancaster by M. *Nowel*, and M. *Bannester*, two of his Majesties Justices of Peace in the same Countie. *viz.*

73 The (translated) indictment refers to the Jacobean Witchcraft Act of 1604. This is a new way for Potts to present a case, and one wonders why he did not use it previously in presenting Anne Chattox. Most pamphleteers had no access to such documents of record, but only to pre-trial material which was usually discarded after the trial.

74 A mistake – unusual in this most careful of pamphlets.

The Examination and voluntarie confession of ELIZABETH DEVICE, *taken at the house of* JAMES WILSEY *of the Forrest of Pendle, in the Countie of Lancaster, the seven and twentieth day of Aprill: Anno Reg.* JACOBI, *Angl. &c. decimo, & Scotiae* xlv.

Before ROGER NOWEL, *and* NICHOLS BANNESTER, *Esquires; two of his Majesties Justices of the Peace within the same Countie.* viz.

The said *Elizabeth Device*, Mother of the said *James*,[75] being examined, confesseth and saith.

THat at the third time her Spirit, the Spirit *Ball*, appeared to her in the shape of a browne Dogge, at, or in her Mothers house in Pendle Forrest aforesaid: about foure yeares agoe the said Spirit bidde this Examinate make a picture of Clay after the said *John Robinson*, alias *Swyer*, which this Examinate did make accordingly at the West end of her said Mothers house, and dryed the same picture away within a weeke or thereabouts, and about a {F4v} weeke after the Picture was crumbled or mulled away; the said *Robinson* dyed.

The reason wherefore shee this Examinate did so bewitch the said *Robinson* to death, was: for that the said *Robinson* had chidden and becalled this Examinate, for having a Bastard child with one *Seller*.

And this Examinate further saith and confesseth, that shee did bewitch the said *James Robinson* to death, as in the said *Jennet Device* her examination is confessed.

And further shee saith, and confesseth, that shee with the wife of *Richard Nutter*, and this Examinates said Mother, joyned altogether, and did bewitch the said *Henrie Mytton* to death.

The Examination and Evidence of JENNET DEVICE, *Daughter of the said* ELIZABETH DEVICE, *late Wife of* JOHN DEVICE, *of the Forrest of Pendle, in the Countie of Lancaster.*

Against ELIZABETH DEVICE *her Mother, Prisoner at the Barre upon her Arraignement and Triall.* viz.[76]

THe said *Jennet Device*, being a yong Maide, about the age of nine yeares, and commanded to stand up to give evidence against her Mother, Prisoner at the Barre: Her Mother, according to her accustomed manner, outragiously cursing, cryed out against the child in such fearefull manner, as all the Court did not a little wonder at her, and so amazed the child, as with weeping

75 This, and the opening words of the examination, suggest that it begins part-way through. It is probably also more linked to statements by James Device (and Jennet Device on F4v) than we can now see, and therefore it may well not be Elizabeth's first examination but a subsequent one, as Potts suggests in his narration F2v–F3.

76 This child's evidence is described as being reported from the trial, but, given its form, vocabulary and context in the story of the Devices' confessions, it seems much more likely to be taken from a previous examination (see G, where this is mentioned). Perhaps, like Brian Darcy, Potts preferred to keep the dates of child evidence vague, especially where it prompted adults to confess.

teares {G} shee cryed out unto my Lord the Judge, and told him, shee was not able to speake in the presence of her Mother.

This odious Witch was branded with a preposterous marke in Nature,[77] even from her birth, which was her left eye, standing lower then the other; the one looking downe, the other looking up, so strangely deformed, as the best that were present in that Honorable assembly, and great Audience, did affirme, they had not often seene the like.

No intreatie, promise of favour, or other respect, could put her to silence, thinking by this her outragious cursing and threatning of the child, to inforce her to denie that which she had formerly confessed against her Mother, before M. *Nowel*: Forswearing and denying her owne voluntarie confession, which you have heard, given in evidence against her at large, and so for want of further evidence to escape that, which the Justice of the Law had provided as a condigne[78] punishment for the innocent bloud shee had spilt, and her wicked and devilish course of life.

In the end, when no meanes would serve, his Lordship commanded the Prisoner to be taken away, and the Maide to bee set upon the Table in the presence of the whole Court, who delivered her evidence in that Honorable assembly, to the Gentlemen of the Jurie of life and death, as followeth. *viz.*

Jennet Device, Daughter of *Elizabeth Device*, late Wife of *John Device*, of the Forrest of Pendle aforesaid Widdow, confesseth and saith, that her said Mother is a Witch, and that this shee knoweth to be true; for, that {Gv} shee hath seene her Spirit sundrie times come unto her said Mother in her owne house, called *Malking-Tower*, in the likenesse of a browne Dogge, which shee called *Ball*; and at one time amongst others, the said *Ball* did aske this Examinates Mother what she would have him to doe: and this Examinates Mother answered, that she would have the said *Ball* to helpe her to kill *John Robinson* of *Barley*,[79] alias *Swyre*: by helpe of which said *Ball*, the said *Swyer* was killed by witch-craft accordingly; and that this Examinates Mother had continued a Witch for these three or foure yeares last past. And further, this Examinate confesseth, that about a yeare after, this Examinates Mother called for the said *Ball*, who appeared as aforesaid, asking this Examinates Mother what shee would have done, who said, that shee would have him to kill *James Robinson*, alias *Swyer*, of Barlow aforesaid, Brother to the said *John*: whereunto *Ball* answered, hee would doe it; and about three weekes after, the said *James* dyed. And this Examinate also saith, that one other time shee was present, when her said Mother did call for the said *Ball*,[80] who appeared in manner as

77 A mark contrary to the natural order.

78 Deserved, appropriate.

79 Barley is the closest village to Pendle Hill, a mile south-east.

80 A marginal note reads 'Her Spirit' – although we have just been given this information in the text. Perhaps the material has been cut and reordered in order to match the indictments closely, and in its original sequence it was no longer clear what Ball was.

aforesaid, and asked this Examinates Mother what shee would have him to doe, whereunto this Examinates Mother then said shee would have him to kill one *Mitton* of the Rough-Lee,[81] whereupon the said Ball said, he would doe it, and so vanished away, and about three weekes after, the said *Mitton* likewise dyed.

{G2} *The Examination of* JAMES DEVICE, *sonne of the said* ELIZABETH DEVICE: *Taken the seven and twentieth day of Aprill*, Annoq; Reg. Regis JACOBI Angliae, &c. Decimo ac Scotiae, xlv.

Before ROGER NOWEL *and* NICHOLAS BANESTER, *Esquires, two of his Majesties Justices of the Peace, within the Countie.* viz.

THe said *James Device* being examined, saith, That he heard his Grand-mother say, about a yeare agoe, That his mother, called *Elizabeth Device*, and others, had killed one *Henry Mitton* of the Rough-Lee aforesaid, by Witchcraft. The reason wherefore he was so killed, was for that this Examinates said Grand-mother *Old Demdike*, had asked the said *Mitton* a penny; and he denying her thereof, thereupon she procured his death, as aforesaid.

And he, this Examinate also saith, That about three yeares ago, this Examinate being in his Grand-mothers house, with his said mother; there came a thing in shape of a browne dogge, which his mother called *Ball*, who spake to this Examinates mother, in the sight and hearing of this Examinate, and bad her make a Picture of Clay like unto *John Robinson*, alias *Swyer*, and drie it hard and then crumble it by little and little; and as the said Picture should crumble or mull away, so should the said *Jo. Robinson* alias *Swyer* his body decay and weare away. And within two or three dayes after, the Picture shall so all be wasted, and mulled away; so then the said *John Robinson* should die presently. Upon the agreement be-{G2v}-twixt the said dogge and this Examinates mother; the said dogge suddenly vanished out of this Examinates sight. And the next day, this Examinate saw his said mother take Clay at the West-end of her said house, and make a Picture of it after the said *Robinson*, and brought into her house, and dried it some two dayes: and about two dayes after the drying thereof this Examinates said mother fell on crumbling the said Picture of Clay, every day some, for some three weekes together; and within two dayes after all was crumbled or mulled away, the said *John Robinson* died.

Being demanded by the Court, what answere shee could give to the particular points of the Evidence against her, for the death of these severall persons; Impudently shee denied them, crying out against her children, and the rest of the Witnesses against her.

But because I have charged her to be the principall Agent, to procure a solemne meeting at *Malking-Tower* of the Grand-witches, to consult of some speedy course for the deliverance of her mother, *Old Demdike*, her daughter, and other Witches at Lancaster: the speedie Execution of Master *Covell*, who

81 Roughlee is a village near Blacko, two miles south-east of Pendle Hill.

little suspected or deserved any such practise or villany against him: The blowing up of the Castle, with divers other wicked and divellish practises and murthers; I shall make it apparant unto you, by the particular Examinations and Evidence of her owne children, such as were present at the time of their Consultation, together with her owne Examination and Confession, amongst the Records of the Crowne at Lancaster, as hereafter followeth.

{G3} *The voluntary Confession and Examination of* ELIZABETH DEVICE, *taken at the house of* JAMES WILSEY, *of the Forrest of Pendle, in the Countie of Lancaster, the seven and twentieth day of Aprill,* Annoq; Reg. Regis JACOBI Angliae, &c. Decimo, & Scotiae Quadragesimo quinto.

Before ROGER NOWEL and NICHOLAS BANISTER, *Esquires, two of his Majesties Justices of the Peace within the same Countie.* viz.

THe said *Elizabeth Device* being further Examined, confesseth, that upon Good-Friday last, there dined at this Examinates house, called *Malking-Tower*, those which she hath said are Witches, and doth verily think them to be Witches: and their names are those whom *James Device* hath formerly spoken of to be there. And she further saith, that there was also at her said mothers house, at the day and time aforesaid, two women of Burneley Parish, whose names the wife of *Richard Nutter* doth know. And there was likewise there one *Anne Crouckshey* of Marsden:[82] And shee also confesseth, in all things touching the Christening of the Spirit, and the killing of Master *Lister* of Westbie,[83] as the said *James Device* hath before confessed; but denieth of any talke was amongst them the said Witches, to her now remembrance, at the said meeting together, touching the killing of the Galoer,[84] or the blowing up of Lancaster Castle.[85]

{G3v} *The Examination and Evidence of* JENNET DEVICE, *daughter of the said* ELIZABETH DEVICE, *late wife of* JOHN DEVICE, *of the Forrest of Pendle, in the Countie of Lancaster.*

Against ELIZABETH DEVICE, *her Mother, prisoner at the Barre, upon her Arraignement and Triall,* viz.

THe said *Jennet Device* saith, That upon Good Friday last there was about twentie persons (whereof onely two were men, to this Examinates remembrance) at her said Grandmothers house, called Malking-Tower aforesaid, about twelve of the clocke: all which persons this Examinates said mother told her, were Witches, and that they came to give a name to *Alizon Device* Spirit, or Familiar, sister to this Examinate, and now prisoner at Lancaster. And also this Examinate saith, That the persons aforesaid had to their dinners

82 Marsden is now Nelson, four miles south-east of Pendle Hill.

83 Westby is in Yorkshire, near Gisburn, four miles north of Pendle Hill in an area known as Craven.

84 *Sic.*

85 There are clearly missing pieces of text here.

Beefe, Bacon, and roasted Mutton; which Mutton (as this Examinates said brother said) was of a Wether[86] of *Christopher Swyers* of Barley: which Wether was brought in the night before into this Examinates mothers house by the said *James Device*, this Examinates said brother: and in this Examinates sight killed and eaten, as aforesaid. And shee further saith, That shee knoweth the names of sixe of the said Witches, *viz.* the wife of *Hugh Hargraves* under Pendle,[87] *Christopher Howgate* of Pendle, unckle to this Examinate, and *Elizabeth* his wife, and *Dicke Miles* his wife of the Rough-Lee; *Christopher Jackes* of Thorny-holme,[88] and his wife: and the names {G4} of the residue shee this Examinate doth not know, saving that this Examinates mother and brother were both there. And lastly, she this Examinate confesseth and saith, That her mother hath taught her two prayers: the one to cure the bewitched, and the other to get drinke; both which particularly appeare.[89]

The Examination and Evidence of JAMES DEVICE, *sonne of the said* ELIZABETH DEVICE, *late wife of* JOHN DEVICE, *of the Forrest of Pendle, in the Countie of Lancaster.*

Against ELIZABETH DEVICE, *his Mother, prisoner at the Barre, upon her Arraignement and Triall,* viz.

THe said *James Device* saith, That on Good-Friday last, about twelve of the clocke in the day time, there dined in this Examinates said mothers house, at Malking-Tower, a number of persons, whereof three were men, with this Examinate, and the rest women; and that they met there for three causes following (as this Examinates said mother told this Examinate) The first was, for the naming of the Spirit, which *Alizon Device*, now prisoner at Lancaster, had: But did not name him, because shee was not there. The second was, for the deliverie of his said Grandmother, olde *Dembdike*; this Examinates said sister *Allizon*; the said {G4v} *Anne Chattox*, and her daughter *Redferne*; killing the Gaoler at Lancaster; and before the next Assises to blow up the Castle there: and to that end the aforesaid prisoners might by that time make an escape, and get away. All which this Examinate then heard them conferre of.

And he also sayth, That the names of the said Witches as were on Good-Friday at this Examinates said Grandmothers house, and now this Examinates owne mothers, for so many of them as hee did know, were these, *viz.* The wife of *Hugh Hargreives* of Burley; the wife of *Christopher Bulcock* of the Mosse end,[90] and *John* her sonne; the mother of *Myles Nutter*;[91] *Elizabeth*, the wife of *Christopher Hargreives*, of Thurniholme; *Christopher Howgate*, and

86 Castrated male sheep.
87 A farm near Barley.
88 A farm near Roughlee.
89 Potts acknowledges his own editing with this 'cross-reference'.
90 A farm near Newchurch.
91 Alice Nutter (see P) almost certainly also called 'Dick Miles wife', just as Christopher Hargreives may well be Christopher Jackes (see Lumby, 45).

Elizabeth, his wife; *Alice Graye* of Coulne, and one *Mould-heeles* wife, of the same: and this Examinate, and his Mother. And this Examinate further sayth, That all the Witches went out of the said House in their owne shapes and likenesses. And they all, by that they were forth of the dores, gotten on Horsebacke, like unto Foales, some of one colour, some of another; and *Prestons* wife was the last: and when shee got on Horsebacke, they all presently vanished out of this Examinates sight. And before their said parting away, they all appointed to meete at the said *Prestons* wives[92] house that day twelve-moneths; at which time the said *Prestons* wife promised to make them a great Feast. And if they had occasion to meete in the meane time, then should warning be given, that they all should meete upon *Romleyes* Moore.[93]

{H} And here[94] they parted, with resolution to execute their devillish and bloudie practises, for the deliverance of their friends, untill they came to meete here, where their power and strength was gone. And now finding her Meanes was gone, shee cryed out for Mercie. Whereupon shee being taken away, the next in order was her sonne *James Device*, whom shee and her Mother, old *Dembdike*, brought to act his part in this wofull Tragedie.

{Hv} THE ARRAIGNMENT *and Triall of* JAMES DEVICE, *Sonne of* ELIZABETH DEVICE, *of the Forrest of Pendle, within the Countie of Lancaster aforesaid, Laborer, for Witchcraft; Upon Tuesday the eighteenth of August, at the Assises and generall Gaole-Deliverie holden at Lancaster.*

Before *Sir* EDWARD BROMLEY *Knight, one of his Majesties Justices of Assise at Lancaster.*

James Device.

THis wicked and miserable Wretch, whether by practise, or meanes, to bring himselfe to some untimely death, and thereby to avoide his Tryall by his Countrey, and just judgement of the Law; or ashamed to bee openly charged with so many devillish practises, and so much innocent bloud as hee had split (*sic*); or by reason of his Imprisonment so long time before his Tryall (which was with more favour, commiseration, and reliefe then hee deserved) I know not: But being brought forth to the {H2} Barre, to receive his Triall before this worthie Judge, and so Honourable and Worshipfull an Assembly of Justices for this service, was so insensible, weake, and unable in all thinges, as he could neither speake, heare, or stand, but was holden up when hee was brought to the place of his Arraignement, to receive his triall.

This *James Device* of the Forrest of Pendle, being brought to the Barre, was there according to the forme, order, and course, Indicted and Arraigned; for that hee Felloniously had practised, used, and exercised divers wicked and devillish Arts, called *Witch-crafts, Inchauntments, Charmes*, and *Sorceries,* in

92 A marginal note reads '*Executed at Yorke the last Assises*'. See the final section of this pamphlet.

93 Moorland in Yorkshire, east of Gisburn.

94 The printer amends this to 'there'.

and upon one *Anne Towneley*, wife of *Henrie Towneley* of the Carre,[95] in the Countie of Lancaster Gentleman, and her by force of the same, felloniously had killed. *Contra pacem, &c.*

The said *James Device* was the second time Indicted and Arraigned in the same manner and forme, for the death of *John Duckworth*, by witch-craft. *Contra pacem, &c.*

To these two severall Indictments upon his Arraignment, he pleaded not guiltie, and for the triall of his life put himselfe upon God and his Countrie. So as now the Gentleman of the Jurie of life & death stand charged to finde, whether he be guiltie of these, or either of them.

Whereupon Master *Nowel* humbly prayed Master *Towneley* might be called, who attended to prosecute and give evidence against him for the Kings Majestie, and that the particular examinations taken before him and others, might be openly published & read in Court, in the hearing of the Prisoner. {H2v} But because it were infinite to bring him to his particular Triall for every offence, which hee hath committed in his time, and every practice wherein he hath had his hand: I shall proceede in order with the Evidence remayning upon Record against him, amongst the Records of the Crowne; both how, and in what sort hee came to be a witch: and shew you what apparant proofe there is to charge him with the death of these two severall persons, for the which hee now standeth upon his triall for al the rest of his devillish practises, incantations, murders, charmes, sorceries, meetings to consult with Witches, to execute mischiefe (take them as they are against him upon Record:) Enough, I doubt not. For these with the course of his life will serve his turne to deliver you from the danger of him that never tooke felicitie in any things, but in revenge, bloud, & mischiefe with crying out unto God for vengeance; which hath now at the length brought him to the place where hee standes to receive his Triall with more honor, favour, and respect, then such a Monster in Nature doth deserve; And I doubt not, but in due time by the Justice of the Law, to an untimely and shamefull death.[96]

{H3} *The Examination of* JAMES DEVICE, *sonne of* ELIZABETH DEVICE, *of the Forrest of Pendle, in the Countie of Lancaster, Labourer. Taken the seven and twentieth day of Aprill, Annoq Reg. Regis* JACOBI, *Angliae, &c. xo. & Scotiae Quadragesimo quinto.*

Before ROGER NOWEL, *and* NICHOLAS BANNESTER, *Esquires: two of his Majesties Justices of Peace within the said Countie.*

HE saith, that upon Sheare Thursday was two yeares,[97] his Grand-Mother *Elizabeth Sothernes*, alias *Dembdike*, did bid him this Examinate goe to the

95 Near Nelson, four miles south-east of Pendle Hill.

96 This anxious passage suggests problems with the textual evidence against James Device which are obvious throughout this section.

97 Two years ago. Sheare Thursday is the Thursday before Good Friday.

church to receive the Communion (the next day after being Good Friday) and then not to eate the Bread the Minister gave him, but to bring it and deliver it to such a thing as should meet him in this way homewards: Notwithstanding her perswasions, this Examinate did eate the Bread: and so in his comming homeward some fortie roodes off the said Church, there met him a thing in the shape of a Hare, who spoke unto this Examinate, and asked him whether hee had brought the Bread that his Grand-mother had bidden him, or no? whereupon this Examinate answered, hee had not: and thereupon the said thing threatned to pull this Examinate in peeces, and so this examinate thereupon marked himselfe to God,[98] and so the said thing vanished out of this Examinates sight. And within some foure daies after that, there appeared in this Examinates sight, hard by the new Church in Pendle, a thing like unto a browne {H3v} *Dogge*, who asked this Examinate to give him his Soule, and he should be revenged of any whom hee would: whereunto this Examinate answered, that his Soule was not his to give, but was his *Saviour Jesus Christs*, but as much as was in him this Examinate to give, he was contented he should have it.

And within two or three daies after, this Examinate went to the Carre-Hall, and upon some speeches betwixt Mistris *Towneley* and this examinate; Shee charging this Examinate and his said mother, to have stolne some Turves of hers, badde him packe the doores:[99] and withall as he went forth of the doore, the said Mistris *Towneley* gave him a knock betweene the shoulders: and about a day or two after that, there appeared unto this Examinate in his way, a thing like unto a black dog, who put this Examinate in minde of the said Mistris *Towneleys* falling out with him this Examinate; who bad this Examinate make a Picture of Clay, like unto the said Mistris *Towneley*: and that this Examinate with the helpe of his Spirit (who then ever after bidde this Examinate to call it *Dandy*) would kill or destroy the said Mistris *Towneley*: and so the said dogge vanished out of this Examinates sight. And the next morning after, this Examinate tooke Clay, and made a Picture of the said Mistris *Towneley*, and dried it the same night by the fire: and within a day after, hee, this Examinate began to crumble the said Picture, every day some, for the space of a weeke: and within two daies after all was crumbled away; the said Mistris *Towneley* died.

And hee further saith, That in Lent last one *John Duckworth* of the Lawnde, promised this Examinate an old shirt: and within a fortnight after, this Examinate {H4} went to the said *Duckworthes* house, and demanded the said old shirt; but the said *Duckworth* denied him thereof. And going out of the said house, the said Spirit *Dandy* appeared unto this Examinate, and said, Thou didst touch the said *Duckworth*; whereunto this Examinate answered, he did not touch him: yes (said the Spirit againe) thou didst touch him, and

98 Crossed himself – in a Catholic fashion.
99 Probably to 'go away', as in 'to be sent packing'.

therfore I have power of him: whereupon this Examinate joyned with the said Spirit, and then wished the said Spirit to kill the said *Duckworth*: and within one weeke, then next after, *Duckworth* died.

This voluntary Confession and Examination of his owne, containing in it selfe matter sufficient in Law to charge him, and to prove his offences, contained in the two severall Indictments, was sufficient to satisfie the Gentlemen of the Jury of Life and Death, that he is guiltie of them, and either of them: yet my Lord *Bromley* commanded, for their better satisfaction, that the Witnesses present in Court against any of the Prisoners, should be examined openly, *viva voce*, that the Prisoner might both heare and answere to every particular point of their Evidence; notwithstanding any of their Examinations taken before any of his Majesties Justices of Peace within the same Countie.[100]

Herein do but observe the wonderfull work of God; to raise up a yong Infant, the very sister of the Prisonr,[101] *Jennet Device*, to discover, justifie and prove these things against him at the time of his Arraignement and Triall, as hereafter followeth. *viz.*

{H4v} *The Examination and Evidence of* JENNET DEVICE *daughter of* ELIZABETH DEVICE, *late wife of* JOHN DEVICE *of of*[102] *the Forrest of Pendle, in the Countie of Lancaster.*

Against JAMES DEVICE, *Prisoner at the Barre, upon his Arraignement and Triall.* viz.

BEing examined in open Court, she saith, That her brother *James Device*, the Prisoner at the Barre, hath beene a Witch for the space of three yeares: about the beginning of which time, there appeared unto him, in this Examinates mothers house, a Black-Dogge, which her said brother called *Dandy*.[103] And further, this Examinate confesseth, & saith: That her said brother about a twelve month since, in the presence of this Examinate, and in the house aforesaid, called for the said *Dandy*, who thereupon appeared; asking this Examinates brother what he would have him to doe. This Examinates said brother then said, he would have him to helpe him to kill

100 The scrupulous nature of the trial is one of the pamphlet's most often restated points. Here Bromley is presented as adopting a belt-and-braces approach. But curiously Potts does not use the evidence of the victim's relative (whom we are told on H2 is present), relying instead on more questionable child evidence to support the otherwise unsubstantiated confession of the accused. This omission of independent adult evidence occurs again (for example I2) and is here attributed to Potts. Why some documents are repeated *ad nauseam* whilst other key documents are omitted altogether is a mystery: Lumby suggests that here the Catholic Towneley forbade Potts from using his evidence for anti-Catholic propaganda (Lumby, 145). But it is unclear whether he would have known anything about Potts's account whilst it was in preparation or had the power to give such an order.

101 *Sic.*

102 *Sic.*

103 A marginal note reads '*Dandy*'.

old Mistris *Towneley* of the Carre: whereunto the said *Dandy* answered, and said, That her said brother should have his best helpe for the doing of the same; and that her said brother, and the said *Dandy*, did both in this Examinates hearing, say, they would make away the said Mistris *Towneley*. And about a weeke after, this Examinate comming to the Carre-Hall, saw the said Mistris *Towneley* in the Kitchin there, nothing well: whereupon it came into this Examinate minde, that her said brother, by the help of *Dandy*, had brought the said Mistris *Towneley* into the state she then was in.

{I} Which Examinat, although she were but very yong, yet it was wonderfull to the Court, in so great a Presence and Audience, with what modestie, governement, and understanding, shee delivered this Evidence against the Prisoner at the Barre, being her owne naturall brother, which he himselfe could not deny, but there acknowledged in every particular to be just and true.

But behold a little further, for here this bloudy Monster did not stay his hands: for besides his wicked and divellish Spels, practises, meetings to consult of murder and mischiefe, which (by Gods grace) hereafter shall follow in order against him; there is yet more bloud to be laid unto his charge. For although he were but yong, and in the beginning of his Time, yet was he carefull to observe his Instructions from *Old Demdike* his Grand-mother, and *Elizabeth Device* his mother, in so much that no time should passe since his first entrance into that damnable Arte and exercise of Witchcrafts, Inchantments, Charmes and Sorceries, without mischiefe or murder. Neither should any man upon the least occasion of offence given unto him, escape his hands, without some danger. For these particulars were no sooner given in Evidence against him, when he was againe Indicted and Arraigned for the murder of these two. *viz.*

James Device of the Forrest of Pendle aforesaid, in the Countie of Lancaster, Labourer, the third time Indicted and Arraigned for the death of *John Hargraves* of Gould-shey-booth, in the Countie of Lancaster, by Witchcraft, as aforesaid. *Contra &c.*

To this Inditement upon his Arraignement, he pleaded thereunto not guiltie: and for his Triall put himselfe upon God and his Countrey, &c.

{Iv} *James Device* of the Forrest of Pendle aforesaid, in the County of Lancaster, Labourer, the fourth time Indicted and Arraigned for the death of *Blaze Hargreves* of Higham, in the Countie of Lancaster, by Witchcraft, as aforesaid. *Contra Pacem, &c.*

To this Indictment upon his Arraignement, he pleaded thereunto not guiltie; and for the Triall of his life, put himselfe upon God and the Countrey, &c.

Hereupon *Jennet Device* produced, sworne and examined, as a witnesse on his Majesties behalfe, against the said *James Device*, was examined in open Court, as followeth. *viz.*

The Examination and Evidence of JENNET DEVICE *aforesaid.*

Against JAMES DEVICE, *her brother, Prisoner at the Barre, upon his Arraignement and Triall.* viz.

Being sworne and examined in open Court, she saith, That her brother *James Device* hath beene a Witch for the space of three yeares: about the beginning of which time, there appeared unto him, in this Examinates mothers house, a Blacke-Dogge, which her said brother called *Dandy*, which *Dandy* did aske her said brother what he would have him to doe, whereunto he answered, hee would have him to kill *John Hargreives*, of Gold-shey-booth: whereunto *Dandy* answered that he would doe it; since which time the said *John* is dead.[104]

{I2} And at another time this Examinate confesseth and saith, That her said brother did call the said *Dandy*: who thereupon appeared in the said house, asking this Examinates brother what hee would have him to doe: whereupon this Examinates said brother said, he would have him to kill *Blaze Hargreives* of Higham: whereupon *Dandy* answered, hee should have his best helpe, and so vanished away: and shee saith, that since that time *Hargreives* is dead; but how long after, this Examinate doth not now remember.

All which things, when he heard his sister upon her Oath affirme, knowing them in his conscience to bee just and true, slenderly[105] denyed them, and thereupon insisted.

To this Examination were diverse witnesses examined in open Court *viva voce*, concerning the death of the parties, in such manner and forme, and at such time as the said *Jennet Device* in her Evidence hath formerly declared to the Court.

Which is all, and I doubt not but matter sufficient in Law to charge him with, for the death of these parties.

For the proofe of his Practises, Charmes, Meetings at Malking-Tower, to consult with Witches to execute mischiefe, Master *Nowel* humbly prayed, his owne Examination, taken and certified, might openly be read; and the rest in order, as they remaine upon Record amongst the Records of the Crowne at Lancaster: as hereafter followeth, *viz.*

{I2v} *The Examination of* JAMES DEVICE, *Sonne of* ELIZABETH DEVICE, *of the Forrest of Pendle: Taken the seven and twentieth day of Aprill aforesaid,* Before ROGER NOWEL *and* NICHOLAS BANESTER *Esquires, two of his Majesties Justices of Peace within the said Countie,* viz.

ANd being examined, he further saith, That upon Sheare-Thursday last, in the evening, he this Examinate stole a Wether from *John Robinson* of Barley, and brought it to his Grand-mothers house, old *Dembdike*, and there killed it: and that upon the day following, being Good Friday, about twelve of the clocke in the day time, there dined in this Examinates mothers house a number of persons, whereof three were men, with this Examinate, and the

104 The immediate flawless repeating of words used before on H4v suggests the pamphlet's inaccuracy in describing its text. This is not a shorthand record of Jennet's courtroom evidence but a patchwork constructed of various documents – a view borne out by the opening sentence of the next page.

105 Unconvincingly.

rest women; and that they met there for three Causes following, as this Examinates said Mother told this Examinate.

1 The first was, for the naming of the Spirit which *Alizon Device*, now prisoner at Lancaster, had, but did not name him, because she was not there.

2 The second Cause was, for the deliverie of his said Grand-mother, this Examinates said sister *Alizon*; the said *Anne Chattox*, and her daughter *Redferne*; killing the Gaoler at Lancaster; and before the next Assises to blow up the Castle there, to the end the aforesaid persons might by that meanes make an escape & get away: all which this Examinate then heard them conferre of.

3 And the third Cause was, for that there was a wo-{I3}-man dwelling in Gisborne Parish, who came into this Examinates said Grandmothers house, who there came and craved assistance of the rest of them that were then there, for the killing of Master *Lister* of Westby, because (as shee then said) he had borne malice unto her, and had thought to have put her away at the last Assises at Yorke, but could not: and this Examinate heard the said woman say, That her power was not strong ynough to doe it her selfe, being now lesse then before time it had beene.

And also, that the said *Jennet Preston* had a Spirit with her like unto a white Foale, with a blacke spot in the forhead.

And he also saith, That the names of the said Witches as were on Good-Friday at this Examinates said Grand-mothers house, & now this Examinates owne mothers, for so many of them as he did know, were these, *viz.* the wife of *Hugh Hargreives* of Barley; the wife of *Christopher Bulcock* of the Mosse end, and *John* her sonne; the mother of *Myles Nutter*; *Elizabeth*, the wife of *Christopher Hargreives*, of Thurniholme; *Christopher Howgate*, and *Elizabeth* his wife; *Alice Graye* of Coulne, and one *Mould-heeles* wife of the same: and this Examinate, and his Mother. And this Examinate further saith, That all the said Witches went out of the said House in their owne shapes and likenesses. And they all, by that they were forth of the dores, were gotten on Horsebacke, like unto Foales, some of one colour, some of another; and *Prestons* wife was the last: and when shee got on Horsebacke, they all presently vanished out of this Examinates sight. And before their said parting away, they all appointed to meete at the said *Prestons* {I3v} wives house that day twelve-moneths; at which time the said *Prestons* wife promised to make them a great Feast. And if they had occasion to meete in the meane time, then should warning be given, that they all should meete upon *Romleyes* Moore.

The Examination and Evidence of JENNET DEVICE.

Against JAMES DEVICE *her said Brother, Prisoner at the Barre, upon his Arraignement and Triall: Taken before* ROGER NOWEL, *and* NICHOLAS BANNESTER, *Esquires: two of his Majesties Justices of Peace within the said Countie*. viz.

SHee saith, that upon Good-Friday last there was about twentie persons, whereof only two were men, to this Examinates remembrance, at her said Grand-mothers house, called *Malking-Tower* aforesaid, about twelve of the clock: all which persons this Examinates said Mother told her were Witches, and that they came to give a name to *Alizon Device* Spirit or Familiar, Sister to this Examinate, and now Prisoner, in the Castle of Lancaster: And also this Examinate saith, that the persons aforesaid had to their Dinners, Beefe, Bacon, and rosted[106] Mutton, which Mutton, as this Examinates said brother said, was of a Weather of *Robinsons* of Barley: which Weather was brought in the night before into this Examinates mothers house, by the said *James Device* {I4} this Examinates said brother, and in this Examinates sight killed, and eaten, as aforesaid: And shee further saith, that shee knoweth the names of sixe of the said Witches, *viz.* the wife of the said *Hugh Hargreives*, under Pendle: *Christopher Howget*, of Pendle, Uncle to this Examinate: and *Dick Miles* wife, of the Rough-Lee: *Christopher Jacks*, of Thorne-holme, and his Wife: and the names of the residue shee this Examinate doth not know, saving that this Examinates Mother and Brother were both there.

The Examination of ELIZABETH DEVICE, *Mother of the said* JAMES DEVICE, *of the Forrest of Pendle: Taken the seven and twentieth day of Aprill aforesaid.*

Before ROGER NOWEL, *and* NICHOLAS BANNESTER, *Esquires; as aforesaid.* viz.

BEing examined, the said *Elizabeth* saith and confesseth, that upon Good-Friday last there dined at this Examinates house, those which she hath said to be Witches, and doth verily thinke to bee Witches, and their names are those, whom *James Device* hath formerly spoken of to be there.

And shee also confesseth in all things touching the Christning of her Spirit, and the killing of Master *Lister* of Westby, as the said *James Device* confesseth. But denieth that any talke was amongst them the said Witches, to her now remembrance, at the said meeting together, {I4v} touching the killing of the Gaoler at Lancaster; blowing up of the Castle, thereby to deliver old *Dembdike* her Mother; *Alizon Device* her Daughter, and other Prisoners, committed to the said Castle for Witchcraft.

After all these things opened, and delivered in evidence against him; Master *Covil*, who hath the custodie of the Gaole at Lancaster, having taken great paines with him during the time of his imprisonment, to procure him to discover his practizes, and such other Witches as he knew to bee dangerous: Humbly prayed the favour of the Court, that his voluntarie confession to M. *Anderton*, M. *Sands* the Major[107] of Lancaster, M. *Covel*, and others, might openly bee published and declared in Court.

The voluntarie confession and declaration of JAMES DEVICE, *Prisoner in the Castle at Lancaster.*

Before WILLIAM SANDS, *Maior of Lancaster*, JAMES ANDERTON, *Esquire, one of his Majesties Justices of Peace within the Countie of Lancaster:*

106 *Sic.*
107 Mayor.

And THOMAS COVEL, *Gentleman, one of his Majesties Coroners in the same Countie.* viz.

James Device, Prisoner in the Castle at Lancaster, saith; That his said Spirit *Dandie*, being very earnest with {K[108]} him to give him his soule, He answered, he would give him that part thereof that was his own to give: and thereupon the said Spirit said, hee was above CHRIST JESUS, and therefore hee must absolutely give him his Soule: and that done, hee would give him power to revenge himselfe against any whom he disliked.

And he further saith, that the said Spirit did appeare unto him after sundrie times, in the likenesse of a Dogge, and at every time most earnestly perswaded him to give him his Soule absolutely: who answered as before, that he would give him his owne part and no further. And hee saith, that at the last time that the said Spirit was with him, which was the Tuesday next before his apprehension, when as hee could not prevaile with him to have his Soule absolutely granted unto him, as aforesaid; the said Spirit departed from him, then giving a most fearefull crie and yell, and withall caused a great flash of fire to shew about him: which said Spirit did never after trouble this Examinate.

William Sands,

James Anderton.

Tho. Covel, Coroner.

The said *Jennet Device*, his Sister, in the very end of her Examination against the said *James Device*, confesseth and saith, that her Mother taught her two Prayers: the one to get drinke, which was this. *viz.*

Crucifixus hoc signum vitam Eternam. Amen.[109]

{Kv} And shee further saith, That her Brother *James Device*, the Prisoner at the Barre, hath confessed to her this Examinate, that he by this Prayer hath gotten drinke: and that within an houre after the saying of the said Prayer, drinke had come into the house after a very strange manner. And the other Prayer, the said *James Device* affirmed, would cure one bewitched, which shee recited as followeth. *viz.*

A Charme.

Upon Good-Friday, I will fast while I may
Untill I heare them knell
Our Lords owne Bell,
Lord in his messe[110]
With his twelve Apostles good,
What hath he in his hand

108 There is no signature J.
109 The sign of Christ's cross gives eternal life (Rosen, 366, n. 21).
110 In company eating together – archaic term for a banquet.

Ligh in leath wand:[111]
What hath he in his other hand?
Heavens doore key,
Open, open Heaven doore keyes,
Steck, steck hell doore.[112]
Let Crizum child
Goe to it Mother mild,
What is yonder that casts a light so farrandly,[113]
Mine owne deare Sonne that's naild to the Tree,
He is naild sore by the heart and hand,
And holy harne Panne,[114]
Well is that man
That Fryday spell can,
His Child to learne;
A Crosse of Blew, and another of Red,
{K2} As good Lord was to the Roode.
Gabriel *laid him downe to sleepe*
Upon the ground of holy weepe:
Good Lord came walking by,
Sleep'st thou, wak'st thou Gabriel,
No Lord I am sted with sticke and stake,[115]
That I can neither sleep nor wake:
Rise up Gabriel *and goe with me,*
The stick nor the stake shall never deere thee.[116]
Sweete Jesus our Lord, Amen.

James Device[117]

What can be said more of this painfull Steward, that was so carefull to provide Mutton against this Feast and solemne meeting at *Malking-Tower*,

111 An obscure phrase: ligh might suggest 'lying' or 'liege' ('lige') – neither of which makes obvious sense here. Leath can mean 'to make peace', 'to cause cessation', 'rest' or to 'soften or mitigate' – ideas associated with Christ's tempering of humankind's punishment for the Fall. A wand is a supple stick – sometimes with religious and magical associations (*OED*). Perhaps as a whole the phrase *might* mean: 'he has in his hand lordship (or liege-lord's authority) in the form of a peace-making wand'?

112 Rosen glosses this as 'stick, stick' (367).

113 Pleasantly.

114 This may read 'barne' or (most likely) 'harne' – in either case the words refer to the brain-pan, or skull (*OED*; see Rosen, 367, n. 24 for variants).

115 Rosen suggests 'stayed' (367).

116 Harm, hurt.

117 Rosen splits the 'charm' into four sections: the first three lines, from lines 4–13, from lines 14–22, and line 23 onwards. This seems to make the most textual sense of the jumbled images here. See her note (366, n. 22) for discussion of the folk and liturgical roots of the rhymes.

of these hellish[118] and divellish band of Witches, (the like whereof hath not been heard of) then hath beene openly published and declared against him at the Barre, upon his Arraignement and Triall: wherein it pleased God to raise up Witnesses beyond expectation to convince[119] him; besides his owne particular Examinations, which being shewed and read unto him; he acknowledged to be just and true. And what I promised to set forth against him, in the beginning of his Arraignment and Triall, I doubt not but therein I have satisfied your expectation at large, wherein I have beene very sparing to charge him with anything, but with sufficient matter of Record and Evidence, able to satisfie the consciences of the Gentlemen of the Jury of Life and Death; to whose good consideration I leave him, with the perpetuall Badge and Brand of as dangerous and malicious a Witch, as ever lived in these parts of Lancashire, of his time, and spot-{K2v}-ted with as much Innocent bloud, as ever any Witch of his yeares.

After all these proceedings, by direction of his Lordship, were their severall examinations, subscribed by every one of them in particular, shewed unto them at the time of their Triall, & acknowledged by them to be true, delivered to the gentlemen of the Jury of Life & Death, for the better satisfaction of their consciences: after due consideration of which said severall examinations, confessions, and voluntary declarations, as well of themselves as of their children, friends and confederates, The Gentlemen delivered up their Verdict against the Prisoners, as followeth. *viz.*

The Verdict of Life and Death.

WHo found *Anne Whittle*, alias *Chattox*, *Elizabeth Device*, and *James Device*, guiltie of the severall murthers by Witchcraft, contained in the Indictments against them, and every of them.

{K3} THE WITCHES OF SALMESBURY.[120]

The Arraignement and Triall of JENNET BIERLEY, ELLEN BIERLEY, *and* JANE SOUTHWORTH *of Salmesbury, in the County of Lancaster; for Witchcraft upon the bodie of* GRACE SOWERBUTTS, *upon Wednesday the nineteenth of August: At the Assises and generall Gaole-delivery holden at Lancaster.*

Before *Sir* EDWARD BROMLEY *Knight, one of his Majesties Justices of Assise at Lancaster: As hereafter followeth.* viz.

Jennet Bierley.

Ellen Bierley.

Jane Southworth.

Thus have we for a time left the Graund Witches of the Forrest of Pendle, to the good consideration of a verie sufficient Jury of worthy Gentlemen of

118 The printer amends this to ‘this hellish’.

119 Overcome, convict.

120 Salmesbury, now Samlesbury, is a town near Preston, about thirteen miles south-west from Pendle Hill.

their Countrey. We are now come to the famous Witches of Salmesbury, as the Countrey called them, {K3v} who by such a subtill practise and conspiracie of a Seminarie Priest, or, as the best in this Honorable Assembly thinke, a Jesuite, whereof this Countie of Lancaster hath good store, who by reason of the generall entertainement they find, and great maintenance they have, resort hither, being farre from the Eye of Justice, and therefore, *Procul a fulmine*;[121] are now brought to the Barre, to receive their Triall, and such a young witnesse prepared and instructed to give Evidence against them, that it must be the Act of GOD that must be the means to discover their Practises and Murthers, and by an infant: but how and in what sort Almightie GOD delivered them from the stroake of Death, when the Axe was layd to the Tree, and made frustrate the practise of this bloudie Butcher, it shall appeare unto you upon their Arraignement and Triall, whereunto they are now come. Master *Thomas Covel*, who hath charge of the prisoners in the Castle at Lancaster, was commaunded to bring forth the said

Jennet Bierley,
Ellen Bierley,
Jane Southworth,

to the Barre to receive their Triall.

Indictment.

THe said *Jennet Bierley, Ellen Bierly*, and *Jane Southworth* of Salmesbury, in the Countie of Lancaster, {K4} being indicted, for that they and every one of them felloniously had practised, exercised, and used diverse devillish and wicked Arts, called *Witchcrafts, Inchauntments, Charmes*, and *Sorceries*, in and upon one *Grace Sowerbutts*: so that by meanes thereof her bodie wasted and consumed, *Contra formam Statuti &c. Et Contra Pacem dicti Domini Regis Coronam & dignitatem & c.*[122]

The Prisoners being now at the Barre upon their Triall, *Grace Sowerbutts*, the daughter of *Thomas Sowerbutts*, about the age of foureteene yeares, was produced to give Evidence for the Kings Majestie against them: who standing up, she was commaunded to point out the Prisoners, which shee did, and said as followeth, *viz.*

{K4v} *The Examination and Evidence of* GRACE SOWERBUTTS, *daughter of* THOMAS SOWERBUTTS, *of Salmesbury, in the Countie of Lancaster Husband-man, upon her Oath,*

Against JENNET BIERLEY, ELLEN BIERLEY, *and* JANE SOUTHWORTH, *prisoners at the Barre, upon their Arraignement and Triall,* viz.

THe said *Grace Sowerbutts* upon her oath saith, That for the space of some yeares now last past shee hath beene haunted and vexed with some women, who have used to come unto her: which women, shee sayth, were *Jennet*

121 Far from threat – literally, lightening.

122 Against the form of the statute, and against the peace of the said lord, the King, his crown and dignity.

Bierley, this Informers Grand-mother; *Ellen Bierley*, wife to *Henry Bierley*; *Jane Southworth*, late the wife of *John Southworth*, and one *Old Doewife*,[123] all of Salmesburie aforesaid. And shee saith, That now lately those foure women did violently draw her by the haire of the head, and layd her on the toppe of a Hay-mowe, in the said *Henry Bierlyes* Barne. And shee saith further, That not long after the said Jennet Bierley did meete this Examinate neere unto the place where shee dwelleth, and first appeared in her owne likenesse, and after that in the likenesse of a blacke Dogge, and as this Examinate did goe over a style, shee picked[124] her off: howbeit shee saith shee had no hurt then, but rose againe, and went to her Aunts in Osbaldeston, and returned backe againe to her Fathers house the same night, being fetched home by her father. And she saith, That in her way home-wards shee did then tell her Father {L} how shee had beene dealt withall both then and at sundry times before that; and before that time she never told any bodie thereof: and being examined why she did not, she sayth, she could not speake thereof, though she desired so to doe. And she further sayth, That upon Saterday, being the fourth of this instant Aprill, shee this Examinate going towards Salmesburie bote,[125] to meete her mother, comming from Preston, shee saw the said *Jennet Bierley*, who met this Examinate at a place called the Two Brigges, first in her owne shape, and afterwards in the likenesse of a blacke Dogge, with two legges, which Dogge went close by the left side of this Examinate, till they came to a Pitte of Water, and then the said Dogge spake, and persuaded this Examinate to drowne her selfe there, saying it was a faire and an easie death:[126] Whereupon this Examinate thought there came one to her in a white sheete, and carried her away from the said Pitte, upon the comming whereof the said blacke Dogge departed away; and shortly after the said white thing departed also: And after this Examinate had gone further on her way, about the length of two or three Fields, the said blacke Dogge did meete her againe, and going on her left side, as aforesaid, did carrie her into a Barne of one *Hugh Walshmans*, neere there by, and layed her upon the Barne-floore, and covered this Examinate with Straw on her bodie, and Haye on her head, and the Dogge it selfe lay on the toppe of the said Straw, but how long the said Dogge lay there, this Examinate cannot tell, nor how long her selfe lay there: for shee sayth, That upon her lying downe there, as aforesaid, her Speech and Senses were taken from her: and the first {Lv} time shee knew where shee was, shee was layed upon a bedde in the said *Walshmans* house, which (as shee hath since beene told) was upon the Monday at night following: and shee was also told, That shee was found and taken from the

123 We hear no more of this woman.

124 Pitched.

125 A boat over the River Ribble, which runs between Preston and Samlesbury?

126 This is another story of what sounds like an obsessing, potentially possessing, spirit curiously blending with the traditional witchcraft accusation. Here the witch is the 'spirit'.

place where shee first lay, by some of her friends, and carried into the said *Walshmans* house, within a few houres after shee was layed in the Barne, as aforesaid. And shee further sayth, That upon the day following, being Tuesday, neere night of the same day, shee this Examinate was fetched by her Father and Mother from the said *Walshmans* house to her Fathers house. And shee saith, That at the place before specified, called the Two Brigges, the said *Jennet Bierley* and *Ellen Bierley* did appeare unto her in their owne shapes: whereupon this Examinate fell downe, and after that was not able to speake, or goe, till the Friday following: during which time, as she lay in her Fathers house, the said *Jennet Bierley* and *Ellen Bierley* did once appeare unto her in their owne shapes, but they did nothing unto her then, neither did shee ever see them since. And shee further sayth, That a good while before all this,[127] this Examinate did goe with the said *Jennet Bierley*, her grand-mother, and the said *Ellen Bierley* her Aunt, at the bidding of her said Grand-mother, to the house of one *Thomas Walshman*, in Salmesbury aforesaid. And comming thither in the night, when all the house-hold was abed, the doores being shut, the said *Jennet Bierley* did open them, but this Examinate knoweth not how: and beeing come into the said house, this Examinate and the said *Ellen Bierley* stayed there, and the said *Jennet Bierley* went into the Chamber {L2} where the said *Walshman* and his wife lay, & from thence brought a little child, which this Examinate thinketh was in bed with it[128] Father and Mother: and after the said *Jennet Bierley* had set her downe by the fire, with the said child, shee did thrust a naile into the navell of the said child: and afterwards did take a pen and put it in at the said place, and did suck there a good space, and afterwards laid the child in bed againe: and then the said *Jennet* and the said *Ellen* returned to their owne houses, and this Examinate with them. And shee thinketh that neither the said *Thomas Walshman*, nor his wife knew that the said child was taken out of the bed from them. And shee saith also, that the said child did not crie when it was hurt, as aforesaid: But she saith, that shee thinketh that the said child did thenceforth languish, and not long after dyed. And after the death of the said child; the next night after the buriall thereof, the said *Jennet Bierley* & *Ellen Bierley*, taking this Examinate with them, went to Salmesburie Church, and there did take up the said child, and the said *Jennet* did carrie it out of the Church-yard in her armes, and then did put it in her lap and carryed it home to her owne house, and having it there did boile some therof in a Pot, and some did broile on the coales, of both which the said *Jennet* and *Ellen* did eate, and

127 The reader, already alerted by Potts's warning, can see why this story might be seen as suspicious: it lacks chronological unity, and the most shocking episode is added as a vaguely dated afterthought. This unconvincing shape is unusual, even among stories whose content might seem to us equally fantastic. Clearly part of Grace's story is a second examination (L2v) but even this does not explain its confused shape, unless Potts has edited elements of it as with other examinations. However, see note 148.

128 *Sic.*

would have had this Examinate and one *Grace Bierley*, Daughter of the said *Ellen*, to have eaten with them, but they refused so to doe: And afterwards the said *Jennet* and *Ellen* did seethe[129] the bones of the said child in a pot, & with the Fat that came out of the said bones, they said they would annoint themselves, that thereby they might sometimes change themselves into other shapes.[130] And after all this being done, they said they {L2v} would lay the bones againe in the grave the next night following, but whether they did so or not, this Examinate knoweth not: Neither doth shee know how they got it out of the grave at the first taking of it up. And being further sworne and examined,[131] she deposeth & saith, that about halfe a yeare agoe, the said *Jennet Bierley, Ellen Bierley, Jane Southworth*, and this Examinate (who went by the appointment of the said *Jennet* her Grand mother) did meete at a place called Red banck, upon the North-side of the water of Ribble, every Thursday and Sonday at night by the space of a fortnight, and at the water side there came unto them, as they went thether, foure black things, going upright, and yet not like men in the face: which foure did carrie the said three women and this Examinate over the Water, and when they came to the said Red Banck they found some thing there which they did eate. But this Examinate saith, shee never saw such meate; and therefore shee durst not eate thereof, although her said Grand mother did bidde her eate. And after they had eaten, the said three Women and this Examinate danced, every one of them with one of the black things aforesaid, and after their dancing the said black things did pull downe the said three Women, and did abuse their bodies, as this Examinate thinketh, for shee saith, that the black thing that was with her, did abuse her bodie.[132]

The said Examinate further saith upon her Oth, That about ten dayes after her Examination taken at Blackborne,[133] shee this Examinate being then come to her Fathers house againe, after shee had beene certaine dayes at her Unckles house in Houghton: *Jane Southworth* widow, did meete this Examinate at her Fathers house dore {L3} and did carrie her into the loft, and there did lay her upon the floore, where shee was shortly found by her Father and brought downe, and laid in a bed, as afterwards shee was told: for shee saith, that from the first meeting of the said *Jane Southworth*, shee this Examinate

129 Boil.

130 Here the content of the statement is very unusual. There is no other case of blood-sucking cannibal witches in the English (or Scottish, or translated European) pamphlets of this period, and all the supporting details – the making of witches' ointment, and transformation into other shapes – are rare and here have an unusually coherent exotic and gory context. They probably come from French or German demonology.

131 This seems to be a re-swearing – because of magisterial disbelief even as the examination is taken?

132 This statement is not followed up at all, although one would expect further questioning. In another context this would be a damning admission of sex with the devil.

133 Blackburn, a town six miles east of Samlesbury.

had her speech and senses taken from her. But the next day shee saith, shee came somewhat to her selfe, and then the said Widow *Southworth* came againe to this Examinate to her bed-side, and tooke her out of bed, and said to this Examinate, that shee did her no harme the other time, in respect of that shee now would after doe to her, and thereupon put her upon a hey-stack, standing some three or foure yards high from the earth, where shee was found after great search made, by a neighbours Wife neare dwelling, and then laide in her bed againe, where she remained speechlesse and senselesse as before, by the space of two or three daies: And being recovered, within a weeke after shee saith, that the said *Jane Southworth* did come againe to this Examinate at her fathers house and did take her away, and laid her in a ditch neare to the house upon her face, and left her there, where shee was found shortly after, and laid upon a bedde, but had not her senses againe of a day & a night, or thereabouts. And shee further saith, that upon Tuesday last before the taking of this her Examination, the said *Jane Southworth* came to this Examinates Fathers house, and finding this Examinate without the doore, tooke her and carried her into the Barne, and thrust her head amongst a companie of boords that were there standing, where shee was shortly after found and laid in a bedde, and remained in her old fit till the Thursday at night following.

{L3v} And being further examined touching her being at Red-bancke, shee saith, That the three women, by her before named, were carried backe againe over Ribble, by the same blacke things that carried them thither; and saith that at their said meeting in the Red-bancke, there did come also divers other women, and did meete them there, some old, some yong, which this Examinate thinketh did dwell on the North-side of Ribble, because she saw them not come over the Water: but this Examinate knew none of them, neither did she see them eat or dance, or doe any thing else that the rest did, saving that they were there and looked on.

These particular points of Evidence being thus urged against the Prisoners: the father of this *Grace Sowerbutts* prayed that *Thomas Walshman*, whose childe they are charged to murther, might be examined as a witnes upon his oath, for the Kings Majestie, against the Prisoners at the Barre: who upon this strange devised accusation, delivered by this impudent wench, were in opinion of many of that great Audience guilty of this bloudie murther, and more worthy to die then any of these Witches.

{L4} *The Examination and Evidence of* THOMAS WALSHMAN, *of Salmesbury, in the Countie of Lancaster, Yeoman.*

Against JENNET BIERLEY, ELLEN BIERLEY, *and* JANE SOUTHWORTH, *Prisoners at the Barre, upon their Arraignement and Triall, as followeth.* viz.

THe said Examinate, *Thomas Walshman*, upon his oath saith, That hee had a childe died about Lent was twelve-month, who had been sicke by the space of a fortnight or three weekes: which childe when it died was about a yeare old; But how it came to the death of it this Examinate knoweth not. And he further saith, that about the fifteenth of Aprill last, or thereabouts, the said *Grace Sowerbutts* was found in this Examinates fathers Barne, laid under a little hay and straw, and from thence was carried into this Examinates house, and there laid till the Monday at night following: during which time shee did not speak, but lay as if she had beene dead.[134]

{L4v} *The Examination of* JOHN SINGLETON: *Taken at Salmesbury, in the Countie of Lancaster, the seventh day of August*: Anno Reg. Regis JACOBI Angliae, Franciae, & Hiberniae, Fidei Defensor. &c. Decimo & Scotiae, xlvi. Before ROBERT HOULDEN,[135] *Esquire, one of his Majesties Justices of Peace in the County of Lancaster.*

Against JENNET BIERLEY, ELLEN BIERLEY, *and* JANE SOUTHWORTH, *which hereafter followeth.*

THe said Examinate upon his oath saith, That hee hath often heard his old Master, Sir *John Southworth* Knight, now deceased, say, touching the late wife of *John Southworth*, now in the Gaole, for suspition of Witchcraft: That the said wife was as he thought an evill woman, and a Witch: and he said that he was sorry for her husband, that was his kinsman, for he thought she would kill him. And this Examinate further saith, That the said Sir *John Southworth* in his comming or going betweene his owne house at Salmesbury, and the Towne of Preston, did for the most part forbeare to passe by the house, where the said wife dwelled, though it was his nearest and best way; and rode another way, only for feare of the said wife, as this Examinate verily thinketh.

{M} *The Examination of* WILLIAM ALKER *of Salmesbury, in the Countie of Lancaster, Yeoman: Taken the fifteenth day of Aprill*, Anno Reg. Regis JACOBI, Angliae, Franciae, & Hiberniae, Decimo & Scotiae, quadragesimo quinto.

Before ROBERT HOULDEN, *one of his Majesties Justices of Peace in the County of Lancaster: Against* JENNET BIERLEY, ELLEN BIERLEY, *and* JANE BIERLEY,[136] *which hereafter followeth.* viz.

THe said Examinate upon his oath saith, That hee hath seene the said Sir *John Southworth* shunne to meet the said wife of *John Southworth*, now Prisoner in the Gaole, when he came neere where she was. And hath heard the said Sir *John Southworth* say, that he liked her not, and that he doubted she would bewitch him.

Here was likewise *Thomas Sowerbutts*, father of *Grace Sowerbutts*, examined upon his oath, and many other witnesses to little purpose: who being examined

134 The brevity of this statement, its (far from unusual, but exceptionally extreme) appearance of having been elicited by questions, and its non-committal content all suggest an informant unwilling to inform – a key gap in any prosecution.

135 Robert Holden was Nicholas Bannester's son-in-law, and a Catholic, from Haslingden (a town twelve miles south-east of Samlesbury).

136 Should presumably read 'Southworth' – unless it is an alias and she is related to the other women?

by the Court, could depose little against them: But the finding of the wench upon the hay in her counterfeit fits: wherfore I leave to trouble you with the particular declaration of their Evidence against the Prisoners, In respect there was not any one witnes able to charge them with one direct matter of Withcraft;[137] nor prove any thing for the murther of the childe.[138]

Herein, before we come to the particular declaration of that wicked and damnable practise of this Jesuite or Seminary. I shall commend unto your examination and judgement some points of her Evidence, wherein you {Mv} shal see what impossibilities are in this accusation brought to this perfection, by the great care and paines of this officious Doctor, Master *Tompson* or *Southworth*,[139] who commonly worketh upon the Feminine disposition, being more passive then Active.

The particular points of the Evidence of GRACE SOWERBUTTS, *viz.*

Evidence.

THat for the space of some yeares she hath been haunted and vexed with some women, who have used to come to her.

The Jesuite forgot to instruct his Scholler how long it is since she was tormented: it seemes it is long since he read the old Badge of a Lyer, *Oportet mendacem esse memorem.*[140] He knowes not how long it is since they came to church, after which time they began to practise Witchcraft. It is a likely thing the Torment and Panges of Witchcraft can be forgotten, and therefore no time can be set downe.

Shee saith that now lately these foure women did violently draw her up by the haire of the head, and lay her on the top of a Hay-mow.

Heere they use great violence to her, whome in another place they make choice to be of their counsell, to go with them to the house of *Walshman* to murther the childe. This courtesie deserves no discovery of so foule a Fact.

{M2} *Not long after, the said* Jennet Bierley *did meete this Examinate neere unto the place where she dwelled, and first appeared in her owne likenesse, and after that in the likenesse of a blacke Dogge.*

Uno & eodem tempore,[141] shee transformed her selfe into a Dogge. I would know by what meanes any Priest can maintaine this point of Evidence.

And as shee went over a Style, shee picked her over, but had no hurt.

137 *Sic.*

138 The accusation appears to be unsupported. Potts implies that no witnesses told the usual stories of acts of *maleficium*, and none provided the appropriate circumstantial evidence to make up for Thomas Walshman's unwillingness to accuse the women of his child's murder. But see note 148.

139 The name suggests a family feud, as with Sir John Southworth's suspicion of his relative's wife.

140 Liars need good memories.

141 At one and the same time. Potts is probably alluding to transubstantiation here as well as questioning the plausibility of witch transformation.

This is as likely to be true as the rest, to throw a child downe from the toppe of a House, and never hurt her great toe.[142]

She rose againe; had no hurt, went to her Aunt, and returned backe againe to her Fathers house, being fetched home.

I pray you observe these contrarieties, in order as they are placed, to accuse the Prisoners.[143]

Saterday the fourth of this instant Aprill.

Which was about the very day the Witches of the Forrest of Pendle were sent to Lancaster. Now was the time for the Seminarie to instruct, accuse, and call into question these poore women: for the wrinckles of an old wives face is good evidence to the Jurie against a Witch. And how often will the common people say *(Her eyes are sunke in her head,* GOD *blesse us from her.)* But old *Chattox* had *Fancie*, besides her withered face, to accuse her.[144]

{M2v} *This Examinate did goe with the said* Jennet Bierley *her Grand-mother, and* Ellen Bierley *her Aunt, to the house of* Walshman, *in the nighttime, to murther a Child in a strange manner.*

This of all the rest is impossible, to make her of their counsell, to doe murther, whome so cruelly and barbarously they pursue from day to day, and torment her. The Witches of the Forrest of Pendle were never so cruell or barbarous.

And she also saith, the Child cried not when it was hurt.

All this time the Child was asleepe, or the Child was of an extraordinarie patience, *o inauditum facinus*![145]

After they had eaten, the said three women and this Examinate danced every one of them with one of the Blacke things: and after, the Blacke things abused the said women.

Here is good Evidence to take away their lives. This is more proper for the Legend of Lyes, then the Evidence of a witnesse upon Oath, before a reverend and learned Judge, able to conceive this Villanie, and finde out the practise. Here is the Religious act of a Priest, but behold the event of it.[146]

She describes the foure Blacke things to goe upright, but not like Men in the face.

142 This is, says Potts, as believable as a story in which a child was thrown from a house top, and hurt not even her big toe. Why is it so incredible to him?

143 Potts's point here is unclear to me. What is his argument?

144 Potts's defensive last sentence illustrates perfectly the problems of proof involved in cases of witchcraft. To modern eyes there is no distinction to be made between 'these poore women' and 'old Chattox'. But it suits Potts to make one, on religious grounds, even though he must (jokingly?) call the devil as a witness to do so – a surprisingly weak rhetorical move with an ambiguous tone.

145 Oh, unheard of action (or crime)!

146 In looking for comparable incredible tales, Potts gestures towards the *Golden Legend*, a collection of stories of the lives of saints. But maybe his rhetorical move here also shows that this kind of demonological tale is too (allegedly) Catholic and too European to be believed.

The Seminarie mistakes the face for the feete: For *Chattox* and all her fellow Witches agree, the Devill is cloven-footed: but *Fancie* had a very good face, and was a very proper Man.

{M3} *About tenne dayes after her Examination taken at Black-borne, then she was tormented.*

Still he pursues his Project: for hearing his Scholler had done well, he laboured she might doe more in this nature. But notwithstanding, many things are layd to be in the times when they were Papists: yet the Priest never tooke paines to discover them, nor instruct his Scholler, untill they came to Church. Then all this was the Act of GOD, to raise a child to open all things, and then to discover his plotted Tragedie. Yet in this great discoverie, the Seminarie forgot to devise a Spirit for them.

And for *Thomas Walshman*, upon his Oath he sayth, That his Child had beene sicke by the space of a fortnight, or three weekes, before it died. And *Grace Sowerbutts* saith, they tooke it out of the bedde, strucke a nayle into the Navell, sucked bloud, layd it downe againe, and after, tooke it out of the Grave, with all the rest, as you have heard. How these two agree, you may, upon view of their Evidence, the better conceive, and be able to judge.[147]

How well this project, to take away the lives of three innocent poore creatures by practise and villanie; to induce a young Scholler to commit perjurie, to accuse her owne Grand-mother, Aunt, &c. agrees either with the Title of a Jesuite, or the dutie of a Religious Priest, who should rather professe Sinceritie and Innocencie, then practise Trecherie: But this was lawfull; for they are Heretikes accursed, to leave the companie of Priests; to frequent Churches, heare the word of GOD preached, and professe Religion sincerely. {M3v} But by the course of Times and Accidents, wise men observe, that very seldome hath any mischievous attempt beene under-taken without the direction or assistance of a Jesuite, or Seminarie Priest.

Who did not condemne these Women upon this evidence, and hold them guiltie of this so foule and horrible murder?[148] But Almightie God, who in his providence had provided meanes for their deliverance, although the Priest

147 Again Potts marches determinedly past an arguable point in search of an obscure one.

148 Potts implies that only the judge's intervention saved the accused. Is this flattery, or did the audience truly accept this story with all the flaws which Potts so anxiously – but confusingly – points out? It seems certain that we are not hearing the full story. A few lines later the judge refers to the involvement of a Jesuit without this having been mentioned in court as far as we are aware. Three main possibilities present themselves: one, the judge was always aware of the case's flaws and/or the alleged Catholic plot (perhaps because of magisterial suspicions?); two, the judge discovered the Catholic plot and the case collapsed; three, the court seized on the 'Catholic plot' to save its collective face when the case fortuitously collapsed due to unusual evidence. If foreknowledge or discovery of the plot is the key feature, the form of the evidence and its content is not nearly as important as Potts suggests. This idea – that evidence is discredited not because it is unusual or insufficient but because it is Catholic – might explain the sense we get of a complex argument against the evidence being made over-eagerly by one who is not

by the helpe of the Devill, had provided false witnesses to accuse them; yet GOD had prepared and placed in the Seate of Justice, an upright Judge to sit in Judgement upon their lives, who after he heard all the evidence at large against the Prisoners for the Kings Majestie, demanded of them what answere they could make. They humbly upon their knees with weeping teares, desired him for Gods cause to examine *Grace Sowerbuts*, who set her on, or by whose meanes this accusation came against them.

Immediately the countenance of this *Grace Sowerbuts* changed: The witnesses being behinde, began to quarrell and accuse one an other. In the end his Lordship examined the Girle, who could not for her life make any direct answere, but strangely amazed, told him, shee was put to a Master to learne, but he told her nothing of this.

But here as his Lordships care and paines was great to discover the practises of these odious Witches of the Forrest of Pendle, and other places, now upon their triall before him: So was he desirous to discover this damnable practise, to accuse these poore Women, and bring their lives in danger, and thereby to deliver the innocent.

{M4} And as he openly delivered it upon the Bench, in the hearing of this great Audience: That if a Priest or Jesuit had a hand in one end of it, there would appeare to bee knaverie, and practise in the other end of it. And that it might the better appeare to the whole World, examined *Thomas Sowerbuts*, what Master taught his daughter: in generall termes, he denyed all.

The Wench had nothing to say, but her Master told her nothing of this. In the end, some that were present told his Lordship the truth, and the Prisoners informed him how shee went to learne with one *Thompson* a Seminarie Priest, who had instructed and taught her this accusation against them, because they were once obstinate Papists, and now come to Church. Here is the discoverie of this Priest, and of his whole practise. Still this fire encreased more and more, and one witnesse accusing an other, all things were laid open at large. In the end his Lordship tooke away the Girle from her Father, and committed her to M. *Leigh*, a very religious Preacher,[149] and M. *Chisnal*, two Justices of the Peace, to be carefully examined. Who tooke great paines to examine her of every particular point: In the end they came into the Court, and there delivered this Examination as followeth.

{M4v} *The Examination of* GRACE SOWERBUTS, *of Salmesburie, in the Countie of Lancaster, Spinster: Taken upon Wednesday the 19. of August* 1612.

completely in control of his material. For the modern mind it is indeed puzzling that Potts can accept stories of speaking animal familiars, witches vanishing on foals and young girls exposing their grandmother's guilt simply because these were adjudged true by the court, whilst cavilling at some of these points of evidence here (see especially M2). The reader must decide what matters here: unusual evidence, Catholic plot or both? The case presents a circular problem of past mentalities and reasoning, and their representation.

149 Leigh was the Rector of Standish (twelve miles south of Samlesbury) since 1586, and a distinguished godly preacher with royal connections (Lumby, 146).

Annoq Reg. Regis, JACOBI *Angliae, Franciae, & Hiberniae, Fidei Defensoris, &c. decimo & Scotiae,* xlvi.

Before WILLIAM LEIGH, *and* EDWARD CHISNAL, *Esquires; two of his Majesties Justices of Peace in the same Countie: At the Assizes and generall Gaole deliverie, holden at Lancaster.*

By *Direction of Sir* EDWARD BROMLEY *Knight, one of his Majesties Justices of Assize at Lancaster.*

BEing demanded whether the accusation shee laid upon her Grand-mother, *Jennet Bierley, Ellen Bierley* and *Jane Southworth,* of Witchcraft, *viz.* of the killing of the child of *Thomas Walshman,* with a naile in the Navell, the boyling, eating, and oyling, thereby to transforme themselves into divers shapes, was true; shee doth utterly denie the same; or that ever shee saw any such practises done by them.

Shee further saith, that one Master *Thompson,* which she taketh to be Master *Christopher Southworth,* to whom shee was sent to learne her prayers, did perswade, counsell, and advise her, to deale as formerly hath beene said against her Grand-mother, Aunt, and *Southworths* wife.

{N} And further shee confesseth and saith, that shee never did know, or saw any Devils, nor any other Visions, as formerly by her hath beene alleaged and informed.

Also shee confesseth and saith, That shee was not throwne or cast upon the Henne-ruffe,[150] and Hay-mow in the Barne, but that shee went up upon the Mow her selfe by the wall side.

Being further demanded whether shee ever was at the Church, shee saith, shee was not, but promised her after to goe to the Church, and that very willingly.

Signum, + Grace Sowerbuts.

William Leigh.

Edward Chisnal.

{Nv} *The Examination of* JENNET BIERLEY, ELLEN BIERLEY, *and* JANE SOUTHWORTH, *of Salmesburie, in the Countie of Lancaster, Taken upon Wednesday the nineteenth of August* 1612. *Annoq Reg. Regis* JACOBI *Angliae, Franciae, & Hiberniae, Fidei Defensoris, &c. decimo & Scotiae,* xlvi.

Before WILLIAM LEIGH, *and* EDWARD CHISNAL, *Esquires; two of his Majesties Justices of Peace in the same Countie: At the Assizes and generall Gaole deliverie, holden at Lancaster.*

By *Direction of Sir* EDWARD BROMLEY *Knight, one of his Majesties Justices of Assize at Lancaster.*

Jennet Bierley being demanded what shee knoweth, or hath heard, how *Grace Sowerbuts* was brought to *Christopher Southworth,* Priest; shee answereth, that shee was brought to M. *Singletons*[151] house by her owne Mother, where the

150 The *OED* casts no light on this term.

151 See L4v.

said Priest was, and that shee further heard her said Mother say, after her Daughter had been in her fit, that shee should be brought unto her Master, meaning the said Priest.[152]

And shee further saith, that shee thinketh it was by and through the Counsell of the said M. *Thomson*, alias *Southworth*, Priest, That *Grace Sowerbuts* her Grand-child accused her of Witchcraft, and of such practises as shee is accused of: And thinketh further, the cause why the said *Thompson*, alias *Southworth* Priest, should practise with the Wench to doe it was for that shee went to the Church.

{N2} *Jane Southworth* saith shee saw Master *Thompson*, alias *Southworth*, the Priest, a month or sixe weekes before she was committed to the Gaole; and had conference with him in a place called Barne-hey-lane, where and when shee challenged him for slandering her to bee a Witch: wherunto he answered, that what he had heard thereof, he heard from her mother and her Aunt: yet shee, this Examinate, thinketh in her heart it was by his procurement, and is moved so to thinke, for that shee would not be disswaded from the Church.

Ellen Bierley saith, Shee saw Master *Thompson*, alias *Southworth*, sixe or eight weeks before she was committed, and thinketh the said Priest was the practiser with *Grace Sowerbutts*, to accuse her of Witchcraft, and knoweth no cause why he should so doe, but because she goeth to the Church.

Signum, + Jennet Bierley.
Signum, + Jane Southworth.
Signum, + Ellen Bierley.
William Leigh.
Edward Chisnal.

{N2v} These Examinations being taken, they were brought into the Court, and there openly in the presence of this great Audience published, and declared to the Jurie of Life and Death; and thereupon the Gentlemen of their Jury required to consider of them. For although they stood upon their Triall, for matter of Fact of Witchcraft, Murther, and much more of the like nature: yet in respect all their Accusations did appeare to bee practise: they were now to consider of them, and to acquit them. Thus were these poore Innocent creatures, by the great care and paines of this honorable Judge, delivered from the danger of this conspiracie; this bloudie practise of this Priest laid open: of whose fact I may lawfully say; *Etiam si ego tacuero clamabunt lapides.*[153]

These are but ordinary with Priests and Jesuites: no respect of Bloud, kindred, or friendship, can move them to forbeare their Conspiracies: for when he had laboured treacherously to seduce and convert them, and yet could doe no good; then devised he this meanes.

152 This sounds like a possession case, demanding exorcism – again, the story is incomplete.
153 Even if I remain silent, the stones will cry out.

God of his great mercie deliver us all from them and their damnable conspiracies: and when any of his Majesties subjects, so free and innocent as these, shall come in question grant them as honorable a Triall, as Reverend and worthy a Judge to sit in Judgement upon them; and in the end as speedie a deliverance. And for that which I have heard of them; seene with my eyes, and taken paines to Reade of them: My humble prayer shall be to God Almightie. Ut Convertantur ne pereant. Aut confundantur ne noceant.[154]

To conclude, because the discourse of these three women of Salmesbury hath beene long and trouble-{N3}-some to you; it is heere placed amongst the Witches, by special order and commaundement, to set forth to the World the practise and conspiracie of this bloudy Butcher. And because I have presented to your view a Kalender in the Frontispiece of this Booke, of twentie notorious Witches: I shall shew you their deliverance in order, as they came to their Arraignement and Triall every day, and as the Gentlemen of every Jury for life and death stood charged with them.

{N3v} THE ARRAIGNMENT *and Triall of* ANNE REDFERNE, *Daughter of* ANNE WHITTLE, *alias* CHATTOX, *of the Forrest of Pendle, in the Countie of Lancaster, for Witchcraft; upon Wednesday the nineteenth of August, at the Assises and Generall Gaole-deliverie, holden at Lancaster,*

Before *Sir* EDWARD BROMLEY *Knight, one of his Majesties Justices of Assise at Lancaster.*

Anne Redferne.

SUch is the horror of Murther, and the crying sinne of Bloud, that it will never bee satisfied but with Bloud. So fell it out with this miserable creature, *Anne Redferne*, the daughter of *Anne Whittle*, alias *Chattox*: who, as shee was her Mother, and brought her into the World, so was she the meanes to bring her into this danger, and in the end to her Execution, for much Bloud spilt, and many other mischiefes done.

For upon Tuesday night (although you heare little of her at the Arraignement and Triall of old *Chattox*, her Mother) yet was shee arraigned for the murther of {N4} *Robert Nutter*, and other: and by the favour and mercifull consideration of the Jurie, the Evidence being not very pregnant against her, she was acquited, and found Not guiltie.[155]

Such was her condition and course of life, as had she lived, she would have beene very dangerous: for in making pictures of Clay, she was more cunning then any: But the innocent bloud yet unsatisfied, and crying out unto GOD for satisfaction and revenge; the crie of his people (to deliver them from the danger of such horrible and bloudie executioners, and from her wicked and damnable practises) hath now againe brought her to a second Triall, where you shall heare what wee have upon Record against her.

154 Another quotation from Coke: 'that either they may be converted, to the end they perish not, or else confounded, that they hurt not' (Cobbett, II, 184).

155 She was presumably indicted jointly with her mother.

This *Anne Redferne*, prisoner in the Castle at Lancaster, being brought to the Barre, before the great Seat of Justice, was there, according to the former order and course, indicted and arraigned, for that she felloniously had practised, exercised, and used her devillish and wicked Arts, called *Witchcrafts, Inchauntments, Charmes,* and *Sorceries*, in and upon one *Christopher Nutter*, and him the said *Christopher Nutter*, by force of the same Witchcrafts, felloniously did kill and murther, *Contra formam Statuti &c. Et Contra Pacem &c.*

Upon her Arraignement to this Indictment, she pleaded *Not-Guiltie*; and for the triall of her life put her selfe upon GOD and the Countrey.

So as now the Gentlemen of the Jurie of Life and Death stand charged with her as with others.

The Evidence against Anne Redferne, *Prisoner at the Barre.*

{N4v} *The Examination of* ELIZABETH SOTHERNES, alias OLD DEMBDIKE, *taken at the Fence, in the Forrest of Pendle, in the Countie of Lancaster, the second day of Aprill,* Anno Reg. Regis JACOBI, Angliae, &c. decimo, & Scotiae xlv.

Against ANNE REDFERNE (*the daughter of* ANNE WHITTLE, alias CHATTOX) *Prisoner at the Barre*:

Before ROGER NOWEL *of Reade, Esquire, one of his Majesties Justices of Peace within the said Countie.*

THis Examinate saith, That about halfe a yeare before *Robert Nutter* died, as this Examinate thinketh, this Examinate went to the house of *Thomas Redferne*, which was about Midsummer, as shee this Examinate now remembreth it: and there, within three yards of the East end of the said house, shee saw the said *Anne Whittle* and *Anne Redferne*, wife of the said *Thomas Redferne*, and daughter of the said *Anne Whittle*, the one on the one side of a Ditch, and the other on the other side, and two pictures of Clay or Marle lying by them, and the third picture the said *Anne Whittle* was making. And the said *Anne Redferne*, her said daughter, wrought her Clay or Marle to make the third picture withall, And this Examinate passing by them, a Spirit, called *Tibbe*, in the shape of a blacke Cat, appeared unto her this Examinate, and said, Turne backe againe, and doe as they doe. To whom this Examinate said, What are they do-{O}-ing? Whereunto the said Spirit said, They are making three pictures: whereupon shee asked, whose pictures they were? whereunto the said Spirit said, They are the pictures of *Christopher Nutter, Robert Nutter*, and *Mary*, wife of the said *Robert Nutter*. But this Examinate denying to goe backe to helpe them to make the pictures aforesaid, the said Spirit seeming to be angrie therefore, shot[156] or pushed this Examinate into the Ditch; and so shedde the milke which this Examinate had in a Kanne, or Kitt: and so thereupon the Spirit at that time vanished out of this Examinates sight. But presently after that, the said Spirit appeared unto this

156 Violently threw.

Examinate again in the shape of a Hare, and so went with her about a quarter of a myle, but said nothing unto her this Examinate, nor shee to it.

The Examination of MARGARET CROOKE.

Against *the said* ANNE REDFERNE: *Taken the day and yeare aforesaid,*

Before ROGER NOWEL *aforesaid, Esquire, one of his Majesties Justices of the Peace in the Countie of Lancaster.*

THis Examinate, sworne & examined upon her oath,[157] sayth, That about eighteene or nineteene yeares agoe, this Examinates brother, called *Robert Nutter*, about Whitsontide the same yeare, meeting with the said *Anne Redferne*, upon some speeches betweene them they fell {Ov} out, as this Examinats said brother told this Examinat: and within some weeke, or fort-night, then next after, this Examinats said brother fell sicke, and so languished untill about Candlemas then next after, and then died. In which time of his sicknesse, he did a hundred times in the least say, That the said *Anne Redferne* and her associates had bewitched him to death. And this Examinate further saith, That this Examinates Father, called *Christopher Nutter*, about Maudlintide[158] next after following fell sicke, and so languished, untill Michaelmas then next after, and then died: during which time of his sicknesse, hee did sundry times say, That hee was bewitched; but named no bodie that should doe the same.

The examination of JOHN NUTTER, *of Higham Booth, in the Forrest of Pendle, in the Countie of Lancaster, yeoman,*

Against *the said* ANNE REDFERNE: *Taken the day and yeare aforesaid,*

Before ROGER NOWEL *Esquire, one of his Majesties Justices of Peace in the Countie of Lancaster.*

THis Examinate, sworne & examined upon his oath, sayth, That in or about Christmas, some eighteene or nineteene yeares agoe, this Examinat comming from Burnley with *Christopher Nutter* and *Robert Nutter*, this Examinates Father and Brother, this Examinate heard {O2} his said Brother then say unto his Father these words, or to this effect. *Father, I am sure I am bewitched by the* Chattox, Anne Chattox, *and* Anne Redferne *her daughter, I pray you cause them to bee layed in Lancaster Castle*: Whereunto this Examinates Father answered, Thou art a foolish Ladde, it is not so, it is thy miscarriage. Then this Examinates Brother weeping, said; nay, I am sure that I am bewitched by them, and if ever I come againe (for hee was readie to goe to Sir *Richard Shuttleworths*, then his Master) I will procure them to bee laid where they shall be glad to bite Lice in two with their teeth.

Hereupon *Anne Whittle*, alias *Chattox*, her Mother, was brought forth to bee examined, who confessed the making of the pictures of Clay, and in the end cried out very heartily to God to forgive her sinnes, and upon her knees intreated for this *Redferne*, her daughter.

157 Is this new phrase original, or added by Potts in the textual aftermath of the Grace Sowerbutts affair?

158 22 July.

Here was likewise many witnesses examined upon oth *Viva voce*, who charged her with many strange practises, and declared the death of the parties, all in such sort, and about the time in the Examinations formerly mentioned.

All men that knew her affirmed, shee was more dangerous then her Mother, for shee made all or most of the Pictures of Clay, that were made or found at any time. Wherefore I leave her to make good use of the little time she hath to repent in: but no meanes could move her to repentance, for as shee lived, so shee dyed.

{O2v} *The Examination of* JAMES DEVICE, *taken the day and yeare aforesaid.*

Before ROGER NOWEL, *and* NICHOLAS BANNESTER, *Esquires: two of his Majesties Justices of Peace within the said Countie of Lancaster.* viz.

THe said Examinate upon his oath saith, That about two yeares agoe, hee this Examinate saw three Pictures of Clay, of halfe a yard long, at the end of *Redfernes* house, which *Redferne* had one of the Pictures in his hand, *Marie* his Daughter had another in her hand, and the said *Redfernes* wife, now prisoner at Lancaster,[159] had an other Picture in her hand, which Picture she the said *Redfernes* wife, was then crumbling, but whose Pictures they were, this Examinate cannot tell. And at his returning back againe, some ten Roods off them there appeared unto him this Examinate a thing like a Hare, which spit fire at him this Examinate.[160]

{O3} THE Arraignment *and Triall of* ALICE NUTTER, *of the Forrest of Pendle, in the Countie of Lancaster, for Witch-craft; upon Wednesday the nineteenth of August, at the Assizes and generall Gaole deliverie, holden at Lancaster.*

Before *Sir* EDWARD BROMLEY *Knight, one of his Majesties Justices of Assize, at Lancaster.*

Alice Nutter.

THe two degrees of persons which chiefly practise Witch-craft, are such, as are in great miserie and povertie, for such the Devil allures to follow him, by promising great riches, and worldly commoditie; Others, though rich, yet burne in a desperate desire of Revenge; Hee allures them by promises, to get their turne satisfied to their hearts contentment, as in the whole proceedings against old *Chattox*: the examinations of old *Dembdike*; and her children, there was not one of them, but have declared the like, when the Devill first assaulted them.[161]

159 A marginal note reads '*Anne Redferne the Witch*'.

160 This ends the case of Anne Redferne. Potts does not give us her examination, or many of the examinations of the later witches, but there is no indication of why this should be.

161 Certainly the material which Potts has given us does not bear out this theory. Anne Chattox described the devil offering gold, silver and worldly wealth (B4v) but other witches, who are also shown as poor and begging, are represented as motivated by revenge alone. Potts's categories of witch are probably based on King James's *Daemonologie* 1.2 and 2.3, which he mentions on T2–T2v.

{O3v} But to attempt this woman in that sort, the Divel had small meanes: For it is certaine that she was a rich woman; had a great estate, and children of good hope: in the common opinion of the world, of good temper, free from envy or malice; yet whether by the meanes of the rest of the Witches, or some unfortunate occasion, shee was drawne to fall to this wicked course of life, I know not:[162] but hither shee is now come to receive her Triall, both for Murder, and many other vilde and damnable practises.

Great was the care and paines of his Lordship, to make triall of the Innocencie of this woman, as shall appeare unto you upon the Examination of *Jennet Device*, in open Court, at the time of her Arraignement and Triall; by an extraordinary meanes of Triall, to marke her out from the rest.

It is very certaine she was of the Grand-counsell at Malking-Tower upon Good-Friday, and was there present, which was a very great argument to condemne her.

This *Alice Nutter*, Prisoner in the Castle at Lancaster: Being brought to the Barre before the Great Seat of Justice; was there according to the former order and course Indicted and Arraigned, for that she felloniously had practised, exercised, and used her divellish and wicked Arts, called *Witchcrafts, Inchantments, Charmes* and *Sorceries*, in and upon *Henry Mitton*: and him the said *Henry Mitton*, by force of the same Witchcrafts, felloniously did kill and murther. *Contra formam Statuti*, &c. *Et Contra Pacem*, &c.

Upon her Arraignement, to this Indictment, shee pleaded not guiltie; and for the triall of her life, put {O4} her selfe upon God and the Countrey.

So as now the Gentlemen of the Jury of life and death stand charged with her, as with others.

The Evidence against Alice Nutter *Prisoner at the Barre.*

The Examination of JAMES DEVICE *sonne of* ELIZABETH DEVICE: *Taken the seven and twentieth day of Aprill*: Anno Reg. Regis JACOBI Angliae, Franciae, & Hiberniae, Fidei Defensor. &c. Decimo & Scotiae, xlvi.

Before ROGER NOWEL *and* NICHOLAS BANESTER, *two of his Majesties Justices of Peace in the Countie of Lancaster. Against Alice Nutter.*

THe said Examinate saith upon his oath, That hee heard his Grand-mother say, about a yeare ago, that his mother, called *Elizabeth Device*, and his Grand-mother, and the wife of *Richard Nutter*, of the Rough-lee aforesaid,[163] had killed one *Henry Mitton*, of the Rough-lee aforesaid, by Witchcraft. The reason wherefore he was so killed, was for that this Examinats said Grand-mother had asked the said *Mitton* a penny: and hee denying her thereof; thereupon shee procured his death as aforesaid.

162 Alice Nutter is often cited as an exceptional 'rich witch', but local historical studies have cast doubt on Potts's representation of her as wealthy. See J.M. Furphy, 'An Anthropological Account of Witchcraft in Early Seventeenth Century England', M.A. dissertation, University of Manchester, 1991, and Gladys Whittaker, *Roughlee Hall: Fact and Fiction* (Nelson: Marsden Antiquarians, 1980).

163 A marginal note reads: '*Alice Nutter* the Prisoner'.

{O4v} *The Examination of* ELIZABETH DEVICE, *mother of the said* JAMES DEVICE.

Against ALICE NUTTER, *wife of* RICHARD NUTTER, *Prisoner at the Barre, upon her Arraignement and Triall.*

Before ROGER NOWEL *and* NICHOLAS BANESTER, *Esquires, the day and yeare aforesaid.*[164]

THis Examinate upon her oath confesseth, and saith, That she, with the wife of *Richard Nutter*, called *Alice Nutter*, Prisoner at the Barre; and this Examinates said mother, *Elizabeth Sotherne*, alias *Old Demdike*; joyned altogether, and bewitched the said *Henry Mitton* to death.

This Examinate further saith, That upon Good-friday last, there dined at this examinats house two women of Burneley Parish, whose names the said *Richard Nutters* wife, *Alice Nutter*, now Prisoner at the Barre, doth know.

{P} *The Examination of* JAMES DEVICE *aforesaid*,

Against *The said* ALICE NUTTER, *the day and yeare aforesaid.*

THe said Examinate upon his oath saith, That upon Good-Friday about twelve of the clocke in the day time, there dined at this Examinats said mothers house, a number of persons, whereof three were men, with this Examinate, and the rest women: and that they mette there for these three causes following, as this Examinats said mother told this Examinate.

The first was for the naming of the Spirit, which *Alizon Device*, now Prisoner at Lancaster, had, but did not name him, because she was not there.

The second cause was, for the deliverie of his said Grand-mother; this Examinates said sister, *Alizon*; the said *Anne Chattox*, and her daughter *Redferne*; killing the Gaoler at Lancaster, and before the next Assizes to blow up the Castle there; to the end that the foresaid Prisoners might by that meanes make an escape, and get away: all of which this Examinate then heard them conferre of.

And he also saith, The names of such Witches as were on Good-Friday at this Examinats said Grand mothers house, and now this Examinates owne mothers, for so many of them as he doth know, were amongst others, *Alice Nutter*, mother of *Myles Nutter*, now Prisoner at the Barre. And this Examinate further saith, That all the said Witches went out of the said house in their {Pv} owne shapes and likenesses; and they all, by that time they were forth of the doores, were gotten on horsebacke, like unto Foales, some of one colour, and some of another; and *Prestons* wife was the last: and when shee got on horseback, they all presently vanished out of this Examinates sight: and before their said parting away, they all appointed to meete at the said *Prestons* wifes house that day twelve month, at which time the said *Prestons* wife promised to make

164 This 'document' is patched together from different parts of Elizabeth Device's evidence. It presumably represents what was given orally in evidence at the trial, using these extracts of written examinations – which is perhaps why it is not properly dated and refers both to the original examinations and to the 'Prisoner at the Barre'.

them a great feast: and if they had occasion to meete in the meane time, then should warning be given to meet upon Romleys Moore.

The Examination and Evidence of JENNET DEVICE, *daughter of* ELIZABETH DEVICE.

Against ALICE NUTTER, *Prisoner at the Barre.*

THe said Examinate saith, That on Good-Friday last, there was about 20. persons, whereof only two were men (to this Examinates remembrance) at her said Grand-mothers house at Malking-Tower, about twelve of the clock; all which persons, this Examinats said mother tould her, were Witches. And she further saith, she knoweth the names of six of them, *viz.* the wife of *Hugh Hargreives* under Pendle, *Christopher Howgate* of Pendle, Uncle to this Examinat and *Elizabeth* his wife; and *Dick Myles* wife of the Rough-Lee,[165] *Christopher Jacks* of Thorniholme, and his wife; and the names of the residue, she this Examinate doth not know.

{P2} After these Examinations were openly read, his Lordship being very suspitious of the accusation of this yong wench *Jennet Device*, commanded one to take her away into the upper Hall, intending in the meane time to make Triall of her Evidence, and the Accusation especially against this woman, who is charged to have beene at Malking-Tower, at this great meeting. Master *Covel* was commanded to set all his Prisoners by themselves, and betwixt every Witch another Prisoner, and some other strange women amongst them, so as no man could judge the one from the other: and these being set in order before the court from the prisoners, then was the Wench *Jennet Device* commaunded to be brought into the Court: and being set before my Lord, he tooke great paines to examine her of every particular Point, What women were at Malking-Tower upon Good-Friday? How she knew them? What were the names of any of them? And how she knew them to be such as she named? In the end being examined by my Lord, Whether she knew them that were there by their faces, if she saw them? she told my Lord she should: whereupon in the presence of this great Audience, in open Court, she went and tooke *Alice Nutter*, this prisoner, by the hand, and accused her to be one: and told her in what place shee sat at the Feast at Malking-Tower, at the great assembly of the Witches, and who sat next her: what conference they had, and all the rest of their proceedings at large, without any manner of contrarietie.

Being demaunded further by his Lordship, Whether she knew *Johan a Style*? she alledged, she knew no such woman to be there, neither did she ever heare her name.[166]

{P2v} This could be no forged or false Accusation, but the very Act of GOD to discover her.

165 See note 91.

166 An obvious trick question – names such as 'John o' Nokes' were used as labels for 'person or persons unknown' in court.

Thus was no meanes left to doe her all indifferent[167] favour, but it was used to save her life; and to this shee could give no answere.

But nothing would serve: for old *Dembdike*, old *Chattox*, and others, had charged her with innocent bloud, which cries out for Revenge, and will be satisfied. And therefore Almightie GOD, in his Justice, hath cut her off.

And here I leave her, untill shee come to her Execution, where you shall heare shee died very impenitent; insomuch as her owne children were never able to move her to confesse any particular offence, or declare any thing, even in *Articulo Mortis*:[168] which was a very fearefull thing to all that were present, who knew shee was guiltie.

{P3} THE ARRAIGNMENT *and Triall of* KATHERINE HEWIT, *Wife of* JOHN HEWIT, *alias* MOULD-HEELES, *of Coulne, in the Countie of Lancaster Clothier, for Witchcraft; upon Wednesday the nineteenth of August, at the Assises and Generall Gaole-deliverie, holden at Lancaster,*

Before *Sir* EDWARD BROMLEY *Knight, one of his Majesties Justices of Assise at Lancaster.*

Katherine Hewit.

WHo but Witches can be proofes, and so witnesses of the doings of Witches? since all their Meetings, Conspiracies, Practises, and Murthers, are the workes of Darkenesse: But to discover this wicked *Furie*, GOD hath not onely raised meanes beyond expectation, by the voluntarie Confession and Accusation of all that are gone before, to accuse this Witch (being Witches, and thereby witnesses of her doings) but after they were committed, by meanes of a Child, to discover her to be one, and a Principall in that wicked assembly at Malking-Tower, to devise such a damnable course for the deliverance of their friends at {P3v} Lancaster, as to kill the Gaoler, and blow up the Castle, wherein the Devill did but labour to assemble them together, and so being knowne to send them all one way: And herein I shall commend unto your good consideration the wonderfull meanes to condemne these parties, that lived in the world, free from suspition of any such offences, as are proved against them: And thereby the more dangerous, that in the successe wee may lawfully say, the very Finger of God did point them out. And she that never saw them, but in that meeting, did accuse them, and by their faces discover them.

This *Katherine Hewyt*, Prisoner in the Castle at Lancaster, being brought to the Barre before the great Seate of Justice, was there according to the former order and course Indicted and Arraigned, for that she felloniously had practized, exercised, and used her Devillish and wicked Arts, called *Witch-crafts, Inchantments, Charmes*, and *Sorceries*, in, and upon *Anne Foulds*; and the same *Anne Foulds*, by force of the same witch-craft, felloniously did kill and murder. *Contra formam Statuti, &c. Et contra Pacem dicti Domini Regis, &c.*

167 Impartial, disinterested.

168 Her dying speeches.

Upon her Arraignement to this Indictment, shee pleaded not guiltie; And for the triall of her life put her selfe upon God and her Countrie.
So as now the Gentlemen of the Jurie of life and death, stand charged with her as with others.
The Evidence against Katherine Hewyt, *Prisoner at the Barre.*
{P4} *The Examination of* JAMES DEVICE, *Sonne of* ELIZABETH DEVICE, *taken the seven and twentieth day of Aprill,* Anno Reg. Regis JACOBI, Angliae, Franciae, & Hiberniae, decimo, & Scotiae quadragesimo quarto.
Before ROGER NOWEL, *and* NICHOLAS BANNESTER, *Esquires; two of his Majesties Justices of Peace in the Countie of Lancaster.*
Against KATHERINE HEWYT, *alias* MOULD-HEELES *of Colne.* viz.
THis Examinate saith, that upon Good-Friday last, about twelve of the Clock in the day time, there dined at this Examinates Mothers house a number of persons: And hee also saith, that they were Witches; and that the names of the said Witches, that were there, for so many of them as he did know, were amongst others *Katherine Hewyt*, wife of *John Hewyt*, alias *Mould-heeles*, of Colne, in the Countie of Lancaster Clothier; And that the said Witch, called *Katherine Hewyt*, alias *Mould-heeles*, and one *Alice Gray*, did confesse amongst the said Witches at their meeting at *Malkin-Tower* aforesaid that they had killed *Foulds* wifes child, called *Anne Foulds*, of Colne: And also saith, that they had then in hanck[169] a child of *Michael Hartleys* of Colne.[170]
And this Examinate further saith, that all the said Witches went out of the said house in their own shapes and likenesses, and by that time they were gotten forth {P4v} of the doores, they were gotten on Horse-back like unto foales, some of one colour, some of an other, and the said *Prestons* wife was the last: And when shee got on Horse-back, they all presently vanished out of this Examinates sight. And before their said parting away they all appointed to meete at the said *Prestons* wifes house that day twelve Moneths: at which time the said *Prestons* wife promised to make them a great feast, and if they had occasion to meete in the meane time, then should warning be given that they all should meete upon Romlesmoore.
The Examination and Evidence of ELIZABETH DEVICE, *Mother of the said* JAMES DEVICE,

169 'To hanck' means to catch, noose or have power to restrain – here, it clearly means a magical power over a victim. Potts's use is cited in the *OED*, suggesting that it is unusual in print.

170 Here is just one of many examples of Potts's cavalier pick-and-mix editing, which is particularly rife in the Devices' statements – presumably because he is attempting to recreate what they said in court. The removal of the repeated list of names (as in the evidence against Alice Nutter and others) may be a relief to the sated reader, but what else is silently missing, and from where does the material which Potts adds come? It may be from other examinations, other parts of the same examination, from what was said in court, or Potts may be adding material from his own 'knowledge'. We are certainly not reading exactly what each witch/witness said.

Against KATHERINE HEWYT, *alias* MOULD-HEELES, *Prisoner at the Barre upon her Arraignement and Triall, taken the day and yeare aforesaid.* viz.

THis Examinate upon her oath confesseth, that upon Good-Friday last there dyned at this Examinates house, which she hath said are Witches, and verily thinketh to bee Witches, such as the said *James Device* hath formerly spoken of; amongst which was *Katherine Hewyt*, alias *Mould-heeles*, now Prisoner at the Barre: and shee also saith, that at their meeting on Good-Friday at *Malkin-Tower* aforesaid, the said *Katherine Hewyt*, alias *Mould-heeles*, and *Alice Gray*, did confesse, they had kil-{Q}-led a child of *Foulds* of Colne, called *Anne Foulds*, and had gotten hold of an other.

And shee further saith, the said *Katherine Hewyt* with all the rest, there gave her consent with the said *Prestons* wife for the murder of Master *Lister*.

The Examination and Evidence of JENNET DEVICE,

Against KATHERINE HEWYT, *alias* MOULD-HEELES, *Prisoner at the Barre.*

THe said Examinate saith, That upon Good-Friday last, there was about twentie persons, whereof two were men to this Examinates remembrance, at her said Grand-mothers house, called *Malkin-Tower* aforesaid, about twelve of the clock: All which persons this Examinates said mother told her were Witches, and that shee knoweth the names of sixe of the said Witches.

Then was the said *Jennet Device* commanded by his Lordship, to finde and point out the said *Katherine Hewyt*, alias *Mould-heeles*, amongst all the rest of the said Women, whereupon shee went and tooke the said *Katherine Hewyt* by the hand: Accused her to bee one, and told her in what place shee sate at the feast at *Malkin-Tower*, at the great Assembly of the Witches, and who sate next her; what conference they had, and all the rest of their proceedings at large, without any manner of contrarietie: Being demanded further by his Lord-{Qv}-ship, whether *Joane a Downe* were at that Feast, and meeting, or no? shee alleaged shee knew no such woman to be there, neither did shee ever heare her name.

If this were not an Honorable meanes to trie the accusation against them, let all the World upon due examination give judgement of it. And here I leave her the last of this companie, to the Verdict of the Gentlemen of the Jurie of life and death, as hereafter shall appeare.

Heere the Jurie of Life and Death, having spent the most part of the day, in due consideration of their offences; Returned into the Court to deliver up their Verdict against them, as followeth.

The Verdict of Life and Death.

WHo upon their Oathes found *Jennet Bierley*, *Ellen Bierley*, and *Jane Southworth*, not guiltie of the offence of Witch-craft, conteyned in the Indictment against them.

Anne Redferne, guiltie of the fellonie & murder, conteyned in the Indictment against her.

Alice Nutter, guiltie of the fellonie and murder conteyned in the Indictment against her.

And *Katherine Hewyt*, guiltie of the fellonie & murder conteyned in the Indictment against her.

{Q2} Whereupon Master *Covell* was commanded by the Court to take away the Prisoners Convicted, and to bring forth *John Bulcocke, Jane Bulcocke* his mother, and *Alizon Device*, Prisoners in the Castle at Lancaster, to receive their Trialls.

Who were brought to their Arraignement and Triall as hereafter followeth.

{Q2v} THE ARRAIGNMENT *and Triall of* JOHN BULCOCK *and* JANE BULCOCK *his mother, wife of* CHRISTOPHER BULCOCK, *of the Mosse-end, in the Countie of Lancaster, for Witch-craft: upon Wednesday in the after-noone, the nineteenth of August*, 1612. *At the Assizes and generall Gaole delivery, holden at Lancaster.*

Before *Sir* EDWARD BROMLEY, *Knight, one of his Majesties Justices of Assizes at Lancaster.*

John Bulcock, and *Jane Bulcock* his mother.

IF there were nothing to charge these Prisoners withall, whom now you may behold upon the Arraignment and Triall but their poasting in haste to the great Assembly at Malking-Tower, there to advise and consult amongst the Witches, what were to bee done to set at liberty the Witches in the Castle at Lancaster: Joyne with *Jennet Preston* for the murder of Master *Lister*; and such like wicked & divellish practises: {Q3} It were sufficient to accuse them for Witches, & to bring their lives to a lawfull Triall. But amongst all the Witches in this company, there is not a more fearefull and divellish Act committed, and voluntarily confessed by any of them, comparable to this, under the degree of Murder: which impudently now (at the Barre having formerly confessed;) they forsweare, swearing, they were never at the great Assembly at Malking Tower; although the very Witches that were present in that action with them, justifie, maintaine, and sweare the same to be true against them: Crying out in very violent & outragious manner, even to the gallowes, where they died impenitent for any thing we know, because they died silent in the particulars. These of all others were the most desperate wretches (void of all feare or grace) in all this Packe; Their offences not much inferiour to Murther: for which you shall heare what matter of Record wee have against them; and whether they be worthie to continue, we leave it to the good consideration of the Jury.

The said *John Bulcock*, and *Jane Bulcock* his mother, Prisoners in the Castle of Lancaster, being brought to the Barre before the great Seat of Justice: were there according to the former order and course Indicted and Arraigned, for that they felloniously had practised, exercised and used their divellish & wicked Arts, called *Witchcrafts, Inchantments, Charmes* and *Sorceries*, in and upon the body of *Jennet Deane*: so as the body of the said *Jennet Deane*, by force of the said Witchcrafts, wasted and consumed; and after she, the said *Jennet*, became madde. *Contra formam Statuti*, &c. *Et Contra Pacem*, &c.

Upon their Arraignment, to this Indictment they pleaded not guiltie; and for the triall of their lives put {Q3v} themselves upon God and their Countrey. So as now the Gentlemen of the Jurie of Life and Death stand charged with them as with others.

The Evidence against John Bulcock, *and* Jane Bulcock *his mother, Prisoners at the Barre.*

The Examination of JAMES DEVICE *taken the seven and twentieth day of Aprill aforesaid.*

Before ROGER NOWEL *and* NICHOLAS BANESTER, *Esquires, two of his Majesties Justices of Peace in the Countie of Lancaster.*

Against JOHN BULCOCK *and* JANE BULCOCK *his mother.*

THis Examinate saith, That upon Good-Friday, about twelve of the clocke in the day time, there dined at this Examinates said Mothers house a number of persons, whereof three were men with this Examinate, and the rest women, and that they met there for these three causes following, as this Examinates said mother told this Examinate. The first was, for the naming of the Spirit which *Allison Device*, now prisoner at Lancaster had, but did not name him, because shee was not there. The second cause was, for the deliverie of his said Grand-mother; this Examinates said sister *Allison*; the said *Anne Chattox*, and her daughter *Redferne*, killing {Q4} the Gaoler at Lancaster, and before the next Assises to blow up the Castle there, to that end the aforesaid prisoners might by that meanes make an escape, and get away: All which this Examinate then heard them conferre of.

And he also sayth, That the names of such said Witches as were on Good-Friday at this Examinates said Grand-mothers house, and now at this Examinates owne mothers, for so many of them as hee did know, were these, *viz. Jane Bulcock*, wife of *Christopher Bulcock*, of the Mosse end, and *John* her sonne amongst others, &c.

And this Examinate further saith, That all the said Witches went out of the said house in their owne shapes and likenesses: and they all, by that they were forth of the dores, were gotten on horse-backe, like unto Foales, some of one colour, and some of another, and *Prestons* wife was the last: and when shee got on horse-backe, they all presently vanished out of this Examinates sight.

And further he saith, That the said *John Bulcock* and *Jane* his said Mother, did confesse upon Good-Friday last, at the said Malking-Tower, in the hearing of this Examinate, That they had bewitched, at the new-field Edge in Yorkeshire,[171] a woman called *Jennet*, wife of *John Deyne*, besides her Reason; and the said Womans name so bewitched, he did not heare them speake of.[172] And this Examinate further saith, That at the said Feast at Malking-

171 Three miles north of Blacko, just over the Yorkshire–Lancashire border.

172 This seems entirely contradictory. It is also odd that there is no information here from anyone directly connected with the alleged victim.

Tower this Examinate heard them all give their consents to put the said Master *Thomas Lister* of Westby to death. And after Master *Lister* should be made away by Witch-craft, then all the said Witches gave their consents to joyne all together, to hanck Ma-{Q4v}-ster *Leonard Lister*, when he should come to dwell at the Cow-gill,[173] and so put him to death.

The Examination of ELIZABETH DEVICE, *Taken the day and yeare afore-said,*

Before ROGER NOWEL *and* NICHOLAS BANESTER, *Esquires, two of his Majesties Justices of Peace in the Countie of Lancaster,*

Against JOHN BULCOCK, *and* JANE BULCOCK, *his mother.*

THis Examinate saith upon her oath, That she doth verily thinke, that the said *Bulcockes* wife doth know of some Witches to bee about Padyham and Burnley.[174]

And shee further saith, That at the said meeting at Malking-Tower, as afore-said, *Katherine Hewit* and *John Bulcock*, with all the rest then there, gave their consents, with the said *Prestons* wife, for the killing of the said Master *Lister.*

{R} *The Examination and Evidence of* JENNET DEVICE

Against JOHN BULCOCKE *and* JANE *his mother, prisoners at the Barre.*

THe said Examinate, That upon Good-Friday last there was about twentie persons, whereof two were men, to this Examinates remembrance, at her said Grand-mothers house, called Malking-Tower aforesaid: all which persons, this examinates said mother told her were Witches, and that she knoweth the names of sixe of the said Witches.

Then was the said *Jennet Device* commaunded by his Lordship to finde and point out the said *John Bulcock* and *Jane Bulcock* amongst all the rest: where-upon shee went and tooke *Jane Bulcock* by the hand, accused her to be one, and told her in what place shee sat at the Feast at Malking-Tower, at the great Assembly of the Witches; and who sat next her: and accused the said *John Bulcock* to turne the Spitt there; what conference they had, and all the rest of their proceedings at large, without any manner of contrarietie.

Shee further told his Lordship, there was a woman that came out of Craven to that Great Feast at Malking-Tower, but shee could not finde her out amongst all those women.

{Rv} The names of the Witches at the *Great Assembly and Feast at* Malking-Tower, *viz.* upon Good-Friday last, 1612.

Elizabeth Device.

Alice Nutter.

173 A farm two miles south-west of Westby.

174 This is an obviously incomplete examination. It would be interesting to know how 'the said Bulcockes wife' was first mentioned, and how she is connected with some of the later witches who seem unrelated to the Pendle group except by an examination of Anne Chattox. Padiham is a town four miles south of Pendle Hill.

Katherine Hewit, alias *Mould-heeles.*
John Bulcock.
Jane Bulcock.
Alice Graie.
Jennet Hargraves.
Elizabeth Hargraves.
Christopher Howgate,
Sonne to old *Dembdike.*
Christopher Hargraves.
{R2} *Grace Hay*, at Padiham.
Anne Crunckshey, of Marchden.
Elizabeth Howgate.
Jennet Preston, Executed at Yorke for the Murder of Master *Lister.*[175]
With many more, which being bound over to appeare at the last Assizes, are since that time fled to save themselves.

{R2v} THE ARRAIGNMENT *and Triall of* ALIZON DEVICE, *Daughter of* ELIZABETH DEVICE, *within the Forrest of Pendle, in the Countie of Lancaster aforesaid, for Witch-craft.*

Alizon Device.

BEhold, above all the rest, this lamentable spectacle of a poore distressed Pedler, how miserably hee was tormented, and what punishment hee endured for a small offence, by the wicked and damnable practise of this odious Witch, first instructed therein by old *Dembdike* her Grand-mother, of whose life and death with her good conditions, I have written at large before in the beginning of this worke, out of her owne Examinations and other Records, now remayning with the Clarke of the Crowne at Lancaster: And by her Mother brought up in this detestable course of life; wherein I pray you observe but the manner and course of it in order, even to the last period at her Execution, for this horrible fact, able to terrifie and astonish any man living.

This *Alizon Device*, Prisoner in the Castle of Lanca-{R3}-ster, being brought to the Barre before the great Seat of Justice, was there according to the former order and course indicted and arraigned, for that shee felloniously had practised, exercised, and used her Devillish and wicked Arts, called *Witch-crafes,*[176] *Inchantments, Charmes,* and *Sorceries,* in, and upon one *John Law*, a Petti-chapman,[177] and him had lamed, so that his bodie wasted and consumed, &c. *Contra formam Statuti, &c. Et contra pacem dicti Domini Regis, Coronam & Dignitatem, &c.*

175 Some of these were acquitted, some never tried: but they are still believed to have been present.

176 *Sic.*

177 A pedlar and seller of small items – including sometimes pamphlets. Since the Law family is in the cloth trade and John Law is asked for pins, he may have been a mobile cloth-seller and haberdasher.

Upon the Arraignement, The poore Pedler, by name *John Law*, being in the Castle about the Moot-hall, attending to be called, not well able to goe or stand, being led thether by his poore sonne *Abraham Law*: My Lord *Gerard*[178] moved the Court to call the poore Pedler, who was there readie, and had attended all the Assizes, to give evidence for the Kings Majestie, against the said *Alizon Device*, Prisoner at the Barre, even now upon her Triall. The Prisoner being at the Barre, & now beholding the Pedler, deformed by her Witch-craft, and transformed beyond the course of Nature, appeared to give evidence against her; having not yet pleaded to her Indictment, saw it was in vaine to denie it, or stand upon her justification: Shee humbly upon her knees at the Barre with weeping teares, prayed the Court to heare her.

Whereupon my Lord *Bromley* commanded shee should bee brought out from the Prisoners neare unto the Court, and there on her knees, shee humbly asked forgivenesse for her offence: And being required to make an open declaration or confession of her offence: Shee confessed as followeth. *viz.*

{R3v} *The Confession of* ALIZON DEVICE, *Prisoners (sic) at the Barre: published and declared at time of her Arraignement and Triall in open Court.*

SHe saith, That about two yeares agone, her Grand-mother, called *Elizabeth Sothernes*, alias *Dembdike*, did (sundry times in going or walking together, as they went begging) perswade and advise this Examinate to let a Divell or a Familiar appeare to her, and that shee, this Examinate would let him suck at some part of her; and she might have and doe what shee would. And so not long after these perswasions, this Examinate being walking towards the Rough-Lee, in a Close of one *John Robinsons*, there appeared unto her a thing like unto a Blacke Dogge: speaking unto her, this Examinate, and desiring her to give him her Soule, and he would give her power to doe any thing she would: whereupon this Examinate being therewithall inticed, and setting her downe; the said Blacke-Dogge did with his mouth (as this Examinate then thought) sucke at her breast, a little below her Paps,[179] which place did remaine blew halfe a yeare next after: which said Blacke-Dogge did not appeare to this Examinate, untill the eighteenth day of March last: at which time this Examinate met with a Pedler on the high-way, called Colne-field, neere unto Colne: and this Examinate demanded of the said Pedler to buy some pinnes of him; but the said Pedler sturdily answered this Examinate that he would not loose his Packe; and so this Examinate parting with him: presently there appeared to this Examinate the Blacke-Dogge, which appeared unto her as before: which Black {R4} Dogge spake unto this Examinate in English, saying; What wouldst thou have me to do unto yonder man? to whom this Examinate said, What canst thou do at him? and the Dogge answered againe, I can lame him: whereupon this Examinat answered, and said to the said Black Dogge, Lame him: and before the Pedler was gone

178 See T3.
179 Breasts.

fortie Roddes further, he fell downe Lame: and this Examinate then went after the said Pedler; and in a house about the distance aforesaid, he was lying Lame: and so this Examinate went begging in Trawden Forrest that day, and came home at night: and about five daies next after, the said Black Dogge did appeare to this Examinate, as she was going a begging, in a Cloase neere the New-Church in Pendle, and spake againe to her, saying; Stay and speake with me; but this Examinate would not: Sithence which time this Examinat never saw him.

Which agreeth verbatim *with her owne Examination taken at* Reade, *in the Countie of Lancaster, the thirtieth day of March, before Master* Nowel, *when she was apprehended and taken.*[180]

MY Lord *Bromley*, and all the whole Court not a little wondering, as they had good cause, at this liberall and voluntarie confession of the Witch; which is not ordinary with people of their condition and qualitie: and beholding also the poore distressed Pedler, standing by, commanded him upon his oath to declare the manner how, and in what sort he was handled; how he came to be lame, and so to be deformed; who deposed upon his oath, as followeth.

{R4v} *The Evidence of* JOHN LAW, *Pettie Chapman, upon his oath*:

Against ALIZON DEVICE, *Prisoner at the Barre.*

HE deposeth and saith, That about the eighteenth of March last past, hee being a Pedler, went with his Packe of wares at his backe thorow Colne-field: where unluckily he met with *Alizon Device*, now Prisoner at the Barre, who was very earnest with him for pinnes, but he would give her none: whereupon she seemed to be very angry; and when hee was past her, hee fell downe lame in great extremitie; and afterwards by meanes got into an Ale-house in Colne, neere unto the place where hee was first bewitched: and as hee lay there in great paine, not able to stirre either hand or foote; he saw a great Black-Dogge stand by him, with very fearefull firie eyes, great teeth, and a terrible countenance, looking him in the face; whereat he was very sore afraid: and immediately after came in the said *Alizon Device*, who staid not long there, but looked on him, and went away.

After which time hee was tormented both day and night with the said *Alizon Device*; and so continued lame, not able to travell or take paines ever since that time: which with weeping teares in great passion turned to the Prisoner; in the hearing of all the Court hee said to her, *This thou knowest to be too true*: and thereupon she humblie acknowledged the same, and cried out to God to forgive her; and upon her knees with weeping teares humbly prayed him to forgive her that wicked offence; which he very freely and voluntarily did.

{S} Hereupon Master *Nowel* standing up, humbly prayed the favour of the Court, in respect this Fact of Witchcraft was more eminent and apparant

180 It seems likely that this is a transcript of that examination, part of which appears on C as information against Elizabeth Demdike. The date may be confused: on C the examination is said to have been taken on the 13th, but this is before the offence occurred.

then the rest, that for the better satisfaction of the Audience, the Examination of *Abraham Law* might be read in Court.[181]

The Examination of ABRAHAM LAW, *of Halifax,*[182] *in the Countie of Yorke, Cloth-dier, taken upon oath the thirtieth day of March,* 1612.

Before ROGER NOWEL, *Esquire, aforesaid.*

BEing sworne and examined, saith, That upon Saturday last save one, being the one and twentieth day of this instant March, he, this Examinate was sent for, by a letter that came from his father, that he should come to his father, *John Law*, who then lay in Colne speechlesse, and had the left-side lamed all save his eye:[183] and when this Examinate came to his father, his said father had something recovered his speech, and did complaine that hee was pricked with Knives, Elsons[184] and Sickles and that the same hurt was done unto him at Colne-field, presently after that *Alizon Device* had offered to buy some pinnes of him, and she had no money to pay for them withall; but as this Examinates father told this Examinate, he gave her some pinnes.[185] And this Examinate further saith, That he heard his said father say, that the hurt he had in his lamenesse was done unto him by the said *Alizon Device*, by Witchcraft. And this {Sv} Examinate further saith, that hee heard his said Father further say, that the said *Alizon Device* did lie upon him and trouble him. And this Examinate seeing his said Father so tormented with the said *Alizon* and with one other olde woman, whome this Examinates Father did not know as it seemed: This Examinate made search after the said *Alizon*, and having found her, brought her to his said Father yesterday being the nine & twenteth[186] of this instant March: whose said Father in the hearing of this Examinate and divers others did charge the said *Alizon* to have bewitched him, which the said *Alizon* confessing did aske this examinates said Father forgivenesse upon her knees for the same; whereupon this Examinates Father accordingly did forgive her. Which Examinate in open Court upon his oath hee justified to be true.

181 It's unclear why this preamble is important, and why this information (unlike almost all the others, which Potts persistently represents as oral testimony), is described as being read. Since the accused had effectively pleaded guilty, further appearance of witnesses would be very unusual, and seen as wasting time: therefore perhaps a special plea must be made for further evidence to be given – in a different, concise way.

182 A town about eighteen miles south-east of Pendle Hill.

183 This description suggests he had a stroke.

184 Awls.

185 This is the third version of this classic story of refusal of charity. Alizon Device says she asked to *buy* pins but Law would not sell them to her; John Law says she *begged* pins from him and he refused to give her any; Abraham Law says she *was given* pins. This instability should make us question the evidence we hear in pamphlets, and the reliability of the denial story itself as a representation of economic reality. Potts accepts the story in its traditional form on R2v – the pedlar was punished for 'a small offence' (of uncharity), he says.

186 *Sic.*

Whereupon it was there affirmed to the Court that this *John Law* the Pedler, before his unfortunate meeting with this Witch, was a verie able sufficient stout man of Bodie, and a goodly man of Stature. But by this Devilish art of *Witch-craft* his head is drawne awrie, his Eyes and face deformed, His speech not well to bee understood; his Thighes and Legges starcke lame: his Armes lame especially the left side, his handes lame and turned out of their course, his Bodie able to indure no travell: and thus remaineth at this present time.

The Prisoner being examined by the Court whether shee could helpe the poore Pedler to his former strength and health, she answered she could not and so did many of the rest of the Witches: But shee, with others, affirmed, That if old *Dembdike* had lived, shee could and would have helped him out of that great mi-{S2}-serie, which so long he hath endured for so small an offence, as you have heard.

These things being thus openly published against her, and she knowing her selfe to be guiltie of every particular, humbly acknowledged the Indictment against her to be true, and that she was guiltie of the offence therein contained, and that she had justly deserved death for that and many other such like: whereupon she was carried away, untill she should come to the Barre to receive her judgement of death.

Oh, who was present at this lamentable spectacle, that was not moved with pitie to behold it!

Hereupon my Lord *Gerard*, Sir *Richard Houghton*, and others, who much pitied the poore Pedler, At the entreatie of my Lord *Bromley* the Judge, promised some present course should be taken for his reliefe and maintenance; being now discharged and sent away.

But here I may not let her passe; for that I find some thing more upon Record to charge her withall: for although she were but a young Witch, of a yeares standing, and thereunto induced by *Dembdike* her Grand-mother, as you have formerly heard, yet she was spotted with innocent bloud among the rest: for in one part of the Examination of *James Device*, her brother, he deposeth as followeth, *viz.*

{S2v} *The Examination of* JAMES DEVICE, *brother to the said* ALIZON DEVICE. *Taken upon Oath*

Before ROGER NOWEL *Esquire, aforesaid, the thirtieth day of March*, 1612.

J*Ames Device*, of the Forrest of Pendle, in the Countie of Lancaster, Labourer, sworne and examined, sayth, That about Saint *Peters* day[187] last one *Henry Bulcock* came to the house of *Elizabeth Sothernes*, alias *Dembdike*, Grand-mother to this Examinate, and said, That the said *Alizon Device* had bewitched a Child of his, and desired her, that shee would goe with him to his house: which accordingly shee did: and thereupon shee the said *Alizon* fell downe on her knees, and asked the said *Bulcock* forgivenesse; and confessed to him

187 29 June.

that she had bewitched the said Child, as this Examinate heard his said sister confesse unto him this Examinate.

And although shee were never indicted for this offence, yet being matter upon Record, I thought it convenient to joyne it unto her former Fact.

HEre the Jurie of Life and Death having spent the most part of the day in due consideration of their offences, returned into the Court to deliver up their Verdict against them, as followeth.

{S3} *The Verdict of Life and Death.*

WHo upon their Oathes found *John Bulcock* and *Jane Bulcock* his mother, not guiltie of the Felonie by Witch-craft, contained in the Indictment against them.[188]

Alizon Device convicted upon her owne Confession.

Whereupon Master *Covel* was commaunded by the Court to take away the Prisoners convicted, and to bring forth *Margaret Pearson*, and *Isabell Robey*, Prisoners in the Castle at Lancaster, to receive their Triall.

Who were brought to their Arraignement and Trialls, as hereafter followeth, *viz.*

{S3v} THE ARRAIGNMENT *and Triall of* MARGARET PEARSON *of Paddiham, in the Countie of Lancaster, for Witchcraft; the nineteenth of August* 1612, *at the Assises and Generall Gaole-deliverie, holden at Lancaster.*

Before *Sir* EDWARD BROMLEY *Knight, one of his Majesties Justices of Assise at Lancaster.*

Margaret Pearson.

THus farre have I proceeded in hope your patience will endure the end of this discourse, which craves time, and were better not begunne at all, then not perfected.

This *Margaret Pearson* was the wife of *Edward Pearson* of Paddiham, in the Countie of Lancaster; little inferiour in her wicked and malicious course of life to any that hath gone before her: A very dangerous Witch of long continuance, generally suspected and feared in all parts of the Countrie, and of all good people neare her, and not without great cause: For whosoever gave her any just occasion of offence, shee tor-{S4}-mented with great miserie, or cut off their children, goods, or friends.

This wicked and ungodly Witch revenged her furie upon goods, so that every one neare her sustained great losse. I place her in the end of these notorious Witches, by reason her judgement is of an other Nature, according to her offence; yet had not the favour and mercie of the Jurie beene more then her desert, you had found her next to old *Dembdike*; for this is the third time shee is come to receive her Triall; one time for murder by Witch-craft; an other time for bewitching a neighbour; now for goods.[189]

188 But see the printer's *errata* on A4 – 'not guiltie' should read 'guiltie'.

189 Pearson must have been acquitted of earlier charges, or she would not have survived to appear a third time.

How long shee hath beene a Witch, the Devill and shee knowes best.

The Accusations, Depositions, and particular Examinations upon Record against her are infinite, and were able to fill a large Volume; But since shee is now only to receive her Triall for this last offence. I shall proceede against her in order, and set forth what matter we have upon Record, to charge her withall.

This *Margaret Pearson*, Prisoner in the Castle at Lancaster: Being brought to the Barre before the great Seat of Justice; was there according to the course and order of the Law Indicted and Arraigned, for that shee had practised, exercised, and used her divellish and wicked Arts, called *Witchcrafts, Inchantments, Charmes* and *Sorceries*, and one Horse or Mare[190] of the goods and Chattels of one *Dodgeson* of Padiham, in the Countie of Lancaster, wickedly, maliciously, and voluntarily did kill. *Contra formam Statuti, &c. Et contra Pacem dicti Domini Regis. &c.*

{S4v} Upon her Arraignement to this Indictment, shee pleaded not guiltie; And for the triall of her life[191] put her selfe upon God and her Countrie.

So as now the Gentlemen of the Jurie of her offence and death,[192] stand charged with her as with others.

The Evidence against Margaret Pearson, *Prisoner at the Barre.*

The Examination and Evidence of ANNE WHITTLE, *alias* CHATTOX.

Against MARGARET PEARSON, *Prisoner at the Barre.*

THe said *Anne Chattox* being examined saith, That the wife of one *Pearson* of Paddiham, is a very evill Woman, and confessed to this Examinate, that shee is a Witch, and hath a Spirit which came to her the first time in likenesse of a Man and cloven footed, and that shee the said *Pearsons* wife hath done very much harme to one *Dodgesons* goods, who came in at a loope-hole into the said *Dodgesons* Stable, and shee and her Spirit together did sit upon his Horse or Mare, untill the said Horse or Mare died. And likewise, that shee the said *Pearsons* wife did confesse unto this Examinate, that shee bewitched unto death one *Childers* wife, and her Daughter, and that shee the said *Pearsons* wife is as ill as shee.[193]

{T} *The Examination of* JENNET BOOTH, *of Paddiham, in the Countie of Lancaster, the ninth day of August* 1612.

Before NICHOLAS BANNESTER, *Esquire; one of his Majesties Justices of Peace in the Countie of Lancaster.*[194]

190 The A4 *errata* list changes this to 'one Mare'.

191 This matter was not a capital crime, and the printer amends 'for the Triall of her life' to 'for the triall of her offence'.

192 As above, this is inaccurate.

193 As wicked as Chattox herself.

194 This statement describes events after Pearson's arrest and committal (Peel and Southern, 72) although some writers have read the syntax differently and accordingly believe 'Margerie' to be Pearson herself (Lumby, 134). A missing piece of the statement has already referred to Margerie and would have told us who she was. The information was

Jennet, the wife of *James Booth*, of Paddiham, upon her oath saith, That the Friday next after, the said *Pearsons* wife, was committed to the Gaole at Lancaster, this Examinate was carding in the said *Pearsons* house, having a little child with her, and willed the said *Margerie* to give her a little Milke, to make her said child a little meat, who fetcht this Examinate some, and put it in a pan; this examinat meaning to set it on the fire, found the said fire very ill, and taking up a stick that lay by her, and brake it in three or foure peeces, and laid upon the coales to kindle the same, then set the pan and milke on the fire: and when the milke was boild to this Examinates content, she tooke the pan wherein the milke was, off the said fire, and with all, under the bottome of the same, there came a Toade, or a thing very like a Toade, and to this Examinates thinking came out of the fire, together with the said Pan, and under the bottome of the same, and that the said *Margerie* did carrie the said Toade out of the said house in a paire of tonges; But what shee the said *Margerie* did therewith, this Examinate knoweth not.

After this were divers witnesses examined against her in open Court, *viva voce*, to prove the death of the Mare, {Tv} and divers other vild and odious practises by her committed, who upon their Examinations made it so apparant to the Jurie as there was no question; But because the fact is of no great importance, in respect her life is not in question by this Indictment, and the Depositions and examinations are many, I leave to trouble you with any more of them,[195] for being found guiltie of this offence, the penaltie of the Law is as much as her good Neighbours doe require, which is to be delivered from the companie of such a dangerous, wicked, and malicious Witch.

{T2} THE ARRAIGNMENT *and Triall of* ISABELL ROBEY *in the Countie of Lancaster, for Witch-craft: Upon Wednesday the nineteenth of August,* 1612: *At the Assizes and generall Gaole-delivery, holden at Lancaster.*

Before *Sir* EDWARD BROMLEY, *Knight, one of his Majesties Justices of Assizes at Lancaster.*

Isabel Robey.

THus at one time may you behold Witches of all sorts from many places in this Countie of Lancaster which now may lawfully bee said to abound asmuch in Witches of divers kindes as Seminaries, Jesuites, and Papists. Here then is the last that came to act her part in this lamentable and wofull Tragedie, wherein his Majestie hath lost so many Subjects, Mothers their Children, Fathers their Friends, and Kinsfolkes the like whereof hath not beene set forth in any age. What hath the Kings Majestie written and published in his *Daemonologie*, by way of premonition and prevention, which

given only days before the assize itself and it mentions no *maleficium* useful to the court. Presumably it is thought to show the discovery of a familiar?

195 This seems a wholly inadequate explanation from one usually so verbose. The chosen information has no bearing on the offence, and Potts's usual treatment of oral evidence (which he says does relate to it) is to give us the written version. Perhaps some material has been lost by him?

hath not here by the first or last {T2v} beene executed, put in practise or discovered?[196] What Witches have ever upon their Arraignement and Trial made such open liberall and voluntarie declarations of their lives, and such confessions of their offences: The manner of their attempts and their bloudie practises, their meetings, consultations and what not? Therefore I shall now conclude with this *Isabel Robey* who is now come to her triall.

This *Isabel Robey* Prisoner in the Castle of Lancaster being brought to the Barre before the great Seat of Justice was there according to the former order and course Indicted and Arraigned, for that shee Felloniously had practised, exercised and used her Devilish and wicked Artes called *Witchcrafts, Inchantments, Charmes and Sorceries.*

Upon her Arraignment to this Indictment she pleaded not guiltie, and for the triall of her life, put her selfe upon God and her Countrie.

So as now the Gentlemen of the Jurie of life and death stand charged with her as with others.

The Evidence against Isabel Robey *Prisoner at the Barre.*

{T3} *The Examination of* PETER CHADDOCK *of Windle,*[197] *in the Countie of Lancaster: Taken at Windle aforesaid, the* 12. *day of July* 1612. Anno Reg. Regis JACOBI, Angliae, &c. decimo, & Scotiae xlv.

Before *Sir* THOMAS GERRARD *Knight, and Barronet. One of his Majesties Justices of the Peace within the said Countie.*

THe said Examinate upon his Oath saith, That before his Marriage hee heard say that the said *Isabel Robey* was not pleased that hee should marrie his now wife: whereupon this Examinate called the said *Isabel* Witch, and said that hee did not care for her. Then within two dayes next after this Examinate was sore pained in his bones: And this Examinate having occasion to meete Master *John Hawarden* at Peaseley Crosse, wished one *Thomas Lyon* to goe thither with him, which they both did so; but as they came home-wards, they both were in evill case. But within a short time after, this Examinate and the said *Thomas Lyon* were both very well amended.

And this Examinate further saith, that about foure yeares last past, his now wife was angrie with the said *Isabel*, shee then being in his house, and his said wife thereupon went out of the house, and presently after that the said *Isabel* went likewise out of the house not well pleased, as this Examinate then did thinke, and presently after upon the same day, this Examinate with his said wife working in the Hay, a paine and a starknesse[198] fell into the neck of this Examinate which grieved him very {T3v}[199] whereupon this Examinate sent to one *James* a Glover, which then dwelt in Windle, and

196 A great deal, actually, even though Potts has done his best to gloss cases in a way which makes them echo King James's theories.

197 Near St Helens, Merseyside – at least twenty-five miles south-west of Pendle Hill.

198 Stiffness.

199 Should read 'sore' which is omitted from the first line of T3v.

desired him to pray for him, and within foure or five dayes next after this Examinate did mend very well. Neverthelesse this Examinate during the same time was very sore pained; and so thirstie withall, and hot within his body, that hee would have given any thing hee had, to have slaked his thirst, having drinke enough in the house, and yet could not drinke untill the time that the said *James* the Glover came to him, and this Examinate then said before the said Glover, I would to God that I could drinke, where upon the said Glover said to this Examinate, take that drinke, and in the name of the *Father*, the *Sonne*, and the *Holy Ghost*, drinke it, saying; The Devill and Witches are not able to prevaile against GOD and his Word, whereupon this Examinate then tooke the glasse of drinke, and did drinke it all, and afterwards mended very well, and so did continue in good health, untill our Ladie day in Lent was twelve moneth or thereabouts, since which time this Examinate saith, that hee hath beene sore pained with great warch[200] in his bones, and all his limmes, and so yet continueth, and this Examinate further saith, that his said warch and paine came to him rather by meanes of the said *Isabel Robey*, then otherwise, as he verily thinketh.

{T4} *The Examination of* JANE WILKINSON, *Wife of* FRANCIS WILKINSON, *of Windle aforesaid: Taken before the said Sir* THOMAS GERRARD, *Knight and Barronet, the day and place aforesaid. Against the said* ISABEL ROBEY.

THe said Examinate upon her oath saith, that upon a time the said *Isabel Robey* asked her milke, and shee denied to give her any: And afterwards shee met the said *Isabel*, whereupon this Examinate waxed afraid of her, and was then presently sick, and so pained that shee could not stand, and the next day after this Examinate going to Warrington,[201] was suddenly pinched on her Thigh as shee thought, with foure fingers & a Thumbe twice together, and thereupon was sicke, in so much as shee could not get home but on horse-backe, yet soone after shee did mend.

The Examination of MARGARET LYON *wife of* THOMAS LYON *the yonger, of Windle aforesaid: Taken before the said Sir* THOMAS GERRARD, *Knight and Barronet, the day and place aforesaid. Against the said* ISABEL ROBEY.

THe said *Margaret Lyon* upon her Oath saith, that upon a time *Isabel Robey* came into her house and said that *Peter Chaddock* should never mend untill he had asked her forgivenesse; and that shee knew hee would never doe: whereupon this Examinate said, how doe {T4v} you know that, for he is a true Christian, and hee would aske all the world forgivenesse? then the said *Isabel* said, that is all one, for hee will never aske me forgivenesse, therefore hee shall never mend; And this Examinate further saith, that shee being in the house of the said *Peter Chaddock*, the wife of the said *Peter*, who is God-Daughter of the said *Isabel*, and hath in times past used her companie much,

200 Ache.

201 A town six miles south-east of St Helen's.

did affirme, that the said *Peter* was now satisfied, that the said *Isabel Robey* was no Witch, by sending to one *Halseworths*, which they call a wiseman, and the wife of the said *Peter* then said, to abide upon it, I thinke that my Husband will never mend untill hee have asked her forgivenesse, choose him whether hee will be angrie or pleased, for this is my opinion: to which he answered, when he did need to aske her forgivenesse, he would, but hee thought hee did not need, for any thing hee knew: and yet this Examinate further saith, That the said *Peter Chaddock* had very often told her, that he was very afraid that the said *Isabel* had done him much hurt; and that he being fearefull to meete her, he hath turned backe at such time as he did meet her alone, which the said *Isabel* hath since then affirmed to be true, saying, that hee the said *Peter* did turne againe when he met her in the Lane.

{V[202]} *The Examination of* MARGARET PARRE *wife of* HUGH PARRE *of Windle aforesaid. Taken before the said Sir* THOMAS GERARD *Knight and Baronet, the day and place aforesaid. Against the said* ISABEL ROBEY.

THe said Examinate upon her oath saith, that upon a time, the said *Isabel Robey* came to her house, and this Examinate asked her how *Peter Chaddock* did, And the said *Isabel* answered shee knew not, for shee went not to see, and then this Examinate asked her how *Jane Wilkinson* did, for that she had beene lately sicke and suspected to have beene bewitched: then the said *Isabel* said twice together, I have bewitched her too: and then this Examinate said that shee trusted shee could blesse her selfe from all Witches and defied them; and then the said *Isabel* said twice together, would you defie me? & afterwards the said *Isabel* went away not well pleased.

Here the Gentlemen of the last Jurie of Life and Death having taken great paines, the time being farre spent, and the number of the Prisoners great, returned into the Court to deliver up their Verdict against them as followeth. *viz.*

The Verdict of Life and Death.

WHo upon their Oathes found the said *Isabel Robey* guiltie of the Fellonie by Witch-craft, con-{Vv}-tained in the Indictment against her. And *Margaret Pearson* guiltie of the offence by Witch-craft, contained in the Indictment against her.

Whereupon Master *Covell* was commaunded by the Court in the afternoone to bring forth all the Prisoners that stood Convicted, to receive their Judgment of Life and Death.

For his Lordship now intended to proceed to a finall dispatch of the Pleas of the Crowne.[203] And heere endeth the Arraignement and Triall of the Witches at Lancaster.

THus at the length have we brought to perfection this intended Discovery of Witches, with the Arraignement and Triall of every one of them in order,

202 There is no U signature.

203 The criminal (as opposed to civil) cases before the court.

by the helpe of Almightie God, and this Reverend Judge; the Lanterne from whom I have received light to direct me in this course to the end. And as in the beginning, I presented unto their view a Kalender containing the names of all the Witches: So now I shall present unto you in the conclusion and end, such as stand convicted, and come to the Barre to receive the judgement of the Law for their offences, and the proceedings of the Court against such as were acquitted, and found not guiltie: with the religious Exhortation of this Honorable Judge, as eminent in gifts and graces as in place and preeminence, which I may lawfully affirme without base flattery (the canker of all honest and worthie minds) drew the eyes and reverend respect of all that great Audience present, to heare their Judgement, and the end of these proceedings.

{V2} *The Prisoners being brought to the Barre.*

THe Court commanded three solemne Proclamations for silence, untill Judgement for Life and Death were given.

Whereupon I presented to his Lordship the names of the Prisoners in order, which were now to receive their Judgement.

{V2v} The names of the Prisoners at the *Barre to receive their Judgement* of Life and Death.

Anne Whittle, alias *Chattox.*
Elizabeth Device.
James Device.
Anne Redferne.
Alice Nutter.
Katherine Hewet.
John Bulcock.
Jane Bulcock.
Alizon Device.
Isabel Robey.

{V3} THE JUDGEMENT OF THE RIGHT HONORABLE Sir EDWARD BROMLEY, Knight, one *of his Majesties Justices of Assize at Lancaster upon the Witches convicted*, as followeth.

THere is no man alive more unwilling to pronounce this wofull and heavy Judgement against you, then my selfe: and if it were possible, I would to God this cup might passe from me. But since it is otherwise provided, that after all proceedings of the Law, there must be a Judgement; and the Execution of that Judgement must succeed and follow in due time: I pray you have patience to receive that which the Law doth lay upon you. You of all people have the least cause to complaine: since in the Triall of your lives there hath beene great care and paines taken, and much time spent: and very few or none of you, but stand convicted upon your owne voluntarie confessions and Examinations, Ex ore proprio:[204] *Few Witnesses examined against you, but such as were present, and*

204 Out of your own mouths.

parties in your Assemblies. Nay I may further affirme, What persons of your nature and condition, ever were Arraigned and Tried with more solemnitie, had more libertie given to plead or answere to everie particular point of Evidence against you? In conclusion such hath beene the {V3v} *generall care of all, that had to deale with you, that you have neither cause to be offended in the proceedings of the Justices, that first tooke paines in these businesses, nor with the Court that hath had great care to give nothing in evidence against you, but matter of fact; Sufficient matter upon Record, and not to induce or lead the Jurie to finde any one of you guiltie upon matter of suspicion or presumption, nor with the witnesses who have beene tried, as it were in the fire: Nay, you cannot denie but must confesse what extraordinarie meanes hath beene used to make triall of their evidence, and to discover the least intended practice in any one of them, to touch your lives unjustly.*[205]

As you stand simply (your offences and bloudie practises not considered) your fall would rather move compassion, then exasperate any man. For whom would not the ruine of so many poore creatures at one time, touch, as in apparance[206] *simple, and of little understanding?*

But the bloud of those innocent children, and others his Majesties Subjects, whom cruelly and barbarously you have murdered, and cut off, with all the rest of your offences, hath cryed out unto the Lord against you, and sollicited for satisfaction and revenge, and that hath brought this heavie judgement upon you at this time. It is therefore now time no longer wilfully to strive, both against the providence of God, and the Justice of the Land: the more you labour to acquit your selves, the more evident and apparant you make you offences to the World. And unpossible it is that they shall either prosper or continue in this World, or receive reward in the next, that are stained with so much innocent bloud.

The worst then I wish to you, standing at the Barre convicted, to receive your Judgement, is, Remorse, and true Re-{V4}*-pentance, for the safeguard of your Soules, and after, a humble, penitent, and heartie acknowledgement of your grievous sinnes and offences committed both against* GOD *and Man.*

First, yeeld humble and heartie thankes to Almightie GOD *for taking hold of you in your beginning, and making stay of your intended bloudie practises (although* GOD *knowes there is too much done alreadie) which would in time have cast so great a weight of Judgement upon your Soules.*

205 This concern with *in*justice, as in the later Jennet Preston account, is an interesting indication of conflict over witchcraft and its fair trial, and perhaps over the system of criminal justice itself (whose potential flaws Bromley lists, from insufficient time taken over felony trials through magisterial interference to witness perjury). Bromley's section of the pamphlet sets out to defend the court from serious accusations of injustice, rather than to assert unquestioned wisdom, as we might expect. He seems likely to have written this polished, balanced judgement himself – its relationship to what was actually said is, of course, unclear. What is obvious is that the judge's tone differs greatly from Potts's laudatory confidence in the legal system, expressed throughout the main text of the pamphlet.

206 *Sic.*

Then praise GOD *that it pleased him not to surprize or strike you suddenly, even in the execution of your bloudie Murthers, and in the middest of your wicked practises, but hath given you time, and takes you away by a judiciall course and triall of the Law.*

Last of all, crave pardon of the World, and especially of all such as you have justly offended, either by tormenting themselves, children, or friends, murder of their kinsfolkes, or losse of any their goods.

And for leaving to future times the president[207] *of so many barbarous and bloudie murders, with such meetings, practises, consultations, and meanes to execute revenge, being the greatest part of your comfort in all your actions, which may instruct others to hold the like course, or fall in the like sort:*

It only remaines I pronounce the Judgement of the Court against you by the Kings authoritie, which is; You shall all goe from hence to the Castle, from whence you came; from thence you shall bee carried to the place of Execution for this Countie: where your bodies shall bee hanged untill you are dead; And GOD HAVE MERCIE UPON YOUR SOULES: For your comfort in this world I shall commend a learned and worthie Preacher {V4v} to instruct you, and prepare you for an other World: All I can doe for you is to pray for your Repentance in this World, for the satisfaction of many; And forgivenesse in the next world, for saving of your Soules. And God graunt you may make good use of the time you have in this World, to his glorie and your owne comfort.

Margaret Pearson.

THe Judgement of the Court against you, is, You shall stand upon the Pillarie in open Market, at *Clitheroe, Paddiham, Whalley*, and *Lancaster*,[208] foure Market dayes, with a Paper upon your head, in great Letters, declaring your offence, and there you shall confesse your offence, and after to remaine in Prison for one yeare without Baile, and after to be bound with good Suerties, to be of good behaviour.

{X} *To the Prisoners found not guiltie* by the JURIES.

Elizabeth Astley.

John Ramsden.

Alice Gray.

Isabel Sidegraves.

Lawrence Hay.

TO you that are found not guiltie, and are by the Law to bee acquited, presume no further of your Innocencie then you have just cause: for although it pleased God out of his Mercie, to spare you at this time, yet without question there are amongst you, that are as deepe in this Action, as any of them that are condemned to die for their offences:[209] *The time is now for you to forsake the Devill: Remember*

207 Precedent.

208 Clitheroe is three miles east of Pendle Hill, and Whalley four miles south of Clitheroe.

209 This suggestion that the acquitted are as guilty as the condemned is a further indication

how, and in what sort hee hath dealt with all of you: make good use of this great mercie and favour: and pray unto God you fall not againe: For great is your happinesse to have time in this World, to prepare your selves against the day when you shall appeare before the Great Judge of all.

Notwithstanding, the judgement of the Court, is, You shall all enter Recognizances with good sufficient Suerties, to appeare at the next Assizes at Lancaster,[210] and in the meane time to be of the good behaviour. All I can say to you:

{Xv} *Jennet Bierley,*

Ellen Bierley,

Jane Southworth, is, That GOD hath delivered you beyond expectation, I pray GOD you fall not hereafter: And so the Court doth order you shall be delivered.

What more can bee written or published of the proceedings of this honorable Court: but to conclude with the Execution of the Witches, who were executed the next day following at the common place of Execution, neare unto Lancaster. Yet in the end give mee leave to intreate some favour that have beene afraid to speake untill my worke were finished. If I have omitted any thing materiall, or published any thing imperfect, excuse me for that I have done: It was a worke imposed upon me by the Judges, in respect I was so wel instructed in every particular. In hast I have undertaken to finish it in a busie Tearme amongst my other imploiments.

My charge was to publish the proceedings of Justice, and matter of Fact, wherein I wanted libertie to write what I would, and am limited to set forth nothing against them, but matter upon Record, even in their owne Countrie tearmes, which may seeme strange. And this I hope will give good satisfaction to such as understand how to judge of a businesse of this nature. Such as have no other imploiment but to question other mens Actions, I leave them to censure what they please, It is no part of my profession to publish any thing in {X2} print, neither can I paint in extraordinarie tearmes. But if this discourse may serve for your instruction, I shall thinke my selfe very happie in this Service, and so leave it to your generall censure.[211]

of Bromley's pragmatic sense of the legal system – which sits uneasily with Potts's idealism despite the attempt to present verdicts as God's will. Although scandalous to modern sensibilities, Bromley's claim is not unusual. For example, witchcraft stories printed in pamphlets from pre-trial documents often concern those eventually acquitted (Joan Waterhouse in *The Examination and Confession of certayne Wytches*, Mother Staunton in *A Detection of damnable driftes*), although some pamphlets (conscientiously?) omit such matter as, in fact, this one does.

210 Recognisances were documents kept by the court clerks, guaranteeing (with a stated bond which would be forfeited if the agreement were broken) appearance at future sessions of the court – they were also entered by innocent parties such as witnesses required to give evidence.

211 It seems certain from Potts's tone that he intended to conclude his work here. The addition after this peroration of material from the trial of Jennet Preston has traditionally, almost

Da veniam Ignoto non displicuisse meretur, Festinat studiis qui placuisse tibi.[212]
{X2 blank}
{X3} *The* ARRAIGNEMENT AND TRIALL OF JENNET PRESTON, OF GISBORNE IN CRAVEN, in the Countie of Yorke.
At the Assises and Generall Gaole-*Deliverie holden at the Castle of Yorke* in the Countie of Yorke, the xxvii. day of July last past, *Anno Regni Regis* JACOBI *Angliae, &c. Decimo, & Scotiae quadragesimo quinto.*
Before *Sir* JAMES ALTHAM *Knight, one* of the Barons of his Majesties Court of Exchequer; and Sir EDWARD BROMLEY Knight, another of *the Barons of his Majesties Court of Exchequer*; his Majesties Justices of Assise, Oyer and Terminer, *and generall Gaole-Deliverie, in the Circuit of the North-parts.*
LONDON, Printed by W. STANSBY for JOHN BARNES, and are to be sold at his Shoppe neere Holborne Conduit. 1612.[213]
{X3v blank}
{X4} THE ARRAIGNMENT *and Triall of* JENNET PRESTON *of Gisborne in Craven, in the Countie of Yorke, at the Assises and Generall Gaole-deliverie, holden at the Castle of Yorke, in the Countie of Yorke, the seven and twentieth day of July last past.* Anno Regni Regis Jacobi Angliae &c. Decimo & Scotiae xlvi.
Jennet Preston.
MANY have undertaken to write great discourses of Witches and many more dispute and speake of them. And it were not much if as many wrote them as could write at al,[214] to set forth to the world the particular Rites and Secrets of their unlawfull Artes, with their infinite and wonderfull practises which many men little feare till they seaze upon them. As by this late wonderfull discoverie of Witches in the Countie of Lancaster may appeare, wherein I find such apparant matter[215] to satisfie the World, how dangerous and malitious a {X4v} Witch this *Jennet Preston* was, How unfit to live, having once

without comment, been regarded as Potts's – but this editor is inclined to take his words here as his final ones and ascribe the end of the pamphlet to another writer.

212 Potts repeats in compact form his plea that we receive his humble and hurried efforts well, and not according to the displeasure which they perhaps merit.

213 This section of the pamphlet, relating to Jennet Preston, is dated '1612' – *before* the main body of the pamphlet. But, as the text makes clear, it actually post-dates it. Possibly the publisher had already planned to publish the book on Yorkshire witchcraft when he was unexpectedly deluged with Lancashire material, and decided to combine the two. Jonathan Lumby, arguing this case, ingeniously suggests that the wording of the Preston account has been altered to allow it to be used as a postscript to *The Wonderfull Discoverie* (14, 184). Equally, the date may be mistaken and the text may be correct in its assertions. Whatever the case, this final part of the pamphlet is publishable separately, with its own title page and publisher's imprint, although if it *was* published before *The Wonderfull Discoverie*, no copy or record survives.

214 *Sic.*

215 This remark again suggests a new pamphleteer, as does the choppy, confusing nature of his sentences – unlike Potts's usual clarity.

so great mercie extended to her:[216] And againe to exercise her practises, and returne to her former course of life, that I thinke it necessarie not to let the memorie of her life and death die with her; But to place her next to her fellowes and to set forth the Arraignement Triall and Conviction of her, with her offences for which she was condemned and executed.

And although shee died for her offence before the rest, I yet can afford her no better place then in the end of this Booke in respect the proceedings was in an other Countie;

You that were husband to this *Jennet Preston*; her friends and kinsfolkes, who have not beene sparing to devise so scandalous a slander out of the malice of your hearts, as that shee was maliciously prosecuted by Master *Lister* and others; Her life unjustly taken away by practise, and that (even at the Gallowes where shee died impenitent and void of all feare and grace) she died an Innocent woman, because she would confesse nothing:[217] You I say may not hold it strange, though at this time, being not only moved in conscience, but directed, for example sake, with that which I have to report of her, I suffer you not to wander any further; but with this short discourse oppose your idle conceipts able to seduce others: And by Charmes of Imputations and slander, laid upon the Justice of the Land, to cleare her that was justly condemned and executed for her offence;[218] That this *Jennet Preston* was for many yeares well thought of and esteemed by Master *Lister* who afterwardes died for it. Had free accesse to his house, kind respect and entertainment; nothing denied her she {Y} stood in need of. Which of you that dwelleth neare them in Craven but can and will witnesse it? which might have incouraged a Woman of any good condition to have runne a better course.

The favour and goodnesse of this Gentleman Master *Lister* now living, at his first entrance after the death of his Father extended towards her, and the reliefe[219] she had at all times, with many other favours that succeeded from time to time, are so palpable and evident to all man as no man can denie them. These were sufficient motives to have perswaded her from the murder of so good a friend.

But such was her execrable Ingratitude, as even this grace and goodnesse was the cause of his miserable and untimely death. And even in the beginning

216 See Y.

217 Lumby examines the accusation of malicious prosecution, and the connections between the Nowell, Starkey, Bannester and Holden families, and the Lister and Heber families which form an important, though probably not a genuinely conspiratorial, framework behind both accounts.

218 This part of the pamphlet is strongly concerned with defending local justice – with the kind of zeal which suggests a serious breakdown of confidence in it amid public suspicion and active opposition (see also Y). Its tone is very harsh and incisive, which sounds unlike Potts. The writer speaks authoritatively and without the timidity, or the bluster, which is characteristic of Potts.

219 Charity.

of his greatest favours extended to her, began shee to worke this mischiefe, according to the course of all Witches.[220]

This *Jennet Preston*, whose Arraignment and Triall, with the particular Evidence against her I am now to set forth unto you, one that lived at Gisborne in Craven, in the Countie of Yorke, neare Master *Lister* of Westbie, against whom she practised much mischiefe; for having cut off *Thomas Lister* Esquire, father to this gentleman now living, shee revenged her selfe upon his sonne: who in short time received great losse in his goods and cattell by her meanes.

These things in time did beget suspition, and at the Assizes and Generall Gaole deliverie holden at the Castle of Yorke in Lent last past, before my Lord *Bromley*, shee was Indicted and Arraigned for the murder of a Child of one *Dodg-sonnes*,[221] but by the favour and mercifull consideration of the Jurie thereof acquited.

{Yv} But this favour and mercie was no sooner extended towardes her, and shee set at libertie, But shee began to practise the utter ruine and overthrow of the name and bloud of this Gentleman.

And the better to execute her mischiefe and wicked intent, within foure dayes after her deliverance out of the Castle at Yorke, went to the great Assembly of Witches at *Malking-Tower* upon Good-friday last: to pray aide and helpe, for the murder of Master *Lister*, in respect he had prosecuted against her at the same Assizes.

Which it pleased God in his mercie to discover, and in the end, howsoever he had blinded her, as he did the King of AEgypt and his Instruments, for the brighter evidence of his own powerful glory; Yet by a Judiciall course and triall of the Law, cut her off, and so delivered his people from the danger of her Devillish and wicked practises:[222] which you shall heare against her, at her Arraignement and Triall, which I shall now set forth to you in order as it was performed, with the wonderfull signes and tokens of GOD, to satisfie the Jurie to finde her guiltie of this bloudie murther, committed foure yeares since.

{Y2} Indictment.

THis *Jennet Preston* being Prisoner in the Castle at Yorke, and indicted, for that shee felloniously had practised, used, and exercised diverse wicked and devillish Arts, called Witchcrafts, Inchauntments, Charmes, and Sorceries, in

220 This generalising statement of the 'motiveless' and ungrateful malignity attributed to witches in pamphlets from about 1590 suggests that this explanation of witch-attack had crystallised into a commonplace in gentlemanly accounts of them. But Potts's pamphlet shows that other motives (revenge for the denial of charity, for example) were still the mainstay of *court* proceedings against witches, and thus of pamphlets using legal documents to tell their stories.

221 Perhaps the same Dodgson whom Margaret Pearson is accused of harming on S4v (Peel and Southern, 78) – although Padiham and Gisburne are some twelve miles apart.

222 The Lister family are likened to the Israelites – God's chosen people – in Egypt (Exodus 7, etc.).

and upon one *Thomas Lister* of Westby in Craven, in the Countie of Yorke Esquire, and by force of the same Witchcraft felloniously the said *Thomas Lister* had killed, *Contra Pacem, &c.* beeing at the Barre, was arraigned.
To this Indictment upon her Arraignement, shee pleaded not guiltie, and for the Triall of her life put her selfe upon GOD and her Countrey.
Whereupon my Lord *Altham* commaunded Master Sheriffe of the Countie of Yorke, in open Court to returne a Jurie of sufficient Gentlemen of understanding, to passe betweene our Soveraigne Lord the Kings Majestie and her, and others the Prisoners, upon their lives and deaths; who were afterwards sworne, according to the forme and order of the Court, the prisoner being admitted to her lawfull challenge.
Which being done, and the Prisoner at the Barre to receive her Tryall, Master *Heyber*, one of his Majesties Justices of Peace in the same County,[223] having taken great paines in the proceedings against her; and being best instructed of any man of all the particular points of Evidence against her, humbly prayed, the witnesses hereafter following might be examined against her, and the severall Examinations, taken before Master *Nowel*, and certified, might openly bee published against her; which hereafter follow in order, *viz.*
{Y2v} *The Evidence for the Kings Majestie*
Against JENNET PRESTON, *Prisoner at the Barre.*
HEreupon were diverse Examinations taken and read openly against her, to induce and satisfie the Gentlemen of the Jurie of Life and Death, to find she was a Witch; and many other circumstances for the death of Master *Lister*. In the end *Anne Robinson* and others were both examined, who upon their Oathes declared against her, That M. *Lister* lying in great extremitie, upon his death-bedde, cried out unto them that stood about him; that *Jennet Preston* was in the house, looke where shee is, take hold of her: for Gods sake shut the doores, and take her, she cannot escape away. Looke about for her, and lay hold on her, for shee is in the house: and so cryed very often in his great paines, to them that came to visit him during his sicknesse.
Anne Robinson and *Thomas Lister*
Being examined further, they both gave this in evidence against her, That when Master *Lister* lay upon his death-bedde, hee cryed out in great extremitie; *Jennet Preston* lyes heavie upon me, *Prestons* wife lyes heavie upon me; helpe me, helpe me: and so departed, crying out against her.[224]
{Y3} These, with many other witnesses, were further examined, and deposed, That *Jennet Preston*, the Prisoner at the Barre, being brought to M. *Lister*

223 Thomas Heyber or Heber, of Marton in Craven, was related to the Listers by marriage. Thomas Lister the younger married his daughter Jane in 1607/8.

224 The writer clearly is not reproducing documents here. There is no legalese language or format, and Master Lister's words are dramatised rather than reported. The pamphleteer is reconstructing his text, probably from memory, to make it look authoritative. He clearly does not have access to the informations behind this court testimony – but he does have access to Lancashire documents (see Y3v–Zv) including one not used by Potts.

after hee was dead, & layd out to be wound up in his winding-sheet, the said *Jennet Preston* comming to touch the dead corpes,[225] they bled fresh bloud presently, in the presence of all that were there present: Which hath ever beene held a great argument to induce a Jurie to hold him guiltie that shall be accused of Murther, and hath seldome, or never, fayled in the Tryall. But these were not alone: for this wicked and bloud-thirstie Witch was no sooner delivered at the Assises holden at Yorke in Lent last past, being indicted, arraigned, and by the favor and mercie of the Jurie found not guiltie, for the murther of a Child by Witch-craft: but upon the Friday following, beeing Good-Friday, shee rode in hast to the great meeting at Malking-Tower, and there prayed aide for the murther of M. *Thomas Lister*: as at large shall appeare, by the severall Examinations hereafter following; sent to these Assises from Master *Nowel* and others his Majesties Justices of Peace in the Countie of Lancaster, to be given in evidence against her, upon her Triall, *viz.*

{Y3v} *The Examination and Evidence of* JAMES DEVICE, *of the Forrest of Pendle, in the Countie of Lancaster, Labourer, taken at the house of* JAMES WILSEY, *of the Forrest of Pendle in the Countie of Lancaster, the seven and twentieth day of Aprill,* Anno Reg. Regis JACOBI Angliae, &c. Decimo ac Scotiae quadragesimo quinto.

Before ROGER NOWEL, *and* NICHOLAS BANESTER, *Esquires, two of his Majesties Justices of the Peace within the Countie of Lancaster*, viz.

THis Examinate saith, That upon Good-Friday last about twelve of the clocke in the day-time, there dined at this Examinates said mothers house a number of persons, whereof three were men, with this Examinate, and the rest women: and that they met there for these three causes following (as this Examinates said mother told this Examinate): First was for the naming of the Spirit, which *Alizon Device*, now Prisoner at Lancaster, had, but did not name him, because shee was not there. The second cause was for the delivery of his said Grand-mother, this Examinates said sister *Alizon*, the said *Anne Chattox*, and her daughter *Redferne*: Killing the Gaoler at Lancaster; and before the next Assizes to blow up the Castle there; to that end the aforesaid Prisoners might by that meanes make an escape and get away. All of which this Examinate then heard them conferre of. And the third cause was, for that there was a woman dwelling in Gisburne Parish, who came into this Examinates said Grand-mothers {Y4} house, who there came, and craved assistance of the rest of them that were then there, for the killing of Master *Lister* of Westby: because, as she then said, he had borne malice unto her, and had thought to have put her away at the last Assizes at Yorke; but could not. And then this Examinat heard the said woman say, that her power was not strong enough to doe it her selfe, being now lesse then before-time it had beene. And he also further saith, That the said *Prestons* wife had a Spirit with her like unto a white Foale, with a blacke-spot in the forehead. And further, this

225 *Sic.*

examinat saith, That since the said meeting, as aforesaid, this Examinate hath beene brought to the wife of one *Preston* in Gisburne Parish aforesaid, by *Henry Hargreives* of Gold-shey[226] to see whether shee was the woman that came amongst the said Witches, on the said last Good-Friday, to crave their aide and assistance for the killing of the said Master *Lister*: and having had full view of her; hee this Examinate confesseth, That she was the selfe-same woman which came amongst the said witches of the said last Good-Friday, for their aide for the killing of the said Master *Lister*; and that brought the Spirit with her, in the shape of a White Foale, as aforesaid.[227]

And this Examinate further saith, That all the said Witches went out of the said house in their owne shapes and likenesses, and they all, by that they were forth of the doores, were gotten on horse-backe like unto Foales, some of one colour, some of another, and *Prestons* wife was the last; and when she got on horse-backe, they all presently vanished out of this Examinats sight: and before their said parting away, they all appointed to meete at the said *Prestons* wifes house that {Y4v} day twelve-month; at which time the said *Prestons* wife promised to make them a great feast; and if they had occasion to meet in the meane time, then should warning bee given that they all should meete upon Romles-Moore. And this Examinate further saith, That at the said feast at Malking-Tower, this Examinat heard them all give their consents to put the said Master *Thomas Lister* of Westby to death: and after Master *Lister* should be made away by Witchcraft, then al the said Witches gave their consents to joyne altogether to hancke Master *Leonard Lister*, when he should come to dwell at the Sowgill, and so put him to death.

The Examination of HENRIE HARGREIVES *of Goldshey-booth, in the Forrest of Pendle, in the Countie of Lancaster Yeoman, taken the fifth day of May,* Anno Reg. Regis JACOBI Angliae, &c. Decimo, ac Scotiae quadragesimo quinto. Before ROGER NOWEL, NICHOLAS BANNESTER, *and* ROBERT HOULDEN, *Esquires; three of his Majesties Justices of Peace within the said Countie.*

THis Examinat upon his oath saith, That *Anne Whittle*, alias *Chattox*, confessed unto him, that she knoweth one *Prestons* wife neere Gisburne, and that the said *Prestons* wife should have beene at the said feast, upon the said Good-Friday, and that shee was an ill woman, and had done Master *Lister* of Westby great hurt.

{Z} *The Examination of* ELIZABETH DEVICE, *mother of* JAMES DEVICE, *taken before* ROGER NOWEL *and* NICHOLAS BANESTER, *Esquires, the day and yeare aforesaid,* viz.

THe said *Elizabeth Device* upon her Examination confesseth, That upon Good-Friday last, there dined at this Examinats house, which she hath said

226 See E3v.

227 This material, if it was there, was all omitted by Potts. Is it spliced in from another examination, given that the sequence of events is confused: Jennet Preston is first named (as 'Prestons wife') but only afterwards described as being physically identified by Device?

are Witches, and doth verily thinke them to be Witches; and their names are those whom *James Device* hath formerly spoken of to be there.

She also confesseth in all things touching the killing of Master *Lister* of Westby, as the said *James Device* hath before confessed.

And the said *Elizabeth Device* also further saith, That at the said meeting at Malking-Tower, as aforesaid, the said *Katherine Hewyt* and *John Bulcock*, with all the rest then there, gave their consents, with the said *Prestons* wife, for the killing of the said Master *Lister*. And for the killing of the said Master *Leonard Lister*, she this Examinate saith in all things, as the said *James Device* hath before confessed in his Examination.[228]

{Zv} *The Examination of* JENNET DEVICE, *daughter of* ELIZABETH *late wife of* JOHN DEVICE, *of the Forrest of Pendle, in the Countie of Lancaster, about the age of nine yeares or thereabouts, taken the day and yeare aforesaid*: Before ROGER NOWEL *and* NICHOLAS BANESTER, *Esquires, two of his Majesties Justices of Peace in the Countie of Lancaster.*

THe said Examinate upon her Examination saith, that upon Good-friday last there was about twenty persons, whereof only two were men, to this Examinats remembrance, at her said Grand mothers house, called Malking-Tower aforesaid, about twelve of the clocke: all which persons, this Examinates said mother told her were Witches, and that she knoweth the names of divers of the said Witches.

{Z2} AFter all these Examinations, Confessions, and Evidence, delivered in open Court against her, His Lordship commanded the Jurie to observe the particular circumstances; first, Master *Lister* in his great extremitie, to complaine hee saw her, and requested them that were by him to lay hold of her.

After he cried out shee lay heavie upon him, even at the time of his death. But the Conclusion is of more consequence then all the rest, that *Jennet Preston* being brought to the dead corps, they bled freshly, And after her deliverance in Lent, it is proved shee rode upon a white Foale, and was present in the great Assembly at *Malkin Tower* with the Witches, to intreat and pray for aide of them, to kill Master *Lister*, now living, for that he had prosequuted[229] against her.

And against these people you may not expect such direct evidence, since all their workes are the workes of darkenesse, no witnesses are present to accuse them, therefore I pray God direct your consciences.[230]

228 Clearly this is – at last – an abbreviated version of the familiar evidence.

229 *Sic.*

230 Altham's heavy direction of the jury blends into the authorial voice. Is this Altham's own work, or that of someone closely associating themself with his views (see also Z3–Z3v for his echoing and praise of Altham)? On Z2v the writer says he was present at Lancaster for the assizes, and his grasp of legal terminology and procedure seems sound enough for him to be a legal official. He also seems to come from the north (Z3v) and has strong views on jurors' duties. But his identity remains unknown.

After the Gentlemen of the Jurie of Life and Death had spent the most part of the day, in consideration of the evidence against her, they returned into the Court and delivered up their Verdict of Life and Death.

{Z2v} *The Verdict of Life and Death.*

WHo found *Jennet Preston* guiltie of the fellonie and murder by Witchcraft of *Thomas Lister*, Esquire; conteyned in the Indictment against her, &c.

Afterwards, according to the course and order of the Lawes, his Lordship pronounced Judgement against her to bee hanged for her offence. And so the Court arose.

HEre was the wonderfull discoverie of this *Jennet Preston*, who for so many yeares had lived at Gisborne in Craven, neare Master *Lister*: one thing more I shall adde to all these particular Examinations, and evidence of witnesses, which I saw, and was present in the Court at Lancaster, when it was done at the Assizes holden in August following.

My Lord *Bromley* being very suspicious of the accusation of *Jennet Device*, the little Wench, commanded her to looke upon the Prisoners that were present, and declare which of them were present at *Malkin Tower*, at the great assembly of Witches upon Good-Friday last: shee looked upon and tooke many by the handes, and accused them to be there, and when shee had accused all that were there present, shee told his Lordship there was a Woman that came out of Craven that was {Z3} amongst the Witches at that Feast, but shee saw her not amongst the Prisoners at the Barre.

What a singular note was this of a Child, amongst many to misse her, that before that time was hanged for her offence, which shee would never confesse or declare at her death? here was present old *Preston* her husband, who then cried out and went away: being fully satisfied his wife had Justice, and was worthie of death.

To conclude then this present discourse, I heartilie desire you, my loving Friends and Countrie-men, for whose particular instructions this is added to the former of the wonderfull discoverie of Witches in the Countie of Lancaster: And for whose particular satisfaction this is published; Awake in time, and suffer not your selves to be thus assaulted.

Consider how barbarously this Gentleman hath been dealt withall; and especially you that hereafter shall passe upon any Juries of Life and Death, let not your connivence, or rather foolish pittie, spare such as these, to exequute farther mischiefe.

Remember shee was no sooner set at libertie, but shee plotted the ruine and overthrow of this Gentleman, and his whole Familie.

Expect not, as this reverend and learned Judge saith, such apparent proofe against them, as against others, since all their workes, are the workes of darkenesse: and unlesse it please Almightie God to raise witnesses to accuse them, who is able to condemne them?

Forget not the bloud that cries out unto God for revenge, bring it not upon your owne heads.

Neither doe I urge this any farther, then with this, that I would alwaies intreat you to remember, that it is {Z3v} as great a crime (as *Salomon* sayth, *Prov.* 17)[231] to condemne the innocent, as to let the guiltie escape free.
Looke not upon things strangely alledged, but judiciously consider what is justly proved against them.
And that as well all you that were witnesses, present at the Arraignement and Triall of her, as all other strangers, to whom this Discourse shall come, may take example by this Gentleman to prosecute these hellish Furies to their end: labor to root them out of the Commonwealth, for the common good of your Countrey. The greatest mercie extended to them, is soone forgotten.
GOD graunt us the long and prosperous continuance of these Honorable and Reverend Judges, under whose Government we live in these North parts: for we may say, that GOD Almightie hath singled them out, and set them on his Seat, for the defence of Justice.
And for this great deliverance, let us all pray to GOD Almightie, that the memorie of these worthie Judges may bee blessed to all Posterities.
FINIS.

231 Probably 'he that justifieth the wicked, and he that condemneth the just, even they both are abomination to the Lord' (Proverbs 17.15). But also relevant, in the light of the pamphlet's defence of judicial authority, is 'Also to punish the just is not good, nor to strike princes for equity' (17.26).

14

Witches Apprehended (1613)

Printed by William Stansby for Edward Marchant, this pamphlet was entered in the Stationers' Register on 23 January 1613 to John Trundell. Stansby was the printer of Potts's pamphlet of the previous year but produced this much shorter quarto in a more traditional blackletter format. Trundell or Trundle was a prolific publisher based at the sign of Nobody in the Barbican area in 1613, and he had published the first (bad) quarto of *Hamlet* in 1603. Presumably he passed the pamphlet's rights on to Marchant, a bookseller dealing in ballads and ephemera. The text used here is in the Huntington Library, California.

The pamphleteer seems somewhat unengaged by his subject, and is interested in giving an entertaining account, lightly moralised with a number of *exempla* – some of them more effective than others. There are no documents and the style is that of a gentlemanly ramble enlivened with more humour based on witchcraft events. Some of the other themes of previous narrative accounts are also present: the pamphlet describes the attacks made by a mother and daughter on a rich gentleman, Master Enger. It is another example of a family of witches being suspected of persecuting a gentlemanly victim, without a motive which the pamphlet feels is in any way allowable, as in *The Most strange and admirable discoverie* (1593) and *The Witches of Northamptonshire* (1612). There is an unspecified difference between Mother Sutton and Master Enger, followed by a conflict between Enger's servant and the younger woman's son. Enger's attempts to investigate spiral into brutality which is then revenged. But the pamphleteer protests Enger's innocence throughout, and harps instead on the victim's generosity to the women, as in other such accounts.

The pamphlet also echoes *The Witches of Northamptonshire* (1612) when a gentlemanly friend of the victim is shown providing a solution to the conflict by suggesting that the witches should be swum. The step by step description of this procedure which follows was reused in later pamphlets as a manual. The 1613 pamphlet was certainly, then, successful in promoting this method of testing for witchcraft and advertises this aim on its title page together with an illustration showing the test in action.

{A2 (title page)} **Witches Apprehended, Examined and Executed, for notable villanies by them committed both by Land and Water.**
With a strange and most true triall how to know **whether a woman**[1] **be a Witch or not.**
Printed at London for *Edward Marchant,* **and are to be sold at his shop over against the Crosse in Pauls Church-yard. 1613.**
{A2v blank}
{A3} **The severall and damnable practises of Mother** *Sutton,* **and** *Mary* **Sutton** *her daughter of Milton Milles,* **in the Countie of Bedford: who were lately arraigned convicted, and executed.**

PLinie writes of some kinde of Serpentes that dare not approach the wild Ashtree, nay the sight of it is so terrible to them, they flie from it, and will not draw neer the shadowe thereof, but if they be walled round with fire, they will rather runne through to the confusion {A3v} of themselves then endure it.[2] If it were so with us which professe our selves Christians, & should be **Christes sonnes** to imitate our Father, and Saviour in his life, which hee left as a lesson to mankinde his **children** to learne, we should then having reason (part of the inheritance of Angels) be more provident of our proper good then Serpents are, who to avoid the **persecution of their minde**, will endure the affliction of their bodie, and to shunne the verie shadow of the Ashtree, will thrust themselves into torment of fire: So should men, who seeing sinne like a wild Ashtree grow in the world, and that to lurke under the shadow thereof is a **whippe to their conscience**, when to feed on the sappe i damnation to their soules, in this onely like Serpents avoid it for the reliefe of their mindes, though with the painefull dissolution of their bodies: but such is the deafnesse of our eares, that though heaven it selfe speak in thunder to remember us a day shall come when we must give account for our wilfull transgressions, wee not regard it, and such the hardnesse of our hearts, that neither treasons, murthers, witchcrafts, fires, flouds, of all which the impetuous course hath beene such in this age, that we have cause to looke our day of summons is to morrow, if not this houre, yet we are unprepared of our account, and as if it were lawfull that evils should grow, many from one, and one from another, are as corne is fruitfull from one seede to severall eares. So from one sinne we {A4} multiply to divers, not dreading vengeance till our iniquities be numberlesse. As shall appeare by this following discourse.

At a place called Milton three miles from Bedford, was lately dwelling one Mother **Sutton**, who being a widow, and of declining yeares, had her daughter called **Mary Sutton**, (as it was thought by the neighbours thereabouts) resident with

1 An interesting specific gendering.
2 Pliny, *Natural History*, book 16. The prefacer has altered the story somewhat, and goes on rather unskilfully to develop an uneasy analogy of Christians and serpents, with the alleged desirability of destruction by fire as an added symbolic complication in the tangled syntax.

her as a stay and comfort to her age, when she kept her, but as a furtherer to her divellish practises, nay indeed to make her a scholler to the Divell himselfe.
This widow **Sutton** having beene dwelling a long time in the foresaid, towne of Milton, and not suspected as then to have beene a practiser in this divellish exercise of witchcraft, was by the townsmen (being held but poore) for her better reliefe chosen to be the Hogheard, or Hog-keeper. In which service she continued long, not without commendations for her dutifull care had therein. And though many cattell oftentimes miscarried, and were taken with staggerings, frensies, and other diseases to their confusions, and impoverishing of the owners, yet she not till of late suspected to be a cause thereof, though since it hath evidently beene proved against her.
Continuing thus almost for the space of twentie or one and twentie yeares, and in that time had brought her daughter to be as perfect in her divellish charmes as her selfe, there grew some difference betweene a Gentleman of worship cal-{A4v}-led Master **Enger** dwelling at Milton Milles, and this mother **Sutton**, On whom she had vowed to take a strange and actuall revenge for the discontent she had conceived against him, which rancour of hers she thus prosecuted:[3] His horses that were left well in his stable over night, she caused them to be found dead in the morning, some strangled, some having beaten out their braines, others dead, and no cause perceived how. Besides this losse, which for the strangenesse bred some amazement in him, for that it happened not once, but often, this also did second it: when his Swine were in the fields at their troughes eating their meat, some of them would sodainely fall madde, and violently fall to tearing out the guts, and bowels of their fellowes: others by ten and twentie in a company, as if they had been carried with one desire, would leave their feeding, and runne headlong into the Mill dammes, and drowne themselves. So that not by accidentall meanes, but the hellish and most damnable witchcrafts of this Mother **Sutton**, and her daughter, many these harmelesse cattell and Oxen, made as needfull reliefes to the necessitie of man, were thus perplexed, and an honest and worshipfull Gentleman Master **Enger**, from whom she had oftentimes both foode and cloathing, damnified[4] by her meanes to the value of two hundreth pounds in lesse then two yeares.
In the time of these aforesaid losses happened to Master **Enger**, one **Henry Sutton**, the bastard son {B} sonne[5] of **Mary Sutton** (for it is to bee noted, that although she was never married, yet she had three bastards)[6] comming

3 A good example of how a revenge, whilst it is described as such, is turned into motiveless hatred by the pamphleteer's attack on the witch's character – as in *The Witches of Northamptonshire* (1612).
4 Subjected to loss of property.
5 This word is repeated.
6 The source of this is presumably gossip. Sutton's sexual history is deliberately foregrounded at this early stage to discredit her and confirm in advance the later account of her temptation of the victim.

to play himselfe about the Mill damme, fell to throwing in of stones, dirt, and filth, with other such unhappinesse incident to children: Of which having beene often forewarned by an ancient servant of Master **Engers**, who was then about the Milles, and finding the boy notwithstanding his admonishment rather to persever then to desist from his knaverie, he came to him, and giving him a little blow or two on the eare, the boy went home crying, and the ancient fellow went backe to his labour.

This **Henry Sutton** comming home beganne to tell his mother how a man of Master **Engers** (naming him)[7] had beaten him. Whose venomous nature being soone enkindled, though hee had received no hurt,[8] she vowed to take revenge, and thus it followed.

This ancient servant with another of his masters men were on the morrow being Market day at Bedford, appointed by their master to carry a Cart load of corne for the furnishing of the Market. Being on their way at Milton Townes end they espied a goodly faire blacke Sow grazing, who as they drave their Teame still kept pace with them till they came within a mile of Bedford. Where on a sodaine they perceived her to turne twice or thrice about as readily as a Windmill sayle at worke: And as sodainely their horses fell to starting and drawing some one way, some {Bv} another: At last the strongest prevailing, they drewe away the Cart, and corne, and left the Wheeles, and Axeltree behind them. The horses they ranne away with their loade, as if they had beene madde, and the two fellowes after the horses, the horses being affrighted halfe out of their strength, and the fellowes as much madde to see them, downe went one sacke on this side the Cart, and another on that: The horses they ranne as if they would have swelted[9] themselves, and the fellowes after them breathlesse, and sweating to make the wilde Jades[10] stay. All which till the Divell and the Witch had plaide their partes would not serve turne.

At last this Tragicke-Comedie drawing to an end,[11] they made a stand, when the servants bringing them backe, and finding their Axeltree, pinnes, and all things unbroken, tooke up their Corne, made fit their Cart againe, & the

7 The pamphleteer does not know the name. Obviously there are no legal documents behind this narration, and the account of the witches' trial is very scanty, suggesting the pamphleteer was not reporting his material from the court. Perhaps the source for the story is Master Enger or someone who knew of his case and the Suttons, since his afflictions are the sympathetic subject of the pamphlet. The story seems to have been much elaborated, however, by the pamphleteer's rather antiquated euphuism and desire to display his literary talents.

8 Again a pamphleteer defends the victim.

9 Overpowered with heat.

10 Ill-tempered horses. The pamphleteer clearly enjoys the creation of this narration: his pace speeds up in accord with the events he describes, and he breaks into some striking similes.

11 The pamphleteer overtly represents this incident of witchcraft as a literary event: something out of which a funny story can be made, as with the story of Joan Harrison, 'The severall practises of Johane Harrison and her daughter', in *The Most Cruell and Bloody Murther* (1606). This 1613 pamphlet has a moralising aim, but entertainment is clearly

horses drewe as formally as could be: And they went forthwards towards Bedford, mistrusting nothing, though they saw the Sow following and grazing, as they did before.

Being come to Bedford, and having unloaden the Cart, and made sale of the Corne, the one fell to driving the Teame home againe, leaving his ancienter fellow behind him at Bedford who happening into company, fell a carowsing with boone companions like himselfe, and in the height of their cuppes, they as desirous to heare, {B2} as he to tell, he related unto them the manner and forme how his Cart and Wheels were divorct' as hee was comming to Towne: some wondered, all laughed: the company brake up, and this ancient servant tooke his horse with purpose to overtake his fellow, who was gone before with the Cart: Who no sooner was out of Bedford Townes end, but he might behold the same Sow (as neere as he could judge) grazing againe, as if the Divell and the Witch had made her his footman to waite upon him. But the fellow not mistrusting any thing, made his Nagge take a speedie amble, and so to overtake the Cart, while the Sow side by side ranne along by him. When he overtaking his fellow, and had scarce spoken to him, but the horses (as before) fell to their old contention running one from another, onely the horses were better furnished then be fore, for where at first they left both Wheeles and Axeltree behinde them, they now had the Axeltree to take their part, leaving the Wheeles in the high way for the servants to bring after. The horse in this manner comming home, drave all the beholders into amazement, and the servants beginning to have mistrust of the blacke Sow, they watcht whither she went, whom they found to goe into Mother **Suttons** house, of which they told their master, and of all the accidents aforesaid, who made slight of it to them whatsoever he conceived of it himselfe: and saying he supposed they were drunke, they departed.

{B2v} The same old servant of Master **Engers** within a few daies after going to plough, fell into talks of Mother **Sutton**, and of **Mary Sutton** her daughter, of what pranckes hee had heard they had plaide thereabouts in the Countrey, as also what accidents had befallen him and his fellow, as they had passed to and from Bedford. In discoursing of which a Beetle[12] came, and stroke the same fellow on the breast: and hee presently fell into a trance as he was guiding the Plough, the extremitie whereof was such, as his senses altogether distract, and his bodie and minde utterly distempered, the beholders deemed him cleane hopelesse of recoverie, yea his other fellow upon this sodaine sight was stricken into such amazement, as hee stood like a livelesse truncke devided from his vitall spirits, as farre unable to helpe him, as the other was needfull

another purpose – the two are, again, not seen as incompatible, or as unacceptably minimising the serious nature of witchcraft attack. The description of witchcraft as a tragi-comic phenomenon links the writer's perception with contemporary plays such as Thomas Middleton's *The Witch* (*c.*1613–16?).

12 A large hammer.

to be helpt by him. Till at length being somewhat recovered, and awaked from that astonishment, hee made hast homeward, and carried his master word of what had happened.

Upon deliverie of this newes (for hee was a man highly esteemed for his honest and long service) there was much moane made for him in the house, and Master **Enger** himselfe had not the least part of griefe for his extremitie, but with all possible speed hasted into the field, and used helpe to have him brought home. After which he neglected no meanes, nor spared any cost that might ease his servant, or redeeme him from the {B3} misery he was in, but all was in vaine: for his exstasies were nothing lessened, but continued a long time in as grievous perplexitie as at first, yet though they suspected much, they had no certaine proofe or knowledge of the cause: Their meanes were therefore the shorter to cure the effect. But as a thiefe, when hee entereth into a house to robbe, first putteth out the lights, according to that, **Qui male agit, odit lucem**, He that doth evill, hateth light, so these Impes that live in the gunshot of divellish assaults, goe about to darken and disgrace the light of such as are toward, and vertuous, and make the night the instrument to contrive their wicked purposes. For these Witches having so long, and covertly continued to doe much mischiefe by their practises, were so hardened in their lewde and vile proceeding, that the custome of their sinne had quite taken away the sense and feeling thereof, and they spared not to continue the perplexitie of this old servant both in bodie and minde, in such sort that his friends were as desirous to see death ridde him from his extremitie, as a woman great with childe is ever musing upon the time of her deliverie: For where distresse is deepe, and the conscience cleare, **Mors expectatur absque formidine, exoptatur cum dulcedine, excipitur cum devotione**. Death is looked for without feare, desired with delight, and accepted with devotion. As the actes and enterprises of these wicked persons are darke and divellish: so in the perseve-{B3v}-rance of this fellowes perplexitie, hee being in his distraction both of bodie and minde, yet in bed and awake, espied **Mary Sutton**, (the daughter) in a Mooneshine night come in at a window in her accustomed and personall habite, and shape, with her knitting worke in her hands, and sitting downe at his beds feete, sometimes working, and knitting with her needles, and sometimes gazing and staring him in the face, as his griefe was thereby redoubled and increased. Not long after she drewe neerer unto him, and sate by his bedde side (yet all this while he had neyther power to stirre or speake) and told him if hee would consent she should come to bedde to him, hee should be restored to his former health and prosperitie. Thus the Divell strives to enlarge his Kingdome, and upon the necke of one wickednesse to heape another: So that **Periculum probat transeuntium raritas, pereuntium multitudo**: In the dangerous Sea of this world, the rarenesse of those that passe the same over safe, and the multitude of others that perish in their passage, sufficiently prove the perill wee live in: In the Ocean Sea, of foure shippes not one miscaries. In the Sea of this world, of many fowers, not one escapes his particular crosse and calamitie: yet in our greatest weaknesse and debilitie, when the Divell is most busie to tempt us, and seduce us from God, then is God strongest in the hearts of his children, and most readie to bee auxiliant, and helping to {B4} save and uphold them from declining, and falling. Gods liberalitie appeares more, then his rigour, for whom hee drawes out of the Divels throat by faith, hee would have to trample him downe by vertue least he should onely have fled, not foyled his enemie.

This is made showne in his miraculous working with this fellow: for hee that before had neither power to move, or speake, had then presently by divine assistance free power and libertie to give repulse to her assault, and deniall to her filthie and detested motion: and to upbraide her of her abhominable life and behaviour, having before had three bastards and never married. She upon this (seeing her suite cold, and that Gods power was more predominant with him then her divellish practise, vanished, and departed the same way shee came.

She was no sooner gone, but as well as hee could, hee called for his master, told him that now hee could tell him the cause of this vexation: That Mother **Suttons** daughter came in at the window, sate knitting and working by him, and that if hee would have consented to her filthinesse, hee should have beene freede from his miserie, and related all that had happened.

His master was glad of this newes, for that the meanes found out, the matter and manner of his griefe might bee the easier helped, and redres-{B4v}-sed, yet was he distrustfull of the truth, and rather esteemed it an idlenesse of his braine, then an accident of veritie: Neverthelesse he resolved to make proofe thereof.

The next morrow hee tooke company along with him, and went into the fields, where hee found her working, and tending her hogges. There Master **Enger** speaking to her, she was a verie good huswife, and that shee followed her worke night and day: No sir, said she, My huswifery is very slender, neyther am I so good a follower of my worke as you perswade mee: with that, he told her that she was, and that she had beene working at his house the night before. She would confesse nothing, but stood in stiffe deniall upon her purgation: Insomuch as the Gentleman by fayre entreaties perswaded her to goe home with him, to satisfie his man, and to resolve some doubts that were had of her. She utterly refused, and made answere she would not stirre a foote, neyther had they authoritie to compell her to goe without a Constable: Which Master **Enger** perceiving, and seeing her obstinacie to be so great, fell into a greater dislike, and distrust of her then he did before, and made no more a doe, but caused her to bee set upon an horse-backe to be brought to his house. All the company could hardly bring her away, but as fast as they set her up, in despight of them shee would swarve[13] downe, first on

13 Swarm.

the one side, then on the other, till at last they were faine by maine {C} force to joyne together, and hold her violently downe to the horsebacke, and so bring her to the place where this perplexed person lay in his bed. Where being come, and brought by force to his bed-side, he (as directions had beene given unto him) drew blood of her, and presently beganne to amend, and bee well againe. But her assiduitie and continuall exercise in doing mischiefe, did so prevaile with her to doe this fellow further hurt, that watching but advantage, and opportunitie to touch his necke againe with her finger: It was no sooner done, and she departed, but he fell into as great or farre worse vexation then he had before.

The report of this was carried up and downe all Bedford-shire, and this **Marie Suttons** wicked and lewde courses being rumored as well abroad, as in Master **Engers** house, at last it came into the mouth of Master **Engers** sonne, (being a little boy of seven yeares old) who not long after espying old Mother **Sutton** going to the Mill to grinde corne, and remembering what speeches he had heard past of her and her daughter followed the old woman, flinging stones at her, and calling her Witch, which shee observing conceited a rancour, and deadly hatred to this young childe, and purposed not to suffer opportunitie passe to bee revenged. As soone therefore as she had dispatcht at the Mill, she hasted homewards, and could not be quiet till she had grumbled to her daughter what had happened, and {Cv} how the childe had served her: Then conferring how Master **Enger** had used **Mary Sutton** the daughter, and how hir[14] little sonne had used the Mother, they both resolved, and vowed revenge. This conference and consultation of villanie was had, and concluded in the presence, and hearing of **Henry Sutton**, (the Bastard of **Mary Sutton**) little thinking that his fortune should be to give in evidence to breake the necke of his owne Mother and Grandmother.

To effect their divellish purpose to the young childe of Master **Enger**, they called up their two Spirits, whom she called **Dicke** and **Jude**: and having given them sucke at their two Teats which they had on their thighes (found out afterwards by enquirie, and search of women) they gave them charge to strike the little boy, and to turne him to torment. Which was not long in performing, but the childe being distract, was put to such bitter and insupportable misery, as by his life his torments were augmented, and by his death they were abridged. For his tender and unripe age was so infeebled and made weake by that divellish infliction of extremitie, as in five daies, not able longer to endure them, death gave end to his perplexities.

The Gentleman did not so much grieve for the losse and hinderance hee had in his cattell, (which was much) nor for the miserable distresse that his servant had endured (which was more) as that the hopefull daies of his young {C2} sonne were so untimely cut off: (which touched his heart most of all.) Yet did his discretion temper his passions with such patience, that he referred

14 This should presumably read 'his'.

the remembrance of his wrongs to that heavenly power, that permits not such iniquitie to passe unrevealed, or unrevenged.

As hee was thus wrapt in a Sea of woes, there came a Gentleman a friend of his forth of the North, that travelling towards London sojourned with him all night. Hee perceiving Master **Enger** to be full of griefe, was desirous to know the cause thereof, and hee was as unwilling by the discourse of his misfortunes to renewe his many sorrowes, till at last his friends urgent importunacie perswaded him not to passe it over with silence. Upon Master **Engers** relation of what had happened: the Gentleman demaunded if hee had none in suspition that should doe these wronges unto him: Yes, (quoth Master **Enger**) and therewithall hee mamed[15] this **Mary Sutton** and her mother, and told him the particulars of his losses and miseries. His friend understanding this, advised him to take them, or any one of them to his Mill damme, having first shut up the Mill gates that the water might be at highest, and then binding their armes crosse, stripping them into their Smocks, and leaving their legges at libertie, throw them into the water, yet least they should not bee Witches, and that their lives might not be in danger of drow-{C2v}-ning, let there be a roape tyed about their middles, so long that it may reach from one side of your damme to the other, where on each side let one of your men stand, that if she chance to sinke they may draw her up and preserve her. Then if she swimme, take her up, & cause some women to search her, upon which, if they finde any extraordinarie markes about her, let her the second time be bound, and have her right thumbe bound to her left toe, and her left thumbe to her right toe, and your men with the same rope (if need be) to preserve her, and bee throwne into the water, when if she swimme, you may build upon it, that she is a Witch, I have seene it often tried in the North countrey.[16]

The morrow after Master **Enger** road into the fields where **Mary Sutton** (the daughter) was, having some of his men to accompany him, where after some questions made unto her, they assayed to binde her on horse-backe, when all his men being presently stricken lame, Master **Enger** himselfe began to remember, that once rating her about his man, he was on the sodaine in the like perplexitie, and then taking courage, and desiring God to bee his assistance, with a cudgell which he had in his hand, he beate her till she was scarce able to stirre. At which his men presently recovered, bound her to their Masters horse, and brought her home to his house, & shutting up his Mill gates did as before the Gentleman had advised him: when being throwne in the first time {C3} shee sunke some two foote into the water with a fall,

15 Should presumably read 'named'.

16 How much the 'friend' was a real person, and how much a literary construct, is unsure. As we saw in *The Witches of Northamptonshire* (1612) the process of swimming a witch was represented in print in the previous year as occurring in the north Midlands, and there might be a connection here.

but rose againe, and floated upon the water like a planke. Then he commanded her to be taken out, and had women readie that searched her, and found under her left thigh a kind of Teat, which after the Bastard sonne confest her Spirits in severall shapes as Cats, Moales, &c. used to sucke her.

Then was she the second time bound crosse her thumbes and toes, according to the former direction, and then she sunke not at all, but sitting upon the water, turned round about like a wheele, or as that which commonly we call a whirlepoole. Notwithstanding Master **Engers** men standing on each side of the damme with a roape tossing her up and downe to make her sinke, but could not.

And then being taken up, she as boldly as if she had beene innocent asked them if they could doe any more to her: When Master **Enger** began to accuse her with the death of his cattell, the languish of his man, who continued in sorrow both of bodie and mind from Christmasse to Shrovetide, and also the death of his sonne: All which she constantly denied, and stood in defiance with him till being carried towards a Justice, Master **Enger** told her it was bootlesse to stand obstinately upon deniall of those matters, for her owne sonne **Henry** had revealed all, both as touching her selfe and her mother, and of the time and manner of their plotting to torment his little boy: when she heard that, her heart misgave her, she confessed {C3v} all,[17] and acknowledged the Divell had now left her to that shame that is reward to such as follow him. Upon which confession, the mother also was apprehended, and both being committed to Bedford Gaole, many other matters were there produced against them, of long continuance (for they had remained as before, about twentie yeares) in the prosecute[18] of these lewd and wicked practises. But for this matter of Master **Enger** at the last Assises, the evidence of the Bastard son, and the confessions severally taken both of old Mother **Sutton** & her daughter **Mary**, found them guiltie in al former objections. So that arraigned at Bedford on Munday the thirtieth of March last past, they had a just conviction, and on Tuesday the next day after they were executed. **FINIS.**

17 Previously we had been told that Henry Sutton revealed this information *after* these events. Here it appears that as in *A true and just Recorde* (1582) child evidence precedes confession.

18 *Sic.*

15

The Wonderful Discovery of the Witchcrafts of Margaret and Phillip Flower (1619)

This account, with its intense consciousness of status and hierarchy, deals with one of the most high-ranking victims of witchcraft of his era, Francis Manners, Earl of Rutland. Manners probably commissioned or at least approved it, for it is a flattering representation of his nobility and godly resignation in the face of attack by witches, who allegedly killed his sons and endangered his daughter. The earl's family emerges spotless from the narrator's wordy, sycophantic exposition – as we have come to expect from similar accounts. Nevertheless, the witches' appended examinations (as is usual in pre-trial documents) suggest that the earl had given them cause for wishing him ill, by demoting or dismissing one of their number from his service. This motive is not, however, allowed to the witches by the author – they are shown as poor, dishonest, ignorant, atheist and malign, in sharp contrast with their victims and the godly and educated narrator. The pamphleteer's representation of the injustice of the Manners family's sufferings recalls other gentlemanly narratives of 'motiveless' attack from families of witches.

The pamphlet also contains the examinations of three other (Leicestershire) witches, two of whom are cunning women. It is not clear how the two sets are related, but clearly the other women are being asked if they know anything of the Rutland affair, which is said to begin with the bewitching and death of Henry, Lord Roos some three to five years before (accounts differ, he died in 1613). It may be that in the wake of the apprehension of the Flower family (probably in January 1618/19, and because of the illness of the earl's second son Francis, Lord Roos),[1] there was heightened awareness of witchcraft in adjacent counties and care was taken to examine anyone likely to be involved or to be able to provide extra information. Legal records concerning the case are now lost, so we cannot know independently the outcome of either county's assizes.

It is noticeable that the pamphleteer begins his account with a note of caution:

> MY meaning is not to make any contentious Arguments about the discourses, distinction or definition of Witchcraft, the power of

1 There is confusion over the exact timing of events: see the chronology for further details.

> Divells, the nature of Spirits, the force of Charmes, the secrets of Incantation, and such like; because the Scriptures are full of prohibition to this purpose, and proclaimes death to the presumptuous attempters of the same.
>
> (B–Bv)

The writer's interest in demonology, and his desire to paint a glowing picture of the earl, are both tempered by this fearfulness – a note of panic which will recur in the next, and last, witchcraft pamphlet to be published in the period.

The quarto was printed by George Eld for John Barnes, a bookseller who published essays and dictionaries as well as the more usual ephemera. They also produced a ballad entitled *Damnable Practises Of three Lincoln-shire Witches, Joane Flower, and her two Daughters, Margret and Phillip Flower, against Henry Lord Rosse, with others the Children of the Right Honourable the Earle of Rutland, at Beaver Castle, who for the same were executed at Lincolne the 11 March last.* The ballad (appropriately sung to the tune of 'The Ladies Fall') shares the pamphlet's illustration, its concerns and vocabulary, and advertises it at the end of the song:

> There is a booke printed of these Witches, wherein you shall know all their examinations and confessions at large: As also the wicked practises of three other most Notorious Witches in Leceister-shire with all their examinations and confessions.

The ballad (*STC* 11106) was one of those collected by Samuel Pepys and can be seen in facsimile in W.G. Day, ed., *The Pepys Ballads* (Cambridge: D.S. Brewer, 1987), vol. 1, 132–3. The pamphlet has no entry in the Stationers' Register, but went into two further editions which (mysteriously) omit the examination of 4 February and add a paragraph on testing a witch by swimming 'her' – taken from *Witches Apprehended* (1613). The text used here is in the British Library.

Chronology of events, and the Lincolnshire and Leicestershire documents

Francis Manners became Earl of Rutland in 1612. Henry, Lord Roos died in 1613. However, there is confusion over all the later events, especially the timing of the witches' arrest and trial, and the death of their final victim.

The pamphleteer states that all the Flower family were apprehended 'about Christmas' and taken to Lincoln gaol before re-examination by the earl and others (D2v). Since the pamphlet states that the witches were executed on 11 March 1618, this may be Christmas 1617. But if the pamphlet is using Old Style dating, where the old year ends on 25 March, the preceding Christmas would be that of 1618 and the women would be executed in 1618/19. The pamphlet states that it was published in 1619, which would be logical if it follows closely on the events it reports – as pamphlets usually do. Thus I would date the witches' execution as 11 March 1618/19.

However, the pamphlet also states that the earl, unsuspicious of witchcraft, attended the King at Christmas despite the loss of his *children* (D2). Francis, Lord Roos is also mentioned as one of two lost children on Gv. Yet he cannot have been dead at any Christmas before that of 1620. It is certain that he did not die until 5 March 1619/20, for John Chamberlain mentions his death in a letter dated 11 March 1619/20 (Mary Anne Everett, ed., *Calendar of State Papers Domestic 1619–23* [London, 1858], 129). So in stating that the victim died before a Christmas earlier than 1620, the pamphleteer must be making a mistake (surely a very obvious and damaging one?) or have regarded the boy's illness as sure to be fatal? Two of the suspects clearly state that Francis is alive as they are being questioned – so the story is deeply confused. It seems likeliest that the witches were arrested because of Francis's worsening illness rather than because he had died, or was very near death.

Chamberlain's letter was, therefore, probably written on the first anniversary of the witches' execution, if that happened in 1618/19. Yet Nichols's *History and Antiquities of the County Leicestershire*[2] dates their executions as 11 March 1619/20, placing Francis's death in the midst of the witches' trial. If this were so, the pamphlet's publication date of 1619 would still be valid and it is possible that events might be telescoped in this way. But the dating of the execution in 1618, given by the pamphlet, would have to be ignored, and this would not account for the confusion surrounding the witches' apprehension, Christmas, and Francis's death. Unhelpfully, the specific dates and days given by the witches do not fit any of the possible years in which events could have taken place. Therefore it seems likely that events follow the pattern outlined below, but the reader should bear in mind the dating problem and its implications for the account. Its incoherence, and indeed self-contradiction, seems unnecessary and somewhat suspicious.

1618/19?

Lincolnshire

'about' 22 Jan. Margaret Flower examination (no named questioners)
accuses Joan Flower, Phillip Flower, confesses self,
says they killed Henry and bewitched Francis, Lords Roos,
but Francis 'will mend againe'
says attacked earl, countess
and Lady Katherine

2 John Nichols, *History and Antiquities of the County of Leicester*, 4 vols (London, 1795–1811), vol. II, part 1, 49.

4 Feb.	Phillip Flower examination (by Pelham, Butler) accuses Joan Flower, Margaret Flower of killing Henry, Lord Roos and attacking rest of family
4 Feb.	Margaret Flower examination (no named questioners) accuses Joan Flower of killing Henry, Lord Roos
25 Feb.	Phillip Flower examination (by Earl of Rutland, Lord Willoughby, George Manners, Pelham) confesses self (possesses spirit)
? 25 Feb.	Margaret Flower gaol examination (no named questioners) confesses self (possesses spirits)

Leicestershire

28 Feb.	Joan Willimot examination (by Amcotts) accuses Joan Flower of attacking Francis, Lord Roos, who is still alive
1 Mar.	Anne Baker examination (by Earl of Rutland, George Manners [Lincolnshire justices], Fleming)
2 Mar.	Anne Baker examination (by Fleming)
2 Mar.	Joan Willimot examination (by Amcotts) mentions death of Henry, Lord Roos but accuses no one
3 Mar.	Anne Baker examination (by George Manners, Fleming)
11 Mar.	Lincolnshire witches executed
17 Mar.	Ellen Greene examination (by Hastings, Fleming) accuses Willimot
17 Mar.	Joan Willimot examination (by Hastings, Fleming) accuses Gamaliel Greete, Margaret Flower generally, accuses Joan Flower of killing Henry, Lord Roos

5 March 1619/20 Francis, Lord Roos dies.

{A (title page)[3]} **THE WONDERFUL DISCOVERIE OF THE Witchcrafts of** *Margaret* **and** *Phillip Flower*, **daughters of** *Joan Flower* **neere** *Bever*[4] *Castle*: **Executed at Lincolne,** *March* **11. 1618.**[5]

3 This is all there is of signature A. The pamphlet text, without appearing incomplete in any way, starts on B.

4 Belvoir.

5 The pamphleteer seems to be using the traditional dating system, in which the year date changes at Lady Day, 25 March. Therefore his '11 March 1618' is in what we would refer to as 1619, explaining the publication date of the pamphlet as being simply *later* in 1619. See note 65 and chronology.

Who were specially arraigned and condemned[6] **before Sir** *Henry Hobart,*[7] **and Sir** *Edward Bromley,* **Judges of Assise, for confessing themselves actors in the destruction of** *Henry* **Lord** *Rosse,*[8] **with their damnable practises against others the Children of the Right Honourable FRANCIS Earle of** *Rutland.*[9]

Together with the severall Examinations and Confessions of *Anne Baker, Joan Willimot,* **and** *Ellen Greene,* **Witches in** *Leicestershire.*

Printed at London by *G. Eld* **for** *J. Barnes,* **dwelling in the long [Walke] neere Christ-Church. 1619.**

{B} **THE WONDERFULL** *DISCOVERIE OF THE* **Witch-craftes of** *Margaret* **and** *Phillip* **Flower,** *Daughters of* **Joan Flower, by BEAVER CASTLE, and executed at LINCOLNE the 11.** *of March.* **1618.**[10]

MY meaning is not to make any contentious Arguments about the discourses, distinction or definition of Witchcraft, the power of Divells, the nature of Spirits, the force of Charmes, the secrets of Incantation, and such like; because the Scriptures are full of prohibition to this purpose, and proclaimes death to the presumptuous attemp-{Bv}-ters of the same: Besides both Princes (yea our owne learned and most judicious King)[11] Philosophers, Poets, Chronologers, Historiographers, and many worthy Writers, have concurred and concluded in this; that divers impious and facinorous[12] mischiefes have beene effectuated through the instruments of the Divell, by permission of God, so that the actors of the same have carried away the opinion of the world, to doe that which they did by Witchcraft, or at least to be esteemed Witches, for bringing such and such things to passe: For howsoever the learned have charactred delinquents in this kinde by titles of sundry sortes, and most significant attributes; as *Pythonissae* dealing with artificiall Charmes; *Magi* anciently reputed so, for extraordinary wisedome and knowledge in the secrets of simples and hearbes; *Chaldei*, famous for Astronomy and Astrology;

6 Presumably a separate arraignment took place, because of the status of the victims. As we have seen in Potts's *Discoverie*, well-connected families and high-profile cases could sometimes command special attention and extra time in an otherwise impersonal and overcrowded system. See also *The Most strange and admirable discoverie* (1593) for exceptional treatment of such a family.

7 Henry Hobart (also known as Hubbard) had been Attorney General from 1606 until 1613, when he became Lord Chief Justice of Common Pleas. Thus he was a very eminent judge indeed (*DNB*). For Bromley, see Potts's *Wonderfull Discoverie*.

8 Lord Roos of Hamlake, a title newly claimed by the Earl of Rutland in 1616.

9 Francis Manners, sixth Earl. He was prominent at the court of King James, and entertained him at Belvoir on becoming Earl of Rutland in 1612, as well as several times in later years (*DNB*).

10 From this point onwards, all text is in Roman font unless otherwise specified.

11 A reference to *Daemonologie* – but the context makes the King look like a presumptuous attempter. The prefacer is deeply anxious about the propriety of demonological writing and is drawn deeper into difficulties here.

12 Grossly criminal.

Necromancers for practising to raise dead bodies, and by them to foretell events of the earth; *Geomantici*, for conversing with Spirits, and using Inchantations; {B2} *Genethliaci*, for presuming on the calculating of Nativities, or if you will, assuming the credit of Figure-casting; *Ventriloqui*, for speaking with hollow voyces as if they were possessed with Divells; *Venefici*, for dealing with Poyson, and either killing or curing that way: For you must understand however the Professors aforesaid practise murther and mischiefe, yet many times they Pretend cures and preservation; with many others, carrying the shew of great learning and admitted knowledge; yet have they all but one familier tearme with us in English called Witches. As for the conceit[13] of wisemen or wise woemen, they are all meerely coseners and deceivers; so that if they make you beleeve that by their meanes you shall heare of things lost or stolne, it is either done by Confederacy, or put off by protraction to deceive you of your money.[14]

Only (as I said before) there bee certaine men and women growne in yeares, and over-growne with Melancholly and Atheisme, who out of a malicious dispositi-{B2v}-on against their betters, or others thriving by them; but most times from a heart-burning desire of revenge, having entertained some impression of displeasure, and unkindnesse, study nothing but mischiefe and exoticke[15] practises of loathsome Artes and Sciences: yet I must needes say, that sometimes the fained reputation of wisedome, cunning, and to be reputed a dangerous and skilfull person, hath so prevailed with divers, that they have taken upon them indeed to know more then God ever afforded any creature,[16] & to performe no lesse then the Creator both of Heaven & earth; making you beleeve with *Medea*, that they can raise tempests, turne the Sunne into blood, pull the Moone out of her Spheare, and saile over the Sea in a cockle shell, according to the Poet.[17]

Flectere si nequeam Superos, Acheronta movebo.

If Art doe faile to move the Gods
consent unto my minde:

13 Idea, notion.

14 These ideas, with the list of various practisers of magic, are almost certainly lifted from Reginald Scot, *The Discoverie of Witchcraft* (1584), especially the definition of an English witch in book 5, chapter 9, but the prefacer will not acknowledge a source which had incurred royal disapproval in *Daemonologie* (xi–xii). Scot, and Johan Weyer's *De praestigiis daemonum*, are echoed in the following paragraph: but their ideas are here used against them, for melancholy is said to be a motivation for real witchcraft, not the cause of a delusion that the sufferer is a witch. See also C.

15 Uncouth or strange.

16 Used in the sense in which George Gifford uses it in his *Dialogue concerning Witches and Witchcraftes* (1593): a created being, as opposed (literally) to their creator.

17 Virgil, *Aeneid*, book 7. This quotation was used by Gifford in the *Dialogue*, which we know the prefacer had read (B4v).

I will the Divells raise, to doe
what they can in their kinde.

{B3} But howsoever speciall[18] persons are transported with an opinion of their owne worth, and prevailing in this kinde, yet by lamentable experience we know too well, what monstrous effects have bene produced, even to the horror of the hearers, and the damnation of their owne soules by such kinde of people: For as it is in the tale of the envious man, that put out one of his eyes to have his companion loose both, so fareth it with them and worse, to give away their soules to bee revenged of their adversaries bodies, wherein the monstrous subtilty of the Divell is so apparant, that it is wonderfull one way to relate, and lamentable another to observe the same. For no sooner shall such motives poyson the inward conceite or apprehension of such damnable Caitiffes:[19] But then steppeth forth the Divell, and not onely sheweth them the way, but prescribeth the manner of effecting the same, with facility and easinesse, assuring that hee himselfe will attend them in some familiar shape of Rat, Cat, Toad, {B3v} Bird, Cricket, &c: yea effectuate whatsoever they shall demaund or desire, and for their better assurance and corroboration of their credulity, they shall have palpable and forcible touches of sucking, pinching, kissing, closing, colling, and such like:[20] whereupon, without any feare of God or Man, knowledge of Christ, hope of redemption, confidence of mercy, or true beleefe that there is any other thing to bee looked after but this present World; according to that Athiesticall position of *Epicurus*.

Ede, bibe, lude, post mortem nulla voluptas.

Eat, drink, sport, play and take thy pleasures rest:
For after death, who knowes what shall be best.[21]

They admit of those execrable conditions of commutation[22] of soules for the entertaining of the spirits, and so fall to their abhominable practises, continuing in the same till God laugh them to scorne, and will by no meanes suffer them to abuse his holy name nor deceive others by their prophane

18 Particular.

19 Villains.

20 Kissing, and embracing around the neck. This list suggests a sexual relationship between familiar and witch rather than the more usual suckling/feeding one.

21 Epicurus's ideas were, of course, more complex than this summing-up phrase suggests. It is more literally translated as 'eat, drink and play, for after death there is no pleasure'. See also Ecclesiastes 8.15 for a biblical recommendation to 'eat, drink and be merry', albeit for different reasons. The prefacer is showing off his translating abilities, but is clearly more interested in making a godly point than in philosophical inquiry.

22 Exchange.

lives {B4} any longer: Witnesse for the generall those infinite Treatises of many of them convinced by Law, and condemned to death, to the fearefull example of all carnall and hypocriticall Christians: but more especially you may over-looke (if you please) that learned Discourse of *Daemonologie*, composed in forme of a Dialogue, by the High and mighty Prince, *JAMES* by the grace of God, King of *England, Scotland, France* and *Ireland, &c.* and printed (as I take it) according to the coppy of *Edenburgh*, 1603.[23] As also a Treatise of Witch-craft made by that learned Mr. *Alexander Roberts* Preacher at Kings-Line[24] in Norfolke, 1615. upon the discovery of the Witch-crafts of *Mary Smith*, wife of *Henry Smith* Glover, with her vocall contract betweene the Divell and her selfe, in sollemne tearmes, and such like imposturing filthinesse: with many hurts and mischiefes which thereby she procured:[25] As also a certaine discovery 1611. made by *John Cotta* Doctor of Phisicke in Northampton of Empericks,[26] woemen about sicke persons: {B4v} Quacksalvers,[27] and fugitives, which seeme to worke juggling wonders, Surgeons, Apothecaries, practisers by spells, the true discovery of Witch-craft, especially in the sicke with many instances in that kind, Wisards, and servants, of Phisitions, who may bee called ministring helpers: To this hee hath added the *Methodian*[28] learned deceiver, or hereticke Phisition, Astrologers, *Ephemerides*-maisters,[29] Conjecters by urine, Travellers, and last of all, the true Artist his right description and election.[30] As also a Dialogue concerning Witches and Witchctaft,[31] composed by *George Gifford*, Minister of Gods word in Maldon, 1603. Wherein the cunning of the Divell is dicovered, both concerning the deceiving of witches, and seducing of others into many great errors:[32] As also an ancient discourse of the fearefull practises of foure notorious French Witches, with the manner of their strange execution.[33] As also the severall and damnable practises of Mother *Sutton* of Milton Miles in the

23 The first Edinburgh edition was in 1597. This edition was printed when James became King of England.

24 Kings Lynn.

25 Alexander Roberts, *A Treatise of Witchcraft* (London, 1616).

26 Practisers according to experience, not 'reason' as embodied in Galenic medicine. One of the three ancient schools of physicians.

27 Ignorant people pretending medical knowledge: quacks.

28 Methodics, another ancient school of physicians: here debased to mean 'those who abuse reason'.

29 Those who predict (from astrological books) the positions of heavenly bodies and practise medicine by this means.

30 This lengthily titled work, from which the prefacer quotes extensively, has two editions: the 1612 *A Short Discoverie of the Unobserved Dangers of severall sorts of ignorant and unconsiderate practisers of phisicke in England* and the 1617 *A True Discovery of the Empiricke with the fugitive Physition and Quacksalver.*

31 *Sic.*

32 This is the second edition of the 1593 *Dialogue.*

33 This work is either lost (there is nothing plausibly like it in the Stationers' Register or the *STC*), or it is untraceable using only the brief description given here.

County of Bedford, and *Mary Sutton* her Daughter, {C} who were arraigned, condemned, and executed for the same:[34] As also 1612. the wonderfull discovery of Witches in Lancashire, being 19. in number, notorious for many infamed actions, and convicted before Sr. *James Altham*, and S. *Edward Bromley*, Barons of the Exchequer, together with the arraignment and triall of *Jennet Preston*, at Yorke, with her fearefull execution for the murthering of Mr. *Lisker*[35] by Witch-craft; with infinite other relations concerning the generall conviction of Witches, and their practises, and condemnation of the particular opinion of some men, who suppose there bee none at all, or at least that they doe not personally or truely effect such things as are imputed unto them, and which out of some dangerous impression of melancholly, vaineglory, or some other diseased operation, they assume to themselves by reason of a former contract with the Divell.[36] And so much for the certainty of Story, and fearefulnesse of the truth concerning the damnable practises of Witches and cunning of the Divell to deceive them.

{Cv} But yet because the mind of man may be carried away with many idle conjectures, either that woemen confessed these things by extremity of torture, or that ancient examples are by this time forgotten (although the particulars are upon record, for the benefit of all posteritie:) Or that they were besides themselves, or subject to some weake devise or other, rather to bring in question the integrity of *Justice*; then to make odious the lives of such horrible offendors. I have presumed to present on the *Stage* of verity for the good of Country & the love of truth, the late wofull Tragedy of the destruction of the *Right Honourable* the *Earle* of *Rutlands* Children, who to his eternall praise proceeded yet both religiously and charitably against the offenders, leaving their prosecution to the law and submitting himselfe, and deplorable case to the providence of God, who afflicteth his best servants with punishments, and many times, sendeth extraordinary vengeance as well on the innocent, as the bad deserver, to manifest his glory: {C2} Therefore by way of Caution I advise thee (gentle Reader) whosoever thou art, to take heede how thou doest either despise the power of God in his Creatures, or vilipend[37] the subtilty and fury of the Divell, as Gods instrument of vengeance, considering that truth in despight of gaine sayers will prevaile, according to that principle: *Magna est veritas & prevalebit.*[38]

The Story followes.

AFter the Right Honourable Sr. *Francis Manners* succeeded his Brother in the Earledome of Rutland:[39] and so not onely tooke possession of Beaver

34 See *Witches Apprehended* (1613).
35 *Sic.* This is of course Thomas Potts's *Discoverie* (1612).
36 Scot, book 3, chapter 10 – see note 14.
37 Speak slightingly of.
38 Truth is great and will prevail.
39 In 1612.

Castle, but of all other his demeanes, Lordships, Townes, Mannors, Lands, and Revennues appropriate to the same Earledome: hee proceeded so honourably in the course of his life, as neither displacing Tenants, discharging servants, denying the accesse of the poore, welcoming of strangers, and performing all the duties of a noble Lord, that {C2v} hee fastened as it were unto himselfe the love and good opinion of the Countrey wherein he walked the more cheerefully and remarkable, because his honourable Countesse marched arme in arme with him in the same race;[40] so that Beaver Castle was a continuall Pallace of entertainment, and a daily receptacle for all sorts both rich and poore, especially such auncient people as neighboured the same; amongst whom one *Joane Flower*, with her Daughters *Margaret* and *Phillip* were not onely relieved at the first from thence, but quickly entertained as Chair-women,[41] and *Margaret* admitted as a continuall dweller in the Castle, looking both to the poultrey abroad and the wash-house within dores: In which life they continued with equall correspondency, till something was discovered to the noble Lady, which concerned the misdemeanour of these women. And although such honourable persons shall not want all sorts of people, either to bring them newes, tales, reports, or to serve their turne in all offices whatsoever; so that it may well {C3} bee said of them, as it is of great Kings and Princes, that they have large hands, wide eares, and piercing sights to discover the unswept corners of their remotest confines, to reach even to their furthest borders, and to understand the secrets of their meanest subjects: yet in this matter, neither were they busie-bodies, flatterers, malicious politicians, underminers, nor supplanters one of anothers good fortune; but went simply to worke, as regarding the honor of the Earle and his Lady, and so by degrees gave light to their understanding to apprehend their complaints. First, that *Joane Flower* the Mother was a monstrous malicious woman, full of oathes, curses, and imprecations irreligious, and for any thing they saw by her, a plaine Atheist; besides of late dayes her very countenance was estranged, her eyes were fiery and hollow, her speech fell[42] and envious, her demeanour strange and exoticke, and her conversation sequestred; so that the whole course of her life gave great suspition that she was a notorious Witch, yea some of her {C3v} neighbours dared to affirme that shee dealt with familiar spirits, and terrified them all with curses and threatning of revenge, if there were never so little cause of displeasure and unkindnesse. Concerning *Margaret*, that shee often resorted from the Castle to her Mother, bringing such provision as they thought was unbefitting for a servant to purloyne, and comming at such unseasonable houres, that they could not but conjecture some mischiefe between them, and that their extraordinary

40 Francis Manners had married Cicely Tufton (then the widow of Sir Edward Hungerford) in 1608.

41 Charwomen, daily house servants.

42 Savage.

ryot & expences, tended both to rob the Lady, & to maintaine certaine deboist[43] and base company which frequented this *Joane Flowers* house the mother, & especially her youngest Daughter. Concerning *Phillip*, that she was lewdly transported with the love of one *Th. Simpson*, who presumed to say, that shee had bewitched him: for hee had no power to leave her, and was as hee supposed marvellously altred both in minde and body, since her acquainted company: these complaints began many yeares before either their conviction, or publique {C4} apprehension: Notwithstanding such was the honour of this Earle and his Lady; such was the cunning of this monstrous woman in observation towards them; such was the subtilty of the Divell to bring his purposes to passe; such was the pleasure of God to make tryall of his servants; and such was the effect of a damnable womans wit and malitious envy, that all things were carried away in the smooth Channell of liking and good entertainment on every side, untill the Earle by degrees conceived some mislike against her; and so, peradventure estranged himselfe from that familiaritie and accustomed conferrences hee was wont to have with her: untill one *Peate*[44] offered her some wrong; against whom shee complained, but found that my Lord did not affect her clamours, and malicious information, untill one Mr. *Vavasor* abandoned her company, as either suspicious of her lewd life, or distasted[45] with his owne misliking of such base and poore Creatures, whom nobody loved but the Earles {C4v} houshold; untill the Countesse misconceiving of her daughter *Margaret*, and discovering some undecencies both in her life and neglect of her businesse, discharged her from lying any more in the Castle, yet gave her 40.s. a bolster, & a mattresse of wooll: commanding her to go home, until the slacknesse of her repayring to the Castle, as shee was wont, did turne her love and liking toward this honourable Earle and his family into hate and rancor: whereupon despighted[46] to bee so neglected, and exprobated[47] by her neighbours for her Daughters casting out of dores,[48] and other conceived displeasures, she grew past all shame and Woman-hood, and many times cursed them all that were the cause of this discontentment, and made her so loathsome to her former familiar friends, and beneficiall acquaintance.

43 Debauched.

44 Also named as 'Peak' on Ev and F4.

45 Disgusted. This mysterious gentleman apparently plays a key, but (deliberately?) obscured, role in events. He may have been a member of the Catholic Vavasor family of Husbands Bosworth (thirty-five miles south-west of Belvoir), connected with the Manners family because of their Catholic sympathies.

46 Maliciously indignant.

47 Upbraided. This succession of latinate and arcane words suggests a writer determined to show off his learning and distance his pamphlet from those compiled by mere hacks.

48 It's not clear where the subject changes from Margaret to Joan Flower, but here the sentence returns to her as the origin of the evil.

When the Divell perceived the inficious[49] disposition of this wretch, and that she and her Daughters might easily bee made instruments to enlarge his Kingdome, and bee as it were the executioners of his vengeance; {D} not caring whether it lighted upon innocents or no, he came more neerer unto hem, and in plaine tearmes to come quickly to the purpose, offered them his service, and that in such a manner, as they might easily command what they pleased: For hee would attend you in such prety formes of dog, cat, or Rat, that they should neither be terrified, nor any body else suspicious of the matter. Upon this they agree, and (as it should seeme) give away their soules for the service of such spirits, as he had promised them; which filthy conditions were ratified with abhominable kisses,[50] and an odious sacrifice of blood, not leaving out certaine charmes and conjuartions with which the Divell deceived them, as though nothing could bee done without ceremony, and a solemnity of orderly ratification. By this time doth Sathan triumph, and goeth away satisfied to have caught such fish in the net of his illusions: By this time are these women Divels incarnate, and grow proud againe in their cunning and artificiall power, to doe what mischiefe they listed: By {Dv} this time they have learnt the manner of inchantations, Spells and Charmes: By this time they kill what Cattle they list, and under the covert of flattery and familiar entertainment, keepe hidden the stinging serpent of mallice, and a venomous inclination to mischiefe: By this time is the Earle and his family threatened, and must feele the burthen of a terrible tempest, which from these womens Divellish devises fell uppon him, hee neither suspecting nor understanding the same: By this time both himselfe and his honourable Countesse, are many time subject to sicknesse and extraordinary convulsions, which they taking as gentle corrections from the hand of God, submit with quietnesse to his mercy, and study nothing more, then to glorifie their Creator in heaven, and beare his crosses on earth.

At last, as mallice increased in these damnable Women; so his family felt the smart of their revenge and inficious disposition. For his eldest Sonne *Henry* Lord {D2} *Rosse* sickened very strangely, and after a while died: his next named *Francis* Lord *Rosse* accordingly, was severely tormented by them, and most barbarously and inhumanely tortured by a strange sicknesse; not long after the Lady *Katherine* was set upon by their dangerous and divellish practises, and many times in great danger of life, through extreame maladies and unusuall fits, nay (as it should seeme, and they afterwards confessed) both

49 Corrupted, wicked.

50 Witches in European demonology were thought to kiss the devil's backside. The writer may have encountered this idea in King James's *Daemonologie*, book 2, chapter 3. The King was familiar with the alleged rite from his involvement with the North Berwick trials described in the 1591 pamphlet *Newes from Scotland*. It is unclear from where the writer might have obtained such detailed information about these particular witches, unless from examinations now lost. He may be generalising about what he believes witches do rather than reporting actual confessions – an important difference.

the Earle and his Countesse were brought into their snares as they imagined, and indeed determined to keepe them from having any more children.[51] Oh unheard of wickednesse and mischievous damnation? Notwithstanding all this did the noble Earle attend his Majesty, both at New-market before Christmas, and at Christmas at Whitehall; bearing the losse of his Children most nobly,[52] and little suspecting that they had miscarried by Witch-craft, or such like inventions of the Divell, untill it pleased God to discover the villanous practises of these Woemen, and to command the Divell {D2v} from executing any further vengeance on innocents, but leave them to their shames, and the handes of Justice, that they might not onely be confounded for their villanous practises, but remaine as a notorious example to all ages of his judgement and fury. Thus were they apprehended about Christmas, and carried to Lincolne Jayle, after due examination, before sufficient Justices of the Peace, and discreete Majestrates, who wondred at their audacious wickednes, but *Joane Flower* the Mother before conviction, (as they say)[53] called for Bread and Butter, and wished it might never goe through her if she were guilty of that whereupon shee was examined; so mumbling it in her mouth, never spake more wordes after, but fell downe and dyed as shee was carryed to Lincolne Goale,[54] with a horrible excruciation of soule and body, and was buried at *Ancaster*.[55]

When the Earle heard of their apprehension, hee hasted downe with his brother Sr. *George*,[56] and somtimes examining them himselfe, and sometimes sending them to others; {D3} at last left them to the triall of Law, before the Judges of assise at *Lincolne*; and so they were convicted of murther and executed accordingly, about the 11. of *March*, to the terror of all the beholders, and example of such dissolute and abhominable Creatures, and because you shall have both cause to glorifie God for this discovery, and occasion to apprehend the strangenesse of their lives, and truth of their proceedings: I thought it both meete and convenient to lay open their own Examinations and Evidences against one another, with such apparrant circumstances, as doe not onely shew the cause of their mislike and distasting against the Earle

51 The Manners family are clearly extremely concerned about the male line, and with seeking new power. The accusation that witches had caused infertility was very unusual in English cases. In the absence of further sons, Lady Katherine Manners married the Duke of Buckingham, James's favourite, tying the family more closely to the King – an anxious ambition demonstrated in the next few lines.

52 The pamphleteer seems to have telescoped time here, as on Gv. As Margaret Flower (22 January, F3v) and Joan Willimot (28 February, E3) show, the earl's second son was still alive at Christmas and after. It seems from this slip that the pamphlet was compiled either after his death or in disturbing anticipation of it. Either way, the central story is blurred and self-contradictory. See the chronology.

53 Clear evidence of gossip as a source for this story.

54 *Sic.*

55 A village ten miles north-east of Belvoir, on the road to Lincoln.

56 George Manners, born about 1580, was to succeed his brother as earl in 1632.

and his family; but the manner of their proceedings and revenges, with other particulars belonging to the true and plaine discovery of their villany and Witch-craft.[57]

{D3v} The Examinations of Anne Baker, Joane Willimot, and *Ellen Greene*; as followeth, &c.

{D4} THE EXAMINATION of *Anne Baker* of *Bottesford* in the County of *Leicester*[58] *Spinster*, taken *March*, 1. 1618. by the Right *Honourable, Francis Earle* of *Rutland*, Sir *George Manners Knight*, two of his *Majesties Justices* of the peace for the County of *Lincolne*, and *Samuel Fleming Doctor* of *Divinitie*,[59] one of his *Majesties Justices* of the peace for the County of *Leicester* aforesaid.

SHE saith that there are foure colours of Planets, *Blacke, Yellow, Greene, and Blew, and that Blacke is alwaies death, and that she sawe the Blew* Plannet *strike* Thomas Fairebarne, *the eldest sonne unto* William Fairbarne *of* {D4v} Bottesford *aforesaid by the* Pinfold[60] *there, within the which time the said* William Fairbarne *did beate her and breake her head, whereuppon the said* Thomas Fair-barne *did mend. And being asked who did send that Planet answered it was not I.*

Further shee saith, that shee saw a hand appeare unto her, and that shee heard a voyce in the ayre said unto her: Anne Baker, *save thyselfe, for tomorrow thou and thy maister must be slaine: and the next day her maister and shee were in a Cart together; and suddenly shee saw a flash of fire, and said her prayers, and the fire went away, and shortly after a Crow came and picked upon her cloathes, and shee said her prayers againe, and bad the Crow go to whom he was sent, and the Crow went unto her Maister, and did beat him to death, and shee with her prayers recovered him to life; but hee was sicke a fortnight after, and saith, that if shee had not had more knowledge then her maister, both he and shee and all the Cattell had beene slaine.*

Being examined concerning a Childe of Anne Stannidge, *which shee was suspected to have be-*{E}*-witched to death; saith, the said* Anne Stannidge *did deliver her childe into her hands, and that shee did lay it upon her skirt, but did no harme unto it; And being charged by the Mother of the childe, that upon the burning of the haire and the paring of the nailes of the said childe, the said* Anne Baker *came in and set her downe, and for one houres space could speake nothing; confes-seth shee came into the house of the said* Anne Stannidge *in great paine, but*

57 It is an odd disjunction that the pamphlet now prints examinations of three other witches. It gives the impression that they were the primary focus of attention, when in fact the Flower family's apprehension begins these events.

58 Belvoir is close to the Lincolnshire–Leicestershire border, hence the interest in witches from two counties. Bottesford is four miles north of Belvoir.

59 The Rector of Bottesford since 1581, Fleming was chaplain to the Earl of Rutland (J. Venn and J.A. Venn, *Alumni Cantabrigiensis* [Cambridge: Cambridge University Press, 1927]).

60 Fold for impounding stray animals.

did not know of the burning of the haire and nailes of the said Childe; but said she was so sicke that she did not know whither she went.
Being charged that shee bewitched Elizabeth Hough, *the wife of* William Hough *to death, for that shee angred her in giving her almes of her second bread;*[61] *confesseth that she was angry with her and said she might have given her of her better bread, for she had gone too often on her errands, but more she saith not.*
This Examinat confesseth that shee came to Joane Gylles *house, her childe being sicke, and that shee intreated this Examinat to look on the Child, and to tell her whether it was forspoken or no, and* {Ev} *this Examinate said it was forspoken; but when the said child died she cannot tell.*
And being asked concerning Nortley *carrying of his Child home unto his owne house, where the said* Anne Baker *was, shee asked him, who gave the said Child that loafe, he told her* Anthony Gill, *to whom this Examinate said, he might have had a Child of his owne if hee would have sought in time for it; which words she confessed shee did speake.*[62]
Being blamed by Henry Milles *in this sort: A fire set on you, I have had two or three ill nights; to whom shee made answere, you should have let me alone then, which shee confesseth.*
The said Anne Baker, *March* 2. 1618. *confessed before* Samuel Fleming *Doctor of Divinitie, that about* 3. *yeares agoe, shee went into Northamptonshire, and that at her comming back againe, one* Peakes *wife*[63] *and* Dennis *his wife of Belvoyre told her that my young Lord* Henry *was dead, and that there was a glove of the said Lord buried in the ground; and as that glove did rot and wast, so did the liver of the said Lord rot and wast.*
{E2} *Further shee said, March* 3. 1618. *before Sr.* George Manners *Knight, and* Samuel Fleming *Doctor of Divinity, that shee hath a Spirit which hath the shape of a white Dogge, which shee calleth her good Spirit.*
Samuel Fleming *test.*[64]
{E2v} The Examination of *Joan Willimot*, taken the 28. of *February*, in the 16. yeare of the raigne of our Soveraigne Lord, JAMES, over *England* King &c. and over *Scotland* the 52.[65] before *Alexander Amcotts* Esquire,[66] one of his Majesties Justices of the peace in the said parts and County.

61 Rosen suggests 'two-day-old bread' (375, n. 12)

62 Clearly the questioner has informations before him and has been asking the examinate to respond to each anecdote. The last story sounds as if Baker was a cunning woman, irritated that she had not been consulted in time to save Anthony Gill's child. Now, in a second examination, followed by a third on the next day, the questions alter their focus to probe for material on the Rutland case.

63 Perhaps the same Peak who fell out with Joan Flower. The dating of Henry's death (1613) seems wildly wrong.

64 *Testatur* – he witnesses.

65 This dating puts the examinations in 1618/19.

66 The Amcotts were a Lincolnshire gentry family from Aisthorpe, thirty-five miles north of Belvoir.

THis Examinat saith, that *Joane Flower* told her that my Lord of *Rutland* had dealt badly with her, and that they had put away her Daughter, and that although she could not have her will of my Lord himselfe, yet she had spied my Lords Sonne and had stricken him to the heart. And she saith, that my Lords Sonne was striken with a white Spirit, and that shee can cure some that send unto her, and that some reward her for her paines, and of some she taketh nothing.[67]

{E3} She further saith, that upon Fryday night last, her Spirit came to her and told her that there was a bad woman at *Deeping*[68] who had given her soule to the Divell: and that her said Spirit did then appeare unto her in a more ugly forme then it had formerly done, and that it urged her much to give it something, although it were but a peece of her Girdle, and told her that it had taken great paines for her, but she saith that she would give it nothing, and told it that she had sent it to no place but onely to see how my Lord *Rosse* did,[69] and that her Spirit told her that he should doe well.

{E3v} The Examination of the said *Joan Willimott*, taken the second day of *March* in the yeare abovesaid, before the said *Alexander Amcots*.

THis Examinate saith, That shee hath a Spirit which shee calleth *Pretty*, which was given unto her by *William Berry* of *Langholme*[70] in *Rutlandshire*, whom she served three yeares; and that her Master when hee gave it unto her, willed her to open her mouth, and hee would blow into her a Fairy which should doe her good; and that shee opened her mouth, and he did blow into her mouth; and that presently after his blowing, there came out of her mouth a Spirit, which stood upon the ground in the shape and forme of a Woman, which Spirit did aske of her her Soule, which shee then promised unto it, being willed thereunto by her Master. Shee further confesseth, that shee never hurt any body, but did helpe divers that sent for her, {E4} which were stricken or fore-spoken: and that her Spirit came weekely to her, and would tell her of divers persons that were stricken and forespoken. And shee saith, that the use which shee had of the Spirit, was to know how those did which shee had undertaken to amend; and that shee did helpe them by certaine prayers which she used, and not by her owne Spirit; neyther did she imploy her Spirit in any thing, but onely to bring word how those did which she had undertaken to cure.

And shee further saith, that her Spirit came unto her this last night (as she thought) in the forme of a woman, mumbling, but she could not understand what it said. And being asked whether shee were not in a dreame or

67 Clearly the focus in this examination is primarily on the Flower case and only then on Willimot.

68 Deeping is a collection of villages some twenty-five miles south-east of Belvoir.

69 This must be Francis, Lord Roos since Henry was already dead.

70 Langham, fifteen miles south of Belvoir.

slumber when shee thought shee saw it, shee said no, and that she was as waking as at this present.[71]
Alexander Amcots.
Thomas Robinson test.[72]
{E4v} The Examination of *Joane Willimot* of *Goadby*[73] in the County of *Leicester* Widdow, taken the 17. of *March* by Sir *Henry Hastings* Knight,[74] and *Samuel Fleming* Doctor of Divinitie, two of his Majesties Justices of Peace in the said County of *Leicester.*
SHe saith that she tould one *Cookes* wife of *Stathorne*[75] in the said County Labourer, that *John Patchett* might have had his Child alive, if he would have sought forth for it in time, and if it were not death stricken in her wayes, and that *Patchets* wife had an evill thing within her, which should make an end of her, and that she knew by her Girdle.[76]
She saith further, that *Gamaliel Greete* of *Waltham*[77] in the said County Shepheard, had a Spirit like a white Mouse put into him {F} in his swearing;[78] and that if hee did looke upon any thing with an intent to hurt, it should be hurt, and that hee had a marke on his left arme, which was cut away; and that her own spirit did tell her all this before it went from her.[79]

71 Like John Walsh (*The Examination of John Walsh*, 1566), Willimot defends her fairy beliefs and refuses to be drawn into confessions of malefic witchcraft in these two examinations. Her resistance is more successful, in that the final question of the second examination is a sceptical one, rather than one seeking more evidence of a Satanic pact. Her next examination, some two weeks later and with new questioners, uncovers more conventional material in seeking new suspects and should be read in the light of Ellen Greene's information against her (given before the same justices) on the same day (Fv–F2v). Presumably, like Margaret Flower (G), she was brought from gaol to be questioned.

72 Thomas Robinson was the Rector of Toft-next-Newton, Lincolnshire from 1612, and Rector of Market Deeping, Lincolnshire, from 1618 (Venn, *Alumni Cantabrigiensis*).

73 Goadby is some thirty miles south of Belvoir. It seems far more likely that Willimot lives at Goadby Marwood, five miles south-west of Belvoir.

74 Henry Hastings, of the family of the Earl of Huntingdon, was knighted in 1603 and was MP for Leicestershire from 1620 (*DNB*).

75 Stathern is three miles south-west of Belvoir.

76 Girdles were measured to detect the presence of evil spirits inside the body. Keith Thomas discusses this magical diagnosis in *Religion and the Decline of Magic* (1971; London: Peregrine, 1978), 217–18. See F2 for Patchett. This is further evidence that cunning people were being investigated.

77 Waltham-in-the-Wolds, a mile east of Goadby Marwood.

78 This sounds as if the arrival of the spirit was a response to sin, as with Elizabeth Sawyer (Henry Goodcole, *The Wonderfull Discoverie of Elizabeth Sawyer* [1621] below). Is Greete's mouse an instrument of possession or empowerment? His supposed attributes seem to include the evil eye, and probably a witch's mark, now removed. But, as with many examinations, the significance attached to particular elements of magical beliefs is unclear and appears incoherent: either because it was fluid and negotiable, or because it is being reported by those who do not understand or respect it.

79 Again, material seems to be missing: Willimot's loss of her spirit is not explored as one would expect.

Further she saith, that *Joane Flower*, *Margaret Flower* and shee, did meet about a weeke before *Joane Flowers* apprehension, in *Blackborrow-hill*, and went from thence home to the said *Joan Flowers* house, and there she saw two spirits, one like a Rat, and the other like an Owle; and one of them did sucke under her right eare, as shee thought: and the said *Joan* told her, that her spirits did say that shee should neyther be hanged nor burnt.
Further she saith, that the said *Joan Flower* did take up some earth and spet upon it, and did worke it with her finger, and put it up into her purse, and said though shee could not hurt the Lord himselfe, yet shee had sped his Sonne, which is dead.
H. Hastings.
Samuel Fleming.
{Fv} The Examination of *Ellen Greene* of *Stathorne* in the County of *Leicester*, taken the 17. of *March* 1618. by Sir *Henry Hastings* Kt: and *Samuel Fleming* D. of Divinitie, two of his Majesties Justices of the Peace of his said County.
SHee saith, that one *Joan Willimot* of *Goadby* came about sixe yeares since to her in the Wowlds,[80] and persuaded this Examinate to forsake God, and betake her to the divel, and she would give her two spirits, to which shee gave her consent, and thereupon the said *Joan Willimot* called two spirits, one in the likenesse of a Kitlin, and the other of a Moldiwarp:[81] the first the said *Willimot* called *pusse*, the other *hisse, hisse*, and they presently came to her, & she departing left them with this Examinate, and they leapt on her shoulder, and the kitlin suckt under her right eare on her neck, & the Moldiwarp on the left side in the like place.
{F2} After they had suckt her, shee sent the Kitlin to a Baker of that Towne, whose name shee remembers not, who had called her Witch & stricken her; and bad her said spirit goe and bewitch him to death: the Moldiwarpe shee then bad go to *Anne Dawse* of the same towne and bewitch her to death, because she had called this examinate witch, whore, jade, &c. and within one fortnight after they both dyed.
And further this Examinate saith, that she sent both her spirits to *Stonesby*,[82] to one *Willison* a husbandman, & *Robert Williman* a husbandmans sonne, and bad the Kitlin goe to *Willison* and bewitch him to death, and the Moldywarp to the other, and bewitch him to death, which they did; and within tenne dayes they dyed. These foure were bewitched while this Examinate dwelt at *Waltham* aforesaid.[83]
About three yeares since, this Examinate removed thence to *Stathorne*, where she now dwelt: upon a difference betweene the said *Willimot* and the wife

80 Wolds.
81 A kitten and a mole.
82 A village three miles south-east of Stathern.
83 Missing text is suggested by this remark, as by the casual reference to 'that Towne' earlier on F2.

of *John Patchet* of the said *Stathorne* Yeoman,[84] shee the said *Willimot* called her this Examinate to goe and touch {F2v} the said *John Patchets* Wife and her Childe, which shee did, touching the said *John Patchets* wife in her bed, and the childe in the Grace-wifes arms, and then sent her said spirits to bewitch them to death, which they did, and so the woman lay languishing by the space of a moneth and more, for then shee dyed; the childe dyed the next day after she touched it.

And shee further saith, that the said *Joane Willimot* had a spirit sucking on her, under the left flanke, in the likenesse of a little white Dogge, which this Examinate saith, that she saw the same sucking in Barley-harvest last, being then at the house of the said *Joan Willimot*.

And for her selfe, this Examinate further saith, that shee gave her soule to the Divell to have these spirits at her command; for a confirmation whereof, she suffered them to suck her alwayes as aforesaid about the change and full of the Moone.

H.Hastings.

Samuel Fleming.

{F3} The Examination of *Phillip Flower*, Sister of *Margaret Flower*, and Daughters of *Joane Flower*, before Sr *William Pelham*, and Mr. *Butler*, Justices of the Peace, *Febr.* 4. 1618. Which was brought in at the Assizes as evidence against her Sister *Margaret*.[85]

SHe saith, that her mother and her sister maliced the Earle of *Rutland*, his Countesse, and their Children, because her Sister *Margaret*, was put out of the Ladies service of Laundry, and exempted from other services about the house, whereupon her said sister, by the commaundement of her mother, brought from the Castle the right hand glove of the Lord *Henry Rosse*, which she delivered to her Mother; who presently rubd it on the backe of her Spirit *Rutterkin*, and then put it into hot boyling water, afterward shee pricked it often, and buried it in the yard, wishing the Lord *Rosse* might never thrive, and so her Sister *Margaret* continued with her mother, where shee often saw the cat *Rutterkin* leape on her shoulder, and sucke her necke.

Shee further confessed, that shee heard her mother often curse the Earle and his Lady, and thereupon would boyle feathers and blood together, using many Divellish speeches and strange gestures.

{F3v} The Examination of *Margaret Flower*, Sister of *Phillip Flower &c.* about the 22. of *January*. 1618.[86]

84 See E4v.

85 The pamphleteer obviously attended the assizes. The Pelhams were a Lincolnshire family from Brocklesby, about fifty-five miles north-east of Belvoir. Sir William was married to the daughter of Lord Willoughby of Parham, and was active in local justice and politics (*DNB* entry for Sir William, his father). The Butlers were a large family with branches in both Lincolnshire and Leicestershire – it is not clear just who is referred to here.

86 The uncertainty of date is odd, as this is apparently the first examination and the only one in January. There is no full heading, which suggests missing material and irregular

SHe saith and confesseth, that about foure or five yeare since[87] her Mother sent her for the right hand glove of *Henry* Lord *Rosse*, afterward that her mother bade her goe againe into the Castle of *Beaver*, and bring downe the glove or some other thing of *Henry* Lord *Rosse*, and shee askt what to doe?[88] Her Mother replyed to hurt my Lord *Rosse*: whereupon she brought downe a glove, and delivered the same to her Mother, who stroked *Rutterkin* her Cat with it, after it was dipt in hot water, and so prickt it often, after which *Henry* Lord *Rosse* fell sicke within a weeke, and was much tormented with the same.

She further saith, that finding a glove about two or three yeares since of *Francis* Lord *Rosse*,[89] on a dung hill, she delivered it to her mother, who put it into hot water, and after tooke it out and rubd it on *Rutterkin* the Cat, and bad him goe upwards, and after her mother buried it in the yard, and said a mischiefe light on him, but he will mend againe.

Shee further saith, that her Mother and shee, and her Sister agreed together to bewitch the Earle and his Lady, that they might have no more children: and being demanded the cause of this their mallice and ill will; shee saith, that about foure yeares since {F4} the Countesse (growing into some mislike with her) gave her forty shillings, a bolster, & a mattresse, and bad her lye at home, and come no more to dwell at the Castle; which she not onely tooke in ill part, but grudged at it exceedingly, swearing in her heart to be revenged. After this, her Mother complained to the Earle against one *Peake*, who had offered her some wrong, wherein she conceived that the Earle tooke not her part, as shee expected, which dislike with the rest, exasperated her displeasure against him, and so she watched an opportunity to bee revenged: whereupon she tooke wooll out of the said mattresse, and a paire of gloves, which were given her by Mr. *Vavasor*, and put them into warme water, mingling them with some blood, and stirring it together, then she tooke the wooll and gloves out of the water, and rubd them on the belly of *Rutterkin* her Cat, saying the Lord and the Lady should have more Children, but it would be long first.[90]

recording. Why there are no follow-up examinations recorded between 22 January and 4 February, and none at all of Joan Flower, is a mystery. On Gv the pamphleteer tells us that other examinations were also used at the trial. Both suspected sisters were re-examined in February, and, as we have seen, other suspects were being questioned, and re-examined, about this and other matters as late as 17 March. Can this scantiness of documentation be explained by carelessness, or has a choice been made to exclude certain documents? See the chronology for the dating of each examination story.

87 Again, this dating seems wrong.

88 The disorientated rambling of this sequence of events does not inspire confidence in its usefulness as a record.

89 The younger boy has now succeeded to his brother's title.

90 This modification of the threat of childlessness sounds like a response to pressure of questioning. Clearly anxiety was intense, and the couple did indeed remain childless.

Shee further confesseth, that by her mothers commandement, shee brought to her a peece of a handkercher of the Lady *Katherine* the Earles daughter,[91] and her mother put it into hot water, & then taking it out, rubd it on *Rutterkin*, bidding him flye, and go; whereupon *Rutterkin* whined and cryed Mew: whereupon shee said, that *Rutterkin* had no power over the Lady *Katherine* to hurt her.

{F4v} The Examination of *Phillip Flower*, the 25. of *February*, 1618. before *Francis* Earle of Rutland, *Francis* Lord *Willoughby* of Ersby,[92] Sr. *George Manners*, and Sr. *William Pelham.*

SHee confesseth and saith, that shee hath a Spirit sucking on her in the forme of a white Rat, which keepeth her left breast, and hath so done for three or foure yeares, and concerning the agreement betwixt her Spirit and her selfe, she confesseth and saith, that when it came first unto her, shee gave her Soule to it, and it promised to doe her good, and cause *Thomas Simpson* to love her, if shee would suffer it to sucke her, which shee agreed unto; and so the last time it suckt was on Tuesday at night, the 23. of *February*.

{G} The Examination of *Margaret Flower*, at the same time, &c.

SHee confesseth, that she hath two familiar Spirits sucking on her, the one white, the other black spotted; the white sucketh under her left brest, and the blacke spotted within the inward parts of her secrets. When shee first entertained them she promised them her soule, and they covenanted to doe all things which she commanded them &c.

Shee further saith, that about the 30. of *January*, last past, being Saturday, foure Divells appeared unto her in *Lincolne* Jayle, at eleaven or twelve a clocke at midnight: The one stood at her beds feete, with a blacke head like an Ape, and spake unto her; but what, shee cannot well remember, at which shee was very angry because hee would speake no plainer, or let her understand his meaning: the other three were *Rutterkin*, *Little Robin*, and *Spirit*; but shee never mistrusted them, nor suspected her selfe, till then.

There is another Examination of the said *Margaret Flower*, taken the fourth of *February*, 1618. tending to this effect.[93]

THat being asked what shee knoweth concerning the bewitching of the Earle of Rutland, his wife, and children, shee saith, that it is {Gv} true, that her selfe, her mother, and sister were all displeased with him, especially with the Countesse, for turning her out of service, whereuppon some foure yeare since, her mother commanded her to goe up to the Castle, and bring her the right hand glove of the Lord *Henry Rosse*, the Earles eldest sonne; which glove she

91 Katherine was the child of the earl and his first wife, Frances Knevet.

92 Lord Willoughby of Ersby is, in fact, almost certainly *Robert* Bertie, who succeeded to his barony in 1601. A flamboyant courtier, he was also a soldier (Cokayne, VIII, 15–18, and XII, 679).

93 Presumably another fragment.

found on the rushes in the Nurcery, and delivered the same to her Mother, who put it into hot water, prickt it often with her knife, then tooke it out of the water, and rubd it uppon *Rutterkin*, bidding him height and goe, and doe some hurt to *Henry* Lord *Rosse*, whereupon hee fell sicke, and shortly after dyed, which her Mother hearing of, said it was well: but after shee had rubd the glove on the Spirit *Rutterkin*, shee threw it into the fire and burnt it, &c.

THese Examinations and some others were taken and charily preserved for the contriving of sufficient evidences against them, and when the Judges of Assise came downe to Lincolne about the first weeke of *March*,[94] being Sr. H*enry Hobert*, Lord chiefe Justice of the Common Pleas, and Sr. *Ed: Bromley* one of the Barons of the Exchequer, they were presented unto them, who not onely wondred at the wickednesse of these persons, but were amazed at their practices and horrible contracts with the Divel to damne their owne soules: And although the Right Honourable Earle had sufficient griefe for the losse of his Children; yet no {G2} doubt it was the greater to consider the manner, and how it pleased God to inflict on him in such a fashion of visitation: Besides, as it amazed the hearers to understand the particulars, and the circumstances of this divellish contract, so was it wonderfull to see their desperate impenitency, and horrible distraction, according to the rest of that sort, exclaiming against the Divell for deluding them, and now breaking promise with them, when they stood in most need of his helpe.

Notwithstanding all these aggravations, such was the unparalleled magnanimity, wisedome, and patience of this generous Noble-man, that hee urged nothing against them more then their owne confessions, and so quietly left them to judicall triall, desiring of God mercy for their soules, and of men charity to censure them in their condemnation: but God is not mocked, and so gave them over to judgement, nor man so reformed, but for the Earles sake, they cursed them to that place which they themselves long before had bargained for.

What now remaines (gentle Reader) but for thee to make use of so wonderfull a Story, and remarkable an accident, out of which, to draw to a conclusion, thou maist collect these particulars. First, that God is the supreame commander of all things, and permitteth wonderfull actions in the World, for the tryall of the godly, the punishment of the wicked, and his owne glory: of which man shall never attaine to know the reason or occasion. Secondly, that the Divell is the meere servant and {G2v} agent of God, to prosecute whatsoever hee shall command rather then give leave unto; limiting him yet thus farre in his owne nature, that he can go no further then the bounds

94 The Leicestershire witches were presumably tried at a normal assize in their county, for they were still being examined in mid-March, whilst the Lincolnshire witches were executed (according to the title page) on 11 March 1618. See chronology for further problems with dating.

within which hee is hedged. Thirdly, that this God hath punishments, *ad correctionem*, that is to say, chasticements of the godly, *& ad ruinem, Videlicet*, Judgements against the wicked, wherein yet man must disclaime any knowledge, and forsake prejudicate opinions. For the very just shall be tried like gold, and no man exempted from castigation whom God doth love. Fourthly, that this Divell, though he bee Gods Instrument, yet worketh altogether by deceit: for as hee was a lyer from the beginning; so let no man trust him, because he aymeth at the confusion of all Mankinde. Fiftly, that the wicked, (however they may thrive and prosper for a time) yet in the end are sure to be payed home, either with punishment in this life or in the life to come, or both, as a finall reward of monstrous impiety. Sixtly, that Man in his frailty must not presume of prosperity; but prepare a kinde of stooping under the hand of God, when it pleaseth him to strike or punish us. Seaventhly, that there is no murmuring nor repining against God, but quietly to tolerate his inflictings, whensoever they chance, of which this worthy Earle is a memorable example to all men and Ages. Eightly, that the punishments of the wicked are so many warnings to all irregular sinners to amend their lives, and avoid the judgement to come, by penitency and newnesse of life. Ninthly, that {G3} though man could bee content to passe over blasphemies and offences against the Statutes of Princes, yet God will overtake them in their own walks, and pull them backe by the sleeve into a slaughter-house, as here you know the evidences against these people tooke life and power from their owne Confessions. Tenthly, and last of all, that private opinion cannot prevaile against publique censures: for here you see the learned and religious Judges cryed out with our Saviour, *Ex ore tuo.*[95] Therefore though it were so, that neither Witch nor Divell could doe these things, yet *Let not a Witch live*, saith God,[96] and *Let them dye* (saith the Law of England) *that have conversation with spirits, and presume to blaspheme the name of God with spels and incantation.*[97] O then you sonnes of men, take warning by these examples, and eyther direct your steps from the broad way of destruction, and inrecoverable gulph of damnation, or with *Josuahs* counsell to *Achan*,[98] blesse God for the discovery of wickednesse, and take thy death patiently, as the prevention of thy future judgement, and saving innocents from punishment, who otherwise may be suspected without a cause.

Utinam tam facile vera invenire possem, quam falsa convincere.[99] *FINIS.*

95 'Out of thine own mouth will I judge thee, thou wicked servant', Luke 19.22 (Rosen, 384, n. 20). Particularly apt in this case.

96 'Thou shalt not suffer a witch to live', Exodus 22.18.

97 A summary of elements of James I's 1604 Witchcraft Act (1 James I.c.12).

98 Presumably 'And Joshua said unto Achan, My son, give, I pray thee, glory to the Lord God of Israel, and make confession unto him . . .', Joshua 7.19.

99 'If only I could find out the truth as easily as I can show up the lies!' – adapted from Cicero, *De Finibus Bonorum et Malorum* (ed. and trans. H. Rackham [London: Loeb, 1931], Book 1, 2.13). Quoted in Rosen, 384, n. 22.

16

Henry Goodcole, *The wonderfull discoverie of Elizabeth Sawyer, a Witch* (1621)

This is the only witchcraft pamphlet of the period which is by an author whose other works are well known. Henry Goodcole (1586–1641) was a writer of pamphlets on crime, based on his access to prisoners in Newgate gaol where he acted as chaplain. Like Margaret Harkett (*The severall factes of Witch-crafte*, 1585) Elizabeth Sawyer was sent for trial at the Old Bailey because she was a suspected felon from Middlesex, and so she was imprisoned in Newgate awaiting execution when Goodcole spoke to her. He visited the condemned daily, as he reports in most of his pamphlets, and heard their stories as part of an attempt to ensure repentance. The resultant texts were published with approval 'by authority' – although it is not known precisely who sanctioned them. This quarto was entered in the Stationers' Register to bookseller William Butler on 27 April 1621 and printed by Augustine Matthewes. The text used here is in the British Library.

Goodcole was born in Clerkenwell, where he seems to have remained throughout his life. There is no evidence that he attended university, and his status as a 'minister of God's word' is rather unclear. His *DNB* entry suggests that he eked out an existence on the margins of church life, rather than obtaining quick preferment, because of his hasty marriage to Anne Tryme in 1606 'by whom he had a daughter rather too soon'. By 1637 he was the curate of St James, Clerkenwell, but he died five years later at the age of fifty-five. His real success in life was thus as a pamphleteer. Goodcole's pamphlets deal with a number of different crimes, in different ways, but each one focuses on a particular sin and its apt punishment – hence his emphasis here on Elizabeth Sawyer's cursing, swearing and blaspheming, which not only brought the devil to her but led her into further verbal sin and, through confession, to execution. Goodcole thus wrote primarily as a concerned cleric warning of the consequences of a sinful life, but as his career in print progressed he also told some remarkably racy stories.

His other pamphlets, and the developments in his style and tone over a writing career lasting nearly twenty years, cast light on his motivations and concerns as the author of *The wonderfull discoverie*. The account of the witch of Edmonton was only his third publication. His first, *A True Declaration of the Happy Conversion, Contrition and Christian Preparation of Francis Robinson* (1618), shows many of the traits which distinguish Goodcole's work, but can also be read as a careful foray into new territory. It was certainly intended to attract attention to him, being ambitiously dedicated to the Lord Chief Justice, and telling the story of a famous counterfeiter of the Great Seal. But its spin, whilst plentiful, is uncontroversial. Its messages are clear: that Robinson fell into his sin by contact with papists, that his downfall should make others wary, and that his unfeigned repentance was both beautiful and effectual – as demonstrated by Goodcole's account of his conversation with the condemned man. This neat conclusion, typically laced with pious comment and prayers, suggests Goodcole's desire to transform news into quasi-parable and to publicise safely his own Protestant godliness and literary talent.

The first pamphlet also highlights his privileged access to prisoners as the gift-horse source of his accounts. His exploitation of this provides a window on the legal system in London (and Middlesex), as in *London's Cry* (1619) which is a compilation of court proceedings against assorted felons. The description of Elizabeth Sawyer's trial is thus placed in context, with its author as a man who has a reverential understanding of the legal system and wishes – like Potts – to demonstrate its justice in action. The tone is rather flat: 'facts' and moralising set side by side as in *The wonderfull discoverie*. But by 1621 Goodcole was beginning to develop his eye for the lurid and sentimental possibilities of print, and for sensational (particularly sexual) detail – an eye which the earnest and distracted Potts entirely lacks. This becomes clear with Goodcole's voyeuristic interest in Elizabeth Sawyer's intimacies with the devil. But, for unknown reasons, Goodcole's promising career as a pamphleteer was interrupted. It may be that *The wonderfull discoverie* did not meet with approval despite its authorised publication. Goodcole's introduction to the pamphlet suggests that he feels witchcraft to be a dangerous subject to discuss publicly, because of 'the diversitie of opinions concerning things of this nature, and that not among the ignorant, but among some of the learned' (A3). Goodcole wrote no more for over a decade, and his sometimes clumsy, and rather tentative venture into print must have seemed to be over.

The wonderfull discoverie is, however, a bridge between Goodcole's earlier works and his more assured later ones. Like all three of Goodcole's later pamphlets, it focused primarily on female criminality and sex-related crime. When Goodcole recommenced writing, he continued in a similar vein to his interest in Elizabeth Sawyer's 'sluttish' and unfeminine behaviour (B3). Wifely adultery was condemned as a sin leading to murder in *The Adultresses Funerall Day* (1635), whilst *Nature's Cruell Step-Dames or Matchlesse Monsters of the Female Sex* (1637) dealt with devil-inspired child murder, bastardy and infanticide. In 1635, Goodcole's most exciting pamphlet told the story of two murderous sexual tricksters under the heading *Heavens Speedie Hue and Cry sent after Lust and Murther*. The account is clearly fascinated by the immorality of its subjects, Tom and Bess, and the vivid portrayal of their dark world: Elizabeth Evans is shown leading gentlemen to secluded places with promises of sex, where her partner

Thomas Sherwood then murders them and steals their possessions. In violent contrast, the moralising so apparent in *The wonderfull discoverie* has bloomed further into pious poetry:

> Thy God feare to offend,
> To him doe dayly pray,
> He will thee send a happy end,
> And live with him for aye.
>
> (C3v)

Goodcole's last three pamphlets, whilst hardly seamless, have a flow and literary ambition missing from much of his earlier work. The sentimentality of the account of Francis Robinson remains, but the awkwardness of tone and construction which characterises *Londons Cry* and *The wonderfull discovery* is largely replaced by a smoother blending of narration and commentary.

Goodcole's profile as an author connects witchcraft pamphlets firmly with the general literature of sin, crime and punishment. But other crime pamphlets seldom use the amount of documentation found in many witchcraft pamphlets, especially those published before 1590. Murder pamphlets, for example, a genre to which Goodcole contributed at least half his publications, are almost exclusively third-person narrations of events with appropriate shocked reaction. They do not make use of pre-trial material or indictments at all, and court reports are brief and rare. In contrast to these, and to Goodcole's other works, *The wonderfull discoverie*'s concern for recording question and answer and printing them as a *recreation* of events is striking. In the Jacobean period, as in the Elizabethan, writing about witchcraft seems to demand higher levels of proof than writing about other crimes. Even though pamphlets have drifted away from the early Elizabethan use of documents with minimal intervention, there is still an anxiety to recreate the moment in more detail than is usual in the reporting of other crimes – an anxiety presumably stemming from the debate about the evidence needed to prove that this exceptional crime had taken place. Goodcole is here creating his own textual evidence of the truth of the crime and the confession, but he fears that even this will not protect him from censure and doubt. As he says:

> For my part I meddle here with nothing but matter of fact, and to that ende produce the Testimony of the living and the dead, which I hope shall be Authenticall for the confirmation of this Narration, and free mee from all censorious mindes and mouthes. It is none of my intent here to discusse, or dispute of Witches or Witchcraft, but desire most therin to be dispensed with all, knowing, that in such a little Treatise as this is, no matter that can be effectuall therein can be comprised; especially, in so short a time of deliberation, as three or foure dayes.
>
> (A3–A3v)

It seems that he was right to be concerned about the intellectual viability of discussions of witchcraft in cheap pamphlets: *The wonderfull discoverie* is the last pamphlet about English witchcraft to be published for twenty-two years.

A number of books and articles deal with the case, the pamphlet and Goodcole as a pamphleteer, but discussion is primarily in the context of the play based on the pamphlet, *The Witch of Edmonton* by John Ford, Thomas Dekker and William Rowley (1621). Examples include Diane Purkiss, 'Testimony and Truth: *The Witch of Edmonton* and *The Witches of Lancashire*' in *The Witch in History* (London and New York: Routledge, 1996), 231–49 and Kristin Jeanne Leuschner's unpublished thesis, 'Creating the "Known True Story": Sixteenth and Seventeenth Century Murder and Witchcraft Pamphlets and Plays' (University of California, 1992), which looks at Goodcole as a censor and shaper of speech and discourse. Discussions of Goodcole's other works can be found in general histories of pamphlet literature such as Sandra Clark, *The Elizabethan Pamphleteers: Popular Moralistic Pamphlets 1580–1640* (London: Athlone Press, 1983) and in studies of crime literature and gender, such as Frances Dolan's *Dangerous Familiars: Representations of Domestic Crime in England 1550–1700* (Ithaca and London: Cornell University Press, 1994).

{A2 (title page)} The wonderfull discoverie of ELIZABETH SAWYER *a Witch, late of* Edmonton, *her* conviction and condemnation and Death.[1]
Together with the relation of the Divels accesse to her, and their conference together.
Written by HENRY GOODCOLE Minister of the Word of God, and her continuall Visiter in the Gaole of Newgate.
Published by Authority.
London, Printed for *William Butler*, and are to be sold at his Shop in Saint *Dunstons* Church-yard, Fleetstreet. 1621.
{A2v blank}
{A3} The Authors Apologie to the *Christian Readers, who wisheth* to them all health and happinesse.
THe Publication of this subject whereof I now write, hath bin by importunitie extorted from me, who would have beene content to have concealed it, knowing the diversitie of opinions concerning things of this nature, and that not among the ignorant, but among some of the learned. For my part I meddle here with nothing but matter of fact, and to that ende produce the Testimony of the living and the dead, which I hope shall be Authenticall for the confirmation of this Narration, and free mee from all censorious mindes and mouthes. It is none of my intent here to discusse, or dispute of Witches or Witchcraft, but desire most therin to be dispensed with {A3v} *all, knowing, that in such a little Treatise as this is, no matter that can be effectuall therein can be comprised; especially, in*

1 All text is in Roman font unless otherwise stated.

so short a time of deliberation, as three or foure dayes.[2] *And the rather doe I now publish this to purchase my peace, which without it being done, I could scarse at any time be at quiet, for many who would take no nay, but still desired of me written Copies of this insuing Declaration. Another reason was to defend the truth of the cause, which in some measure, hath received a wound already, by most base and false Ballets,*[3] *which were sung at the time of our returning from the* Witches *execution. In them I was ashamed to see and heare such ridiculous fictions of her bewitching Corne on the ground, of a Ferret and an Owle dayly sporting before her, of the bewitched woman brayning her selfe, of the Spirits attending in the Prison: all which I knew to be fitter for an Ale-bench then for a relation of proceeding in Court of Justice. And thereupon I wonder that such lewde Balletmongers should be suffered to creepe into the Printers presses and peoples eares.*

And so I rest at your opinions and judgements

Your well-wisher in the Lord Jesus,

HENRY GOODCOLE

{A4} A true declaration *of the manner of proceeding against* ELIZABETH SAWYER late of Edmonton Spinster, and the evi*dence of her Conviction.*

A Great and long suspition was held of this person to be a witch, and the eye of Mr. *Arthur Robinson*, a worthy Justice of Peace, who dweleth at *Totnam*[4] neere to her, was watchfull over her, and her wayes, and that not without just cause; stil having his former long suspition of her, by the information of her neighbours that dwelt about her: from suspition, to proceed to great presumptions, seeing the death of Nurse-children and Cattell, strangely and suddenly to happen.[5] And to finde out who should bee the author of this mischiefe, an old ridiculous custome was used, which was to plucke the Thatch of her house, {A4v} and to burne it, and it being so burnd, the author of such mischiefe should presently then come: and it was observed and affirmed to the Court, that *Elizabeth Sawyer* would presently frequent the house of them that burnt the thatch which they pluckt of her house, and come without any sending for.[6]

This triall, though it was slight and ridiculous, yet it setled a resolution in those whom it concerned, to finde out by all meanes they could endeavour,

2 The note of panic here seems genuine: although Goodcole is also making conventional claims about unwilling authorship. Witchcraft seems to become a dangerous subject to discuss in the later Jacobean years.

3 Ballads.

4 Tottenham, then a small town a mile south of Edmonton and five miles north of the City of London.

5 The syntax wavers here: the JP is the focus of the account but the subject seems to change from him to the witch's neighbours, who are thus responsible for the 'old ridiculous custome' in the next sentence.

6 Goodcole firmly sets his account in the context of court proceedings here, as later, although in doing so he is forced to acknowledge that not all evidence presented to the court is good.

her long and close carried[7] Witchery, to explaine it to the world; and being descried,[8] to pay in the ende such a worker of Iniquity, her wages, and that which shee had deserved, (namely, *shame* and *Death*)[9] from which the Divell, that had so long deluded her, did not come as shee said, to shew the least helpe of his unto her to deliver her: but being descried in his waies, and workes, immediately he fled, leaving her to shift and answere for her selfe, with publike and private markes on her body as followeth.

1 Her face was most pale & ghoast-like without any bloud at all, and her countenance was still dejected to the ground.

2 Her body was crooked and deformed, even bending together, which so happened but a little before her apprehension.

3 That tongue which by cursing, swearing, blaspheming, and imprecating, as afterward she {B} confessed, was the occasioning cause, of the Divels accesse unto her, even at that time, and to claime her thereby as his owne, by it discovered her lying, swearing, and blaspheming; as also evident proofes produced against her, to stop her mouth with Truths authority: at which hearing, she was not able to speake a sensible or ready word for her defense, but sends out in the hearing of the Judge, Jury, and all good people that stood by, many most fearefull imprecations for destruction against her selfe then to happen, as heretofore she had wished and indeavoured to happen on divers of her neighbours: the which the righteous Judge of Heaven, whom she thus invocated, to judge then and discerne her cause, did reveale.

Thus God did wonderfully overtake her in her owne wickednesse, to make her tongue to be the meanes of her owne destruction, which had destroyed many before.

And in this manner, namely, that out of her false swearing the truth whereof, she little thought, should be found, but by her swearing and cursing blended, it thus farre made against her, that both Judge and Jurie, all of them grew more and more suspitious of her, and not without great cause: for none that had the feare of God, or any the least motion of Gods grace left in them, would, or durst, to persume[10] so im-{Bv}-pudently, with execrations and false oathes, to affront Justice.

On Saturday, being the fourteenth day of Aprill, *Anno Dom.* 1621. this *Elizabeth Sawyer* late of *Edmonton*, in the County of *Middlesex* Spinster, was arraigned, and indited three severall times at Justice Hall in the Old Baily in *London*, in the Parish of Saint *Sepulchers*, in the Ward of Farrington without: which Inditements were, *viz.*

That shee the said *Elizabeth Sawyer*, not having the feare of God before her eyes, but moved and seduced by the Divell, by Diabolicall helpe, did out of

7 Secretly practised.

8 Discovered.

9 'For the wages of sin is death', Romans 6.23.

10 *Sic.* As is often the case in Goodcole's work, this sentence is curdled by a desire to moralise.

her malicious heart, (because her neighbours where she dwelt, would not buy Broomes of her) would therefore thus revenge her selfe on them in this manner, namely, witch to death their Nurse Children and Cattell. But for brevities sake I here omit formes of Law and Informations.[11]

She was also indited, for that shee the said *Elizabeth Sawyer*, by Diabolicall helpe, and out of her malice afore-thought, did witch unto death *Agnes Ratcleife*, a neighbour of hers, dwelling in the towne of *Edmonton* where shee did likewise dwell, and the cause that urged her thereunto was, because that *Elizabeth Ratcliefe*[12] did {B2} strike a Sowe of hers in her sight, for licking up a little Soape where shee had laide it, and for that *Elizabeth Sawyer* would be revenged of her, and thus threatned *Agnes Ratcleife*, that it should be a deare blow unto her, which accordingly fell out, and suddenly; for that evening *Agnes Ratcleife* fell very sicke, and was extraordinarily vexed, and in a most strange manner in her sicknesse was tormented, Oath whereof, was by this *Agnes Ratcleifes* Husband, given to the Court, the time when shee fell sicke, and the time when shee died, which was within foure dayes after she fell sicke: and further then related, that in the time of her sicknesse his wife *Agnes Ratcleife* lay foaming at the mouth, and was extraordinarily distempered, which many of his neighbors seeing as well as himselfe, bred suspition in them that some mischiefe was done against her, and by none else, but alone by this *Elizabeth Sawyer* it was done; concerning whom the said *Agnes Ratcleife* lying on her death-bed, these wordes confidently spake: namely, that if shee did die at that time shee would verily take it on her death, that *Elizabeth Sawyer* her neighbour, whose Sowe with a washing-Beetle[13] she had stricken, and so for that cause her malice being great, was the occasion of her death.

{B2v} To prove her innocency, she put her selfe to the triall of God and the Countrey, and what care was taken both by the honourable Bench[14] and Jury, the judicious standers by can witnesse: and God knowes, who will reward it.

The Jury hearing this Evidence given upon oath by the husband of the above named *Agnes Ratcliefe*, and his wives speeches relating to them likewise an oath, as she lay on her death-bed, to be truth, that shee had said unto her husband; Namely, that if she dyed at that time, shee the said *Elizabeth Sawyer*

11 This suggests that Goodcole had access to the documents or had noted their contents in court: this may be the source of some of his later additional information on Sawyer. His basic understanding of the legal system is evident – and at least he tells the reader what he is omitting here.

12 Presumably a mistake.

13 Implement for pounding washing.

14 The bench in London sessions of gaol delivery was composed of the aldermen of the City of London, the recorder and the mayor. They, as members of the commission of gaol delivery, were empowered to act as justices of gaol delivery, like their counterparts at the regional assizes.

was the cause of her death; and maliciously did by her Witchery procure the same.

This made some impression in their mindes, and caused due and mature deliberation, not trusting their owne judgements, what to doe, in a matter of such great import, as life, they deemed might be conserved.

The Foreman of the Jury asked of Master *Heneage Finch* Recorder,[15] his direction, and advice, to whom hee Christianlike thus replyed, namely, *Doe it as God shall put in your hearts.*

Master *Arthur Robinson*, a worshipfull Justice of Peace dwelling at *Totnam*, had often & divers times, upon the complaints of the neighbours against this *Elizabeth Sawyer*, laboriously and carefully examined her, and stil his suspition was strengthened against her, that doubtlesse shee was {B3} a Witch. An Information was given unto him by some of her Neighbours, that this *Elizabeth Sawyer* had a private and strange marke on her body, by which their suspition was confirmed against her, and hee sitting in the Court in that time of her triall, informed the Bench thereof, desiring the Bench to send for women to search her, presently before the Jury did goe forth to bring in the verdict, concerning *Elizabeth Sawyer*, whether that shee was guilty or no: to which motion of his, they most willingly condescended.

The Bench commanded officers appointed for those purposes, to fetch in three women to search the body of *Elizabeth Sawyer*, to see if they could finde any such unwonted marke, as they were informed of: one of the womens names was *Margaret Weaver*, that keepes the Sessions House for the City of *London*, a widdow of an honest reputation, and two other grave Matrons, brought in by the Officer out of the streete, passing by there by chance, were joyned with her in this search of the person named, who fearing and perceiving shee should by that search of theirs be then discovered, behaved her selfe most sluttishly and loathsomely towards them, intending thereby to prevent their search of her, (which my pen would forbeare to write {B3v} these things for modesties sake, but I would not vary in what was delivered to the Bench, expressly & openly spoken) yet neverthelesse, nicenesse they laid aside, and according to the request of the Court, and to that trust reposed in them by the Bench, they all three severally searched her, and made severally their answer unto the Court being sworne thereunto to deliver the truth. And they all three said, that they a little above the Fundiment[16] of *Elizabeth Sawyer* the prisoner, there indited before the Bench for a Witch, found a thing like a Teate the bignesse of the little finger, and the length of halfe a finger, which was branched at the top like a teate, and seemed as though

15 The recorder of London was empowered to act as the presiding judge. Heneage Finch, a member of an ambitious family who became the Counts of Winchilsea, had been recorder for only a few months, but had long experience as a lawyer and Member of Parliament (*DNB*).

16 Anus.

one had suckt it, and the bottome thereof was blew, and the top of it was redde. This view of theirs, and answere that she had such a thing about her, which boldly shee denied, gave some insight to the Jury, of her: who upon their consciences returned the said *Elizabeth Sawyer*, to be guilty, by diabolicall help, of the death of *Agnes Ratcliefe* onely, and acquitted her of the other two Inditements. And thus much of the meanes that brought her to her deserved death and destruction.

I will addresse to informe you of her preparation to death, which is alone pertinent to my function, and declare unto you her Confession *ver*-{B4}-*batim*,[17] out of her owne mouth delivered to me, the Tuesday after her conviction, though with great labour it was extorted from her, and the same Confession I read unto her at the place of her execution, and there shee confessed to all people that were there, the same to be most true, which I shall here relate.

And because it should not bee thought that from me alone this proceeded, I would have other testimony thereof to stop all contradictions of so palpable a verity, that heard her deliver it from her owne mouth in the Cappel[18] of *Newgate* the same time.

In testimony whereof, the persons that were then present with mee at her Confession, have hereunto put to their hands, and if it be required, further to confirme this to be a truth, will bee ready at all times to make oath thereof.

{B4v blank}

{C} A true Relation of the confession *of* Elizabeth Sawyer *Spinster*, after her conviction of Witchery, ta*ken on Tuesday the* 17. *day of* Aprill, Anno 1621. in the Gaole of Newgate, where *she was prisoner, then in the presence and hearing of divers persons, whose names to verifie the same are here subscribed to this ensuyng confession, made unto me* Henry Good-cole *Minister of the word of God,* Ordinary[19] *and* Visiter *for the Gaole of Newgate. In dialogue manner are here expressed the persons that she murthered, and the cattell that she destroyed by the helpe of the Divell.*

In this manner was I inforced to speake unto her, because she might understand me, and give unto me answere, according to my demands, for she was a very ignorant woman.[20]

17 As always, a disputable claim – especially given Goodcole's obvious interests as questioner, recorder and editor.

18 Chapel.

19 Chaplain.

20 Goodcole's recording of his questions is very useful in determining what kinds of interrogation witches may have been subject to, but it is interesting that he feels compelled to defend it as unusual. Presumably he believes it to be insufficiently Socratic – simplistic and inartistic? Certainly his other pamphlets are in the form of coherent narratives. But he may also be concerned that the reader will think his questions are inappropriate – see his marginal notes throughout this text.

Question.
B*Y what meanes came you to have acquaintance with the Divell, and when was the first time that you saw him, and how did you know that it was the Divell?*[21]
Answere.
The first time that the Divell came unto me was, when I was cursing, swearing and blasphe-{Cv}-ming; he then rushed in upon me, and never before that time did I see him, or he me: and when he, namely the Divel, came to me, the first words that hee spake unto me were these: *Oh! have I now found you cursing, swearing, and blaspheming? now you are mine.*[22] A wonderfull warning to many whose tongues are too frequent in these abhominable sinnes; I pray God, that this her terrible example may deter them, to leave and distaste them, to put their tongues to a more holy language, then the accursed language of hell. The tongue of man is the glory of man, and it was ordained to glorifie God: but worse then brute beasts they are, who have a tongue, as well as men, that therewith they at once both blesse and curse.[23]
Question.
What sayd you to the Divell, when hee came unto you and spake unto you, were you not afraide of him? if you did feare him, what sayd the Divell then to you?[24]
Answere.
I was in a very greate feare, when I saw the Divell, but hee did bid me not to feare him at all, for hee would do me no hurt at all, but would do for mee whatsoever I should require of him, and as he promised unto me, he alwayes did such mischiefes as I did bid him to do, both on the bodies of Christians[25] and beastes: if I did bid him vexe them to death, as oftentimes I did {C2} so bid him, it was then presently by him so done.
Question.
Whether would the Divell bring unto you word or no, what he had done for you, at your command; and if he did bring you word, how long would it bee, before he would come unto you againe, to tell you?
Answere.
He would alwayes bring unto me word what he had done for me, within the space of a weeke, he never failed me at that time, and would likewise do it to Creatures and beasts two manner of wayes, which was by scratching or pinching of them.

21 This question assumes a great deal, as do many of Goodcole's heavily loaded inquiries.
22 A marginal note reads: 'A Gentleman by name Mr. Maddox standing by, and hearing of her say the word blaspheming, did aske of her, three or foure times, whether the Divell sayd have I found you blaspheming, and shee confidently sayd, I [aye].'
23 There has been no answer to the third part of the question. It is difficult to imagine how Goodcole asked these questions: singly, in blocks?
24 Here Goodcole answers his own question.
25 This word suggests Goodcole's input in shaping the text even after he has asked his highly prescriptive questions.

Question.
Of what Christians and Beastes, and how many were the number that you were the cause of their death, and what moved you to prosecute them to the death?
Answere.
I have bene by the helpe of the Divell, the meanes of many Christians and beasts death, the cause that moved mee to do it, was malice and envy, for if any body had angred me in any manner, I would be so revenged of them, and of their cattell. And do now further confesse, that I was the cause of those two nurse-childrens death, for the which I was now indited and acquited, by the Jury.[26]
{C2v} Question.
Whether did you procure the death of Agnes Ratcliefe, *for which you were found guilty by the Jury?*
Answere.
No, I did not by my meanes procure against her the least hurt.
Question.
How long is it since the Divell and you had acquaintance together, & how oftentimes in the weeke would hee come and see you, and you company with him?
Answere.
It is eight yeares since our first acquaintance; and three times in the weeke, the Divell would come and see mee, after such his acquaintance gotten of me; he would come sometimes in the morning, and sometimes in the evening.
Question.
In what shape would the Divell come unto you?
Answere.
Alwayes in the shape of a dogge and of two collars, sometimes of blacke and sometimes of white.[27]
Question.
What talke had the Divel and you together, when that he appeared to you, and what did he aske of you, and what did you desire of him?[28]
{C3} *Answer.*[29]
He asked of me, when hee came unto me, how I did, and what he should doe for mee, and demanded of mee my soule and body; threatning then to

26 This portrayal of jury error is an interesting gamble, particularly in view of the next question and its answer. It is one thing for Potts to show the judge haranguing the acquitted on the grounds that they are as guilty as the convicted: this very specific reversal of jury decisions described by the condemned felon is another matter, and Goodcole offers no comment on it.

27 This may be intended to read 'two colours'. Sawyer later suggests the dog was either white or black (Dv). But the text makes its own sense here.

28 This is not in italics.

29 The spelling changes here, and later is further abbreviated. This suggests haste and compositor fatigue, as well as reminding us of the variable numbers of people between the reader and original events, and of the arbitrary nature of their impact.

teare me in peeces, if that I did not grant unto him my soule and my body which he asked of me.

Question.

What did you after such the Divells asking of you, to have your Soule and Body, and after this his threatning of you, did you for feare grant unto the Divell his desire?

Answer.

Yes, I granted for feare unto the Divell his request of my Soule and body; and to seale this my promise made unto him, I then gave him leave to sucke of my bloud, the which hee asked of me.

Queston.[30]

In what place of your body did the Divell sucke of your bloud, and whether did hee himselfe chuse the place, or did your selfe appoint him the place? tell the truth, I charge you, as your[31] *will answere unto the Almighty God, and tell the reason if that you can, why he would sucke your bloud.*[32]

Answer.

The place where the Divell suckt my bloud was a little above my fundiment, and that place chosen by himselfe; and in that place by continuall drawing, there is a thing in the {C3v} forme of a Teate, at which the divell would sucke mee. And I asked the Divell why hee would sucke my bloud, and hee sayd it was to nourish him.

Question.

Whether did you pull up your coates or no when the Divell came to sucke you?[33]

Answer.

No, I did not, but the Divell would put his head under my coates, and I did willingly suffer him to doe what hee would.

Question.

How long would the time bee, that the Divill would continue sucking of you, and whether did you endure any paine, the time that hee was sucking of you?

Answer.

He would be suckinge of me the continuance of a quarter of an howre, and when hee suckt mee, I then felt no paine at all.

Question.

What was the meaning that the Divell when hee came unto you, would sometimes speake, and sometimes barke.[34]

30 *Sic.*

31 *Sic.*

32 Goodcole inserts a marginal note: 'I demanded this question of her to confirme the wemens search of her, concerning, that she had such a marke about her, which they upon their oathes informed the court, that truth it was, she had such a marke'.

33 Goodcole's marginal note here defends him from any implication that he is asking prurient questions for their own sake: 'This I asked of her very earnestly, and shee thus answered me, without any studying for an answer'.

34 Goodcole may have been using Elizabeth Sawyer's examination/s to help him question her,

Answer.
It is thus; when the Divell spake to me, then hee was ready to doe for me, what I would bid him to doe: and when he came barking to mee he then had done the mischiefe that I did bid him to doe for me.
{C4} Quest.
By what name did you call the divell, and what promises did he make to you?
Answ.
I did call the Divell by the name of *Tom*, and he promised to doe for me whatsoever I should require of him.
Quest.
What were those two ferrets that you were feeding on a fourme[35] *with white bread and milke, when divers children came, and saw you feeding of them?*[36]
Answ.
I never did any such thing.
Quest.
What was the white thing that did run through the thatch of your house, was it a spirit or Divell?[37]
Answ.
So farre as I know, it was nothing else but a white Ferret.
Quest.
Did any body else know, but your selfe alone of the Divells comming unto you, and of your practises? speake the truth, and tell the reason, why you did not reveale it to your husband, or to some other friend?
Answ.
I did not tell any body thereof, that the Divel came unto me, neither I durst not; for the Divell charged me that I should not, and said, That if I did tell it to any body, at his next comming {C4v} to me, he then would teare me in pieces.
Quest.
Did the Divell at any time find you praying when he came unto you, and did not the Divell forbid you to pray to Jesus Christ, but to him alone? and did not he bid you pray to him the Divell, as he taught you?[38]

since a marginal note adds: 'I asked this question because she sayd that the Divell did not alwayes speake to her'.

35 Bench.

36 Goodcole's marginal comment suggests he does not have the informations of these witnesses, but is relying on their court testimony: 'I asked this of her, because that some children of a good bignesse, and reasonable understanding, informed the Court, that they had divers times seene her feed two white ferrets with white bread & milk'.

37 Goodcole says: 'I asked this question of her because her husband testified to the Bench, he saw such a white thing runne thorow the thatch of the house, and that he catcht at it, but could not get it, and hee thought it was a white ferret'.

38 Goodcole's marginal note clearly reveals his own origination of this notion: 'Upon my general suspition I asked of her this question.' Again, he answers himself.

Answ.

Yes, he found me once praying, and he asked of me to whom I prayed, and I answered him, to Jesus Christ, and he charged me then to pray no more to Jesus Christ, but to him the Divell, and he the Divell taught me this prayer, *Sanctibicetur nomen tuum*. Amen.[39]

Quest.

Were you ever taught these Latine words before by any person else, or did you ever heare it before of any body, or can you say any more of it?

Answ.

No, I was not taught it by any body else, but by the Divell alone; neither doe I understand the meaning of these words, nor can speake any more Latine words.

Quest.

Did the Divell aske of you the next time he came unto you, whether that you had used to pray unto him, in that manner as he taught you?

Answ.

Yes, at his next comming to me hee asked of me, if that I did pray unto him as he had taught me; and I answered him againe, that sometimes {D} I did, and sometimes I did not, and the Divell then thus threatned me; It is not good for me to mocke him.

Quest.

How long is it since you saw the Divell last?

Answ.

It is three weekes since I saw the Divell.

Quest.

Did the Divell never come unto you since you were in prison? speake the truth, as you will answer unto almighty God.[40]

Answ.

The Divell never came unto me since I was in prison, nor I thanke God, I have no motion of him in my minde, since I came to prison, neither doe I now feare him at all.

Quest.

How came your eye to be put out?[41]

39 Like Agnes Waterhouse, Elizabeth Sawyer's Latin Lord's Prayer ('hallowed be thy name') is taken as evidence of ignorant and papistical devil-worship. Goodcole adds: 'I doe here relate the selfe-same wordes upon this question propounded unto her, what prayer the Divell taught her to say'.

40 Goodcole's marginal note, attacking alternative sources of information, reads: 'I asked this question because it was rumoured that the divel came to her since her conviction and shamelesly printed and openly sung in a ballad, to which many give too much credite'.

41 Goodcole adds a note suggesting that he has knowledge of Sawyer's background, and perhaps that the injury may be a genetic defect. But Sawyer says that it is an injury. He says: 'The reason why I asked this was because her father and mothers eye, one of theirs was out'.

Answ.
With a sticke which one of my children had in the hand: that night my mother did dye it was done; for I was stooping by the bed side, and I by chance did hit my eye on the sharpe end of the sticke.
Quest.
Did you ever handle the Divell when he came unto you?
Answ.
Yes, I did stroake him on the backe, and then he would becke[42] unto me, and wagge his tayle as being therewith contented.
Quest.
{Dv} *Would the Divell come unto you, all in one bignesse?*
Answ.
No; when hee came unto mee in the blacke shape, he then was biggest, and in the white the least; and when I was praying, hee then would come unto me in the white colour.
Quest.
Why did you at your triall forsweare all this, that you now doe confesse?
Answ.
I did it thereby hoping to avoyd shame.
Quest.
Is all this truth which you have spoken here unto me, and that I have now written?
Answ.
Yes, it is all truth, as I shall make answer unto almighty God.
Quest.
What moves you now to make this confession? did any urge you to it, or bid you doe it, is it for any hope of life you doe it?
Answ.
No: I doe it to cleere my conscience, and now having done it, I am the more quiet, and the better prepared, and willing thereby to suffer death, for I have no hope at all of my life, although I must confesse, I would live longer if I might.
{D2} A Relation what shee said[43] at the *place of Execution, which was at Tiborne*, on Thursday, the 19. day of Aprill. 1621.
ALL[44] this beeing by her thus freely confessed after her conviction in the Gaole of Newgate, on Tuesday, the 17. day of Aprill, I acquainted Master Recorder of *London* therewith; who thus directed mee, to take that her confession with me to the place of Execution, and to reade it to her, and to aske of her whether that was truth which shee had delivered to me in the prison,

42 Bow the head.
43 *Sic.*
44 *Sic.* This capitalisation of the first two letters, followed by lower-case letters, is conventional but here happens to look odd.

on Tuesday last, concerning what she said; and how shee dyed I will relate unto you.

Elizabeth Sawyer, you are now come unto the place of Execution; is that all true which you confessed unto mee on Tuesday last, when that you were in prison? I have it here, and will now reade it unto you, as you spake it then unto me, out of your owne mouth: and if it be true, confesse it now to God, and to all the people that are here present.

Answer.

This confession which is now read unto me, by Master *Henry Goodcole* Minister, with my owne mouth I spake it to him on Tuesday last at *Newgate*, and I here doe acknowledge, to {D2v} all the people that are here present, that it is all truth, disiring[45] you all to pray unto Almightie God to forgive me my greevous sinnes.

Question.

By what meanes hope you now to bee saved?

Answer.

By Jesus Christ alone.

Question.

Will you now pray unto Almightie God to forgive unto you all your misdeedes?

Answer.

I, with all my heart and minde.[46]

This was confirmed, in the hearing of many hundreds at her last breath, what formerly shee in prison confessed to me, and at that time spake more heartily, then the day before of her execution, on whose body Law was justly inflicted, but mercy in Gods power reserved, to bestow, when and where hee pleaseth.

My labour thus ended concerning her, to testifie and avouch to the world, and all opposers hereof, this to be true; those that were present with me in the prison, that heard her confession, I have desired here their testimonies, which is as followeth. We whose names are heere subscribed, {D3} doe thereby testifie, that *Elizabeth Sawyer* late of *Edmonton* in the Countie of *Midds.* Spinster, did in our hearing, confesse on Tuesday the 17. of *Aprill*, in the Gaole of *Newgate*, to Master *Henry Goodcoale* Minister of the word of God, the repeated foule crimes, and confirmed it at her death the 19. of *Aprill* following, to be true: and if wee be thereunto required, will bee ready to make faith of the truth thereof, namely that this was her confession being alive, and a litle before her death;[47]

Conclusion.

45 *Sic.*

46 The speeches attributed to Sawyer seem surprisingly devout: they may be inventions, or a carefully rehearsed catechism. Goodcole uses them to dramatise a sensational execution scene, focused partly on repentance but more insistent on the truth of his account.

47 There is no appended list of names here, as promised.

Deare Christians, lay this to heart, namely the cause, and first time, that the Divell came unto her, then, even then when she was cursing, swearing, and blaspheming. The Divell rageth, and mallice reigneth in the hearts of many. O let it not doe so, for heere you may see the fruites thereof, that it is a playne way to bring you to the Divell; nay, that it brings the Divell to you: for it seemed that when shee so fearefully did sweare, her oathes did so conjure him, that hee must leave then his mansion place, and come at this wretches commande and will, which was by her imprecations. Stand on your guard and watch with sobrietie to resist him, the Divell your adversary, who waiteth on you continually, {D3v} to subvert you, that so you, that doe detest her abhominable wordes, and wayes, may never taste of the cup nor wages of shame and destruction, of which she did in this life: from which and from whose power, Lord *Jesus* save, and defend thy little flocke. *Amen*.

Bibliography and further reading

Primary sources

Acts of the Privy Council of England. New Series. Ed. J.R. Dasent. 32 vols. 1890–1907. Nendeln/Liechtenstein: Kraus, 1974.

The Apprehension and confession of three notorious witches. Arreigned and by Justice condemned and executed at Chelmesforde in the Countye of Essex, the 5. day of Julye, last past. 1589. London, 1589.

Arber, Edward, ed. *A Transcript of the Registers of the Company of Stationers in London. 1554–1640.* 5 vols. 1875–94. Gloucester, Mass.: Peter Smith, 1967.

B.G. *A Most Wicked worke of a wretched Witch.* London, 1592.

Batty or Battus, Batholomeus. *The Christian Man's Closet.* Ed. and trans. William Lowth. London, 1581.

Bee, Jesse. *The Most Wonderfull and True Story of a Certaine Witch named Alse Gooderige.* Ed. John Denison. London, 1597.

Belcher, Dabriscourt. *Hans Beer Pot.* London, 1618.

Bodin, Jean. *De la Demonomanie des Sorciers.* 1587. La Roche-sur-Yon: Gutenberg Reprints, 1979.

A briefe Description of the notorious Life of John Lambe, otherwise called Doctor Lambe, together with his ignominious Death. London, 1628.

Collier, John Payne. *Illustrations of Early English Popular Literature.* Vol. 1. 1863. New York: Benjamin Blom, 1966. 2 vols.

Cotta, John. *A short Discoverie of the unobserved Dangers of severall sorts of ignorant and unconsiderate practisers of physicke in England.* London, 1612. Republished as *A true discovery of the empiricke with the fugitive Physition and Quacksalver.* London, 1617.

——, *The Triall of Witchcraft.* London, 1616. Republished as *The Infallible, True and Assured Witch* . . . London, 1625.

Coxe, Francis. *A short Treatise declarynge the detestable wickednesse of magicall sciences* . . . London, 1561.

Dalton, Michael. *The Countrey Justice.* 1619. London: Professional Books. 1973.

Darrell, John. *A true narration of the strange and grevous vexation by the Devil of seven persons in Lancashire and William Somers of Nottingham.* n.p., 1600.

Day, W.G. ed. *The Pepys Ballads.* Cambridge: D.S. Brewer, 1987.

A Detection of damnable driftes, practized by three Witches arraigned at Chelmisforde in Essex, at the Assizes there holden, whiche were executed in Aprill. London, 1579.

The Examination and Confession of certaine Wytches at Chensforde in the Countie of Essex, before the Quenes majesties Judges . . . London, 1566.

The Examination of John Walsh, before Maister Thomas Williams, Commissary to the Reverend father in God William bishop of Excester upon certayne Interrogatories touchyng Wytchcrafte and Sorcerye . . . London, 1566.

Fairfax, Edward. *Daemonologia.* 1621. Ed. William Grainge. Harrogate, 1882.

Galis, Richard. *A Briefe Treatise conteyning the most strange and horrible crueltye of Elizabeth Stile alias Bockingham and hir confederates executed at Abington upon Richard Galis.* London, 1579.

Gifford, George. *A Discourse of the Subtill Practises of Devilles by Witches and Sorcerers.* 1587. Amsterdam and Norwood: Theatrum Orbis Terrarum and Walter J. Johnson, 1977.

——, *A Dialogue Concerning Witches and Witchcraftes.* 1593. Ed. Beatrice White. London: Oxford University Press, 1931.

Goodcole, Henry. *The Adultresses Funerall Day: In flaming, scorching and consuming fire: Or the burning down to ashes of Alice Clarke late of Uxbridge . . . for the unnaturall poisoning of Fortune Clarke her Husband . . .* London, 1635.

——, *Heavens Speedie Hue and Cry sent after Lust and Murther. Manifested upon the suddaine apprehending of Thomas Shearwood and Elizabeth Evans . . .* London, 1635.

——, *Londons Cry: Ascended to God, and entred into the hearts, and eares of men for Revenge of Bloodshedders, Burglaiers and Vagabonds . . .* London, 1619.

——, *Natures Cruell Step-Dames: or Matchlesse Monsters of the Female Sex: Elizabeth Barnes, and Anne Willis. Who were executed . . . for the unnaturall murthering of their owne Children . . .* London, 1637.

——, *A True Declaration of the happy Conversion, contrition and Christian preparation of Francis Robinson . . .* London, 1618.

——, *The Wonderfull Discoverie of Elizabeth Sawyer, a Witch, late of Edmonton, her conviction and condemnation and death.* London, 1621.

Greene, Robert. *Friar Bacon and Friar Bungay.* 1594. Ed. Daniel Seltzer. London: Edward Arnold, 1964.

Harsnett, Samuel. *A Declaration of Egregious Popish Impostures.* London, 1603.

James I and VI. *Daemonologie.* 1597. Ed. G.B. Harrison. London: Bodley Head, 1924.

Lambarde, William. *Eirenarcha or the Office of Justices of Peace.* 1581/2. London: Professional Books, 1972.

Lyly, John. *Euphues: The Anatomy of Wyt.* 1579. Ed. R. Warwick Bond. *Complete Works of John Lyly.* Vol. 1. Oxford: Clarendon Press, 1902. 177–323. 3 vols.

More, George. *A true Discourse concerning the certaine possession and dispossession of 7 persons in one familie in Lancashire.* Middelburg, 1600.

The Most Cruell and Bloody Murther committed by an Inkeepers Wife, called Annis Dell . . . With the severall Witchcrafts, and most damnable practises of one Johane Harrison and her Daughter . . . London, 1606.

The Most strange and admirable discoverie of the three Witches of Warboys . . . London, 1593.

Newes from Scotland. Declaring the Damnable life and death of Doctor Fian, a notable sorcerer . . . London, 1592?

Perkins, William. *A Discourse of the Damned Art of Witchcraft.* 1608. *The Workes of that Famous and Worthie Minister of Christ in the University of Cambridge, Mr. William Perkins.* Vol. 3. Cambridge, 1613. 607–52. 3 vols.

Pliny. *Natural History.* Ed. J. Bostock and H.T. Riley. Vol. 1. London, 1893. 6 vols.

Plutarch. 'Life of Artaxerxes'. Trans. Bernadotte Perrin. London: Heinemann; Cambridge, Mass: Harvard University Press, 1943. 129–203. Vol. 11 of *Plutarch's Lives.* 11 vols. First published 1914–1920.

Potts, Thomas. *The Wonderfull Discoverie of Witches in the Countie of Lancaster.* London, 1612.

A Rehearsall both straung and true, of hainous and horrible actes committed by Elizabeth Stile, Alias Rockingham, Mother Dutten, Mother Devell, Mother Margaret, Fower notorious Witches . . . London, 1579.

Roberts, Alexander. *A Treatise of Witchcraft.* London, 1616.

Scot, Reginald. *The Discoverie of Witchcraft.* 1584. Ed. Brinsley Nicholson. London, 1886.
The Severall Facts of Witchcraft Approved and Laid to the Charge of Margaret Harkett. London, 1585.
Smith, Sir Thomas. *De Republica Anglorum.* Ed. Mary Dewar. Cambridge: Cambridge University Press, 1982.
Swan, John. *A True and Breife Report of Mary Glovers Vexation.* London, 1603.
The Triall of Maist. Dorrell. n.p., 1599.
Virgil, *Aeneid.* Trans. C.J. Billson. 1906. New York: Dover, 1995.
Weyer, Johann. *De Praestigiis Daemonum.* 1583. *Witches, Devils and Doctors in the Renaissance.* Trans. John Shea. Ed. George Mora. Binghampton, New York: Medieval and Renaissance Texts, 1991.
Witches Apprehended, Examined and Executed, for notable villanies by them committed both by Land and Water. London, 1613.
The Witches of Northamptonshire. London, 1612.
The Wonderful Discoverie of the Witchcrafts of Margaret and Phillip Flower, daughters of Joan Flower neere Bever Castle . . . Together with the severall examinations and confessions of Anne Baker, Joan Willimot and Ellen Greene Witches of Leicestershire. London, 1619. Republished as *Strange and Wonderfull Witchcrafts,* London, 1621 and 1635.
A World of Wonders. A Masse of Murthers. A Covie of Cosonages. London, 1595.
W.T. *The Office of the Clerk of Assize.* London, 1682.
W.W, *A True and just Recorde, of the Information, Examination and Confession of all the Witches, taken at S. Oses in the countie of Essex . . .* London, 1582.

Manuscripts

MS Chanter 855B, fos 310–12. Devon Record Office, Exeter.
MS Sloane 972. fo. 7. British Library, London.
PRO, ASSI 35/1/4/7, 35/1/4/12 and 35/1/4/9. Public Record Office, London.

Secondary sources

Acheson, Eric. *A Gentry Community: Leicestershire in the Fifteenth Century.* Cambridge: Cambridge University Press, 1992.
Ankarloo, Bengt, and Gustav Henningsen, eds. *Early Modern European Witchcraft: Centres and Peripheries.* Oxford: Clarendon Press, 1993.
Baker, John. 'Criminal Courts and Procedure at Common Law 1500–1800'. In Cockburn, ed. *Crime in England,* 15–48.
Barnes, T.G. 'Examination before a Justice in the Seventeenth Century'. *Somerset and Dorset Notes and Queries* 27 (1955): 39–42.
Beattie, J.M. *Crime and the Courts in England 1660–1800.* Oxford: Clarendon Press, 1986.
——, 'London Juries in the 1690s'. In J.S. Cockburn and T.A. Green, eds. *Twelve Good Men and True: The Criminal Trial Jury in England 1200–1800.* Princeton: Princeton University Press, 1988, 214–53.
Bennett, Walter. *The Pendle Witches.* Preston: Lancashire County Books, 1993.
Bolton, Diane K. 'Harrow including Pinner'. *The Victoria History of the Counties of England. Middlesex.* Ed. R.B. Pugh. Vol. 4. Oxford: Oxford University Press, 1971, 169–271. 10 vols 1969–95.

Bowler, Hugh, ed. *London Sessions Records 1605–85.* London: Catholic Record Society, 1934.

Briggs, K.M. *A Dictionary of British Folktales in the English Language.* London: Routledge, 1991.

Burn, Richard. *The Ecclesiastical Law.* 4 vols. 9th edn. Corrected by Robert Phillimore. London, 1842.

Cameron, H.K. 'The Brasses of Middlesex Part 24: Northolt, Norwood, Pinner and Ruislip', *Transactions of the London and Middlesex Archaeological Society* 35 (1984), 121–2.

Catholic Enclopaedia, The. 15 vols. New York: Robert Appleton, 1907–.

Clark, Sandra. *The Elizabethan Pamphleteers: Popular Moralistic Pamphlets 1580–1640.* London: Athlone Press, 1983.

Cobbett, William. *Cobbett's Complete Collection of State Trials and Proceedings for High Treason and other Crimes and Misdemeanours from the Earliest Period to the Present Time.* London, 1809.

Cockburn, J.S. *Calendar of Assize Records. Home Circuit Indictments. Elizabeth I and James I.* 10 vols. London: HMSO, 1975–85.

——, 'Early Modern Assize Records as Historical Evidence', *Journal of the Society of Archivists* 5 (1975), 215–31.

——, ed. *Crime in England 1500–1800.* London: Methuen, 1977.

——, *A History of English Assizes 1558–1714.* Cambridge: Cambridge University Press, 1972.

——, *Introduction to Calendar of Assize Records. Home Circuit Indictments. Elizabeth I and James I.* London: HMSO, 1985.

——, rev. of *Prosecuting Crime in the Renaissance* by J.H. Langbein. *Revue d'Histoire du Droit (Legal History Review)* 43 (1975), 347–9.

Cohen, Elizabeth S. 'Court Testimony from the Past: Self and Culture in the Making of Text'. In Marlene Kadar, ed. *Essays on Life Writing: From Genre to Critical Practice.* Toronto, Buffalo, London: University Toronto Press, 1992, 83–93.

Cokayne, G.E. *The Complete Peerage.* rev. edn, ed. H. Arthur Doubleday, Vicary Gibbs, Lord Howard de Walden *et. al.* 13 vols. London: St Catherine's Press, 1910–59.

Collinson, Patrick. *The Elizabethan Puritan Movement.* London: Jonathan Cape, 1967.

Cooper, C.H. and T. Cooper, eds. *Athenae Cantabrigiensis.* Cambridge, 1858.

Cooper, William Durrant, 'The Parish Registers of Harrow on the Hill', *Transactions of the London and Middlesex Archaeological Society* 1 (1860).

Crossley, James. Introduction. *The Discoverie of Witches.* By Thomas Potts. 1612. Chetham Society Old Series 6. Manchester, 1845.

Davies, Ralph. *English Overseas Trade 1500–1700.* London and Basingstoke: Macmillan, 1973.

Davis, Kathy A. 'Elizabethan Witchcraft and Sorcery: The Case of John Walsh (1566), Cunning Man or Catholic?'. MA Diss. University of Exeter, 1995.

Davis, Natalie Zemon, *Fiction in the Archives: Pardon Tales and their Tellers in Sixteenth-Century France.* Stanford: Stanford University Press, 1987.

Dolan, Frances. *Dangerous Familiars: Representations of Domestic Crime in England 1550–1700.* Ithaca and London: Cornell University Press, 1994.

Duff, E. Gordon. *A Century of the English Book Trade.* London: Bibliographical Society, 1905.

Ellis, Sir Henry, ed. *The Visitation of the County of Huntingdon.* London, 1849.

Emmison, F.G. *Elizabethan Life: Wills of Essex Gentry and Merchants.* Chelmsford: Essex County Council, 1978.

——, *Elizabethan Life: Wills of Essex Gentry and Yeomen.* Chelmsford: Essex County Council, 1980.

Ewen, C. L'Estrange. *Witch Hunting and Witch Trials.* London: Kegan Paul, Trench, Trubner, 1929.

——, *Witchcraft and Demonianism*. London: Heath Cranton, 1933.

Farrar, Henry. *The Book of Hurst*. Chesham, Bucks: Barracuda, 1984.

Farrer, W. and J. Brownbill, eds. *Victoria County History: Lancashire*. 9 vols. London: Constable, 1911.

Favret-Saada, Jeanne. *Deadly Words: Witchcraft in the Bocage*. Trans. Catherine Cullen. Cambridge and Paris: Cambridge University Press and Editions de la Maison des Sciences de l'Homme, 1980.

Finch, Mary E., *The Wealth of Five Northamptonshire Families*. Oxford: Northamptonshire Record Society, 1956.

Foster, F.F. *The Politics of Stability*. London: Royal Historical Society, 1977.

Furphy, J.M. 'An Anthropological Account of Witchcraft in Early Seventeenth Century England'. MA Diss. University of Manchester, 1991.

Gibson, Joyce. *Hanged for Witchcraft: Elizabeth Lowys and her Successors*. Canberra: Tudor, 1988.

Gibson, Marion. 'Richard Galis: Witches Autobiography and Horror'. Seminar paper. Institute of Historical Research. London, 23 May 1996.

——, 'Greene's *Friar Bacon and Friar Bungay* and *A Most Wicked Worke of a Wretched Witch*: A Link'. *Notes and Queries* (March 1997), 36–7.

——, 'Mother Arnold: A Lost Witchcraft Pamphlet Rediscovered'. *Notes and Queries* (Sept. 1998), 296–300.

——, 'Devilish Sin and Desperate Death: Northamptonshire Witches in Print and Manuscript'. *Northamptonshire Past and Present* (1998), 15–21.

——, *Reading Witchcraft*. London and New York: Routledge, 1999.

Ginzburg, Carlo. *Ecstasies; Deciphering the Witches' Sabbath*. Trans. Raymond Rosenthal. London: Hutchinson Radius, 1990.

Greg, W.W., ed. *Henslowe's Diary*. London: Bullen, 1904. 2 vols.

Gregory, Annabel. 'Witchcraft, Politics and Good Neighbourhood in Early Seventeenth-century Rye'. *Past and Present* 133 (1991), 31–66.

Harris, Anthony, ed. *A True and Just Recorde of the Information, Examination and Confession of all the Witches, taken at S. Oses. ...* Delmar, New York: Scholars Facsimiles and Reprints, 1981.

Harris, Percy. *London and its Government*. London and Toronto: Dent, 1931.

Herrup, Cynthia. *The Common Peace*. Cambridge: Cambridge University Press, 1987.

Hill, J.W.F. *Tudor and Stuart Lincoln*. Cambridge: Cambridge University Press, 1956.

Hodgett, Gerald A.J. *Tudor Lincolnshire*, vol. 6 of *History of Lincolnshire*, ed. Joan Thirsk. Lincoln: History of Lincolnshire Committee, 1975.

Holmes, Clive. 'Women, Witnesses and Witches'. *Past and Present* 140 (1993), 45–78.

——, 'Popular Culture? Witches, Magistrates and Divines in Early Modern England'. In S.L. Kaplan, ed. *Understanding Popular Culture*. Berlin: Mouton, 1984, 85–111.

——, *Seventeenth Century Lincolnshire*. Lincoln: History of Lincolnshire Committee, 1980.

Hunter, Judith. *A History of Berkshire*. Chichester: Phillimore, 1995.

Hutton, Ronald. *The Stations of the Sun*. Oxford: Oxford University Press, 1996.

Jeaffreson, John Cordy. *Middlesex County Records*. Vols 1–3. London: GLC, 1972. 10 vols. 1886.

Kapferer, Jean-Noel. *Rumors: Uses, Interpretations and Images*. 1987. Trans. Bruce Fink. New Brunswick and London: Transaction Publishers, 1990.

Kittredge, G.L. *Witchcraft in Old and New England*. Cambridge, Mass.: Harvard University Press, 1929.

Langbein, J.H. *Prosecuting Crime in the Renaissance*. Cambridge, Mass.: Harvard University Press, 1974.

Leuschner, Kristin Jeanne. 'Creating the "Known True Story": Sixteenth and Seventeenth Century Murder and Witchcraft Pamphlets and Plays'. Thesis. University California, 1992.

Lowndes, William. *The Bibliographer's Manual of English Literature*. Rev. edn, ed. Henry G. Bohn. 6 vols. London, 1890.
Lumby, Jonathan. *The Lancashire Witch-craze: Jennet Preston and the Lancashire Witches 1612*. Preston: Carnegie, 1995.
Macfarlane, Alan. *Witchcraft in Tudor and Stuart England*. 1970. Prospect Heights, Illinois: Waveland Press, 1991.
——, 'Witchcraft in Tudor and Stuart Essex'. In Cockburn, ed. *Crime in England*, 72–89.
Marshburn, J.H. *Murder and Witchcraft in England 1550–1640*. Norman: University Oklahoma Press, 1971.
McKerrow, R.B. ed. *A Dictionary of Printers and Booksellers in England, Scotland and Ireland, and Foreign Printers of English Books 1557–1640*. 1910. London: Bibliographical Society, 1968.
Metcalfe, Walter. C. ed. *The Visitations of Essex*. 2 vols. London, 1878.
Neale Dalton, John, ed. *The Manuscripts of St. George's Chapel, Windsor Castle*. Windsor: The Dean and Canons of St George's Chapel, 1957.
Nichols, John. *History and Antiquities of the County of Leicester*. 4 vols. London, 1795–1811.
Notestein, Wallace. *A History of Witchcraft in England from 1558–1718*. 1911. New York: Apollo, 1968.
Oliver, George. *Lives of the Bishops of Exeter*. Exeter, 1861.
Ollard, S.L. *Fasti Wyndesoriensis: The Dean and Canons of Windsor*. Windsor: The Dean and Canons of St George's Chapel, 1950.
Oxford English Dictionary. Ed. J.A. Simpson and E.S.C. Weiner. 2nd edn. 20 vols. Oxford: Clarendon Press, 1989.
Page, William, and P.H. Ditchfield, eds. *Victoria County History: Berkshire*. 4 vols. 1907. London: Institute of Historical Research, 1972.
Peel, Edgar, and Pat Southern. *The Trials of the Lancashire Witches*. 1969. Nelson: Hendon, 1994.
Plomer, Henry R. *A Dictionary of Booksellers and Printers who Were at Work in England, Scotland and Ireland 1641–1667*. 1907. London: Bibliographical Society, 1968.
Pollard, A.W. and G.R. Redgrave, with Katherine Pantzer. *A Short-title Catalogue of Books Printed in England, Scotland and Ireland 1475–1640* (*STC*). 2nd edn. 3 vols. London: Bibliographical Society, 1986–91.
Purkiss, Diane. *The Witch in History*. London and New York: Routledge, 1996.
Roberts, Gareth. 'John Walsh'. Unpublished lecture, 1989.
Rosen, Barbara. *Witchcraft in England 1558–1618*. 1969. Amherst: University Massachusetts Press, 1991.
St. George, Richard. *A Visitation of the County Palatine of Lancaster . . . 1613*. Ed. F.R. Raines. Chetham Society, 1871.
Shaaber, M.A. *Some Forerunners of the Newspaper in England 1476–1622*. London: Cass, 1966.
Sharpe, J.A. *Instruments of Darkness: Witchcraft in England 1550–1750*. London: Hamish Hamilton, 1996.
Sheils, W.J. *The Puritans in the Diocese of Peterborough 1558–1610*. Northampton: Northamptonshire Record Society, 1979.
Singleton, Barbara. 'Witchcraft in Middlesex 1563–1736', M.Phil, University of Reading, 1996.
South, Raymond. *The Book of Windsor*. Chesham, Bucks.: Barracuda, 1977.
——, *Royal Castle, Rebel Town*. Chesham, Bucks.: Barracuda, 1981.
Sperling, C.F.D. 'Justices of the Peace for Essex 1585', *The East Anglian*. New Series 3 (1889–90), 314–16.
Spufford, Margaret. *Small Books and Pleasant Histories: Popular Fiction and its Readership*. London: Methuen, 1981.

Stephen, Leslie, and Sidney Lee. *The Dictionary of National Biography*. 22 vols. Oxford: Oxford University Press, 1921–2.

Sterry, Wasey, ed. *The Eton College Register 1441–1698*. Eton: Spottiswoode and Ballantyne, 1943.

Summers, Montague. *History of Witchcraft and Demonology*. London: Kegan Paul, 1926.

Thomas, Keith. *Religion and the Decline of Magic*. 1971. London: Peregrine, 1978.

Tighe, Robert R., and James E. Davis. *The Annals of Windsor*. London, 1858.

Unsworth, C.R., 'Witchcraft Beliefs and Criminal Procedure in Early Modern England'. In Thomas Watkin, ed. *Legal Record and Historical Reality*. London: Hambledon, 1989, 71–98.

Venn, J., and J.A. Venn, eds. *Alumni Cantabrigienses*. 4 vols. Cambridge: Cambridge University Press, 1927.

Watt, Tessa. *Cheap Print and Popular Piety*. Cambridge: Cambridge University Press, 1991.

Whittaker, Gladys. *Roughlee Hall: Fact and Fiction*. Nelson: Marsden Antiquarians, 1980.

Index